The Post

CW01464939

'Festa and Carey's collection is a model of the best work being produced in these fields at present, as well as a roadmap for future work to be undertaken. *Postcolonial Enlightenment* cannot be recommended strongly enough, whether to readers already expert in or new to this area of study.'

Devoney Looser, *SEL*

'a varied and sophisticated response to what has become known as the "global eighteenth century".... *The Postcolonial Enlightenment* is a valuable book.'

Robert Jones, *Textual Practice*

'This is an unusually interesting volume of essays.... The collection aims to explore the potential fruitfulness of a certain creative anachronism, if not paradox, in thinking the Enlightenment post-colonially.... The editors and authors must be congratulated for maintaining a fine tension between sympathetic and critical exploration of postcolonial techniques throughout.'

James Delbourgo, *Eighteenth-Century Studies*

'*The Postcolonial Enlightenment* epitomises the kind of stimulating results that an inter-disciplinary effort can help produce through cross-fertilisation of methods, theories and objects of study.... Early and late modernists alike will appreciate the laudable epistemological effort which the various authors have made in order to unweave the complex and sometimes contradictory concepts and political implications which have been all too often conveniently packaged under the umbrella term "Enlightenment"'.

Berny Sèbe, *The Journal of Imperial and Commonwealth History*

'This collection undoubtedly challenges many contemporary critical orthodoxies and initiates new reading practices in 18th-century studies'

Íde Corley, *Journal of Postcolonial Writing*

'*The Postcolonial Enlightenment*...brings together an impressive array of scholars working in the fields of eighteenth-century and postcolonial studies, as well as in the rich but...underexplored territory where these fields meet.'

Zak Sitter, *Eighteenth-Century Fiction*

The Postcolonial Enlightenment

Eighteenth-Century Colonialism and Postcolonial Theory

EDITED BY

Daniel Carey and Lynn Festa

OXFORD
UNIVERSITY PRESS

OXFORD
UNIVERSITY PRESS

Great Clarendon Street, Oxford OX2 6DP

Oxford University Press is a department of the University of Oxford.
It furthers the University's objective of excellence in research, scholarship,
and education by publishing worldwide. Oxford is a registered trade mark of
Oxford University Press in the UK and in certain other countries

© The several contributors 2009

The moral rights of the authors have been asserted

First published 2009
First published in paperback 2013

British Library Cataloguing in Publication Data
Data available

Library of Congress Cataloging in Publication Data
Data available

ISBN 978–0–19–922914–7 (Hbk)
ISBN 978–0–19–967759–7 (Pbk)

ACKNOWLEDGEMENTS

Over the last thirty years, postcolonial critiques of European imperial practices have transformed our understanding of colonial ideology, resistance, and cultural contact. The Enlightenment has played a complex but often unacknowledged role in this discussion, alternately reviled and venerated as harbinger of colonial dominion and avatar of liberation, as target and shield, as shadow and light. This volume brings together two arenas—eighteenth-century studies and postcolonial theory—in order to interrogate the role and reputation of Enlightenment in the context of early European colonial ambitions and postcolonial interrogations of these imperial projects.

The conversations that resulted in this volume began at a conference held at the William Andrews Clark Memorial Library in Los Angeles. We are grateful to Peter Reill, director of the UCLA Center for Seventeenth- and Eighteenth-Century Studies, for his enthusiasm, encouragement, and generous sponsorship of the event, and to Doris L. Garraway and Sven Trakulhun, with whom we jointly organized the conference. We also want to express our gratitude to the staff of the Center and Library, especially Candis Snoddy, Anna Huang, and Marina Romani. Prior to this, our initial encounters and discussions occurred in the context of the International Seminar on the Eighteenth Century, for which we wish to thank Byron Wells and Philip Stewart, who brought us together, and to Vicki Cutting at the American Society for Eighteenth-Century Studies.

At Oxford University Press we have been fortunate to work with Andrew McNeillie, Jacqueline Baker, and Rachel Platt, who have provided wonderful editorial support. We want to thank our production editor, Fiona Vlemmiks, our copy-editor, Fiona Little, and our indexer, Tom Broughton-Willett, whose diligence and care have been enormous.

Our debts to friends, colleagues, institutions, and funding bodies are many. We especially want to mention the assistance of the Bodleian Library in Oxford and its staff, particularly James Allan and Vera Ryhajlo, and the library of Columbia University. Daniel Carey is indebted to the Irish Research

Council for the Humanities and Social Sciences for the award of a Government of Ireland fellowship, which supported his research. Lynn Festa is grateful to the English departments at the University of Wisconsin, Madison, and Harvard University for the junior faculty research leave which enabled her to work on this volume. Finally, we are most grateful to our contributors, for their generosity and patience throughout the publication process.

The essays in this collection address a set of issues of both historical significance and current import. By documenting assumptions and ideas from an earlier period, the vocabulary used to refer to racial, ethnic, and cultural groups in this volume reflects historical usage. Thus, rather than correcting terms such as 'black' or 'Oriental', as OUP house style would dictate, we have generally stayed with the idiom of the era to avoid introducing unnecessary anachronism.

The cover illustration is taken from Bernard Picart, *Cérémonies et coutumes religieuses de tous les peuples du monde* (new edn, Paris, 1738), vi, reproduced by permission of the Keeper of Special Collections, Bodleian Library, University of Oxford, shelfmark Vet. E6 b.8 (t.6) (between p. 228 and p. 229). The scheme for these volumes, which first appeared in Amsterdam, originated with the printer Jean-Frédéric Bernard. The plates were the work of Picart, a Protestant exile from France who settled in Holland. This plate, 'Diverses Pagodes et Penitences des Faquirs', is signed 'B Picart del. 1729' (i.e. *delineavit* or designed). It depicts an idol in a shrine, below a draping Banyan tree. The idol is a distorted and oversized rendition by Picart of a goddess, identified in his plate as 'Mamaniva' (probably a corruption of 'Mahadevi', the Great Goddess). On one side, figures who have come to offer prayers are marked on the forehead; on the other side, offerings of rice are made. The scene also depicts Indian ascetics (sadhus) of different sects, referred to by Picart as *Faquirs*, performing various 'austerities', involving fire, standing, or raising the arms for vast periods of time. The long-haired, naked figures are Shaiva sadhus and those with shaved heads are probably Digambar Jain monks. The figure with a broom in the middle, whose mouth and nose are covered by a cloth, is a Svetambar Jain monk, who must wear the mask and sweep with a broom in order to avoid killing any 'petits insectes' by inadvertently inhaling or stepping on them. Picart's source for all of this was *Les six voyages de Jean Baptiste Tavernier*, 2 vols (Paris, 1676). We are grateful to Dolf Hartsuiker for his expertise in making these identifications.

CONTENTS

NOTES ON CONTRIBUTORS

Siraj Ahmed is Assistant Professor of English and Comparative Literature at Lehman College, City University of New York. His work includes *The Stillbirth of Capital: Enlightenment Writing and Colonial India* (2012) and essays in *Critical Inquiry* and *Representations*. His next book will be *Archaeology of Babel: Critical Method and Colonial Law*.

Srinivas Aravamudan is Dean of Humanities at Duke University and the author of *Tropicopolitans: Colonialism and Agency, 1688–1804* (1999; winner of the MLA prize for best first book, 2000); *Guru English: South Asian Religion in Cosmopolitan Contexts* (2006); and *Enlightenment Orientalism: Resisting the Rise of the Novel* (2012). His essays have appeared in *Diacritics, ELH, Social Text, Novel, South Atlantic Quarterly, Boundary 2, Eighteenth-Century Studies, Eighteenth-Century Fiction*, and other venues. He has also edited *Slavery, Abolition, and Emancipation*, vol. 6: *Fiction* (1999); William Earle, *Obi; or the History of Three-Fingered Jack* (2005); and a special issue of *PMLA* on War (2009).

Daniel Carey is Professor of English at the National University of Ireland, Galway. He is author of *Locke, Shaftesbury, and Hutcheson: Contesting Diversity in the Enlightenment and Beyond* (2006) and has edited *Richard Hakluyt and Travel Writing in Early Modern Europe* (2012), *The Empire of Credit: The Financial Revolution in the British Atlantic World, 1688–1815* (2011), *Asian Travel in the Renaissance* (2004), and *Les voyages de Gulliver: mondes lointains ou mondes proches* (2002).

Lynn Festa is Associate Professor of English at Rutgers University. She is the author of *Sentimental Figures of Empire in Eighteenth-Century Britain and France* (2006). She has published essays on eighteenth-century colonialism in *Romance Quarterly, Romanic Review*, and *Studies on Voltaire and the Eighteenth Century*.

Doris L. Garraway is Associate Professor of French at Northwestern University. She is the author of *The Libertine Colony: Creolization in the Early French Caribbean* (2005) and editor of *Tree of Liberty: Cultural Legacies of the Haitian Revolution in the Atlantic World* (2008). Her articles on colonial and postcolonial Francophone Caribbean writing have appeared in various journals including *Eighteenth-Century Studies, Research in African Literatures, The International Journal of Francophone Studies, Small*

Suvir Kaul is A. M. Rosenthal Professor of English at the University of Pennsylvania, and author of *Eighteenth-Century British Literature and Postcolonial Studies* (2009), *Poems of Nation, Anthems of Empire: English Verse in the Long Eighteenth Century* (2000; winner of the Walker Cowen Memorial Prize), and *Thomas Gray and Literary Authority: Ideology and Poetics in Eighteenth-Century England* (1992). He has edited a collection of essays entitled *The Partitions of Memory: The Afterlife of the Division of India* (2001) and has also co-edited an interdisciplinary volume entitled *Postcolonial Studies and Beyond* (2005).

David Lloyd is Distinguished Professor of English at the University of California, Davis. His works include *Irish Times: Essays on the History and Temporality of Irish Modernity* (2007), *Ireland after History* (2000), *Culture and the State* (1998; with Paul Thomas), *Anomalous States: Irish Writing and the Postcolonial Moment* (1993), and *Nationalism and Minor Literature* (1987). His most recent book is *Irish Culture and Colonial Modernity, 1800–2000* (2011).

Felicity Nussbaum is Distinguished Professor of English at UCLA, and the author most recently of *Rival Queens: Actresses, Performance, and the Eighteenth-Century British Theater* (2010; selected as a CHOICE outstanding academic title). Among her other published books are *The Limits of the Human: Fictions of Anomaly, Race and Gender in the Long Eighteenth Century* (2003); *Torrid Zones: Maternity, Sexuality and Empire* (1995), and *The Autobiographical Subject* (1989). Her edited and co-edited books include *The Arabian Nights in Historical Context: Between East and West* (2008) and *The Global Eighteenth Century* (2003).

Karen O'Brien is Vice-Principal and Professor of English Literature at King's College, London. She is the author of *Narratives of Enlightenment: Cosmopolitan History from Voltaire to Gibbon* (1997) and *Women and Enlightenment in Eighteenth-Century Britain* (2009), co-editor of *The Oxford History of the Novel*, vol. 2: *1750–1820* (forthcoming, Oxford University Press), as well as the author of articles on literature and the British Empire, including 'Poetry against Empire: Milton to Shelley' (Warton Lecture, British Academy, 2001). She is currently co-editing *The Cambridge Companion to Edward Gibbon*.

Sven Trakulhun is Assistant Professor of History at Zurich University, and author of *Siam und Europa: Das Königreich Ayutthaya in westlichen Berichten 1500–1670* (Siam and Europe: The Kingdom of Ayutthaya in Western Accounts 1500–1670) (2006), and editor of *Das eine Europa und die Vielfalt der Kulturen: Beiträge zur Kulturtransferforschung in Europa 1600–1850* (One Europe and the Variety of Cultures: Essays on Cultural Transmission in Europe, 1500–1850) (2003). He is currently working on a book on *Asian Revolutions: Europe and the Rise and Fall of*

LIST OF ILLUSTRATIONS

Introduction

Some Answers to the Question: 'What is Postcolonial Enlightenment?'

Lynn Festa and Daniel Carey

One of the great eighteenth-century statements about the possibilities and promise of colonial Enlightenment appears in the French *philosophe* Condorcet's *Outlines of a History of the Progress of the Human Mind*. '[T]he love of truth', Condorcet proclaims,

will naturally extend its regards, and convey its efforts to remote and foreign climes. These immense countries will afford ample scope for the gratification of this passion. In one place will be found a numerous people, who, to arrive at civilization [*pour se civiliser*], appear only to wait till we shall furnish them with the means; and who, treated as brothers by Europeans, would instantly become their friends and disciples. In another will be seen nations crouching under the yoke of sacred despots or stupid conquerors, and who, for so many ages, have looked for some friendly hand to deliver them.[1]

Conferring a shared moral and epistemic purpose on the global aspirations of Enlightenment, the personified love of truth naturally and inexorably spreads

---

[1] Jean-Antoine-Nicolas de Caritat, Marquis de Condorcet, *Esquisse d'un tableau historique des progrès de l'esprit humain* (Paris: Garnier-Flammarion, 1988), 269; trans. as *Outlines of a History of the Progress of the Human Mind* (London: J. Johnson, 1795), 324.

itself to remote and foreign terrains. Alternately tendering friendship and deliverance, Europeans carry the means of civilization to a host of nations awaiting their arrival. Distant peoples, Condorcet tells us, will immediately recognize the superior merits of Enlightened civility, and embrace their kinship with their new-found brothers. Others, less ready for this moment by virtue of tyrannical political conditions, nonetheless will welcome the promise of liberation that truth extends equally to them. Written in 1794 and published in 1795, Condorcet's book is temporally poised at a period of transition to a post-millennial future: truth has not yet done this work but its influence will be unhindered by indigenous resistance—for who or what could possibly oppose the advancement of truth across the globe? Yet the confident tone of Condorcet's text is undermined by a historical irony: having fallen foul of the revolutionaries whose cause he had sought to advance, the author died in prison under suspicious circumstances— suicide or murder—eighteenth months before the appearance of his book. The promise, it seems, was unravelling at home even before it made its way abroad.

The suspicion that assertions like Condorcet's inevitably generate for contemporary readers owes less to an appreciation of the *philosophe*'s historical predicament than it does to the remarkable progress of postcolonial theory. Over the last thirty years, the sustained critique of European colonial ideologies and practices initiated by figures like Edward Said and Gayatri Spivak has led to a re-evaluation of long-held justifications and assumptions that underwrote the European colonial presence in Africa, America, and Asia. Yet the role of Enlightenment, whether as ideology, aspiration, or time-period, has been surprisingly neglected in this argument. It is as if Enlightenment were already a known quantity and its agency in certain kinds of Western domination already understood. The critique of Enlightenment within postcolonial theory has largely been performed on an ad hoc basis, with haphazard attention to the diversity of texts and contexts that shaped the period and its thought. Conversely, the introduction of postcolonial theory into the field of eighteenth-century studies has generally left Enlightenment relatively untouched.

This volume is designed to draw together two subjects—Enlightenment and postcolonial theory—that are central to current considerations of global modernity. This engagement is both more fruitful and more problematic than critics have traditionally allowed, whether their scholarly home lies in the domain of eighteenth-century studies or postcolonial theory. In reappraising some of the texts and traditions that bind these periods or fields together, the essays in this collection seek both to determine the usefulness of postcolonial theory for reading the Enlightenment and the eighteenth century, and to explore the insights that alternative views of the historical and philosophical phenomenon of Enlightenment may offer to postcolonial theory. Thus Condorcet's statement provides a useful point of departure, not only because it appears at a stage of transition from the eighteenth to the nineteenth century, but also because it serves as a reminder of the vulnerabilities of certain Enlightenment ideals even at the moment of their enunciation.

In this introduction we describe some of the roles allotted to Enlightenment within postcolonial theory as well as the way postcolonial theory has shaped eighteenth-century studies. The need for a more systematic and nuanced account of the relation between the two has become apparent as postcolonial theory has emerged as an important mode of enquiry into the cultural, political, economic, and literary impact of imperial expansion by European states across much of the globe. The incorporation of postcolonial theory into the field of eighteenth-century studies has helped to illuminate the resistant practices of indigenous populations and the uneven development of early modern categories of gender, race, and nation; it has opened up new avenues to critique the omissions and aspirations of Enlightenment thought. Yet despite the centrality of empire in eighteenth-century literary and historical studies today, the surge of interest in the colonial practices and discourses of the era has, with few exceptions, not yet led to a significant reappraisal of the category of Enlightenment from which the age sometimes takes its name. Although scholarship on Enlightenment has increasingly recognized the diversity of contexts—whether Catholic or Protestant, national or regional, high or popular, radical or more restrained—in and from which religious, political, philosophical, and scientific versions of Enlightenment emerged, scholars, as Dorinda Outram notes, 'have yet to come to grips with the relation between the Enlightenment and the creation of a global world'.[2] The Enlightenment made

---

[2] Dorinda Outram, *The Enlightenment* (2nd edn, Cambridge: Cambridge University Press, 2005), 8. Scholarly attention has emphasized Enlightened denunciations of intolerance, tyranny, and superstition, coupled with a praise of reason, science, and cosmopolitan citizenship. Others have explored qualitative degrees of radicalism in the period and various subcultures of Enlightenment, or defined different strands associated with distinct national traditions. More 'material' or social studies have looked at modes of transmission of ideas through book and salon culture,

plural has remained curiously parochial, bound to its European origins and contained within these contexts.[3]

We begin with current invocations and definitions of Enlightenment, before turning to the role these accounts of Enlightenment play within postcolonial theory. The charges levelled against Enlightenment in postcolonial theory do not always acknowledge tensions and disparities within the

clandestinity, and notions of civility and the public sphere. For national accounts of the Enlightenment, see Roy Porter and Mikuláš Teich (eds), *Enlightenment in National Context* (Cambridge: Cambridge University Press, 1981); H. F. May, *The Enlightenment in America* (New York: Oxford University Press, 1976); A. Owen Aldridge, *The Ibero-American Enlightenment* (Urbana: University of Illinois Press, 1971); David A. Bell, Ludmila Pimenova, and Stéphane Pujol (eds), *La Recherche dix-huitièmiste: raison universelle et culture nationale au siècle des Lumières / Eighteenth-Century Research: Universal Reason and National Culture during the Enlightenment* (Paris: Honoré Champion, 1999). On the material processes through which Enlightenment ideas were disseminated across rank and nation, see e.g. Robert Darnton, *The Business of Enlightenment: A Publishing History of the 'Encyclopédie'* (Cambridge, Mass.: Harvard University Press, 1979); Roger Chartier, *Cultural History: Between Practices and Representations*, trans. Lydia Cochrane (Ithaca: Cornell University Press, 1988), and the work of members of the *Annales* School. On religious and anti-religious strains of Enlightenment, see J. G. A. Pocock, *Barbarism and Religion*, esp. ii: *Narratives of Civil Government* (Cambridge: Cambridge University Press, 1999); Peter Gay, *The Enlightenment: An Interpretation*, i: *The Rise of Modern Paganism* (New York: Vintage, 1966); G. C. Becker, *The Heavenly City of the Eighteenth-Century Philosophers* (1932; New Haven: Yale University Press, 1977); Frank Manuel, *The Eighteenth Century Confronts the Gods* (Cambridge, Mass.: Harvard University Press, 1959); Gerald R. Cragg, *Reason and Authority in the Eighteenth Century* (Cambridge: Cambridge University Press, 1964); and Robert R. Palmer, *Catholics and Unbelievers in Eighteenth-Century France* (1939; New York: Cooper Square Publishers, 1961).

[3] For some important exceptions and recent opening out of discussion, see Charles W. J. Withers, *Placing the Enlightenment: Thinking Geographically about the Age of Reason* (Chicago: University of Chicago Press, 2007) and Jorge Cañizares-Esguerra's discussion of European attempts to understand indigenous, pre-Conquest histories in eighteenth-century Mexico in *How to Write the History of the New World: Histories, Epistemologies, and Identities in the Eighteenth-Century Atlantic World* (Stanford: Stanford University Press, 2001); on Spanish relations with indigenous peoples in the period, see David J. Weber, *Bárbaros: Spaniards and their Savages in the Age of Enlightenment* (New Haven: Yale University Press, 2005). For a global model, see Richard Grove, *Green Imperialism: Colonial Expansion, Tropical Island Edens, and the Origins of Environmentalism, 1600–1860* (Cambridge: Cambridge University Press, 1995); for discussion of German traditions, see John H. Zammito, *Kant, Herder and the Birth of Anthropology* (Chicago: University of Chicago Press, 2002) and Sankar Muthu, *Enlightenment against Empire* (Princeton: Princeton University Press, 2003); on the French tradition, see ibid.; Anthony Pagden, *European Encounters with the New World: From Renaissance to Romanticism* (New Haven: Yale University Press, 1993); Harry Liebersohn, *Aristocratic Encounters: European Travelers and North American Indians* (Cambridge: Cambridge University Press, 2001); Tzvetan Todorov, *On Human Diversity: Nationalism, Racism, and Exoticism in French Thought*, trans. Catherine Porter (Cambridge, Mass.: Harvard University Press, 1993); Henry Vyverberg, *Human Nature, Cultural Diversity, and the French Enlightenment* (New York: Oxford University Press, 1989); Michèle Duchet, *Anthropologie et*

period; instead, they serve to constitute Enlightenment as a unified construct that in its turn enables one to see the 'West' and its colonial projects as animated by a common purpose. The second section of the introduction traces the way postcolonial thought has illuminated some of the gaps or suppressions in Enlightenment historiography itself. By bringing out the centrality of empire to eighteenth-century studies, postcolonial theory has cast new aspects of the period into relief; in the process, it has suggested new structures of periodization and new definitions of modernity. Yet—as we discuss in the final section—scholars who employ postcolonial theory in studies of an earlier period must be wary of the perils as well as the potential profits of anachronism. By drawing together Enlightenment studies and postcolonial theory, the contributors to this volume seek to interrogate the conceptual tools used within both fields and to devise new ones. In enlarging the temporal and geographic framework in and through which we read, we may open up alternative genealogies for categories, events, and ideas that, if left unscrutinized, will continue to bask in the sanctified glow of seeming historical inevitability.

I Provincializing Enlightenment

Postcolonial theory invites us to reconsider the Enlightenment both as an eighteenth-century phenomenon and as a concept that bears on modern political formations. At the same time, Enlightenment as it is described in postcolonial theory has all too easily become a cluster of ideals alternately venerated and reviled, but rarely systematically interrogated. Like the Europe that Dipesh Chakrabarty seeks to provincialize, the 'Enlightenment' as

histoire au siècle des Lumières (Paris: F. Maspero, 1971); on the Enlightenment and the wider world, see Outram, *The Enlightenment*, ch. 5, and G. S. Rousseau and Roy Porter (eds), *Exoticism in the Enlightenment* (Manchester: Manchester University Press, 1990); on representations of native peoples in the period and themes of savagery and primitivism, see Peter Hulme, 'The Spontaneous Hand of Nature: Savagery, Colonialism, and the Enlightenment', in Peter Hulme and and Ludmilla Jordanova (eds), *The Enlightenment and its Shadows* (London: Routledge, 1990), 15–34; Mary Louise Pratt, *Imperial Eyes: Travel Writing and Transculturation* (London: Routledge, 1992), chs 2 and 3; Ter Ellingson, *The Myth of the Noble Savage* (Berkeley: University of California Press, 2001); Pocock, *Barbarism and Religion*, iv: *Barbarians, Savages, and Empires* (Cambridge: Cambridge University Press, 2005).

constituted in postcolonial theory is 'an imaginary figure that remains deeply embedded in *clichéd and shorthand forms* in some everyday habits of thought'.[4] One purpose of this introduction is to explore the nature and persistence of these clichés.

If some postcolonial characterizations reduce Enlightenment to a laundry list of stances, it is perhaps because studies of Enlightenment themselves all too often fall into a circular logic, either creating a restrictive set of characteristics and only considering those eighteenth-century philosophers who exemplify them, or selecting a list of philosophers and defining Enlightenment from there. The notion that Paul Hazard's *Crise de la conscience européenne* might better have been called, as some critics have suggested, the *Crise de la conscience de quelques européens*, cautions us against exaggerating the uniformity of Enlightenment; if the category cannot be representative of northern Europe or even the French, still less can it be representative of the West more generally. And of course, the question of which thinkers should be considered as representative of the Enlightenment is still up for dispute. The movement of names like Hobbes, Rousseau, Burke, in and out of the Enlightenment circle looks at times like a game of theoretical hokey-cokey.

Jonathan Israel's *Radical Enlightenment* has recently disputed the trajectory of Enlightenment from its Cartesian and Hobbesian progenitors through Locke, Newton, Rousseau, and Voltaire in favour of Spinoza, Bayle, and Diderot, pushing the heyday of 'high' Enlightenment from 1750–1800 to 1650–1750 and emphasizing the transnational, pan-European nature of the movement. The significance of Israel's assertions in the context of our argument involves not only his interrogation of which thinkers—and which political agendas—will be seen as definitive, but also how Enlightenment can, if understood as an homogenous concept, become an obstacle for thinking about the eighteenth century. It is more constructive, as Judith Shklar has argued, to consider Enlightenment as 'a state of intellectual tension rather than a sequence of similar propositions'.[5] For, once consolidated into a coherent ideological programme, 'Enlightenment' may be easily converted into a monolithic political agenda: 'in escaping the false unity of "The Enlightenment,"' as

[4] Dipesh Chakrabarty, *Provincializing Europe: Postcolonial Thought and Historical Difference* (Princeton: Princeton University Press, 2000), 4.
[5] Judith N. Shklar, 'Politics and the Intellect', in Stanley Hoffmann (ed.), *Political Thought and Political Thinkers* (Chicago: University of Chicago Press, 1998), 94.

J. G. A. Pocock puts it, 'we escape the error of regarding "it" as culminating in "The Enlightenment Project," a construct invented by both left and right in order that they may denounce it'.[6] This volume seeks to acknowledge the tensions within Enlightenment thought in order to reorientate the relation between eighteenth-century studies and postcolonial theories.

The terms 'postcolonial' and 'Enlightenment' share a kinship to the extent that both simultaneously describe a period, a kind of political order, a cluster of ideas, a theoretical purchase point, and a mode of thinking. The volatility here makes for an uncertain referent: when applied to people (or nations), to scholars, to rulers or states, to a world situation, to an epistemological or psychic framework, 'Enlightened' and 'postcolonial' mean different things.[7] (Global political and economic trends suggest that we might adapt a phrase of Kant's in this context and say that we live in an 'age of postcolonialism' but not yet in a postcolonial age.) Both 'postcolonial' and 'Enlightenment' are often construed as historical or temporal breaking points that mark and open up a political and epistemic shift; both are identified with cultural and intellectual stances that create and are created by these transformations. Both postcolonial studies and Enlightenment are simultaneously positive programmes and modes of oppositional critique, defining themselves in relation to ideologies and political regimes that they resist. Most important, neither can be spoken of properly as homogeneous. The Scottish

---

[6] J. G. A. Pocock, 'Enthusiasm: The Antiself of Enlightenment', in Lawrence Klein and Anthony La Vopa (eds), *Enthusiasm and Enlightenment in Europe, 1650–1850* (San Marino: Henry E. Huntington Library and Art Gallery, 1998), 7. Among the right-wing critics of the Enlightenment 'project', one might list Eric Voegelin, *From Enlightenment to Revolution*, ed. John H. Hallowell (Durham, NC: Duke University Press, 1975) and John Gray, *Enlightenment's Wake: Politics and Culture at the Close of the Modern Age* (London: Routledge, 1995), although Gray's work can be difficult to place politically; on the left, one might situate Max Horkheimer and Theodor Adorno, *Dialectic of Enlightenment*, trans. John Cumming (New York: Continuum, 1999) and much of Foucault's work. See also Sven-Eric Liedman, *The Postmodern Critique of the Project of Enlightenment* (Amsterdam: Rodopi, 1997). These writers, as Darrin McMahon points out, are 'united by their willingness to overlook the Enlightenment's contemporary opponents'. Darrin McMahon, *Enemies of the Enlightenment: The French Counter-Enlightenment and the Making of Modernity* (Oxford: Oxford University Press, 2001), 13.

[7] On this point, see Arif Dirlik, 'The Postcolonial Aura: Third World Criticism in the Age of Global Capitalism', *Critical Inquiry*, 20/2 (1994), 328–56. For deliberations over the referent of 'postcolonial', see also Ella Shohat, 'Notes on the "Post-Colonial"', in Fawzia Afzal-Khan and Kalpana Seshadri-Crooks (eds), *The Pre-Occupation of Postcolonial Studies* (Durham, NC: Duke University Press, 2000), 126–39.

Enlightenment does not replicate the French or the German as if each were the expression of a master idea, any more than South Africa or India should be seen as simple variations on a postcolonial theme. The diversity of local instantiations of the terms 'Enlightenment' and 'postcolonial' make the use of a definite article misleading (*the* Enlightenment, *the* postcolonial). The implications of their ostensible singularity differ in each case, as suggested by the kind of mix-and-match pairing that uses, for example, 'the Enlightenment' as a seemingly unified cluster of ideas to define 'the postcolonial' as a political programme that repudiates these ideas.

'The Enlightenment' has taken a beating in recent years at the hands of both poststructuralist and postcolonial theorists. (It is hard to imagine how one might pronounce the words 'Enlightenment universal subject' without a faint sneer.) The accusations levelled against Enlightenment within postcolonial theory might go something like this: irremediably Eurocentric, the ideas grouped under the rubric of Enlightenment are explicitly or implicitly bound up with imperialism. In its quest for the universal, Enlightenment occludes cultural difference and refuses moral and social relativity.[8] Inasmuch as its values are identified as coextensive with modernity, the Enlightenment naturalizes a teleology in which all roads lead inexorably to an episteme associated with the West. Frozen in the dark backward and abysm of the 'primitive' or 'savage', non-Western populations are stripped of the agency and historicity that underwrites civilized advancement. The doctrine of progress, in turn, legitimates imperial conquest under the guise of the civilizing mission, while the celebration of reason disqualifies other belief systems as irrational or superstitious.[9] Enlightenment becomes alternately

[8] As Pheng Cheah remarks, 'It is a historical repetition in colonial space that reveals the particularistic limits of the European Enlightenment's universalist ambitions.' *Spectral Nationality: Passages of Freedom from Kant to Postcolonial Literatures of Liberation* (New York: Columbia University Press, 2003), 3. Luke Gibbons describes a contrasting case in the United Irishmen at the end of the eighteenth century. Despite a commitment to Enlightenment notions of liberty, they nonetheless attempted to preserve the cultural distinctness and autonomy of the Gaelic population. 'Towards a Postcolonial Enlightenment: The United Irishmen, Cultural Diversity and the Public Sphere', in Clare Carroll and Patricia King (eds), *Ireland and Postcolonial Theory* (Cork: Cork University Press, 2003), 81–91.

[9] See e.g. Walter Mignolo, '(Post)Occidentalism, (Post)Coloniality, and (Post)Subaltern Rationality', in Afzal-Khan and Seshadri-Crooks (eds), *The Pre-Occupation of Postcolonial Studies*, 86–118; and more generally, Walter Mignolo, *Local Histories/Global Designs: Coloniality, Subaltern Knowledges, and Border Thinking* (Princeton: Princeton University Press, 2000).

the engine of a relentlessly totalizing historical spirit and the ideological sugar coating designed to disguise the bitter nature of empire from both its victims and its perpetrators. Cast in these terms, any vestiges of 'the Enlightenment' that remain within a theory become a sign of insufficient liberation. Thus Fanon's famous evocation of an Enlightenment concept of the human in the conclusion to *The Wretched of the Earth* marks his failure to recognize and repudiate its alluring but false promise.[10]

Without wishing to treat all critique as always already internal to the Enlightenment itself, it is worth noting that some of the charges levelled against Enlightenment by postcolonial theorists have been made before, either by the dialectical movement within certain Enlightenment texts or by writers of the Counter-Enlightenment. The postcolonial indictment of Enlightenment at times seems to echo in a critical vein the laudatory assertions made without irony or reservation by earlier scholars, such as Hazard's declaration that Enlightenment Europe personifies 'Plus que tout autre continent, la condition humaine'.[11]

In concluding the critique of Enlightenment with the assertion that it is indelibly stamped by Western values, however, postcolonial critics stop too soon: they disregard the way the concept of Enlightenment becomes the means of constituting a pan-European entity, creating the monolith of the 'West'. For postcolonial thought, the notion of Enlightenment bestows a singularity of purpose, a unity of ideas, that allows for Europe to be seen as a consolidated entity engaged in a shared project. In this sense, Enlightenment serves some of the same constitutive functions that Edward Said attributes to Orientalism as a 'collective notion identifying "us" Europeans as against all "those" non-Europeans'.[12] Neil Lazarus has recently argued that 'The concept

---

[10] Frantz Fanon, *The Wretched of the Earth*, pref. by Jean-Paul Sartre, trans. Constance Farrington (New York: Grove Press, 1968), 311–16.

[11] Paul Hazard, *La Pensée européenne au dix-huitième siècle: de Montesquieu à Lessing*, 3 vols (Paris: Boivin & Cie, 1946), ii, 261. For a recent instance of Enlightenment historiography attendant to Europe rather than a wider frame of reference, see Louis Dupré, *The Enlightenment and the Intellectual Foundations of Modern Culture* (New Haven: Yale University Press, 2004). Dupré's preface conjoins the events of 9/11 to the fact that Islam 'never had to go through a prolonged period of critically examining the validity of its spiritual vision, as the West did during the eighteenth century', making the dubious assertion that Enlightenment 'permanently inured us against one thing: the willingness to accept authority uncritically' (p. ix).

[12] Edward Said, *Orientalism* (New York: Vintage Books, 1978), 7.

of "the West" as it is used in postcolonial theory...has no coherent or credible referent. It is an ideological category masquerading as a geographic one.'[13] If the 'West,' as Lazarus claims, has become oddly detached from any specific territories or terrains, so too has Enlightenment become abstracted from its textual and historical origins, serving instead as a kind of place-holder for a set of putatively European ideas or ideals. The elusiveness of the Enlightenment as a kind of invisible colossus is thus paradoxically part of its utility for postcolonial thinkers.

Of course, one could argue that, from the point of view of the eighteenth century's successors, the commonly held perception of a unified Enlightenment legacy—or the fact of its palpable impact on the experience and education of so many—matters more than the accuracy of the account or the nuances of the original debates. The battle of postcolonial critics against this artificial or constructed foe would therefore be just as valid if not more so.[14] By showing the variety and inconsistency of positions in relation to these key terms and assumptions, the essays in this collection suggest alternative strategies for resisting or questioning this alleged inheritance.

At present, the repudiation of Enlightenment in postcolonial theory is simultaneously ubiquitous and elusive: like a divinity without anthropomorphism, what Pheng Cheah has termed the 'monolithic bogeyman' of Enlightenment is everywhere and nowhere in postcolonial theory.[15] (A minor but telling sign of the simultaneous centrality and insignificance of Enlightenment may be found in a cursory survey of the index of recent anthologies and summations of postcolonial theory: a surprising number skip from 'Eagleton, Terry' to 'Fanon, Frantz' without a pause for 'Enlightenment'.) All too often a single aspect of Enlightenment thought—or a single thinker or even a single essay such as Kant's 'What is Enlightenment?'—is invited to stand for the entire concept or

---

[13] Neil Lazarus, 'The Fetish of "the West" in Postcolonial Theory', in Crystal Bartolovich and Neil Lazarus (eds), *Marxism, Modernity and Postcolonial Studies* (Cambridge: Cambridge University Press, 2002), 44. Gayatri Spivak ironizes the matter in referring to 'codename "West"'. *A Critique of Postcolonial Reason: Toward a History of the Vanishing Present* (Cambridge, Mass.: Harvard University Press, 1999), 6.

[14] John Gray's swinging critique in *Enlightenment's Wake*, although motivated by post-Soviet rather than postcolonial concerns, is nonetheless a bold example of deliberately totalizing the Enlightenment. For his defence of this approach, despite an acknowledgement of widespread variations in thought of the period, see ibid. 122–4.

[15] Cheah, *Spectral Nationality*, 267.

period.[16] Worse still, 'Enlightenment' is made into a kind of shorthand notation for a group of familiar abstractions: rationalism, universalism, equality, human rights, and science. At times 'Enlightenment' and 'post-Enlightenment' seem to be used interchangeably, as if nineteenth-century liberal political thought were a seamless continuation of eighteenth-century philosophy.[17] As Gayatri Spivak puts it, 'philosophy has been and continues to be travestied in the service of the narrativization of history'.[18]

Spivak's *Critique of Postcolonial Reason* is an important example of postcolonial work that grapples with the legacy of Enlightenment thought through an insistence on the ethical imperatives of a critical reading practice that is neither dismissive of nor subservient to the traditions on which it draws. Spivak's 'mistaken' (her word) reading of Kant—what she terms a 'scrupulous travesty'—interprets his works (as well as Hegel and Marx) 'as remote discursive precursors, rather than as transparent or motivated repositories of "ideas" ' in order to find 'a constructive rather than disabling complicity between our position and theirs'.[19] The centrality of Kant to Spivak's critique is telling: much postcolonial work continues to focus on Kant and the German Enlightenment.[20] Thus Tsenay Serequeberhan confers what might be termed a strategic essence upon Enlightenment thought in order to critique the obstacles that Eurocentrism places before African philosophy in his reading of 'Kant—and by extension the Occidental tradition'.[21] Kant here serves as a kind of place-holder (though not a straw man) in Serequeberhan's careful account of the exclusion,

---

[16] See James Schmidt, 'What Enlightenment Project?,' *Political Theory*, 28/6 (2000), 734–57.

[17] For recent work critical of such a move, see Uday Singh Mehta, *Liberalism and Empire: A Study in Nineteenth-Century British Liberal Thought* (Chicago: University of Chicago Press, 1999); and Jennifer Pitts, *A Turn to Empire: The Rise of Imperial Liberalism in Britain and France* (Princeton: Princeton University Press, 2005).

[18] Spivak, *Critique of Postcolonial Reason*, 9.

[19] Ibid. 9, 13, 13–14.

[20] Spivak acknowledges, if obliquely, what might be deemed a paradox, namely that German states were not actively engaged in colonial projects at this time, while German scholars nonetheless participated significantly in 'nascent discourses of comparative philology, comparative religion, even comparative literature' (*Critique of Postcolonial Reason*, p. 8). One might note, however, the extensive enrolment of individuals from German states in the Dutch East-India Company. For further considerations see Daniel Carey and Sven Trakulhun in Chapter 7.

[21] Tsenay Serequeberhan, 'The Critique of Eurocentrism and the Practice of African Philosophy', in Emmanuel Chukwudi Eze (ed.), *Postcolonial African Philosophy: A Critical Reader* (Oxford: Blackwell, 1997), 142.

or rather 'negated inclusion' of the figure of the African in Kant's anthropological history. Emmanuel Chukwudi Eze's 'The Color of Reason' likewise articulates the necessity for African philosophers to grapple with the 'universalist conjunction of metaphysics and anthropology', while tracing the cross-pollination of thought among disparate (European) nations and disciplines. In this way he conjoins Kant's endeavour to define the essence of man with Linnaeus's and Buffon's natural histories, Cook's *Voyages* and other travel narratives, and Rousseau's anti-Enlightenment writings. Bridging the gap between Kant's 'pure' philosophy and his 'pragmatic' anthropology, Eze argues that what Kant 'essentializes is not a specific *what of* "man," but—albeit, a specific—*what for*'.[22] In linking Kant's philosophical method to the immaterial location of difference, Eze offers new ways of prising open Enlightenment thought.

One of the most subtle and thoughtful readings of the problematic status of Enlightenment in postcolonial thought has been offered by Dipesh Chakrabarty in his influential *Provincializing Europe*:

Concepts such as citizenship, the state, civil society, public sphere, human rights, equality before the law, the individual, distinctions between public and private, the idea of the subject, democracy, popular sovereignty, social justice, scientific rationality, *and so on* all bear the burden of European public thought and history. One simply cannot think of political modernity without these and other related concepts that found a climactic form in the course of the European Enlightenment and the nineteenth century. These concepts entail an unavoidable—and in a sense indispensable—universal and secular view of the human. The European colonizer of the nineteenth century both preached this Enlightenment humanism at the colonized and at the same time denied it in practice.[23]

(Even in Chakrabarty's otherwise nuanced account, it is hard not to wonder what the 'and so on' appended to his list of 'ideas' entails.) Chakrabarty's attempt to provide a history of subaltern resistance that cannot be assimilated into the master narratives of progress or modernity wrests postcolonial histories from the domination of an indelibly Eurocentric framework (although, as Amitav Ghosh has pointed out, the omission of events like the

---

[22] Emmanuel Chukwudi Eze, 'The Color of Reason: The Idea of "Race" in Kant's Anthropology', in Eze (ed.), *Postcolonial African Philosophy*, 125–6.

[23] Chakrabarty, *Provincializing Europe*, 4 (emphasis added).

1857 Sepoy Revolt from the book is 'multiply interesting because the rea-soning of the insurgents was *not* entirely opaque to "reason" as it was in so many other anti-colonial insurgencies'.[24]). In his correspondence with Chakrabarty on *Provincializing Europe*, Ghosh questions the implications of some of Chakrabarty's claims, calling for a recognition of alternative geneal-ogies for the egalitarian and liberatory ideas often associated with the Enlightenment:

we should not reflexively assume that the egalitarian and liberatory impulses of nineteenth-century India came solely or even primarily from Enlightenment roots . . . [Moreover, i]nasmuch as Indians appropriated certain aspects of Enlighten-ment it was *against* the will and weight of the Empire, and it would have happened (as in Thailand and Japan) whether there was an Empire or not.[25]

The debate reminds us that the question of who reads and how they read matters as much as what is read. As Chakrabarty, in his reply, neatly puts it, 'To acknowledge our debt to the ideas of the Enlightenment is not to thank colonialism for bringing them to us'.[26] Both authors signal the need to consider ideas in relation to policies and practices that reinforce them. Thus Ghosh argues that a consideration of race would recognize its role in creating an intractable barrier converting the 'not-yet' of the historical processes Chakrabarty analyses into a 'never'. Drawing attention to practices and policies as well as quotidian experiences and differences among colonies, classes, and occupations, the dialogue between Chakrabarty and Ghosh serves to emphasize the material as well as discursive premises of colonial and postcolonial history.

In reminding us not to put the theoretical cart before the historical horse, such formulations point out the complicated relation between the discursive and the pragmatic, the ideological and the material. Postcolonial notions of Enlightenment, so often predicated on a purely ideational construction of the phenomenon, provide some hint of the institutional location of many academics working on these questions in English departments (the bread and butter of literary scholars remains, even in the wake of cultural studies and

---

[24] Amitav Ghosh and Dipesh Chakrabarty, 'A Correspondence on *Provincializing Europe*', *Radical History Review*, 82 (2002), 147.

[25] Ibid. 157.

[26] Ibid. 164.

New Historicism, largely text-based). Too narrow a focus on the ideational or discursive forms of Enlightenment (*pace* Foucault) may occlude the complicity not only of knowledge and power, but also of power and capital. As Partha Chatterjee puts it,

> ever since the Age of Enlightenment, Reason in its universalizing mission has been parasitic upon a much less lofty, much more mundane, palpably material and singularly invidious force, namely the universalist urge of capital. From at least the middle of the eighteenth century, for two hundred years, Reason has travelled the world piggyback, carried across oceans and continents by colonial powers eager to find new grounds for trade, extraction and the productive expansion of capital.[27]

Yet even Chatterjee's call for a recognition of the economic underpinnings of the universalizing force of reason personifies reason as an abstraction with agency and intention. Abstractions of course possess social power, but the ways in which they are historically instantiated deserves further reflection. The material effects of capitalism and modernity can be easily disregarded when these terms are treated as self-evident, self-consummating abstractions.[28] At the same time, the conception of Enlightenment as an all-powerful paradigm that shapes every aspect of intellectual modernity seems to leave little ground for critique. David Scott's *Conscripts of Modernity* offers ways for the postcolonial critic to get beyond what Scott (following Foucault) terms the 'blackmail' of the Enlightenment: 'the obligation to either affirm or disaffirm a normative commitment to the Enlightenment's idea of itself while at the same time acknowledging that the very terrain of that disavowal, the very mode of critique that sustains it, is part of his inheritance of the Enlightenment'.[29] Scott traces in C. L. R. James's revisions to *The Black Jacobins* a series of shifts from a resistant form of anticolonialism defined exclusively as a mode of overcoming—in which liberation is envisioned solely as a negation of bondage in a tale of Romantic redemption and 'history rides a triumphant and seamlessly progressive rhythm'—to a tragic mode in which the relation between past, present, and future becomes a 'broken series of paradoxes and reversals in which human action is ever open

---

[27] Partha Chatterjee, *Nationalist Thought and the Colonial World: A Derivative Discourse* (Minneapolis: University of Minnesota Press, 1986), 168.

[28] See the essays in Bartolovich and Lazarus (eds), *Marxism, Modernity and Postcolonial Studies*.

[29] David Scott, *Conscripts of Modernity: The Tragedy of Colonial Enlightenment* (Durham, NC: Duke University Press, 2004), 180.

to unaccountable contingencies—and luck'.[30] Tragic openness (and exposure) in the face of the uncertainties of the postcolonial present, Scott argues, may offer a way around the impasse of the Enlightenment project and enable pursuit of 'the political project of creating institutional conditions for the positive work of freedom'.[31]

The notion that Scott so compellingly repudiates—that contemporary injustices are the fulfilment or extension of an 'Enlightenment project' (or, alternatively, an indication of its failure)—has an additional flaw: it attributes devices and desires to thinkers who did not, invariably, advance a consistent programme. The demonization of a concept or a movement often makes it more coherent than it really is. The ability to consolidate Enlightenment into an ideological programme depends on disregarding form and context while attending to content: reading through the difficult and at times deliberately paradoxical construction of Enlightenment texts in order to mine a single (and sometimes singular) nugget that can serve as a synecdochal representation of the entirety of the period and its thought. Doris Garraway's discussion in this volume of Enlightenment colonial critique in France, like Daniel Carey and Sven Trakulhun's exploration of German anthropology in the period, suggests that a more nuanced reading of texts and traditions discloses contradictory impulses involving a distinctive mixture of complicity, apology, and critique.

The reluctance to engage with Enlightenment texts leads to an unthinking replication of the Romantic and nineteenth-century repudiation of Enlightenment (itself shaped by events like the Haitian Revolution). As Sankar Muthu points out,

It is perhaps by reading popular nineteenth-century political views of progress, nationality, and empire back into the eighteenth century that 'the Enlightenment' as a whole has been characterized as a project that ultimately attempted to efface or marginalize difference, a character that has hidden from view the anti-imperial strand of Enlightenment-era political thought.[32]

This approach leapfrogs over the closing decades of the century, disregarding the ambivalent responses of Enlightenment writers to the cataclysmic events in the American colonies, metropolitan France, and the sugar island of Saint

---

[30] Ibid. 13.   [31] Ibid. 214.
[32] Muthu, *Enlightenment against Empire*, 6.

Domingue. That the age of Enlightenment is also sometimes characterized as the age of revolutions reminds us that we cannot approach the century through texts alone.[33] The Haitian Revolution—simultaneously the extension or consummation of Enlightenment principles regarding the rights of man and a reminder that these rights were unevenly distributed across the globe—was also, as Michel-Rolph Trouillot observes, a colonial riposte whose expression was not necessarily to be found on the page:

> The Haitian Revolution expressed itself mainly through its deeds, and it is through political practice that it challenged Western philosophy and colonialism... [I]ts intellectual and ideological newness appeared most clearly with each and every political threshold crossed, from the mass insurrection (1791) to the crumbling of the colonial apparatus (1793), from general liberty (1794) to the conquest of the state machinery (1797–98), from Louverture's taming of that machinery (1801) to the proclamation of Haitian independence with Dessalines (1804). Each and every one of these steps—leading up to and culminating in the emergence of a modern 'black state', still largely part of the unthinkable until the twentieth century—challenged further the ontological order of the West and the global order of colonialism.[34]

Trouillot's analysis of the erasure of the Haitian Revolution from history exposes the blindness of Enlightenment and post-Enlightenment *bien-penseurs*: their incapacity to see the ways their thought inhibits recognition of the agency and institutions of others. Yet Trouillot also exposes the way modern scholarly methods occlude the resistance of indigenous and colonial populations (while confining their history to their reactions to European incursions). The challenge that the Haitian Revolution offered to the edifice of Enlightenment thought occurred as much in practice as in print. Sibylle Fischer's study of non-elite and radical responses to the Haitian Revolution across the Caribbean makes elements of Trouillot's silenced archive visible, filling in gaps in the historical and cultural record in order to claim that the denied or disavowed

---

[33] Recent scholarship on the relationship between Enlightenment and the French Revolution has emphasized the social networks and associations among the *philosophes* rather than the ideas they propagated as sources of the Revolution. See François Furet, *Interpreting the French Revolution*, trans. Elborg Forster (Cambridge: Cambridge University Press, 1981); Keith Baker, *Inventing the French Revolution: Essays on French Political Culture in the Eighteenth Century* (Cambridge: Cambridge University Press, 1990).

[34] Michel-Rolph Trouillot, *Silencing the Past: Power and the Production of History* (Boston: Beacon Press, 1995), 89.

history of revolutionary antislavery is a constitutive element of a heterogeneous modernity, rather than a strangely intractable barrier hindering the consummation of an as-yet unfinished project of Enlightenment. As Fischer notes, reading for the 'silences and gaps that punctuate the historical record' requires a transnational perspective on literature, culture, and politics that might also enable us to glimpse 'what might have been lost when culture and emancipatory politics were finally forced into the mold of the nation-state; and to think what might have happened if the struggle against racial subordination had carried the same prestige and received the same attention as did the struggle against colonialism and other forms of political subordination'.[35] At stake in such work, as Paul Gilroy puts it, is the opportunity 'to transcend the unproductive debate between a Eurocentric rationalism which banishes the slave experience from its accounts of modernity while arguing that the crisis of modernity can be resolved from within, and an equally occidental antihumanism which locates the origins of modernity's current crises in the shortcomings of the Enlightenment project'.[36] By traversing scholarly domains normally kept discrete, the essays in this volume collectively offer means for rethinking both the relationship between metropole and colony in the period and the conceptual tools used to understand the practice as well as the theory of Enlightenment.

II Enlightenment without others

If postcolonial theory too often obscures the nuances of Enlightenment texts, influential formulations of Enlightenment have not, in general, acknowledged colonialism. None of the major studies—Cassirer, Gay, Foucault, Horkheimer and Adorno—explicitly analyses the colonial projects of the eighteenth century,[37] while recent accounts of Counter-Enlightenment—

---

[35] Sybille Fischer, *Modernity Disavowed: Haiti and the Cultures of Slavery in the Age of Revolution* (Durham, NC: Duke University Press, 2004), 2–3.

[36] Paul Gilroy, *The Black Atlantic: Modernity and Double Consciousness* (Cambridge, Mass: Harvard University Press, 1993), 54.

[37] In 'What is Enlightenment?' Foucault asks what 'mankind' or *Menschheit* means in Kant's essay: 'Are we to understand that the entire human race is caught up in the process of Enlightenment? ... Or are we to understand that it involves a change affecting what constitutes

Darrin McMahon's *Enemies of the Enlightenment: The French Counter-Enlightenment and the Making of Modernity* (2001) and Graeme Garrard's *Counter Enlightenments: From the Eighteenth-Century to the Present* (2006)—barely glance at the postcolonial critique of Enlightenment.[38]

If we look more carefully at some of the leading figures of Enlightenment, we see that some important strands of Enlightenment thought nonetheless provided resources for objections to imperial expansion, to slavery, and to other forms of power in colonial contexts.[39] Diderot's contributions to Raynal's *Histoire philosophique des deux Indes*, like his *Supplément au voyage de Bougainville*, include a vociferous defence of indigenous populations and a sustained interrogation of the underlying assumptions that legitimated imperial enterprise. 'Contrary to what is sometimes assumed,' as Robert Young points out, 'there was a strong tradition of anti-colonialism in the Europe of the eighteenth and nineteenth centuries, a radical tradition that some of the more blimpish representations within postcolonial writings today of the ideology of imperialism neglect.'[40] Sankar Muthu's exploration of the anti-imperial strain in the writings of Diderot, Kant, and Herder in *Enlightenment against Empire* (2003), like the essays by Doris Garraway, Karen O'Brien, and Daniel Carey and Sven Trakulhun included in this collection, reminds us that not all Enlightenment writers supported empire, nor did all critics of

the humanity of human beings?' Although he acknowledges that the Enlightenment creates relations of domination with non-European peoples, he does not pursue this question further. Michel Foucault, 'What is Enlightenment?', in *The Foucault Reader*, ed. Paul Rabinow (New York: Pantheon, 1984), 35.

[38] Garrard does summarize John Gray's critique of the Enlightenment project in *Enlightenment's Wake* but does not explicitly conjoin it to postcolonial theory. For his part, Gray echoes Horkheimer and Adorno's critique of Enlightenment in his claim that 'the Westernising impulse it [the Enlightenment project] embodied has transmitted to nearly all cultures the radical modernist project of subjugating nature by deploying technology to exploit the earth for human purposes.... Westernisation impacts on the world's non-Occidental cultures in the late modern period as a form of revolutionary nihilism'. *Enlightenment's Wake*, 178; quoted in Graeme Garrard, *Counter-Enlightenments: From the Eighteenth-Century to the Present* (London: Routledge, 2006), 120. Yet one difficulty with Gray's position is that he acknowledges the exception of America, which has not, in his assessment, given in to nihilism, despite the fact that it is the Enlightenment country par excellence in his account and has shown no reticence in exploiting the earth for human purposes.

[39] Not least Condorcet in *Réfléxions sur l'esclavage des Nègres* (Neufchatel, 1781).

[40] Robert Young, *Postcolonialism: An Historical Introduction* (Oxford: Blackwell, 2001), 74.

Enlightenment oppose colonial enterprise—even supposing (as we do not) that a pro/anti binary is adequate to the question.

Attention to earlier episodes of commerce, exploration, and expansion allows us to assess the usefulness and limits of postcolonial theory by asking how unexamined models of periodization shape the very questions we are able to pose. On one level, the Enlightenment creates a timeline for the floating temporal frames that construct postcolonial theory. Given the omnipresence of 'colonial' practice, as Aijaz Ahmad has pointed out, the term 'colonialism' risks becoming 'a transhistorical thing, always present and always in process of dissolution in one part of the world or another'.[41] Enlightenment furnishes the necessary prehistory to the dominant timeline of European empire, locating the point from which the history of the colony and thence the post-colony can begin. Enlightenment also becomes a pivot point between an initial wave of imperial activity—the Spanish and Portuguese conquest of the Americas, the French, English, and Dutch colonial endeavours in the New World, as well as expanding trade and settlement networks in East and South-East Asia and the Indian subcontinent—and the nineteenth-century empires of the British, French, Belgians, and Germans. If Enlightenment thus alternately serves as the 'before' of the nineteenth-century 'after' and as the intellectual turn-down service readying the room for the arrival of the imperial barbarians, this is in part because of a periodizing move that seems to make Enlightenment the theory and the nineteenth century the practice. This implicitly casts the temporal 'before' in a causal as well as chronological relation to what follows, as in Patrick Williams and Laura Crisman's suggestion that 'The Enlightenment's universalizing will to knowledge (for better of worse) feeds Orientalism's will to power.'[42]

In order to think through the difficulties with such a claim, we might reflect on the rhetorical convenience of periodization while also questioning the limits of universalism as an attribute of Enlightenment. We need, in that sense, to investigate rival claims about the period which assert, on the one hand, that 'Whatever was not universal was ipso facto erroneous, a limited,

[41] Aijaz Ahmad, 'The Politics of Literary Postcoloniality', *Race and Class*, 36/3 (1995), 9.

[42] Patrick Williams and Laura Chrisman, introduction in Patrick Williams and Laura Chrisman (eds), *Colonial Discourse and Postcolonial Theory: A Reader* (New York: Columbia University Press, 1994), 8.

partial vision that had to be transcended by a larger, universal one'[43] and, on the other, those who with Seyla Benhabib object to 'false generalizations about the West itself, [alleging] the homogeneity of its identity, the uniformity of its developmental processes, and the cohesion of its value systems'.[44] In this vein, Sankar Muthu has described 'the multiplicity of universalisms across eighteenth-century European political thought, each with distinct foundational claims, varying relationships to conceptualizations of human diversity and to humanity . . . and different political orientations toward the nature and limits of state power in theory and in practice'.[45] By pluralizing our concept of universalism, it may become possible to turn some of Enlightenment's most enduringly monolithic ideas on their heads. The logic subtending these models of periodization would then become apparent.

The revised account of Enlightenment offered by Jonathan Israel, for example, allows us to think about the ways in which the sense of the universal in 1680 was profoundly different from that existing in 1780. With global expansion, the test cases for universalism changed. The encounter with new populations radically altered concepts of human nature, both fostering exclusions grounded in the taxonomic projects of ethnography and natural history and generating more elastic and plural ideas of humanity. One manifestation of this can be found in changing representations of Native American peoples over the course of the period. Although the terms of discussion were often set by developments in European and colonial political relations (and in political theory, as Srinivas Aravamudan argues in Chapter 1),[46] it is nonetheless striking to see emerging attributions of political coherence to North American tribes, notably the Five Nations, identified as republican groupings with warrior citizens (as opposed to the

[43] Lionel Gossman, 'What Was Enlightenment?', in Denis Hollier (ed.), *A New History of French Literature* (Cambridge, Mass.: Harvard University Press, 1989), 487.

[44] Seyla Benhabib, ' "Nous" et "les autres": The Politics of Complex Cultural Dialogue in a Global Civilization', in Christian Joppke and Steven Lukes (eds), *Multicultural Questions* (Oxford: Oxford University Press, 1999), 44. She observes that theorists like Rawls, Rorty, and Derrida—one might add Gayatri Spivak—have sought to distinguish universalism from essentialism, although, as Benhabib notes, it is not clear that 'moral and legal universalisms can be defended without a strong commitment to the normative content of reason'.

[45] Muthu, *Enlightenment against Empire*, 266.

[46] Especially the Seven Years War (sometimes called the French and Indian War) and the American Revolution.

savage motif, predicated on a series of conventional ethnographic privations, being *sine fide, sine rege, sine lege*).[47] The struggle over religious toleration within Europe proper likewise suggests the willingness to accept that not all truths are universally acknowledged. As Daniel Carey and Sven Trakulhun demonstrate in Chapter 7, Locke, who upheld reason as a faculty common to all, remained an advocate of toleration (with the signal exclusion of Catholics), arguing that 'the diversity of opinions' in such matters 'cannot be avoided'.[48] Bayle's concept of toleration was also allied to notions of rationality while synthesizing the sceptical tradition's commitment to a certain kind of irreducible diversity.[49] The Enlightenment repudiation of superstition may be seen as elevating a modern rational scientific spirit over 'premodern' belief systems, but the *philosophes*, for their part, also revolted against oppressive Church hierarchies and blind doctrine, promoting a spirit of religious tolerance and fostering an interest (of an admittedly proto-anthropological cast) in alternative systems of belief.

Although a recognition of the plurality of Enlightenment thought opens up additional possibilities for thinking about the colonial history of the period and about the categories underlying that history, it should not lead to a vision of Enlightenment as an arena of delighted free play, a time before categories of human identity and difference assumed discernibly (or prototypically) modern forms. (It is also important, conversely, not to treat nineteenth-century versions of these categories as set in stone.) Ideas of human difference—what we now denominate race, sexual difference, gender, class or rank, and nation—were differently organized, not non-existent, during the eighteenth century. Exemplary work by Srinivas Aravamudan, Laura Brown, Pamela Cheek, Jonathan Lamb, Felicity Nussbaum, Sue Peabody, Roxann Wheeler, and Kathleen Wilson, among others, suggests that the genealogies of these key concepts are anything but straightforward.[50] At the same time, we must be

[47] See Cadwallader Colden, *The History of the Five Indian Nations* (New York, 1727), later expanded in London editions of 1747, 1750, and 1755. Colden drew on the writings of Lahontan and La Potherie. For an example of prior ethnography based on privation, see Thomas Morton, *New English Canaan, or New Canaan* (London, 1637), 27.

[48] John Locke, *A Letter concerning Toleration*, trans. William Popple, ed. James Tully (Indianapolis: Hackett, 1983), 55.

[49] See Daniel Carey, *Locke, Shaftesbury, and Hutcheson: Contesting Diversity in the Enlightenment and Beyond* (Cambridge: Cambridge University Press, 2006).

[50] Srinivas Aravamudan, *Tropicopolitans: Colonialism and Agency, 1688–1804* (Durham, NC: Duke University Press, 1999); Laura Brown, *Ends of Empire: Women and Ideology in Early Eighteenth-Century*

careful to avoid representing what comes after the Enlightenment as somehow richer, more troubled, more complex—a move from the naive eighteenth century to the sentimental nineteenth, which, in its sadness, knows all
that has come before. To make this move is to do an injustice to the internal
tensions within the Enlightenment; it is to disregard the dissonance that
interrupts the chorus of voices clamouring for certain ideals. Such an approach merely assigns to the whole period Roland Barthes's characterization
of Voltaire as 'le dernier des écrivains heureux'.[51]

III Postcolonial Enlightenment(s)

In the past few decades, scholars have emphasized the centrality of global
relations to understanding the eighteenth century, analysing the way European metropolitan identities and ideals during the period were wrought
from engagement with the greater world.[52] The need for primary historical
and theoretical research has been sufficiently great that much of current

English Literature (Ithaca: Cornell University Press, 1993); Pamela Cheek, *Sexual Antipodes: Enlightenment Globalization and the Placing of Sex* (Stanford: Stanford University Press, 2003); Julia Douthwaite, *Exotic Women: Literary Heroines and Cultural Strategies in Ancien Régime France* (Philadelphia: University of Pennsylvania Press, 1992); Felicity Nussbaum, *The Limits of the Human: Fictions of Anomaly, Race, and Gender in the Long Eighteenth Century* (Cambridge: Cambridge University Press, 2003) and *Torrid Zones: Maternity, Sexuality and Empire in Eighteenth-Century English Narratives* (Baltimore: Johns Hopkins University Press, 1995); Sue Peabody, *'There are no slaves in France': The Political Culture of Race and Slavery in the Ancien Régime* (New York: Oxford University Press, 1996); Roxann Wheeler, *The Complexion of Race: Categories of Difference in Eighteenth-Century British Culture* (Philadelphia: University of Pennsylvania Press, 2000); and Kathleen Wilson, *The Island Race: Englishness, Empire, and Gender in the Eighteenth Century* (London: Routledge, 2002). On eighteenth-century discussions of race, see Nicholas Hudson, 'From "Nation" to "Race": The Origin of Racial Classification in Eighteenth-Century Thought', *Eighteenth-Century Studies*, 29 (1996), 247–64; and Pierre Boulle, 'In Defense of Slavery: Eighteenth-Century Opposition to Abolition and the Origins of a Racist Ideology in France', in Frederick Krantz (ed.), *History from Below: Studies in Popular Protest and Popular Ideology in Honour of George Rudé* (Montreal: Concordia University, 1985), 221–41.

[51] Roland Barthes, 'Le dernier des écrivains heureux', in *Essais critiques* (Paris: Éditions du Seuil, 1964), trans. Richard Howard as 'The Last Happy Writer', *Critical Essays* (Evanston, Ill.: North-western University Press, 1972), 83–9.

[52] See the essays in Felicity A. Nussbaum (ed.), *The Global Eighteenth Century* (Baltimore: Johns Hopkins University Press, 2003) and Kathleen Wilson (ed.), *A New Imperial History: Culture, Identity and Modernity in Britain and the Empire, 1660–1840* (Cambridge: Cambridge University Press, 2004).

scholarship has focused on archival recovery: the identification of texts, practices, and events eclipsed by time, by disciplinary protocols, and by the political and intellectual investments of institutions and individuals. Although important work in the field of eighteenth-century studies has drawn on postcolonial theory in its investigation of the literature, art, and history of the period, there has been little sustained critical investigation into Enlightenment per se. The theoretical premises upon which this body of work has been built also deserve greater attention. At times concepts drawn from postcolonial theory are parachuted into analyses of eighteenth-century texts without sufficient recognition of the perils of anachronism. Many of the concepts (ambiguity, hybridity, mimicry) and forms (nation, race, gender) that today anchor postcolonial theory rely on categories of difference that not only do not remain stable across time and space, but also do not exist in a recognizably 'modern' form during the Enlightenment.[53] The myriad shapes assumed by early imperial enterprises challenge any attempt to make generalizations about the history of colonialism.

The ways in which eighteenth-century scholars have borrowed from postcolonial theory have illuminated the field, yet such borrowings create certain methodological problems. The abstractions that often constitute the heuristic value of theory have occasionally obscured the diversity of historical experience, power relations, and practices of resistance. Preoccupation with the notion of 'otherness' within European discourses has, for example, limited the attention given to native historical, material, or narrative traditions. Colonies frequently changed hands in the course of ongoing political, religious, and economic conflicts that marked the shifting balance of power among emerging nation states; European powers held tenuous sway over both their internal and external colonies. No one imperial domain was stable; none constituted a consistent other. The shifting alignment of colonies and the adroitness with which indigenous groups played one European force off another makes it difficult to assert the existence of facile binaries of Western and non-Western. The tenacity of these binaries is evident even today in the assumption that, in Arif Dirlik's words, 'the hybridity to which postcolonial criticism refers is uniformly between the post*colonial* and the First World', rather than between postcolonial thinkers or bodies of work.[54]

---

[53] See Doris L. Garraway in Chapter 6.
[54] Arif Dirlik, 'The Postcolonial Aura', 342.

To employ postcolonial theory as one of the primary tools in discussions of eighteenth-century practices may allow elements of material analysis (above all of gender, class, and sexuality) to be subsumed under a postcolonial rationale, as scholars fall into the trap of writing to the theory, rather than to the history or to the text. The tendency to constitute the agency of empire in terms of nation states has occluded categories of sex/gender, rank, language, ethnicity, religion, and region. (The immixture of peoples and interests in the administrative and military apparatus of empire—the Scots and Irish who peopled the British army in India and the Americas, the African sailors who served in the navy, the West Indian Creoles of European and African descent who served in colonial militias—suggests the difficulty of reducing the agents of empire to the mere implements of the state.) Conversely, to discuss eighteenth-century practices without questioning our allegiance to a particular theoretical paradigm merely reproduces the very systems one would study or critique. Of course we must also be attentive to the way in which the analysis of contradictions in Enlightenment discourses, and even the use of concepts drawn from postcolonial theory, may be used to create a more palatable vision of eighteenth-century colonialism. As Joanna Brooks has contended, 'declaring the "hybridity" or "fluidity" of eighteenth-century racial identities wrongly suggests the ephemerality, immateriality, or evanescence of race in the eighteenth-century Atlantic world. . . . The inconsistency of learned discourses about race in eighteenth-century Europe does not correlate with the instrumental power of race in eighteenth-century America'.[55]

It is our hope that an engagement between postcolonial theory and Enlightenment colonialisms may allow us to qualify theoretical concepts—even to elaborate new categories—so as to move beyond the impasse created by the polarization of the two fields. By reconsidering the historical and theoretical location of, for example, the 'Orient' or the 'Black Atlantic' (as in Felicity Nussbaum's essay), the collection reconsiders organizing concepts that structure current thinking. The attempt to make both centre and periphery plural allows us to recognize multiple points of entry into discourses of Enlightenment as well as the possibility of alternative genealogies and teleologies. But the volume aims to do more than reiterate the

---

[55] Joanna Brooks, *American Lazarus: Religion and the Rise of African-American and Native American Literatures* (New York: Oxford University Press, 2003), 16.

plurality of colonialism and theory. The casual addition of the letter 's' to the words 'Enlightenment' and 'postcolonialism' can simply multiply the objects of study without interrogating the way these several discourses strive against one another. Thus David Lloyd argues that we must read political economy in relation to the discourse of the aesthetic, while Siraj Ahmed insists that we cannot understand eighteenth-century Orientalism without recognizing its implication in the violent transformation of Indian property law. Srinivas Aravamudan scrutinizes the way the elevation of particular historical examples may necessitate the occlusion of rival forms of sovereignty in Hobbes's political theory, while the essays by Karen O'Brien (Chapter 8) and by Daniel Carey and Sven Trakulhun (Chapter 7) address the way scientific, theological, and anthropological discourses produce different structures of universalism within an Enlightenment too often read for its singularity. The need for sustained engagement between histories of eighteenth-century colonial activity, Enlightenment, and postcolonial theory arises from an imperative to think through *how* the relative value of these forms of difference is produced, not just what these forms of difference might be. The contributors seek not to create a history of diversity—comparing pre-given objects of ethical, aesthetic or ethnological interest in order to display, appreciatively, the relativism of all knowledge—but instead to address how historical and cultural differences are structured. The point is not to reify what constitutes identities in order to compare them, but to address how they are made, examining processes of differentiation rather than celebrating difference.

The essays both offer innovative readings of texts by canonical writers ranging from Defoe and Behn to Burke and Diderot, and draw on a body of less familiar works in order to expand our understanding of the texture and scope of eighteenth-century literature. Reading current postcolonial theory against the foundational work of philosophers from Hobbes, Bayle, and Locke to Montesquieu, Kant, and Herder allows for a historical reappraisal of the theoretical insights of leading contemporary critics. In addressing the bond—even complicity—between Enlightenment colonialism and postcolonial theory, these essays take up issues central not only to literature, history, and philosophy but also to natural history, religion, law, and the emerging sciences of man.

The book is structured in three parts, the first of which explores the contexts and relations of 'Subjects and Sovereignty'. Srinivas Aravamudan's

'Hobbes and America', Chapter 1, initiates the discussion by investigating the neglected connection between Hobbes's political thought and his perspective on colonies and subject peoples. Postcolonial theory exposes the shaping (if occluded) role of colonial history in Hobbes's theory of state-formation, allowing Aravamudan to provide a theoretical genealogy of the Enlightenment concept of 'sovereignty'. Although Hobbes's theoretical speculation at first glance may seem abstracted from precise historical anchorage in colonial enterprises—'America' is often understood as a kind of evacuated placeholder for the state of nature in conjectural history—Aravamudan focuses on two early imperial ventures in which Hobbes had some hand. Hobbes's philosophical theory looks different depending on whether one tries to tie it to Bermuda or Virginia as the instantiating example. Whereas the *res nullius* of Bermuda offered the unfettered and unclaimed bounty of a pure state of nature, the existence of native forms of sovereignty in Virginia obliges Hobbes to write over the presence of indigenous political society, and to insist upon a radical break between modern sovereignty and a premodern state of nature—a radical break that allows the theory to efface both other histories and the history of its own emergence in negotiation with these histories. Even as the differential nature of colonial states in Bermuda and Virginia—what might be termed the configuration of a colonial referent— reshapes the theory at those moments in which that referent is allowed to resurface, that suppression must also be understood as the precondition for the theory and an enabling alibi for colonial practices.

In proferring a nuanced account of the theoretical accommodations and suppressions necessitated by differences between these examples, Aravamudan usefully capitalizes on postcolonial critiques of metropolitan etiologies of concepts like 'sovereignty' that separate domestic from overseas political history. Hobbes's ostensibly dehistoricized account of sovereignty and subjection has an imperial valence that must be recognized. Aravamudan shows how the centrality not only of the state but also of private corporate structures to colonization introduces pluralistic notions of sovereignty into Hobbes's theory. In the process, the essay opens up a set of broader methodological questions about the historical, visual, and material underpinnings of theory, showing how certain forms of imaginative embodiment (the state in the form of the Leviathan, colonial ventures in the form of the corporation, sovereignty in the form of oceanic versus territorial dominion) draw abstract entities and relations into our conceptual purview.

David Lloyd likewise takes up the relationship between theories of political economy and forms of aesthetic representation in a discussion of the predicament of the subject in Chapter 2, 'The Physiological Sublime: Pleasure and Pain in the Colonial Context'. Rather than deriving the category of the universal subject from political economy, however, Lloyd turns to the aesthetic: not the self-possessed body or the labouring body but the body that registers pleasure and pain. Postcolonial theory, for which the late eighteenth century marks a threshold, is thus furnished with an unexpected inheritance. Lloyd seeks to find a way around a particular problem within postcolonial theory: how is it possible to construct an account of human subjecthood that steers clear of the claims of representative universality that underwrite Western aesthetics and ethics, on the one hand, while avoiding the anthropological tendency to render the person as the expression, rather than the autonomous agent, of cultural formations, on the other? Postcolonial theory, Lloyd argues, must return not only to political philosophy, but also to Enlightenment discourses of aesthetics—to the moment in which aesthetic discourse furnishes the grounds for the elimination of the body as the condition for the formalization of the subject—in order to find a way out of this impasse.

For Lloyd, the distance that separates Edmund Burke from Immanuel Kant, theoretically and politically, opens on to a more divided eighteenth century. Whereas for Kant, the universality of aesthetic judgement issues from the subject's transcendence of the physical body—the subject's exemption from the pressing exigencies of immediate, physical necessity, and his or her apprehension of the abstracted formal (rather than material) properties of the aesthetic object—for Burke, the universality of aesthetic judgement issues from the shared sensory properties of the body that experiences pleasure and pain. Inasmuch as the savage's subjection to the immediacy of the senses echoes the theoretical subordination to the immediacy of sensation from which Kant's aesthetic theory seeks to emancipate itself, Lloyd argues, Kant's aesthetic subject must be understood as an essential component in the postcolonial critique of the framing of the subject and of history in narratives of progressive development. By contrast, the centrality of the body to Burke's account of aesthetic pleasure, Lloyd contends, means that the universal claims of taste issue from what might be called the physical rather than the subjective universality of the human. Drawing on the racial phenomenology elaborated in Fanon's *Black Skins, White Masks*, Lloyd shows how the appearance of the body of a black woman in Burke's *Enquiry* fissures a text that sought to locate the universality of aesthetic response in the universality of the sensible body. Reading Burke through Fanon exposes the racial blind spot in Burke's model of corporeal sensation as the basis for the universality of taste. The body, which is for Kant material that must be transcended, and which is for Burke the foundation of aesthetic universality, is the site of an irrefutable and irrepressible difference that cannot be assimilated to the declared norms of aesthetic universality. The black body challenges the claims both of the white subject and of the aesthetic to universality by showing that this universality is grounded, in both cases, in the exclusion, and even destruction, of that body's difference. Conjoining Fanon's description of the body as the site that registers the violent effects of a racialized culture to these eighteenth-century models of the aesthetic, Lloyd interrogates the recalcitrance of the colonial body to the normative descriptions of the subject and its history derived from Enlightenment thought.

Together, these essays expose how purportedly universal models of political and aesthetic subjecthood depend upon the occlusion of colonial subjects that nevertheless prove to possess shaping force over the theory. Both Aravamudan and Lloyd address the way in which historical instantiations—rival forms of native sovereignty for Hobbes, the example of the black woman's body for Burke—irrupt into and disrupt the abstract workings of the theory. The second part of the book continues this discussion of the tension between theoretical form and historical context by addressing the degree of compatibility between 'Enlightenment Categories and Postcolonial Classifications'. To what degree do the concepts gleaned from modern theoretical paradigms fit into or onto eighteenth-century modes of ordering and understanding the world? What are the perils and profits of courting anachronism? How might a more nuanced grasp of the eighteenth-century construction of certain crucial modern categories such as Orientalism complicate postcolonial usages of these terms, and vice versa?

Daniel Carey focuses in Chapter 3 on *Robinson Crusoe*, 'the most durable literary creation of the Enlightenment', as Dorinda Outram calls it.[56] Examining the tension in postcolonial criticism of the novel between what Edward Said terms contrapuntal reading, in which the colonial margin or subtext is

[56] Dorinda Outram, *The Enlightenment* (Cambridge: Cambridge University Press, 1995), 63.

revealed to be integral to the constitution of the centre or the whole, and what might be called a palimpsestuous reading, which discovers in an earlier text the traces of a philosophical or historical tradition yet to come, Carey argues that the tendency in modern criticism to read the relationship between Friday and Crusoe as exemplary of slavery (and to bracket other elements of the novel) allows the novel to be inserted into a kind of 'progress narrative' in which all roads lead to the Hegelian master/slave dialectic. The emphasis on slavery, that is, may lapse into a form of theoretical fetishism, in which the broader structure of colonial oppression is analysed through a particular figure ossified into representative singularity—one that occludes the multifarious, dynamic accounts of the notion of 'master' and 'servant' current at the time at which Defoe was writing. In examining how *Crusoe* as a test case is appropriated into a philosophical tradition of Enlightenment of which it may or may not be part, Carey shows how literary texts may be deployed as the ideological handmaidens to the philosophy of the Enlightenment, and interrogates the powers and limits of postcolonial theory in rereading eighteenth-century literary texts.

Felicity Nussbaum also finds reasons for cautioning against the importation of fixed or assumed categories into a reading of late seventeenth- and eighteenth-century texts in 'Between "Oriental" and "Blacks So Called"', 1688–1788' (Chapter 4). Postcolonial theory traditionally separates 'Orientals' and 'Blacks' into distinct subjects of colonialism, yet Orientalism and abolition converge as contemporaneous signs of modernity. Nussbaum locates, by contrast, a group of exemplary works that occupy spaces in-between. In a challenge both to familiar forms of periodization and to assumptions about the 'causation' of Orientalism, she argues that Orientalism and abolitionist discourses arise *in distinct relation to each other*, and that Orientalist discourse in England may become more coherent and legible in part *because* the British slave trade is ended and African slaves are no longer (the principal) abject.

Whereas Nussbaum justly insists upon the imperative to understand Orientalism in relation to the metropolitan discourse of abolition, Siraj Ahmed argues in Chapter 5, 'Orientalism and the Permanent Fix of War', that we must consider the motives and East India Company policies underlying Orientalist scholarship and the material consequences that scholarship authorized in order to challenge characterizations of late eighteenth-century Orientalism within both postcolonial and eighteenth-century criticism. Scholars of eighteenth-century Orientalism, Ahmed notes, have often questioned Said's influential account of Orientalism's complicity with the imperial project, drawing attention to the extraordinary respect shown by the first generation of Orientalists towards the Indian jurisprudence, theology, and culture that they studied. Yet these claims, Ahmed argues, have disregarded the role played by Orientalism in the East India Company's transformation of Indian property law—in particular, its role in the 1793 Permanent Settlement that locked a distinctively modern structure of military fiscalism in place. Only in this context, Ahmed claims, is it possible to grasp the historical significance of the aims and ends to which late eighteenth-century Orientalism was put. As Ahmed suggests, Orientalism's scholarly-textual tendency to reify Indian history complemented and made possible the Company's military-fiscal need to 'fix' the Indian economy so that it would provide a reliable source of capital that could serve as collateral in global financial networks that helped the Company (and later the British state) to pay for the unprecedented costs of modern warfare. Ruined colonial and postcolonial economies, he argues, are thus not aberrations within modernity's trajectory, but constitutive elements thereof.

The three essays that make up the final part of the book, 'Nation, Colony, and Enlightenment Universality', question the oft-made assumption that the critique of colonialism in eighteenth-century literature is always antagonistic to Enlightenment. Doris L. Garraway takes the French tradition as the point of focus in Chapter 6, 'Of Speaking Natives and Hybrid Philosophers: Lahontan, Diderot, and the French Enlightenment Critique of Colonialism'. Why did the philosophical and literary expression of Enlightenment so often take place with ventriloquized foreigners opposing colonial rule? Baron de Lahontan's 1703 *Dialogues avec un Sauvage* and Denis Diderot's 1772 *Supplément au Voyage de Bougainville*, both constructed around the dialogue form, represent the breakdown of colonial discourses by the putative object of colonial command, anticipating some of the most influential critiques in contemporary postcolonial theory, including colonial mimicry and hybridity. Although it is critical to see the reinscription of colonial power dynamics in appropriating native 'speech', Garraway argues, Diderot also subtly thematizes the very impossibility of recovering the voice of the Other. Inasmuch as the Enlightenment public sphere was both constituted and critiqued through dialogue, the incorporation of the speaking native enlarges the scope of that conversation while modelling forms of contestation and critique that were foreclosed by the French absolutist state.

Daniel Carey and Sven Trakulhun's 'Universalism, Diversity, and the Postcolonial Enlightenment' (Chapter 7) addresses the different registers—religious, political, historical, and geographic—on which Enlightenment writers sought to understand the differences among peoples in a moment of increasing global contact. Emphasizing a strain of Enlightenment thought often disregarded in postcolonial theory—the discourse on religious tolerance in the works of John Locke, Pierre Bayle, and Shaftesbury—Carey and Trakulhun offer a comparative account of the various ways in which writers of the German, French, and British Enlightenment sought alternately to accommodate and to disallow diversity. Whereas the discourse on religion fostered tolerance of difference, stadial theories of historical progress assimilated all peoples into a common diachronic trajectory, while emerging concepts of race anchored difference in synchronically possessed distinguishing traits. Subtending each of these theories, Carey and Trakulhun show, were different notions of the shared (or not shared) properties of human beings. The essay emphasizes the plurality of Enlightenment thought on these matters, as well as the importance of situating the theories of these *philosophes* in the precise contexts from which they emerged. Thus by locating the diverging takes on cultural difference in the writings of Immanuel Kant and Johann Gottfried Herder in the context of contemporary debates about anthropology, ethnography, and universal history, Carey and Trakulhun open up the way in which postcolonial critiques of German Enlightenment thought—above all, of Kant—have at times occluded or obscured contradictions and nuances within the broader body of work. In the process, they suggest some of the ways in which Enlightenment thought may itself offer a way out of the impasse between, on the one hand, a univocal Enlightenment universalism that annihilates heterogeneity, mapping all peoples and all nations on to a similar progressive trajectory towards European modernity, and, on the other hand, the universality and portability of attractive Enlightenment concepts such as citizenship, human rights, democracy, and popular sovereignty.

Karen O'Brien's essay, ' "These Nations Newton Made his Own": Poetry, Knowledge, and British Imperial Globalization' (Chapter 8), likewise tackles postcolonial indictments of unilinear Enlightenment progress narratives, but O'Brien turns to the tension between an account of universality that seeks to harness all cultures to a unitary historical trajectory in which all roads lead to Europe (or to capitalism or to global modernity) and the celebration, by some postcolonial critics, of the possibilities and resources offered by an inclusive cosmopolitanism that imagines a global civil society able to supersede the narrowly defined borders of national interest. O'Brien offers a genealogy of Enlightenment cosmopolitanism centred not on the transnational identities and identifications celebrated in some recent postcolonial criticism, but rather on the creation, synthesis, and dissemination of scientific and poetic knowledge. Eighteenth-century British writers, O'Brien shows, capitalized upon the aesthetic possibilities of a global and scientific way of seeing the world, proferring visions in which poetry and natural philosophy become partners in processes of mental awakening and civilization. Focusing on the way in which conceptions of deductive and inductive knowledge central to the Newtonian English Enlightenment were placed in the service of imagining commercial circulation and British global endeavours in the poetry of Mark Akenside, James Thomson, and William Cowper, O'Brien charts a shift from a distinctively Newtonian global consciousness that depicts Britain as promulgating a worldwide knowledge order grounded in universally shared scientific law to a more cosmopolitan notion of global citizenship, in which awareness of the consequences of imperial activity produces more refined models of moral agency. She traces the multiple and multifarious ways in which eighteenth-century writers sought to use the discourses of Enlightenment science and aesthetics to transform the contemporary fact of transoceanic commercial networks and imperial conquests into an order of knowledge or an order of universal citizenship. In the process, she offers an account of the terms and methodologies that eighteenth-century writers used to produce what will paradoxically prove to be plural notions of the ostensibly singular universality of the Enlightenment and the globalization that it is said to mandate and authorize.

The book concludes with a polemical 'Coda' by Suvir Kaul entitled 'How to Write Postcolonial Histories of Empire?', which tackles contemporary apologetic historiography that attempts to recuperate British imperialism as a virtuous exercise. Such narratives, written to frame American responsibilities in the new millennium, have a particular importance because of their accessibility to a wider public through magazine journalism and trade publishing. Kaul identifies new responsibilities and imperatives for postcolonial critics, who must look to the eighteenth century as much as to the nineteenth or twentieth in order to provide alternatives to such comforting and comfortable accounts of colonial experience.

Kaul's observations about the pernicious assumptions that preside over even well-intentioned scholarship serve as a salutary reminder that the notion of 'postcolonial Enlightenment' might be easily misconstrued as projecting the historical and philosophical trajectory of the West on to other nations, cultures, peoples. It is crucial to acknowledge, in closing, the paradoxical if not anachronistic status of our volume's title. There is no such thing as a Postcolonial Enlightenment, and this collection does not aim to invent one (or even many). We must bear in mind Homi Bhabha's caution against theory's use of 'texts within the familiar traditions and conditions of colonial anthropology either to universalize their meaning within its own cultural and academic discourse, or to sharpen its internal critique of the Western logocentric sign, the idealist subject, or indeed the illusions and delusions of civil society',[57] lest the colonial or postcolonial contexts of eighteenth-century studies become the theoretical testing ground or last frontier through which the dominion of Enlightenment—or of its critique—becomes complete.

[57] Homi K. Bhabha, 'The Commitment to Theory', in *The Location of Culture* (London: Routledge, 1994), 31.

Part One

Subjects and Sovereignty

1

Hobbes and America

Srinivas Aravamudan

In [the state of nature] there is no place for Industry; because the fruit thereof is uncertain: and consequently no Culture of the Earth; no Navigation, nor use of the commodities that may be imported by Sea; no commodious Building; no Instruments of moving, and removing such things as require much force; no Knowledge of the face of the Earth; no account of Time; no Arts; no Letters; no Society; and which is worst of all, continuall feare, and danger of violent death; And the life of man, solitary, poore, nasty, brutish, and short...

It may peradventure be thought, there was never such a time, nor condition of warre as this; and I believe it was never generally so, over all the world: but there are many places, where they live so now. For the savage people in many places of America, except the government of small Families, the concord whereof dependeth on naturall lust, have no government; and live at this day in that brutish manner, as I said before.

Thomas Hobbes, *Leviathan*[1]

I would like to thank the John Carter Brown Library and the American Council for Learned Societies for a fellowship during 2006–7 that enabled me to conduct some of the research for this essay.

[1] Thomas Hobbes, *Leviathan*, ed. Richard Tuck (Cambridge: Cambridge University Press, 1991), 89. All further parenthetical citations of *Leviathan* in the text refer to this edition.

> . . . in the beginning, all the world was *America*, and more so than that is now.
>
> John Locke, *Second Treatise of Government*[2]

Without argument, these quotations rank high in the roster of famous sentences culled from political philosophy. The first, by Thomas Hobbes, is the cheerless but strikingly conjectural description of human life before the establishment of civil and political government. In this 'time of Warre, where every man is Enemy to every man', there is minimal security, production, settlement, and trade. Human beings in the state of nature derive none of the secondary benefits of civilization, such as culture, arts, letters, and general knowledge. In this primordial state, human life is hardly worth living: 'solitary, poore, nasty, brutish, and short'. Hobbes associates this miserable condition with that of the North American Indians in the seventeenth century.[3]

Locke's 'America' is also a synonym for 'Nature', but not that of the Hobbesian permanent war of all against all. Locke's New World is pure potentiality, waiting for European settlement. While Hobbes's natural men need to subject themselves to 'a common Power to keep them all in awe', their government rises instantaneously. Once men decide to concede their natural liberty, they begin to enjoy the fruits of sociability, including prop-

[2] John Locke, *Two Treatises of Government*, ed. Peter Laslett (Cambridge: Cambridge University Press, 1988), 301 ('Second Treatise' §49).

[3] The idea of American life as primitive and solitary already originates in Hobbes's *De cive* (*On the Citizen*), published privately in Latin in 1642 and generally in 1647. Hobbes derives perpetual war in the state of nature from the radical equality of the contestants, alleging that 'the present century presents an example of this in the Americans'. See Thomas Hobbes, *On the Citizen*, ed. and trans. Richard Tuck and Michael Silverthorne (Cambridge: Cambridge University Press, 1998), 30. Noel Malcolm suggests that perpetual war is not presented as historically real but more in the manner of an asymptotic limit. That may well be so; nevertheless, indigenous Americans are Hobbes's favourite illustration of this asymptote. See Noel Malcolm, *Aspects of Hobbes* (Oxford: Clarendon Press, 2002), 452. For a nuanced reading of the state of nature as lacking in sovereignty and contractual obligations rather than all the other features of civility, see François Tricaud, 'Hobbes's Conception of the State of Nature from 1640 to 1651: Evolution and Ambiguities', in G. A. J. Rogers and Alan Ryan (eds), *Perspectives on Thomas Hobbes* (Oxford: Clarendon Press, 1988), 107–23. Tricaud suggests that Hobbes emphasized contracts in *De cive* and sovereignty in *Leviathan*. However, as the above passage from *Leviathan* demonstrates, there are 'knock-on' effects on these other areas as well. For Locke, see also John Dunn, *The Political Thought of John Locke: An Historical Account of the Argument of the 'Two Treatises of Government'* (Cambridge: Cambridge University Press, 1969).

erty. Unlike Hobbes, Locke allows for the production of value in the state of nature, where human beings still toil and mix their labour with the land, creating property. Out of the slow process of mastering nature arises society, and from society, government.

Both these differing accounts of the move from nature to government are mythical moments occurring within English narratives of political philosophy. Neither verifiable nor falsifiable, hypotheses concerning natural law work in the manner of narrative thought-experiments backed up by occasional real-world examples. Such accounts—largely if not entirely fictional—allow political philosophers to address questions about the origin, nature, structure, end, foundation, and legitimacy of the state, questions that cannot be answered only through a strict examination of the historical record.[4] Did society pre-exist the state, or do concepts of 'society' and 'government' co-implicate each other? Is Nature without government a permanent state of war, as Hobbes designates 'America', or is it the mute repository of potentiality preferred by Locke? Why was 'America' such a powerful site for the origin myths of seventeenth-century English political philosophy? By focusing on the continent as well as the myth, were political philosophers such as Hobbes and Locke escaping history or supplementing it?

The Hobbesian and Lockean use of 'America' as an ideologeme of conjectural history anticipates many different kinds of thought-experiment in Enlightenment writing. While it might initially appear that such abstract theoretical speculation is unmoored from historical reference, this essay argues that we can uncover the suppressed colonial contexts and occluded premises of writers such as Hobbes, and by doing so fashion an alternate genealogy of key Enlightenment concepts such as 'sovereignty'. The specific history of colonies such as Virginia and Bermuda sheds new light on the larger imperial and postcolonial significance of Hobbes's theory. The insights of postcolonial theory make visible the manner in which the specific theories that arose during the Enlightenment also provided alibis for ongoing colonial practices at the time.[5]

---

[4] I refer abbreviatedly to the brilliant analytical aspects of Norberto Bobbio, *Thomas Hobbes and the Natural Law Tradition*, trans. Daniela Gobetti (Chicago: University of Chicago Press, 1993).

[5] Locke was much more active in colonial policy, as secretary to Lord Shaftesbury, secretary to the Lords Proprietors of Carolina, secretary to the Council of Trade and Plantations, and member of the Board of Trade, as well as being an investor in the Royal African Company and the

Since the Enlightenment, British political historiography has featured a Whig history of internal liberty and a Tory history of external empire along parallel lines. After decolonization, the analysis of the development of British state-building has proceeded on insular lines, with the New British History, linked to the Cambridge School of Political Thought, focusing on 'the history of the state in its domestic or municipal capacities', to the exclusion of 'external relations of states'. Meanwhile, postcolonial historians have taken over the task of accounting for 'overseas' history, earlier the bailiwick of imperial historians. Despite these long-standing patterns of historiography, the origins of domestic state-building and imperial history cannot be truly separated. The early modern British state featured a federation of multiple kingdoms (the four nations of England, Wales, Scotland, and Ireland) in practice, even if, in theory, a composite monarchy supposedly integrated these separate polities into one. England's eventual hegemony over its Celtic fringe parallels Britain's indirect rule over overseas colonies. The focus on state sovereignty, therefore, is a freeze-frame within an imperial-national-regional movement of sovereignties. For this reason, postcolonial interventions take aim at metropolitan etiologies that separate 'domestic' from 'overseas' political history. This naturalized separation is an especially major ideological obstacle when approaching British studies.[6] Keeping these caveats in mind, we can be aware of how much Hobbes's political philosophy also looks forward to empire other than just in its commonly understood sense as a path-breaking rationalization of the state. Rather than imagining colonialism and imperialism as supplementary activities beyond the territory of the nation state, the Hobbesian framework

---

Company of Merchant Adventurers. The topic of Locke and America is much more frequently discussed, given his influence on the American Revolution. Hobbes, on the other hand, did have a brief but significant interaction with American colonial ventures, even though the topic of Hobbes and colonial America still remains slightly more elusive. Mentions are much fewer in the extensive Hobbes literature. For a compelling reading of Locke in the American context, see James Tully, 'Rediscovering America: The *Two Treatises* and Aboriginal Rights', in *An Approach to Political Philosophy: Locke in Contexts* (Cambridge: Cambridge University Press, 1993), 137–78.

[6] For a succinct account of the limitations of the Cambridge School, see Martine Julia van Ittersum, *Profit and Principle: Hugo Grotius, Natural Rights Theories and the Rise of Dutch Power in the East Indies, 1595–1615* (Boston and Leiden: Brill, 2006), pp. xxxviii–xliv. David Armitage's work is a salutary exception. See David Armitage, *The Ideological Origins of the British Empire* (Cambridge: Cambridge University Press, 2000) and also Michael Hechter, *Internal Colonialism: The Celtic Fringe in British National Development, 1536–1966* (Berkeley: University of California Press, 1975).

considers state-formation and imperial activity in the early modern period as conjoint. While Hobbes also shows that the two are analytically separable, he is just as keen to demonstrate how they bleed into each other in practice.

There is, of course, an earlier history of the American colonial encounter, recapitulated into a developmental narrative of political evolution through an encounter with European political reasoning, involving the theologians of the School of Salamanca. Foremost among these thinkers was Francisco de Vitoria, whose *De Indis* argued that the Indians of the New World were human beings, and not subhuman as his rhetorical adversary Juan Ginés de Sepúlveda had notoriously asserted. By recognizing the humanity of the Indian, Vitoria and his followers could assert that the Spanish Crown had full licence to appropriate territories if it met resistance when desiring to access markets or preach conversion. Unlike the Spanish attitude to the Moors as infidels and therefore as inveterate enemies, the recognition of a common humanity between Spaniards and Indians put Americans lower on a developmental scale, analogous to children. This form of Catholic theological reasoning based on natural law took the educability of the Indians as its organizing principle, whereas Protestant responses to North America took an agriculturalist bias while promulgating a non-developmental natural-law individualism in the place of Aristotelian ideas concerning relational degrees of similitude among members of different cultures. Ignoring family structures and rationales, atomistic individualism was used to explain how people alienated their autonomy in the state of nature.[7]

I will argue that the interchange between English political philosophy and northern North America (which is what Hobbes and Locke mostly mean by the loose designation 'America') was a complex dialectic between new developments in politics and history, whether deemed to be theory-in-the-mind or facts-on-the ground. Northern North America was no random site for such theorizations. More than a century after the Spanish encounter with the Americas, English Protestant political theory needed the impetus of recent events stemming from colonial ventures to be able to come up with new justifications for sovereignty that had implications for both state and empire. If Hobbes and Locke were putting forward, each in his own way,

[7] For an excellent discussion of Vitoria and the School of Salamanca, see Anthony Pagden, *The Fall of Natural Man: the American Indian and the Origins of Comparative Ethnology* (Cambridge: Cambridge University Press, 1982).

secularizing accounts of the social contract between sovereign and subject, English colonial ventures to the New World were at the same time justifying their operations through sovereignty doctrines that gave them cover against initial setbacks. While Vitoria and his followers had insisted that theology was the technically appropriate discipline to ascertain the identity of the Indian and provide the basis for rationalizations of Spanish conquest in the Americas, Hobbes and, to some extent, Locke after him turned to the deductive and demonstrative nature of political philosophy as their resource. Could we speculate that this type of early modern political philosophy was a *via media* between the theological vein chosen by Vitoria and the mere particulars of travel narratives concerning colonial ventures from which no obvious theory of sovereignty (*imperium*) or property (*dominium*) could be derived? Political philosophy was still largely deductive, in the manner of theology, but it could also occasionally open itself to inductive and secularizing forms of reasoning from the examples of colonialism and settlement provided by New World travel narratives. At this moment of theoretical inception, Grotius's strong formative influence on Hobbes and Locke cannot be overstated. As Martine van Ittersum suggests, Grotian natural law justified Dutch commercial intervention into areas of Spanish and Portuguese imperial monopoly, even as these very arguments, when generalized, allowed European colonialists to enslave natives for not performing their obligations under the formula for enforcing contracts, or *pacta sunt servanda*.[8]

In what follows, I will first sketch the importance of the early colonial history of Virginia and Bermuda, activities that crucially contextualize Hobbes's political thought in addition to his obvious obsession with the English Civil War. Theorizing sovereignty from Bermuda would be to start from a pure nature of inexhaustible bounty without humanity at all, the purest version of Lockean 'America'. Theorizing from Virginia, on the other hand, meant that Hobbes has to occlude or write over the presence of native forms of sovereignty, and indeed political society, and instead cast his lot with a notion of radical break between modern sovereignty and a premodern state of nature. It is with this idea of a radical break that theory effaces other histories, as well as the history of its own emergence in dialogue with those discourses. While *Leviathan* was Hobbes's greatest English literary

---

[8] See van Ittersum, *Profit and Principle*, p. xxii.

accomplishment, *De cive* was much better known in France and on the Continent during the Enlightenment as the result of Samuel Sorbière's 1649 translation.[9] In the next section, I will demonstrate that Hobbes's dehistoricized and contingent account of sovereignty and subjection has an undeniably imperial and trans-continental valence in both *De cive* and *Leviathan*, showing that Hobbes demonstrates the close links leading from national to imperial sovereignty. Hobbes goes about expending considerable theoretical energy defining the political implications of these dimensions in terms of the new artificial person of the corporation that bridges nation and empire. The artificial person, for Hobbes, defines the very notion of the sovereign, but is also theorized as analogical with the corporation, the private commercial entity composed of fewer individuals than an entire polity, but nonetheless different from a single individual or an extant social form such as the family. Furthermore, Hobbes is presciently aware of the oceanic futures of England's empire in *Leviathan*. These discussions will cumulatively demonstrate that Hobbes imagines a political framework that makes the ideological transition from English nation to British Empire.[10]

I The early colonial history of Virginia and Bermuda

Colonial America served as interpretive occasion, historical example, and mythical construct for Hobbes. His relationship to an incipient 'authority of

---

[9] *De cive* was much more widely known on the Continent than *Leviathan*. Rousseau was mostly influenced by *De cive*, which went through multiple Latin editions. The Latin *Leviathan* was available only through Hobbes's *Opera omnia*. A full French translation of *Leviathan* was not available until 1971. I owe this information to Richard Tuck, 'Hobbes and Democracy', in Annabel Brett and James Tully with Holly Hamilton-Bleakley (eds), *Rethinking the Foundations of Modern Political Thought* (Cambridge: Cambridge University Press, 2006), 172.

[10] See Quentin Skinner, *The Foundations of Modern Political Thought*, 2 vols (Cambridge: Cambridge University Press, 1978); Richard Tuck, 'Hobbes and Democracy', in Brett and Tully with Bleakley (eds), *Rethinking the Foundations of Modern Political Thought*, 171–90; Armitage, *The Ideological Origins of the British Empire*; and David Armitage, 'Hobbes and the Foundations of Modern International Thought', in Brett and Tully with Bleakley (eds), *Rethinking the Foundations of Modern Political Thought*, 219–35.

experience' was not pure rejection, but a complex and surreptitious attitude.[11] Hobbes knew more about the structure of North American indigenous groups than the famous quotation from *Leviathan* reveals. From 1622 to 1624, he was intimately involved in the affairs of the Virginia Company and the Bermuda (Somers Island) Company on behalf of his Oxford classmate and eventual patron, William Cavendish, the second Earl of Devonshire. It is tempting to wonder if the younger Hobbes ever met the well-travelled and intellectually minded Thomas Harriot, who sailed on Ralegh's Roanoke expedition as a mathematician trained at Oxford, and who later continued to teach outgoing missionaries and settlers Algonquian languages while a retainer of the Earl of Northumberland in Syon House in London from 1607 to 1621.[12] In the ongoing relationship then developing between Bermuda and Virginia, there was an interaction between a colony on uninhabited land, and one that was verging on the conquest of rival states and territories. If in the case of Jamestown, economic activities were impossible without various forms of violence against indigenous Americans, in the case of Bermuda, economic activities commenced first, provided that military backup could be developed against piracy and Spanish threats. Strategically positioned, the Bermudas were a natural gateway to the Atlantic seaboard from Newfoundland to the lower Caribbean basin. Given Hobbes's intimate involvement with Virginia Company and Bermuda Company affairs, Noel Malcolm suggests that, 'the problem of the American Indian in Hobbes's works ... is akin to the problem of the dog that did not bark in the night: why did Hobbes make so little use of his special knowledge?' It would be my argument here that this background is not just a missing context that Hobbes puzzlingly did not use, but evidence of

[11] Despite his stint as an amanuensis to Francis Bacon, Hobbes was never an empiricist or an inductive thinker. Nevertheless, early in his career he was deeply concerned with questions surrounding history, translating Thucydides' *History of the Peloponnesian War* later that decade. See Richard Schlatter (ed.), *Hobbes's Thucydides* (New Brunswick, NJ: Rutgers University Press, 1975). Hobbes went from a humanistic phase to a scientific one by the early 1630s, when he was struck by the power of the Pythagorean theorem in Euclidean geometry and Cartesian advances in physics and optics. *Elements of Law* (1641), *De cive* (1647), and *Leviathan* (1651) are remarkable texts of political philosophy in dialogue with contemporary science. For a powerful discussion of the developing authority of experience in colonial America, see Jim Egan, *Authorizing Experience: Refigurations of the Body Politic in Seventeenth-Century New England Writing* (Princeton: Princeton University Press, 1999).
[12] See John W. Shirley, *Thomas Harriot: A Biography* (Oxford: Clarendon Press, 1983); and Robert Fox (ed.), *Thomas Harriot: An Elizabethan Man of Science* (Burlington, Vt.: Ashgate, 2000).

an active writing-over or effacement on the part of Hobbes, analogical to and prefigurative of the bad faith that motivated Locke's mobilization of the trope of 'America', as James Tully has argued.[13]

Early English voyagers in North America were aware that they had entered into a populated region with complex political structures and alliances—after all, the Algonquian name for their territory was Tsenacom-macah, meaning 'densely inhabited land'.[14] In addition to the Powhatan or Pamunkey area, mistakenly described as Wingandacoa to Walter Ralegh, John Smith's *General History of Virginia* mentions several fiefdoms including Menatonon, Secotan, and Pomouik, and a number of clans including the Sasquesahanocks, the Massawomekes, the Monacans, Rapahanocks, and the Mannahoacks. The military chieftains of these groups were collectively referred to as 'werowances', but the English often failed to comprehend that the werowances were 'outside' military chiefs, just as there was a parallel structure of 'inside' chiefs with equal or greater jurisdiction over the group. Given that the coastal Algonquians followed matrilineal practices, inside chiefs included clan mothers and also older men.[15]

Accounts of the political structure of the native groups by contemporary observers acknowledge them as highly organized, constituting a system of petty states in shifting alliances of mutual conflict and cooperation, war-making and trading.[16] Recent scholarship has also re-centred the American experience in the Chesapeake and the middle colonies as more characteristic of early colonial experience than the long-standing emphasis on Puritan New England.[17] As Karen Ordahl Kupperman describes the more general implications of early English observations in Virginia,

[13] Noel Malcolm, 'Hobbes, Sandys, and the Virginia Company', in *Aspects of Hobbes*, 75. For Tully on Locke see n. 5 above.

[14] Most of the early voyages are collected in Samuel Purchas, *Hakluytus Posthumus or Purchas His Pilgrimes*, 4 vols (London, 1625).

[15] See Alden T. Vaughan, *Transatlantic Encounters: American Indians in Britain, 1500–1776* (Cambridge: Cambridge University Press, 2006).

[16] As Smith says about their war-making against each other, 'When they intend any warres, the Werowances vsually haue the advice of their Priests and Coniurers, and their allies, and ancient friends, but chiefly the Priests determine their resolution.' See John Smith, *The Generall Historie of Virginia, New-England and the Summer Isles* (London, 1631), 32.

[17] See Philip Gura, 'The Study of Colonial American Literature, 1966–87: A Vade Mecum', *William and Mary Quarterly*, 3rd ser., 45 (1988), 305–41; and Jack Greene, *Pursuits of Happiness: The Social Development of Early Modern British Colonies and the Formation of American Culture* (Chapel Hill: University of North Carolina Press, 1988).

American natives were social beings, possessing all the characteristics necessary to civility: community life and the family structure, hierarchy, and orderliness that made it possible; care for the morrow by cultivating and preserving foods, and all informed by a religious sensibility that honored the human dependence on supernatural forces in the universe.[18]

In the early phase, the English were supplicants rather than conquerors. John Smith observes that 'they [the Algonquians] seldome make warre for lands or goods, but for women and children, and principally for revenge'.[19] These ethnographic observations are supplemented by knowledge of other cultural details such as royal funerary rituals and burial sites. Villages are shown as neatly laid out and there is a sophisticated deployment of agricultural practices. Hobbes was almost certainly aware of Smith's and Harriot's narratives as well as favourable representations of Algonquian settlements such as John White's watercolours, which were, in turn, reproduced in Theodore de Bry's engravings for Harriot's Virginian narrative.[20] Smith recognizes the existence of magistrates and a form of monarchy, while 'one as Emperour ruleth ouer many Kings or Governours'.[21] Furthermore, 'they all know their severall lands, and habitations, and limits, to fish, foule, or hunt in, but they hold all of their great Werowance, Powhatan [Wahunsonacock], vnto whom they pay tribute of skinnes, beads, copper, pearle, deere, turkies, wild beasts, and corne. What he commandeth they dare not disobey in the least thing.'[22] Thomas Harriot had already reported that the most powerful werowances controlled up to eighteen different towns each in their respective areas of jurisdiction. But some of these perceptions were already misrecognitions that imagined outside chiefs as paramount chiefs.[23]

While the existence of revenge raids and territorial skirmishes (and occasional charges of cannibalism) among the Algonquians confirms that the

---

[18] Karen Ordahl Kupperman, *Indians and English: Facing Off in Early America* (Ithaca: Cornell University Press, 2000), 144.

[19] Smith, *The Generall Historie of Virginia, New-England and the Summer Isles*, 33.

[20] For the most exhaustive catalogue raisonné, see Paul Hulton and David Beers Quinn, *The American Drawings of John White, 1577–1590*, 2 vols (London: The Trustees of the British Museum and Chapel Hill: University of North Carolina Press, 1964). See also Kim Sloan, *A New World: England's First View of America* (London: The British Museum Press, 2007).

[21] Smith, *The Generall Historie of Virginia, New-England and the Summer Isles*, 37.

[22] Ibid. 38.

[23] Thomas Harriot, *A briefe and true report of the new found land of Virginia* (Frankfurt, 1590), 25.

mid-Atlantic coast of North America was by no means a peaceful region, it is still a far cry from the hyperbolical notion of a war of all against all, without property, territorial jurisdiction, or political subjection, as Hobbes appears to suggest.[24] The political system, as it had evolved in the region, contained many of the key ingredients for the laws of war and peace as specified for European polities by international lawyers such as Vitoria and Gentili earlier, and Grotius, whose *De jure belli ac pacis* / *On the Law of War and Peace* was about to appear in 1625. All these authors describe rival states' need for mutual recognition and their search for political equilibrium amid economic production, trading, and making war and peace.[25] The presence of the first English settlers introduced another fledgling state. The Virginia Company was a statelet established by private capital with royal assent, and introduced into a situation of territorial competition and co-optation with older rivals within the rudimentary Amerindian inter-state structure.

By the 1610s, Jamestown was in danger of collapse, partly as a result of petty jealousies and internal political anarchy. Walter Ralegh's Roanoke colony had also failed for lack of supplies. Smith complains bitterly that 'nothing [is] so difficult as to establish a Common wealth so farre remote from men and meanes, and where mens mindes are vntoward as neither doe well themselues, nor suffer others'.[26] An early sermon, by William Symonds, was very critical of the first depredations made by the colonists: 'Why is there no remedie, but assoone as we come on land, like Wolues, and Lyons, and Tygres, long famished, we must tear in peeces, murther, and torment the naturall inhabitants with cruelties never read, nor heard of before?'[27] The settlement nonetheless stabilized as a result of skilful pressure diplomacy and military threats made by Smith, who managed to turn his own temporary captivity in the Powhatan

---

[24] The natives 'who very bruitishly and cruelly doe dayly eate and consume one another, through their emulations, warres, and contentions'. Robert Cushman, *A Sermon Preached at Plimmouth* (London, 1622), 18. Of course the most systematic refutation of the persistent savage war myth can be found in Francis Jennings, *The Invasion of America: Indians, Colonialism, and the Cant of Conquest* (Chapel Hill: Published for the Institute of Early American History and Culture, University of North Carolina Press, 1975).

[25] These Amerindian inter-state rivalries could certainly merit comparison with discussions in Thucydides, if not with the ongoing Thirty Years War that raged through Europe in the first decades of the seventeenth century until the Treaty of Westphalia in 1647 established a rudimentary system of European inter-state adjudication.

[26] Smith, *The Generall Historie of Virginia, New-England and the Summer Isles*, 45.

[27] William Symonds, *Virginia. A Sermon Preached at White-Chappel* (London, 1609), 14.

village of Werowocomoco (when about to undergo the *huskanaw* ceremony for integration into the group) into an agreement with the outside chief Wahunsonacock for more amicable trading relations.[28] A peaceful period followed from 1614 until 1622, with several experiments involving coexistence and unsuccessful attempts to convert the natives to Christianity. Insatiable land demands by settlers during these years were also inexorably squeezing the coastal Algonquians. Despite this temporary stabilization, the annual setbacks of the Virginia Company, which included a monetary drain on capital as well as the high mortality rates of the settlers, had been creating political pressure back in London. The initial merchant-adventurers were still to see the profits they had hoped for when they invested.

Meanwhile, the accidental settling of Bermuda following a shipwreck in 1609 brought up a different possibility of colonization of land where there was genuinely no human habitation. It was in the initial Bermudan writings of George Somers, Thomas Gates, and Silvester Jourdain that the mythical original of the Lockean idea of a virginal America full of miraculous bounty arose. The birds on the island had never encountered predators, let alone human beings. Lewes Hughes, a minister who was one of the colony's most enthusiastic backers, reports that 'the silly wilde birds coming in so tame into my Cabbin, and goe so familiarly betweene my feet, and round about the Cabbin, and into the fire, with a strange lamentable noyse, as though they did bemoane vs, and bid vs, take, kill, roast and eate them'.[29] The fortuitous colonization of Bermuda—until then characterized by the Spaniards as an enchanted Isle of Devils—became the new site of hopes that were being dashed to the ground in Virginia. Comparing it with 'the poore *Virginian* plantation', Silvester Jourdain describes Bermuda as 'one of the sweetest Paradises that be vpon the earth'.[30] Hughes, ever the indefatigable clergyman, thanks the Almighty for fortifying the Bermudas with formidable rocks and shoals and for 'reserving and keeping these Ilands ever since the beginning of the world, for the English Nation'.[31] These were stock sentiments expressed by many

---

[28] Kupperman, *Indians and English*, 114. For information regarding the plotting around Pocahontas, see Ralph Hamor, *A True Discovrse of the Present Estate of Virginia* (London, 1615).

[29] Lewes Hughes, *A Plaine and True Relation of the Goodness of God towards the Sommer Ilands* (London, 1621), B1r.

[30] Silvester Jourdain, *A Plaine Description of the Barmudas, Now Called Sommer Ilands* (London, 1613), A3r.

[31] Hughes, *A Plaine and True Relation*, A3r. See also Lewes Hughes, *A Letter Sent into England from the Summer Ilands* (London, 1615).

contemporary writers.[32] The islands also become the target for speculative projects involving fishing expeditions—a 1615 pamphlet proposes to build 100 'buses' (or herring boats) and breed 600 mariners to fill these boats. As such a large fishing operation would be prey to pirates, the pamphlet also argues for warships to protect the buses.[33]

Hobbes enters this thicket of colonial debates as a surrogate for his patron Lord Cavendish, Earl of Devonshire. While active in assisting his patron with Virginia and Bermuda business from 1619, on 19 June 1622 Hobbes formally became a shareholder of the Virginia Company, and he attended at least thirty-seven meetings over the next two years.[34] While a faction under Thomas Smythe had controlled company affairs from 1606 to 1619, a rival group under Edwin Sandys and the Earl of Southampton had seized control under a reformist agenda. Hobbes's patron belonged to Sandys's group. Taking over from Smythe's control, the Sandys faction assigned Hobbes administrative jobs such as the need to draft responses to letters of complaint from Virginian settlers, letters probably similar to that from an earlier correspondent for whom the grapes were sour, both literally and metaphorically.[35]

Sandys was a dangerous associate for the naturally fearful Hobbes. As a Member of Parliament, Sandys had earned the lifelong enmity of King James after giving an electrifying speech in favour of 'elective' rather than 'succes-

---

[32] 'These Islands may seem, as well in the strange manner of their discovery, as in respect of their strength and situation, to be ordained and reserved by the providence of God, not so much for themselves (being small) as for the more easy and commodious planting of other parts of this new world; and especially of *Virginia*.' See John Speed, *The Theatre of the Empire of Great-Britaine* (London, 1676), 42.

[33] E[dward] S[harpe], *Britaines Busse* (London, 1615). The Somers Island Company was incorporated on 29 June 1615, and 'company colonization' formally began. The first black slave arrived in Bermuda in 1616 to labour in the pearl fisheries offshore, and according to some this was the first instance of African slavery on a New World English settlement. Wesley Frank Craven, *An Introduction to the History of Bermuda* (Bermuda: Bermuda Maritime Museum Press, 1990), 91.

[34] 'It pleaseth the Right Hono[ble] the Lord Cauendish to passe ouer one of his shares of land in Virginia unto M[r] Hobbs w[ch] being allowed by the Auditors was also approued and ratified by the Court', quoted in Malcolm, *Aspects of Hobbes*; see Susan Myra Kingsbury (ed.), *Records of the Virginia Company*, 4 vols (Washington, DC: Library of Congress, 1906–35), iv, 40.

[35] A Virginian alderman complains to Nicholas Ferrar, Sandys's treasurer, that Virginia's promoters had tricked too many dupes into investing there, even though 'the Grapes were sower, and the Country not proper for Wynes, the Mulbery Trees in Virginia had a prickle in their leaves which destroyed the Silkwormes when they grew to bigness, and as for the

sive' kingship on 21 May 1614.[36] Some overblown rumours circulated that Sandys's 'intention was to erect a free state in Virginia', but the record is silent on what if anything the monarchist Hobbes thought of these supposed predilections in Sandys's circle.[37] What is certain is that small investors had coalesced around Sandys's successful wresting of control of the company from the larger capital investors such as Smythe and Lord Rich, even though Sandys's ally Cavendish was also a large investor.

The moment of Hobbes's formal entry into the Company deliberations on 19 June was circumstantially significant. News had just come to London by the *Seaflower* a few days earlier about the killing of approximately 340 English settlers during an insurrection led by the new Powhatan outside chief, Opechancanough, on 22 March. By August, the Company was recommending 'wherefore as they haue merited let them haue a p_r petuall warre wth out peace or truce'. Urging full extermination by October, the Company nonetheless suggested that the young be preserved, 'whose bodies may, by labo^r and service become profitable, and theire minde not overgrowne wth evill Customes, be reduced to civilitie, and afterwarde to Christianitie'.[38] In December, John Martin wrote that the Indians had to be brought under subjection by military means but they ought not to be fully extirpated 'least the woods and wild beasts should over runn them [the colonists]'.[39] Edward Waterhouse was to see the massacre as beneficial to the colony because of the ensuing sympathy factor it generated in England.[40] While it took a full year for the impact of the massacre to be felt fully in the Company courts and

---

converting of ye Infidells it was a thing impossible they being ye cursed race of Cham . . . the world had been too long deluded by Virginia'. Nicholas Ferrar, *Sir Thomas Smith's Misgovernment of the Virginia Company* (Cambridge: Roxburghe Club, 1990), 12. Hobbes may have helped draft some of the company documents attributed to Lord Cavendish, as has been speculated with respect to publications such as *Horae subsecivae*.

[36] The King is supposed to have remarked, 'the Virginia Company was a seminary for a seditious Parliament'. See Wesley Frank Craven, *Dissolution of the Virginia Company: The Failure of a Colonial Experiment* (New York: Oxford University Press, 1932), 17.

[37] Ibid. 277.

[38] 'Letter to Governor and Council in Virginia, Aug 1, 1622', in Kingsbury (ed.), *Records of the Virginia Company*, iii, 672.

[39] John Martin, 'The Manner Howe to Bringe the Indians into Subiection', in Kingsbury (ed.), *Records of the Virginia Company*, iii, 706.

[40] Edward Waterhouse, *A Declaration of the State of the Colony and Affaires in Virginia With a Relation of the Barbarous Massacre in the Time of Peace* (London, 1622), 33.

English public opinion, the intersection of the ideas of reduction and religious re-education in the company documents is intriguing, as I will discuss further in the next section. Writing soon after the 1622 uprising, Samuel Purchas would suggest that agricultural settlement was the key: 'the very names of a Colony and Plantation doe import a reasonable and seasonable culture'.[41]

The revolt nearly finished off the colony as the subsequent famine killed another five to six hundred settlers. Meanwhile, the surviving English settlers fought back ferociously, poisoning around two hundred Indians through drinks provided at a sham peace parley. The goal of the First Indian War of 1622–32 was to expel all natives from the area between the James and York rivers. Captives were sent to the Bermudas as slaves. Proponents of Indian conversion to Christianity, such as the well-known writer-clerics John Donne and Samuel Purchas, also deemed the land available for English occupation.[42] The Sandys–Southampton leadership was rightly blamed for the Virginian catastrophe that disastrously compounded its over-hasty colonization efforts when in charge.[43]

At this point, Hobbes had hardly published, although there is indirect evidence that his translation of Thucydides' *History of the Peloponnesian Wars*, published later in 1629, was begun shortly after the Virginia Company's dissolution. Themes from both Thucydides and Tacitus (arguably the two greatest political influences on Hobbes) ought to have been reflected in relation to descriptions of the political structure of Algonquian groups, indeed present in others' accounts of the Indians, but were puzzlingly not

[41] Samuel Purchas, 'Virginias Verger: Or a Discourse shewing the benefits which may grow to this Kingdome from American English Plantations, and specially those of Virginia and Summer Ilands', in *Hakluytus Posthumus, or, Purchas His Pilgrimes*, 20 vols (Glasgow: James MacLehose and Sons, 1905–7), xix, 239. At this time 'culture' equals 'agriculture'.

[42] See e.g. Purchas, 'Virginias Verger', in *Hakluytus Posthumus*, and John Donne, *A Sermon upon the VIII Verse of the I Chapter of the Acts of the Apostles Preached to the Honourable Company of the Virginian Plantation 13 November 1622* (London, 1622).

[43] Sandys had overseen an over-ambitious programme that blundered by sending 4,000 new settlers during four years without adequate supplies or local housing. Mortality rates ranged from 50 to 75 per cent over the period, and furthermore, the Company had sunk an additional £85,000 on general expenses, and £5,000 into an ironworks without any appreciable return. While Sandys had recommended cohabitation and eventual integration of Indians into English settler society amid a liberalizing regime that abolished martial law, inaugurated a colonial assembly, and introduced English common law, his mismanagement of the company led to the

present in Hobbes's remarks, except indirectly through the frontispiece of his private edition of *De cive*, which I will discuss. Rhetorically speaking, this was not just the case of the dog that did not bark in the night, as Malcolm suggests, but perhaps a deliberate omission.[44] However, other English settlers made up for Hobbes's silence, seeing their Algonquian adversaries in relation to Tacitus's discussion of German and English forebears of modern civilization as enjoying a rude liberty and an indomitable spirit of equality. As Tacitus had remarked about the Germanic tribes, Algonquians also relied on women as their agriculturalists. There was an additional point of commonality in that the unwritten roots of English common law, which supposedly followed hoary Saxon traditions and were formalized for the first time by Coke's massive *Institutes* (1628–41), broadly resembled the Algonquian respect of native traditions and customs that were also inherited but not formalized through writing. In a 1637 work about Massachusetts, the anti-Puritan Thomas Morton suggests through mock-epic style that Americans 'might be the scattered Trojans when Brutus departed Latium', but also alleges, in a negative vein, that Indians 'build houses like the wild Irish'.[45] The colonial propagandist William Wood compares aspects of native culture to English culture in 'quondam times'.[46] As David Armitage suggests, the writings by multiple hands about America in Hakluyt's voyages formed so many 'aetiological fictions' and 'charter histories', whereby Madoc of Wales, Hespéro of Spain, and Japhet from the Bible were variously deemed ancestors of the Americans. Peter Heylyn's *Microcosmus* and also De Bry's *America* discussed similarities between indigenous Americans and Picts, and Roger Williams compares

catastrophic results of high mortality and bankruptcy. Sandys's control was resoundingly defeated by a realignment of factions in favour of the king's supporters after a Royal Investigation conducted in 1623 following the uprising of 1622 and the terrible winter of 1622–3. By 1624 the company charter had been revoked by the King's Bench, and Virginia became the first English royal colony. See Craven, *Dissolution of the Virginia Company* and Alden T. Vaughan, ' "Expulsion of the Salvages": English Policy and the Virginia Policy of 1622', in *The Roots of American Racism: Essays on the Colonial Experience* (New York: Oxford University Press, 1995), 105–27.

[44] Richard Tuck has been a significant proponent of the significance of Hobbes's Tacitism. See Richard Tuck, 'Hobbes and Tacitus,' in G. A. J. Rogers and Tom Sorell (eds), *Hobbes and History* (London: Routledge, 2000), 99–111. See also Richard Tuck, *Philosophy and Government 1572–1651* (Cambridge: Cambridge University Press, 1993), 279–345.

[45] Thomas Morton, *New English Canaan, or New Canaan* (London, 1637), 24, 20.

[46] William Wood, *New Englands Prospect* (London, 1634), 8; see also Egan, *Authorizing Experience*, 59.

Indian culture with that of the Jews and their languages to Greek.[47] We will see, however, that a 'cross-cultural' notion of sovereignty can emerge as a kind of subtractive third language, comprehensible only when straddling two cultures rather than within any one of them. This cross-cultural idea of sovereignty bridges both national and imperial sites. Connecting these separate contexts of Europe and America with each other, the new formulation of sovereignty makes a modest but intriguing appearance in Hobbes's writing almost two decades later.

II The theoretical reduction of America to Company colonization

The colonists hoped to 'reduce' the Algonquians in at least two senses, the first a military one, in which they succeeded, and the second the now archaic sense of 'reduce', which meant to bring them to civility and Christ.[48] Hobbes's reduction was of a theoretical variety. His exposure to Virginian affairs is modestly visible in the private edition of *De cive* (1642). The frontispiece image of this first edition of *De cive* (Figure 1.1) visualizes the move from the state of nature to government. On the right, we see an Algonquian, on a pedestal entitled 'Libertas', based recognizably on John White's watercolours and Theodore De Bry's engravings, offering his allegiance to a European-looking female allegory of sovereignty, standing on a pedestal entitled 'Imperivm'. This image tantalizingly portrays the general categories of subjection and consent as taking place within a broadly American colonial framework.[49] The Algonquian subject represents the choice of natural man, who wishes to escape the ambivalent mixture of natural liberty and anarchic

---

[47] David Armitage, 'The New World and British Historical Thought: From Richard Hakluyt to William Robertson' in Karen Ordahl Kupperman (ed.), *America in European Consciousness, 1493–1750* (Chapel Hill: University of North Carolina Press, 1995), 58.

[48] For an interesting discussion of the multiple senses of the term 'reduction', see Kupperman, *Indians and English*, 130.

[49] See Richard Tuck's brief editorial commentary in Hobbes, *On the Citizen*, ed. and trans. Tuck and Silverthorne, pp. xxiv–xxv; and Richard Ashcraft, 'Leviathan Triumphant: Thomas Hobbes and the Politics of Wild Men', in Edward J. Dudley and Maximillian E. Novak (eds), *The Wild Man Within: An Image in Western Thought from the Renaissance to Romanticism* (Pittsburgh: University of Pittsburgh Press, 1972), 141–82.

Figure 1.1 Thomas Hobbes, *Elementorvm philosophiae sectio tertia de cive* (Paris, 1642), frontispiece. By permission of the William Andrews Clark Memorial Library, University of California, Los Angeles.

violence. Behind the androgynous-looking Algonquian warrior, armed with a bow and arrow, there is a settlement evoking White's and De Bry's Secoton, along with depictions of native warfare. On the left, the European allegory of sovereignty features sword and scales. In the background, peaceful agricultural production is depicted, perhaps as an unintended irony, given that White's drawings and De Bry's plates also show systematic Algonquian agriculture in Pomouik.

European sovereignty, 'Imperivm', is a combination of conquest and contract, demanding sovereign subjection but enforcing an imperial peace. Through this frontispiece, the phylogeny of cultural plurality has been recast as an ontogeny of political universality. Ethnographic observations about family groups have been converted into theoretical speculations about individual behaviour. Conventional patriarchalists and monarchists wished to analogize the state as macrocosm to the family as microcosm. This analogy of concentric dependence from the family to the state, found in both Aristotle and Judaeo-Christian sources as well as neo-patriarchalist accounts of sovereignty such as Robert Filmer's, is replaced by a narrative that occludes the family in place of a radical separation between two moments, a pre-political situation, where the individual is free but in constant fear of violent death, and a properly political moment, when individuals band together to offer their obedience to a sovereign who will protect them from insecurity in exchange for the comforts of government. By thus superimposing a myth regarding the birth of politics on the general background of the European conquest of America, Hobbes simultaneously denies America's political past even as he implies American consent to colonization. This image makes the beginning of politics a transcontinental, cross-cultural, imperial, and ultimately sovereign narrative, divested of history but reimpregnated with myth.

Hobbes rejects entirely the classical tradition that naturalizes government as reintegrating the family unit with the state. His self-regulating radical individualism, by way of a constructivist thought-experiment, combines with a surreptitious citation of recent English colonial experience. Hobbesian theory ultimately eschews both history and the family as bad forms of naturalization that prevent the understanding of government as radical artifice. The sole textual mention of Americans in *De cive* makes them into living anachronisms. They are current-day examples of the past of 'nations, now civilized and flourishing, whose inhabitants then were few, savage, short lived, poor and mean, and lacked all the comforts and amenities of life which *peace* and society afford'.[50] These lines foreshadow the 'solitary, poore, nasty, brutish and short' tag in *Leviathan*. In that later masterpiece, Hobbes grants that

---

[50] Hobbes, *On the Citizen*, 30.

American political structures might have existed in the form of rudimentary family structures: 'for the savage people in many places of America, except the government of small Families, the concord whereof dependeth on naturall lust, have no government' (p. 89). The grammatical structure of the sentence embeds the possible existence of the state in America (they have government of families) as an exceptional subordinate clause inside the main clause (they have no government at all) that negates the very possibility of the exception. This disavowal also goes against classical and medieval European political theory, which had posited the existence of at least three forms of political sovereignty, one based on family, or *ex generatione*, another based on consent, *ex contractu*, and a third based on conquest, or *ex delicto*. In this context, it is interesting to mention Samuel Purchas's contrasting religious ideas concerning the ways in which rights over Virginia were granted to the English that was truly extraordinary in the manner in which it attempted to list all the different arguments by which conquest could be justified: 'right naturall, right nationall, right by first discovery, by accepted trade, by possession surrendred voluntarily, continued constantly, right by gift, by birth, by bargaine and sale, by cession, by forfeiture in that late damnable trechery and massacre, and the fatal possession taken by so many murthered English'.[51]

Hobbes suppresses the family, and combines consent and conquest into the sole model of political sovereignty feasible at all times. The voluntary alienation of man's liberty in the state of nature leads to civility, even as family structures and individuals are relegated to a history of the pre-political. The beginnings of commerce ('chrematistic' society according to Aristotle) are possible only after the initial social contract that underwrites all civilized behaviour. Using very similar premises to Hobbes's, Locke posits an agency theory of the social contract for Hobbes's alienation theory, but in order to maintain an agency theory, Locke has to posit a two-step approach to the problem, whereby society is a secondary construct and includes the possibility of rudimentary social exchange. Government becomes an altogether tertiary outcome. Despite these differences, for both Hobbes and Locke, complex political society is portrayed as a radical departure from the presumable atomism of pre-political individuals and families.[52] Even though

---

[51] Samuel Purchas, 'Virginias Verger', in *Hakluytus Posthumus*, xix, 266.
[52] Locke was certainly much better informed than Hobbes regarding French and Spanish justifications in relation to the colonial settlement of the Americas. See Daniel Carey, *Locke, Shaftesbury, and Hutcheson: Contesting Diversity in the Enlightenment and Beyond* (Cambridge: Cambridge University Press, 2006), ch. 3.

this charge does not sit well in relation to the actual structure of Algonquian states as they were found in the seventeenth century, the supplementary goal for political philosophy from Hobbes to Rousseau is to release the family from a direct role in the understanding of the political bond. While the family is no longer the site for the production of government, it is converted into a crucial propagandistic area for the reproduction of social relations, right philosophical and moral attitudes, and private non-political freedoms detached from the imperative to maintain the public laws. It is no surprise that Locke and Rousseau devoted considerable attention to the theory of education, and while Hobbes did not devote a specific treatise to the subject of pedagogy, he makes several ancillary remarks that relate to the misgovernment of the passions in both *Leviathan* and *Behemoth*. Replacing covenant theology with contractarianism was, for Hobbes, an additional way to secularize religious metaphysics and trim the sails of 'aristocratic aggrandizement' with 'bourgeois diffidence'.[53]

Hobbes reconstructs the political sphere within a single mythic time. The medium of Hobbes's new organicist conception of politics is omeomerous (where part and whole are all part of the same substance) in the Aristotelian sense, best represented visually by the same small individual bodies forming the composite body of the sovereign in the famous frontispiece to *Leviathan* (Figure 1.2).[54] This image reveals the paradox of political philosophy as a form of imaginative social construction that relies on fiction, myth, and rhetorical persuasion, despite Hobbes's explicit protestations against rhetoric.[55]

Hobbes's *Leviathan* was written and published at the mid-point of the Interregnum, almost a decade after the private edition of *De cive*. Trying his best to keep company with the Royalists (who suspected his 'levelling fancy') even while his text subtly rationalizes obedience to Cromwell, Hobbes needs

[53] In an elegant recent study, Victoria Kahn sees Hobbesian contractarianism as a solution to the problem of aristocratic romance that unites literature and politics. This study makes possible the imagination of a rich literary subject of the social contract, rather than the thin rights-bearing liberal subject that has been projected backwards from the nineteenth century. See Victoria Kahn, *Wayward Contracts: The Crisis of Political Obligation in England, 1640–1674* (Princeton: Princeton University Press, 2004), 150.

[54] I owe this insight regarding the omeomerous and the anomeomerous in Aristotle to Bobbio, *Thomas Hobbes and the Natural Law Tradition*.

[55] The best argument about *Leviathan* as a post-humanist text that nonetheless uses eloquence and humanist persuasion in the service of science is in Quentin Skinner, *Reason and Rhetoric in the Philosophy of Hobbes* (Cambridge: Cambridge University Press, 1996).

Non est potestas Super Terram quæ Comparetur ei Iob. 41. 24

LEVIATHAN
Or
THE MATTER, FORME
and POWER of A COMMON-
WEALTH ECCLESIASTICALL
and CIVIL.

By THOMAS HOBBES
of MALMESBVRY.

London
Printed for Andrew Crooke
1651

Figure 1.2 Thomas Hobbes, *Leviathan* (London, 1651), frontispiece. By permission of the Rare Book collection at the Wilson Library, University of North Carolina,

to establish even further distance from both Parliamentary accounts of mixed sovereignty and Sandys's notions of mixed and collective rule in Jamestown and the Bermudas.[56] Hobbes and his new Cavendish patron, the son of his erstwhile classmate, had fully associated with the exiled court in the 1640s when Hobbes was also tutor of mathematics to Prince Charles. Meanwhile, three of Sandys's sons had ended up as Parliamentary officers during the English Civil War. Therefore, even though the collective decision-making of the Virginia Council that went about advising the governor was accepted practice in the 1610s and 1620s and strongly supported by the reformist Sandys faction, Hobbes either misremembers or repudiates earlier inferences that primitive democracy existed in American indigenous societies before the colonial state. While we ought not to confuse rumours about primitive democracy amongst natives with corporate collectivism among settlers in the Virginia colony, there is a sense in which the view from London was so long-distance as to blur the two together as somehow mutually implicated in the colonial wilderness. Hobbes's Tacitean impulses persisted in his being able to imagine democracy as the earliest and least stable form of government in the early *Elements of Law* (1641), but this nod to early republicanism was dropped in the later treatises. While the Algonquians would be the obvious example of this tendency, they are barely visible as the historical example. In light of the famous frontispiece of *Leviathan*, and the less well-known frontispiece from the first edition of *De cive*, the image of an Algonquian elder from De Bry's edition of Harriot (Figure 1.3) appears to foreshadow both frontispieces in striking ways. Given that Hobbes almost definitely knew the De Bry–Harriot text, it is worth pondering whether, several decades later, indigenous forms of sovereignty are being visualized and processed through his earlier exposure to them, even if not discussed extensively. Does the visual reveal what the verbal conceals?

Consent vocabulary dominated intra-European political philosophy even as conquest vocabulary was prevalent with imperial and colonial ventures that took place outside Europe. As Martine van Ittersum demonstrates copiously, Grotian international law was actually composed of two systems, a rational inter-state system for Europe based on positive law, and a flexible

---

[56] For a contemporary criticism of Hobbes's levelling tendencies, see Edward Hyde, Earl of Clarendon, *A Brief View and Survey of the Dangerous and Pernicious Errors to Church and State of Mr. Hobbes's Book, entitled Leviathan* (Oxford, 1676), 71.

Figure 1.3 'An ageed [Pomouik] manne in his winter garment', in Thomas Harriot, *A briefe and true report of the new found land of Virginia of the commodities and of the nature and manners of the naturall inhabitants* (Frankfurt, 1590). Engraving by Theodor De Bry after a watercolour by John White (*c*.1585–6). Courtesy of the John Carter Brown Library at Brown University.

theory of divisible sovereignty and subjective rights based on natural law for imperial activities outside Europe.[57] Hobbes does engage in comparative political history, equating indigenous American political culture with ancient Greek and classical Asian cultures. Speaking about the rise of philosophy, deemed necessary for political culture, Hobbes argues, 'The Savages of America, are not without some good Morall Sentences; also they have a little Arithmetick, to adde, and divide in Numbers not too great: but they are not therefore Philosophers' (p. 459). This is not through innate lack but because of the dictates of material necessity. An agricultural metaphor drives home the point that in primitive societies,

there was no Method; that is to say, no Sowing, nor Planting of Knowledge by it self, apart from the Weeds, and common Plants of Errour and Conjecture: And the cause

---

[57] See van Ittersum, *Profit and Principle*, p. lxi.

of it being the want of leisure from procuring the necessities of life, and defending themselves against their neighbours, it was impossible, till the erecting of great Common-Wealths, it should be otherwise. *Leasure* is the mother of *Philosophy*; and *Common-Wealth* the mother of *Peace*, and *Leasure*. Where first were great and flourishing Cities, there was first the study of Philosophy. (p. 459)

Hobbes goes on to compare the Gymnosophists of India, the Magi of Persia, and the priests of Chaldaea and Egypt as the world's first philosophers. He has a lower opinion of philosophizing in ancient Greece, where, according to him, warring city states prevented the development of leisure. Here, his long study and translation of Thucydides comes into play. 'Moral sentences' also existed in ancient Greece, but not full-fledged philosophy, which arose later when the Athenian armies defeated the Persians and established a Hellenic empire across the archipelago with holdings in Asia and Europe. Common-wealths are the grandmothers of philosophy. Once the later Greek state had 'grown wealthy they that had no employment, neither at home, nor abroad, had little else to employ themselves in, but either in telling and hearing news, or in discoursing of Philosophy publiquely to the youth of the City' (p. 460). The *translatio studii* (arts and letters) can follow only after the establishment of the *translatio imperii* (sovereignty), recapitulating America into a developmental narrative of political evolution.[58]

Moving on from questions surrounding the comparative political history of sovereignty, Hobbes appears to be aware of colonization as proceeding on several tracks, some of which are state-supported and others being privately funded and managed. As a result, the idea of sovereignty has to translate across and account for these different contexts of public and private interest, as well as collective and individual aspiration. While the published record largely appears to be one of an absence of engagement with the content of colonial geography, Hobbes's recognition of the radically innovative nature of company colonization as a structure seems prescient in chapter 22 of *Leviathan*. The recognition of these pre-existing partial bodies poses a problem, as these are anomeomerous structures that can bring pluralistic notions of sovereignty in through the back door just when chapter 16 seemed to impose

[58] For a rich discussion of the development of the *translatio studii* trope in relation to American-ness as a form of diasporic Englishness, see Leonard Tennenhouse, 'Diaspora and Empire', in *The Importance of Feeling English: American Literature and the British Diaspora, 1750–1850* (Princeton: Princeton University Press, 2007), 1–18.

an organic conception across the board.[59] Using Otto Gierke's terminology, territorially created states are forms of *Anstalten*, or externally imposed unities on the people who are found within it, but if the actors are companies, these turn out to be forms of *Körperschaften* or sovereign corporations with a coherent internal unity that is only partially sovereign in the larger context.[60] Company colonization is portrayed as having turned from a mixed public-private venture into an entirely private assignment. Hobbes had acknowledged that partial societies, such as merchants (*sodalitates mercatorum*), are allowed to operate with the permission of the city or state (*permittente civitate sua*). While Grotius had used the term 'system' to discuss a confederation of states, Hobbes uses 'system' to describe any number of sub-state structures, such as men joined together in one interest—whether these are universities, public agencies, corporations, or guilds. These units could also be random multitudes or unforeseen congregations of people who assemble at markets and fairs. Additionally, one could imagine pirates and privateers, as well as rogue merchants operating as another fringe system of quasi-sovereign interactions with other partial or dependent societies within a colonial environment. The corporation's performance of social denaturalization reveals itself differentially in a colonial environment. Through this concept of 'system' (Gk. *Systema*), Hobbes theorizes the supplementary state power of corporations that were becoming efficient extension programmes of the nascent English empire.

Corporations are dependent systems that work in tandem with the state, both tacitly and explicitly. The Virginia Company was both surrogate state actor and non-state entity. Sandys had vastly privatized its holdings in his failed attempt at making the venture profitable: while only seven private plantations were licensed in the first assembly and only six more under

---

[59] For my pursuit of these representational logics in ch. 16 of *Leviathan*, see Srinivas Aravamudan, ' "The Unity of the Representer": Reading *Leviathan* against the Grain', in Alberto Moreiras (ed.), *Thinking Politically*, special issue of *South Atlantic Quarterly*, 104/4 (Fall 2005), 631–53; and also Srinivas Aravamudan, 'Sovereignty: Between Embodiment and Detranscendentalization', *Texas International Law Journal*, 41/3 (2006), 427–46.

[60] See Otto Friedrich von Gierke, *Community in Historical Perspective*, trans. Mary Fischer, ed. Antony Black (Cambridge: Cambridge University Press, 1990). See also Bobbio's discussion of Gierke's notion of *Gennosenschaften* in German law, and Gierke's discussion of Johannes Althusius's study of smaller units of sovereignty including *universitates*, *collegia*, and neighbourhoods (*consociatio propinquorum*).

Smythe, Sandys authorized a further forty-four private plantations.[61] This hasty privatization also led to the straggling of settlements, making them vulnerable to the great uprising of 1622. While the Virginia Company was disbanded a couple of years after the uprising and made into the first royal colony, the experiment of company colonization continued with the Somers Island Company until 1684.

The Virginian colony echoes the Grotian double standard that justified commercial colonists taking natural law into their own hands, also suggested by Hobbes and Locke. Much more spectacular instances of company colonization were to follow with the British East India Company, but such a high-profile venture was already extant with the Dutch East India Company, or Vereenighde Oostindische Compagnie (VOC), whose justification was the context for Grotius's theories. Speaking directly about Virginia and the Bermudas, *Leviathan* relatedly argues that the necessity of proxy representation in the colonial context always inclines in favour of a monarchical rather than a popular form of government: 'For though every man, where he can be present by Nature, desires to participate of government; yet where they cannot be present, they are by nature also enclined, to commit the Government of their common Interest rather to a Monarchicall, then a popular form of Government' (p. 159). Hobbes compares this with Roman imperialism as well, suggesting that democracy was the norm for the metropolis, but that provinces were best governed by praetors or governors. As colonial administration tends to have a privatizing tendency, especially as venture capital is involved, Hobbes resorts to the following analogy: 'those men that have great private estates; who when they are unwilling to take the paines of administring the businesse that belongs to them, choose rather to trust one Servant, than an Assembly either of their friends or servants' (p. 159). Something similar was being advocated through the Virginia Company at the time by Sandys's opponents, who had criticisms regarding the company government by small investors as 'Democraticall and Tumultuous and therefore fit to be altered and reduced to the hands of some few persons'.[62] Shareholder democracy in colonial corporate ventures—not to be confused with political democracy—was introduced by Sandys in the name of efficiency, but is rejected later in *Leviathan* for an autocratic command structure

---

[61] Craven, *Dissolution of the Virginia Company*, 59.
[62] Quoted in Craven, *Dissolution of the Virginia Company*, 283.

that puts imperial sovereignty on a different track from the consensual model of political sovereignty that characterizes the nation. The single moment where the two were perhaps unified, if at all, was in the frontispiece to the private edition of *De cive*. Natural-law universalism, as applied to multiple colonial contexts, was very useful for a theory of sovereignty that combined nation and empire anomeomerously, just as the double standards of the eventual post-Westphalian system favoured the relativism of positive law for the European situation, even while the rest of the world was subjected to the universalizing justifications of natural law.

III From theoretical reduction to oceanic expansion

Britain's capacity to yoke the paradoxical concepts of empire and liberty together later during the eighteenth century depended on the naval separation of territorial state from oceanic empire. The ideas of political freedom merged indistinguishably with the notion of commercial access.[63] This imperial feint is at least as old as Vitoria's. Questions of jurisdiction concerning land would imply evaluating the rights and practices of indigenes, as well as the consequences of settlement and conquest. The same questions, when taken to jurisdiction concerning the seas, would articulate similar questions but not necessarily lead to the same outcomes. Ideas concerning the freedom of the seas were elaborated in Elizabethan times, well before Grotius. However, the Stuart century was one that preferred *mare clausum* to *mare liberum*, partly as a result of Scottish suspicions regarding English depredations into North Sea fisheries. Hobbes himself derived the motif of the oceanic monster, 'Leviathan', from Jewish cabbalistic lore, and especially the book of Job. Leviathan, typically a sea monster or a whale, is the Hobbesian emblem for the demonic power of the state as a mechanism that he characterizes as a 'mortal god' and an 'artificial animal'. To some degree, this identification of the state with a sea monster is counter-intuitive as traditional notions of

---

[63] Commercial access is not to be confused with the doctrine of free trade theorized by Hume and Adam Smith later in the eighteenth century. Universal commercial access, in theory, was in practice often restricted by monopolistic trading agreements. This Grotian move allowed Dutch penetration of areas claimed by the Spanish and Portuguese, even as it also justified new monopolies established in the same areas.

Figure 1.4 Honorius Philoponus [Caspar Plautius], St Brendan's Island, from *Nova typis transacta navigatio: novi orbis Indiae Occidentalis* ([Linz], 1621). Courtesy of the John Carter Brown Library at Brown University.

sovereignty are territorial. The famous Hobbesian image shows the sovereign uniting the temporal and religious powers, and combining the terrestrial and the divine in a radically new way (see Figure 1.2). 1651, the year of the publication of *Leviathan*, also saw the passage of the Cromwellian Acts of Navigation that eventually led to Britain's exercise of Atlantic and, eventually, global imperial sovereignty through maritime domination. Cromwell had later made an imperial effort during the failed Western Design on the Caribbean. The famous image of the island as whale on which a religious service is being conducted, from Honorius Philoponus's account of St Brendan's voyage off the coast of Normandy, visually evokes Hobbes's notion of a state structure that is artificial and natural, monstrous and totalizing, territorial and oceanic, all at once (Figure 1.4).

Relatedly, we can see the reversal of the territorial and the oceanic as a feature of the Bermuda Company logo (Figure 1.5), which includes the traditional image of English territorial sovereignty, the lion. The lion holds up a pennant showing a ship on a stormy sea, suggesting the new combin-

Figure 1.5 Bermuda Company logo, in *Orders and constitutions, partly collected out of his Maiesties letters patents; and partly by authority, and in vertue of the said letters patents: ordained vpon mature deliberation, by the gouernour and company of the city of London, for the plantation of the Summer-Islands: for the better gouerning of the actions and affaires of the said company and plantation. 6. Febr. 1621.* (London, 1622), frontispiece. Courtesy of the John Carter Brown Library at Brown University.

ation of terrestrial and oceanic sovereignty. Another interpretation of this banner image might be as a stylized internal view, where the lion's paws frame the true interior of the sovereign lion as seafaring, not terrestrial. As another Bermudan pamphlet puts it in more artificial terms rather than in relation to lions rampant, 'this great *Machina*, this goodly Engine of our Sea-state'.[64] Other Bermuda Company images reveal the fortifications of the

---

[64] [Robert Kayll], *The Trades Increase* (London, 1615), 33.

islands alongside the map of the tiny archipelago. The Devonshire redoubt is named after Hobbes's patron, Cavendish. Bridges are featured on Nathaniel Rich's mountain and various other forts, the state house, the town of St George, and the king's castle with cannon are also depicted. The state is demonstrated as a martial entity on its outside—perhaps in the manner of the English understanding of the Algonquian outside chief—mirroring the reduction of the state to its ability to protect and defend territory through mechanisms of war.

Hobbes's theory is an interesting parallel to Samuel Purchas's favouring of cosmopolitan justifications for national dominance. Hobbes was probably conversant with Purchas's 'Virginias Verger', published in *Hakluytus Posthumus* (1625), and was at the same time aware of Grotius's proposal for oceanic access in *Mare liberum*, the only chapter of his *De jure praedae / On the Law of Prize and Booty* published in his lifetime. Hobbes was also a personal friend of John Selden, who wrote *Mare clausum* defending James I's and Charles I's attempts to declare the North Atlantic an English zone of sovereignty. Selden's notion of a closed, proprietary ocean was heir to the first maritime theorist of the British Empire, John Dee.[65] Grotius's tract was written to refute Portuguese claims of oceanic sovereignty in the East Indies, especially as Dutch interests were expanding in that zone. Retained by the Dutch East India Company to argue for the law of prize booty in adjudications regarding the Dutch capture of the *Santa Catarina*, a Portuguese ship in the Moluccas in 1602, Grotius refutes the Portuguese title to the East Indies, whether by sovereignty, papal donation, prescription, or custom. Arguing instead from equity and free trade, Grotius wishes to create the ocean as *res nullius* or *res communis*. Sea, like air, according to Grotius, was not intrinsically susceptible to occupation, although it could be subjected to restrictions by mutual agreements and contracts among proximate and interested parties.[66]

In contrast, Hobbes was much more sympathetic to writers such as the Scot William Welwood, who immediately attacked Grotius. Selden's riposte to Grotius, *Mare clausum* (pub. 1635), argued plausibly that seas were always domains of jurisdiction and imperial influence at multiple historical mo-

[65] For a brilliant discussion of this intellectual historical background, see Armitage, *The Ideological Origins of the British Empire*, ch. 4.

[66] See Hugo Grotius, *The Free Sea*, trans. Richard Hakluyt, ed. and introd. by David Armitage (Indianapolis: Liberty Fund, 2004).

ments. Packed with a considerable degree of erudite historical reference, Selden's work demonstrates that oceanic sovereignty was often contested, but just as often enforced and enforceable. Selden's second book divides a putative British Ocean into four cardinal zones, and argues that while British sovereignty was exercised continuously since Roman times over the bounded seas to the south and east, the new empire had to assert its interests in the much more open and vast oceans to the north and the west. Selden argued that the North Atlantic should, for all intents and purposes, be defended as a British Atlantic. Oceanic sovereignty was a Scottish obsession more than an English one and declined by the time of the Glorious Revolution, when Britain fully embraced the notion of the freedom of the seas even as she confidently began asserting commercial empire. The last gasp of Hobbesian and Seldenian ideas concerning *mare clausum* was William Petty's evocative idea of signal ships demarcating oceanic boundaries manned by convicts who would be knitting stockings and communicating by semaphores.[67]

Oceanic sovereignty was crucial as the transition from state to empire. *Leviathan* develops a notion of oceanic sovereignty during the Interregnum, as does the famous English Machiavellian republican text that follows it, James Harrington's *The Commonwealth of Oceana* (1656).[68] Involving the new developments of international mercantile commerce, English sovereignty theory aims to move beyond territorial adjudication and defensible boundaries. Sounding more like the republican Grotius than the Royalist Selden, who would later attempt to refute Grotius, John Donne, in his sermon to the Virginia Company, preaches that 'a man does not become proprietary of the Sea, because hee hath two or three Boats, fishing in it, so neither does a man become Lord of a maine Continent, because hee hath two or three Cottages in the Skirts thereof'.[69] Insisting on the apostolic function of the colonists, Donne rebukes the impatience of those looking for quick profits and instantaneous success. Nonetheless, according to Donne, who also seems

---

[67] See William Welwood, *An Abridgement of all Sea-Lawes* (London, 1613); and John Selden, *Mare clausum* (London, 1635). The work was drafted in 1619. William Petty, 'Of a Mare Clausum', BL Add. Ms 72 866, cited in Armitage, *The Ideological Origins of the British Empire*, 123–4.

[68] James Harrington, *The Commonwealth of Oceana*, ed. J. G. A. Pocock (Cambridge: Cambridge University Press, 1993). David Armitage argues that Harrington was a critic of Cromwell's imperial ambitions, only later recuperated as an imperial apologist. See Armitage, *The Ideological Origins of the British Empire*, 137–9.

[69] Donne, *A Sermon upon the VIII Verse of the Ist Chapter of the Acts of the Apostles*, 22.

to write in the generally Grotian vein, the law of nature and nations deems that new inhabitants can settle vacant land.[70]

Not as moderate as Donne, Hobbes unabashedly defines a colony as a group of men sent out under supervision 'to inhabit a Forraign Country, either formerly voyd of Inhabitants, or made voyd then, by warre' (p. 175). Conquest is in the nature of the process. In another passage, Hobbes counsels restraint, seeing the emigration to and settlement of less populated areas as unavoidable but as needing management. In general, colonists are urged 'not to exterminate those they find there; but constrain them to inhabit closer together, and not range a great deal of ground, to snatch what they find; but to court each little Plot with art and labour, to give them their sustenance in due season' (p. 239). In other words, territories of hunter-gatherers ought to be converted into agricultural settlements. This implication is problematic for the reasons already discussed, given that many of the Algonquian coastal cultures were already, in fact, settled agricultural societies, suffering an invasion from English settlers who were claiming to convert, settle, and civilize those who were already settled and exhibiting the objective characteristics of civility.

All in all, with the theory of the Leviathan as a mortal god or artificial animal, Hobbes is undertaking a poligonic or nation-creating exercise for the modern English imperial state, drawing from the new interpretations of natural law and also the pre-existing materials of the cosmogonic language of the Bible. This mythical construction, leading to either alienation or agency theories of social contract, is yet another sign of the fictional creativity of political philosophy and its many ways of providing different rationales for the state, even as this fictionalization distorts and disavows the complex historical conditions from which it sprang.[71] Hobbes's method eschewed empiricism as well as historical verification for rational deduction. He proposed a brave new world of illimitable (but mortal) sovereignty. It is well known that by using natural-law arguments, Hobbes paradoxically justified legal positivism, and while seeming to take note of theories of democratic consent, he ended up rationalizing sovereign authority. Even while laying the theoretical basis for territorial and corporate forms of

[70] Ibid. 26.

[71] For a full-fledged discussion of Leviathan and other monsters, see Timothy K. Beal, *Religion and its Monsters* (New York: Routledge, 2002).

colonial acquisition, Hobbes also made visible oceanic expansion as a means to imperial growth for which the artificial person of the corporation functioned as a surrogate.

Abraham Cowley's poem to Hobbes positions him as a theoretical conqueror, in fact, 'the great *Columbus* of the *Golden Lands* of *new Philosophies*'. Hobbes's task, according to Cowley, was much harder than Columbus's:

> Thy Task was harder much than his,
> For thy learn'd *America* is
> Not onely found out first by *Thee*,
> And rudely left to *Future Industrie*,
> But thy *Eloquence* and thy *Wit*
> Has *planted*, *peopled*, *built*, and civiliz'd it.[72]

There is no better explanation of why Hobbes, as the founder of modern political philosophy, needed to see America as *terra nullius* to be able to build an integrated defence of conquest and positive law using natural-law premises. Cowley's amazing verses celebrate the audacity of the theorist, and his magisterial sweeping aside of history for the constructionist power of eloquence and wit, indeed for the rhetorical amalgamation of fiction and non-fiction that is political philosophy. Sovereignty is believable through performance. Hobbes's theory initiates a sovereign attitude that erases the historical past, consolidates the national present, and looks forward to an imperial future.

---

[72] 'To Mr. Hobs', in *The Poems of Abraham Cowley*, ed. A. R. Waller (Whitefish, MT: Kessinger Publishing, 2004), 189. Sheldon Wolin suggests that Hobbes's favouring of theoretical over practical knowledge meant that he 'replaced the political heroes by a single figure, the heroic theorist'. Cowley's poem certainly reiterates that movement. See Sheldon Wolin, *Hobbes and the Epic Tradition of Political Theory*, introd. by Richard Ashcraft (Los Angeles: Clark Memorial Library, University of California at Los Angeles, 1970), 14.

2

The Pathological Sublime

Pleasure and Pain in the Colonial Context

David Lloyd

I Aesthetic culture

In the past two decades or so, postcolonial theory has been markedly preoccupied with two categories that underpin the operations of colonial discourse, that of the subject and that of history. Indeed, as Ranajit Guha's magisterial essay 'The Prose of Counter-Insurgency' suggests, the categories are so intimately intertwined as to be virtually inextricable: as there is no subject without a history, so there can be no history without a subject, whether that subject be the human agent who is the cause of historical events, or a personification such as 'civil society' or 'reason'.[1] Rightly or wrongly, for better or worse, we tend to trace these categories to the late eighteenth century, regarding them as the products of an Enlightenment in which they find their determinant forms. Despite the fact that European colonialism, as the violent conquest of the Americas and of parts of Asia and Africa, evidently originates in earlier centuries, the late eighteenth century stands as a kind of threshold for postcolonial theory, marking both the emergence of categories that assert their own universal validity and the

[1] Ranajit Guha, 'The Prose of Counter-Insurgency', in Ranajit Guha and Gayatri Chakravorty Spivak (eds), *Selected Subaltern Studies* (New York: Oxford University Press, 1988), 45–86.

formation of political states in which they are to be instantiated. Paradoxically, since clearly both the subject and history have traceable prehistories, their emergence is seen, even in this moment, as revolutionary, as establishing a new order of things by rupture with a past that nonetheless already contained the very forms now declared for the first time to be self-evident. As Marx notes of that other 'new' discourse of the bourgeoisie, political economy, a discourse that claims universal validity cannot help but descry retroactively in human history the categories that are its own invention.[2] It is not, however, from political economy that I will seek to derive here the categories of the subject and of history, but from the aesthetic: not from the labouring body, but from the body that registers pleasure and pain.

In characterizing the aesthetic as a discourse on the sensible body, I am evidently returning to a notion of the aesthetic that predated its currently predominant usage to denominate reflection on taste, on beauty or the philosophy of art. I do so for several reasons that will, I hope, become clearer in the course of this essay. In the first place, the trajectory by which the aesthetic shifts from a concern with pleasure and pain or disgust to reflection on the properties and characteristics of art is inseparable from a shift in its focus from material objects and their impact on the body as an organ of feeling to questions of form and the judging subject. This formalization of reflection on the beautiful entails various decisive shifts in the discourse on the aesthetic and in its social function. The shift from the properties of the object that affect the subject to the subject that judges simultaneously places the claim for the universal validity of judgements of taste on a new ground, basing them in the disposition of the subject in general rather than in specific characteristics of the object. For this to take place, the judgement, as we shall see further, must be of the formal rather than the material properties of the object, the latter potentially affecting only the idiosyncratic gratifications and desires of the individual. Along with the elimination of the material properties of the object, the corporeal differences of individual subjects must also be discounted and the capacity for aesthetic judgement be predicated on the properties of the subject in general. The aesthetic thus becomes a means to determining the very possibility of a universal subject. This, on the one hand, removes the discrimination of taste from the purview of the learned and

[2] Karl Marx, *A Contribution to the Critique of Political Economy*, trans. S. W. Ryazanskaya, ed. Maurice Dobb (Moscow: Progress Publishers, 1970), 210–13.

wealthy elites and makes it, at least in potential, a field open to all subjects. On the other hand, the aesthetic simultaneously becomes the site for the cultural formation of subjects who accede to universality only through the cultivation of taste. Taste, or the capacity for disinterested contemplative pleasure, becomes an index of development and a means of discriminating a savage subordination to immediate pleasure and the coercive force of objects from the reflective mediations that characterize civilization. At the same time, formalization of the aesthetic object enables the emergence of the autonomous work of art itself, regarded as the product in which materials are entirely subordinated to formal requirements, and aesthetics becomes the philosophy of fine art. Reflection on natural beauty or, indeed, on the beauty of useful commodities is relegated to a secondary place.

The trajectory of the discourse on the aesthetic thus gradually distinguishes a domain we may refer to as that of 'aesthetic culture' (I avoid the term 'high culture' because the distinction between high and low still takes place within the domain of aesthetic judgement). Differentiated (or emancipated) in the first place as the domain of autonomous art from that of useful artifacts (the products of 'arts and crafts' and later of industry whose form is subordinated to their practical purpose), the domain of aesthetic culture will in turn be differentiated from culture understood as the life-ways of whole groups or societies. That such a usage of the term seems first to emerge with early anthropologists like E. B. Tylor, who popularized the term 'primitive culture' in the mid nineteenth century, signals the judgement secreted in the distinction of aesthetic culture from culture-in-general. The emergence of a distinct field of aesthetic culture, made possible by the emancipation of autonomous art from political or religious ends, or even, ideally, from the demand to furnish gratifications, differentiates the civilized or developed society from the primitive or underdeveloped one, as a taste for autonomous art distinguishes the cultivated from the uncultivated individual. The civilized society, with the complex differentiation of spheres that distinguish modernity, *has* culture. The uncivilized, who fail to differentiate the spheres of religion, art, labour, and so forth, *are* culture. What the latter lack most signally is the capacity to separate out the subject as autonomous agent from the forces of nature and the forces of nature in the human that subordinate the individual to the coercive force of its needs and desires. They are the vessels and objects of a nature and a culture that are themselves barely distinguished rather than free, deliberative subjects.

It is this differentiating and, in a quite strict sense, discriminatory function of aesthetic culture that makes it a necessary object of postcolonial theory and which makes critical a rethinking of the aesthetic from the place of the sensible body as a locus of differentiation rather than identity. But it is not only a postcolonial critique of the framing of the subject and of history understood as the history of development (a history that we can term historicist) that is envisaged here. Such a critique, outlined in the previous paragraphs, is fairly straightforward and involves little more than the recognition and the genealogy of aesthetic discourse and its constitutive function in both subject formation and racial or colonial judgement. What is more complicated is the no less necessary and related self-critique of postcolonial theory that its own theoretical terms have come to demand. For postcolonial theory, in its departure from and criticisms of decolonizing nationalism, has equally departed from consideration of the colonial body, object of both epistemological and physical violence and subject to racialization and objectification as the not-yet-emancipated human subject. Where, for a writer of decolonization like Frantz Fanon, the impact of colonial oppression could be read on the very body of the native and in his bodily comportment and the violence of racism registered in the corporeal encounter between white and black, postcolonial theory has retained of such thinking mostly its reading of the psychic traces of colonialism, whether in the form of hybridity, mimicry, or melancholia. Neither the body of the colonized nor the physical violence inflicted by colonialism is its principal object.

There are sound reasons for this shift in postcolonial theory's commitment to the critique of anticolonial nationalisms. The embrace by these movements of a Manichean analysis of colonial structures, together with the formation of restrictive identities for the nation-people, contributed to the post-independence failure of most postcolonial states. But a deeper and more disabling reason lies in the way in which postcolonial theory straddles a dilemma whose terms are in effect given by the tradition of aesthetic discourse. On the one hand, postcolonial theory seeks to offer an account of subjecthood that is not entrammelled in the notions of transcendental universality and representativeness that undergird Western aesthetics and ethics or in their counterpart, nationalist versions of the representative popular subject. On the other hand, if postcolonial theory turns to alternative accounts of culture for another conceptualization of human subjecthood and agency, it slips all too easily into an anthropological model of culture for which the person is the expression rather than the subject of cultural formations. The dilemma is perhaps seen at its clearest in the predicament of subalternity, where the desire to account for subaltern agency founders between the two schools. Since the subaltern is by definition the formation that eludes assimilation to Western forms, it cannot be conceived, even by analogy, as acting 'like a subject' or by way of representative subjects. But to conceive the subaltern as a group formation acting without subjecthood forecloses the possibility of thinking its autonomy or agency in any form, leaving it rather to appear as a kind of automatism operating on the impulse of exterior forces. This is, indeed, the dilemma framed both by Ranajit Guha in 'The Prose of Counter-Insurgency' and by Gayatri Spivak in 'Subaltern Studies: Deconstructing Historiography'.[3] But this strikes me as a dilemma already determined by the framework of a discourse on the aesthetic in which the discrimination between two domains of culture is first established. Hence the need to take postcolonial theory back to the founding moments of that discourse.

In doing so in this essay, I do not propose to resolve that dilemma, which is probably far too deeply inscribed in our disciplinary formation and its material effects to be summarily overcome. I want merely to return to a telling moment in the formation of aesthetic discourse where the grounds for the elimination of the body and for the formalization of the subject are most clearly deduced. That moment is Kant's dismissal in the *Critique of Judgement* (1790) of what he terms the 'physiological' logic of Edmund Burke's earlier *Philosophical Enquiry into the Origin of our Ideas of the Sublime and Beautiful* (1757) just as he himself is establishing the need for a transcendental rather than an empirical deduction of the aesthetic.[4] In what can be no more than a sketch

---

[3] See Guha, 'The Prose of Counter-Insurgency', and Spivak, 'Subaltern Studies: Deconstructing Historiography', in Guha and Spivak (eds), *Selected Subaltern Studies*, 3–32. For further discussion of the problematic of subalternity in these terms, see my 'Representation's Coup', in Swati Chattopadhyay and Bhaskar Sarkar (eds), *The Subaltern and the Popular* (London: Routledge, forthcoming).

[4] For an excellent account of the distinction between Kant and both the British aesthetic tradition and Burke, see Vanessa L. Ryan, 'The Physiological Sublime: Burke's Critique of Reason', *Journal of the History of Ideas*, 62/2 (2001), 265–79. As she remarks, 'at the point where the British tradition seems to come closest to the Kantian, namely, in the writings of Burke, it also most clearly marks its distance from it. Burke is in some ways the least Kantian of eighteenth-century British thinkers. Whereas Kant holds that the sublime allows us to intuit our rational capacity, Burke's physiological version of the sublime involves a critique of reason' (p. 266).

of some moments or nodes in which the political and the historical are linked within aesthetics, I want to suggest that the distance that separates Edmund Burke from Immanuel Kant, theoretically and politically, opens on to a more divided eighteenth century and furnishes resources for thinking how the recalcitrance of the colonial body opposes the normative force of the subject and its history. In order to do so, I will turn to a peculiar moment in Burke's essay where the sudden appearance of a racialized body fissures a text that promised to locate the universality of aesthetic response in the universality of the sensible body itself. In reading the significance of this moment, I return to Fanon's racial phenomenology in *Black Skins, White Masks* in order to elaborate the ways in which the black body appears to present an abyss for white attempts to establish the universality of certain cultural norms and responses. That abyss will appear, however, not as the domain of excluded matter, but as immanent to the system which produces it in seeking to erase difference and materiality themselves.

II The narrative of development

Let me start then with some assertions whose logic I have worked out more fully elsewhere.[5] The first assertion is that, for all its apparent separation out from other domains and its consequent antagonism to what we call political or ideological claims, the domain of the Kantian aesthetic constitutes and regulates the very 'condition of possibility' of the political as a category of modernity. It does so, I would argue, by furnishing an account of the subject that grounds its formal universality in the form of an a priori common sense. The second assertion is that, although that common sense has the appearance of a disposition universally present in all humans, it is nonetheless realized only as the product of a developmental history that we have come to call cultivation or the civilizing process. The first of these assertions is in accord with, but somewhat stronger than, for example, Terry Eagleton's argument for the secretly political significance of the supposedly apolitical

[5] See David Lloyd, 'Kant's Examples', *Representations*, 28 (Fall 1989), 34–54; David Lloyd, 'Analogies of the Aesthetic: The Politics of Culture and the Limits of Materialist Aesthetics', *New Formations*, 10 (Spring 1990), 109–26; and David Lloyd, 'Race under Representation', *Oxford Literary Review*, 13/1–2 (1991), 62–94.

claims of culture, or Hannah Arendt's powerful demonstration of the 'interrelation and mutual dependence' of the spheres of culture and politics.[6] The *Critique of Judgement* is not merely concerned with such interrelations but seeks to give an account of the very conditions of possibility of the political in the demonstration of the transcendental grounds for a 'public' or common sense in the disposition of the judging subject.

As is well known, Kant achieves this in the third critique by locating the properties that are strictly aesthetic—beauty and sublimity—not in the object itself but in the 'disposition' (*Bestimmung*) of the reflecting and judging subject. Unlike the teleological judgement, which is interested in what a thing is for, its actual conformity with a given end, and unlike a moral or ethical judgement, which is interested in whether a thing is good, a pure aesthetic judgement is entirely disinterested and free of subjection either to moral or to mere sensual gratification. It is through aesthetic judgement, or Taste, that the empirical individual becomes the autonomous Subject in a universal sense, a movement that is achieved by the judgement's reflection not upon the object itself but on the formal properties of its mode of representation. In the case of the beautiful, the pleasure which attends the aesthetic judgement derives from the formal accord of the understanding and the imagination (which for Kant is merely the faculty by which sense presentations are borne to us as representations): that is, the pleasure is not in the realization of what a thing is, its concept, but in its 'formal finality', its possibility as a thing with ends. In the case of the sublime, the pleasure derives from the capacity of (practical) reason to apprehend and represent forces or magnitudes in nature that exceed the representative capacity of the imagination itself. The sublime overwhelms the senses and the imagination but is nonetheless a manifestation of the supersensible in the mortal human.

As with the beautiful, the sublime has reference to the state of the judging subject, not to any quality inherent in its object:

Therefore, just as the aesthetic judgement in its estimate of the beautiful refers the imagination in its free play to the *understanding*, to bring out its agreement with the *concepts* of the latter in general (apart from their determination): so in its estimate of a thing as sublime it refers that faculty to *reason* to bring out its subjective accord with

---

[6] Terry Eagleton, *The Ideology of the Aesthetic* (Oxford: Blackwell, 1990); Hannah Arendt, 'The Crisis in Culture: Its Social and Political Significance', in *Between Past and Future: Six Exercises in Political Thought* (New York: Viking, 1961), 218.

ideas of reason (indeterminately indicated), i.e. to induce a temper of mind conformable to that which the influence of definite (practical) ideas would produce upon feeling, and in common accord with it.

This makes it evident that true sublimity must be sought only in the mind of the judging Subject, and not in the Object of nature that occasions this attitude by the estimate formed of it. Who would apply the term 'sublime' even to shapeless mountain masses towering one above the other in wild disorder, with their pyramids of ice, or to the dark tempestuous ocean, or such like things? But in the contemplation of them, without any regard to their form, the mind abandons itself to the imagination and to a reason placed, though quite apart from any definite end, in conjunction therewith, and merely broadening its view, and it feels itself elevated in its own estimate of itself on finding all the might of imagination still unequal to its ideas.[7]

We will return shortly to the implications of this and related passages for the autonomy of the Subject as envisaged by Kant. What is crucial to note here as elsewhere in Kant's painstaking prose is that the disinterest of the aesthetically judging subject is derived from the fact that its reflection is on the mode of its representation as a form rather than on the object represented. It is precisely this formal reflection, the formalization of reflection, that will allow Kant to deduce the existence a priori of a 'common sense' in humans that permits them to make claims of taste 'as if' they could have universal subjective validity.

The relationship between the process of formalization in aesthetic judgement and the positing of a universal common or public sense is spelt out later in section 40:

by the name *sensus communis* is to be understood the idea of a *public* sense, i.e. a critical faculty which in its reflective act takes account (*a priori*) of the mode of representation of every one else, in order, *as it were*, to weigh its judgement with the collective reason of mankind, and thereby avoid the illusion . . . that would exert a prejudicial influence upon its judgement. This is accomplished by weighing the judgement, not so much with actual, as rather with the merely possible, judgements of others, and by putting ourselves in the position of every one else, as the result of a mere abstraction from the limitations which contingently affect our own estimate. This, in turn, is effected by so far as possible letting go of the element of matter, i.e. sensation, in our general state of representative activity, and confining our attention

[7] Immanuel Kant, *Critique of Judgement*, trans. James Creed Meredith (Oxford: Clarendon Press, 1952) (cited in the text hereafter as *CJ*), 104–5, §26.

to the formal peculiarities of our representation or general state of representative activity. (*CJ*, 151, §40)

A series of formalizing and generalizing movements are embedded here: from the sensuous 'presentation' to the representation in the mind; from the 'matter' that is the object of the sensuous presentation to the 'form' of its 'representation'; and, perhaps most importantly, from the actuality of the representation to its potentiality as a representative of representation itself. That is, in the latter case, we invoke the potential judgements of others as a measure of our judgement's possible universality rather than our own or any other actual judgements of taste. The import of this for Kant in his dissociation from Burke will become clear shortly, but at this point it is no less important to stress that what concerns him is the pure formal potentiality that constitutes the realm of 'public' or common sense as one of universal accord. That potentiality of common sense is at once the discovery or product of the discourse on judgement and the ground which allows for judgement's possibility at all. This aporetic paradox of common sense, as at once origin and end of taste, is spelled out by Kant somewhat earlier in the text:

experience cannot be made the ground of this common sense, for the latter is invoked to justify judgements containing an 'ought'. The assertion is not that every one *will* fall in with our judgement, but rather that every one *ought* to agree with it . . . .But does such a common sense in fact exist as a constitutive principle of the possibility of experience, or is it formed by us as a regulative principle by a still higher principle of reason, that for higher ends first seeks to beget in us a common sense? Is taste, in other words, a natural and original faculty, or is it only the idea of one that is artificial and to be acquired by us, so that a judgement of taste, with its demand for universal assent, is but a requirement of reason for generating such a con*sensus*, and does the 'ought', i.e. the objective necessity of the coincidence of the feeling of all with the particular feeling of each, only betoken the possibility of arriving at some sort of unanimity in these matters, and the judgement of taste only adduce an example of the application of this principle? (*CJ*, 85, §22)

Is the common sense that makes the concept of taste possible as a universal rather than a set of idiosyncratic judgements an a priori ground for judgement or is it rather an 'artificial' faculty that must be cultivated as an ethical requirement? As we will see, the resolution of this problem is crucial to the larger claims of the aesthetic as Kant develops it, but as a problem, it derives

from his insistent and systematic dismissal of empirical tests of the universality of judgements of taste. What is common or universal to the human as
subject cannot be derived merely from experience but must have transcendental grounds. The 'ought', by evident analogy with the *Critique of Practical
Reason*, is categorical rather than actually realized or enforced, which thus
saves it from the shadow of coerciveness. These considerations will, of course,
be the principal basis for Kant's critique of Burke.[8]

Kant ostensibly defers this problem until after the analysis of the beautiful
and the sublime and after the argument about the necessity for common sense
as the formal reflection on the mode of representation just cited. In the
following section, however, he resolves the apparent aporia of common sense
in a manner which is surely momentous for subsequent Western thought
about the place of culture in the formation of the subject and, no less, for the
thinking of the possibility of the political. What Kant does is to assume the
latency of that 'common sense' while making its actualization subject to what
we might call a 'narrative of development'. In doing so, he makes a certain form
of historicity intrinsic to the history of the subject: the two categories become
inseparable. In the first place, the narrative of subject formation that folds into a
larger history of human civilization furnishes a kind of master narrative for
a racialized understanding of human development itself. In the second, that
narrative of civilization is universalized in accord with what are posed as the
collective ends of humanity itself. Finally, in grounding it in the sphere of
aesthetic judgements that are political in their effect, he incorporates equally a
set of cultural judgements that determine the level of development of any
given human community, its capacity for autonomy. As the ground of sociality,
this 'common sense' emerges only in society, and is rudimentary at best in
'primitive' or 'savage' states:

Only in society does it occur to him [the human being] to be not merely a man, but a
man refined after the manner of his kind (the beginning of civilization)—for that is

---

[8] Although, as Daniel Carey has shown, the conundrum posed by the desire to establish the
grounds for universal human tastes and moral feeling in the face of manifest diversity in each
sphere exercised British thinkers throughout the eighteenth century, Kant's mode of posing the
question set quite different terms from theirs. From the outset, he rejects the deduction of
common sense from experience rather than predicating it, as the British tradition (whatever its
conclusions) tended to, on nature and the frame of the human senses. See Daniel Carey, *Locke,
Shaftesbury, and Hutcheson: Contesting Diversity in the Enlightenment and Beyond* (Cambridge: Cambridge
University Press, 2006).

the estimate formed of one who has the bent and turn for communicating his pleasure to others, and who is not quite satisfied with an Object unless his feeling of delight in it can be shared in communion with others. Further, a regard to universal communicability is a thing which every one expects and requires from every one else, just as if it were part of an original compact dictated by humanity itself. And thus, no doubt, at first only charms, e.g. colours for painting oneself (roucou among the Caribs and cinnabar among the Iroquois), or flowers, sea-shells, beautifully coloured feathers, then, in the course of time, also beautiful forms (such as canoes, wearing-apparel, &c.) which convey no gratification, i.e. delight of enjoyment, become of moment in society and attract a considerable interest. Eventually, when civilization has reached its height it makes this work of communication almost the main business of refined inclination, and the entire value of sensations is placed in the degree to which they permit of universal communication. (*CJ*, 155–6, §41)

We recognize in this schematic narrative the history of human development that poses the emergence of civil society and the public sphere—'universal communicability'—both as its privileged end and as the process of actualization of a capacity always latent in the human at whatever stage of development. By the same token, however, the constitutive limit of the aesthetic is a cultural difference specified in racial terms and comprehended within this developmental narrative as a state of 'underdevelopment'. The savage—Carib or Iroquois—stands at the threshold of a development that culminates in civil society but is still predominantly subject to the 'charm of sense', as Kant earlier calls it. This heteronomy of the senses over the judgement must be overcome for the full history of the subject to unfold. The savage stands as at once the instance of subjection and as the latent potentiality of the aesthetic. Accordingly, we should not understand the 'native' to be 'foreclosed' from this Kantian history, as Gayatri Spivak has suggested, but rather to be its limit point, at once outside the temporality of civilization and the 'informing' moment of its emergence.[9] For what effectively makes this a racializing judgement rather than, as might be argued, a merely contingent historical or comparative anthropological example is its structural necessity to Kant's account of the development of the civilized subject. The savage, Iroquois or Carib, is required as a permanent instance of the 'not-subject', the object of heteronomy both in the form of natural forces and of

---

[9] Gayatri Chakravorty Spivak, *A Critique of Postcolonial Reason: Toward a History of the Vanishing Present* (Cambridge, Mass.: Harvard University Press, 1999), 4–6.

the immediate gratification of his own desires. The savage is, as Denise da Silva has put it, opposed to 'the subject of transparency, for whom universal reason is an internal guide' as a 'subject of affectability', one subordinated both to reason as its object and to nature as a force that it has yet to master.[10]

For the 'actual' subordination of the savage to the senses corresponds discretely to the theoretical subordination to the immediacy of sensation from which Kant's own aesthetic philosophy, and in particular his analytic of the sublime, seeks to emancipate itself. It is well known that what Kant calls his 'transcendental exposition of aesthetic judgements' (*CJ*, 130, §29) marks a decisive turn away from the eighteenth-century preoccupation with the phenomena of pleasure and pain that formerly constituted the object of aesthetic philosophy as well as its etymological foundation. In seeking to ground the judgements of taste in a priori faculties of the human mind, Kant no less seeks to emancipate the aesthetic from its dangerous subordination to physical gratifications or affects, giving preeminence to formal modes of judgement rather than to the exquisite cultivation of sensation. Even such civilized refinements retain for him the marks of heteronomy, of the force of need and desire that continues to exert its sway through the body over the mind. This consideration explains the peculiar supplement that is inserted at the end of section 29, marked off from the rest of the text by a horizontal bar or boundary. Kant is at pains here to emphasize the distance that separates his analysis from the 'physiological' exposition that is most eminently exemplified in Burke's *Philosophical Enquiry into the Origin of our Ideas of the Sublime and Beautiful.*

---

[10] See Denise Ferreira da Silva, *Toward a Global Idea of Race* (Minneapolis: University of Minnesota Press, 2007), p. xxxix. This work has appeared since I wrote the first version of this essay, but has been invaluable to the clarification of its conceptualization in the course of its revision. It is this distinction that also marks the philosophical difference between Kant's narrative of development and Scottish Enlightenment historicism, influential though the latter may have been on German thought and on Kant himself. For Scottish thinkers, as Carey has argued, 'Difference emerged as a feature of historical predicament, a conclusion that did not militate against the notion of a unified human nature but rather placed societies on a continuum from savagery to civilisation.' See Carey, *Locke, Shaftesbury, and Hutcheson*, 193. Kant's argument is grounded rather in the trajectory of the Subject and its emergence into autonomy out of heteronomy than in empirical history. On the influence of the Scottish Enlightenment in mid-eighteenth-century Germany, and especially in Göttingen, see John H. Zammito, *Kant, Herder and the Birth of Anthropology* (Chicago: University of Chicago Press, 2002), 28.

Kant's objections to the 'physiological' exposition of aesthetic judgements are twofold. In the first place, Burke's analysis of the 'origins' of the sublime and the beautiful remains attached to sensation and therefore to the 'gratification' of the senses from which Kant has been at pains to separate the disinterested and autonomous reflecting Subject. In the second place, and this is yet more telling for Kant, this attribution of delight to the 'charm of the senses', which we have seen to be associated with the condition of the savage, prevents the 'universal accord' that is the standard of taste from being achieved by anything but a coercive exaction of agreement:

> But if we attribute the delight in the object wholly and entirely to the gratification which it affords through charm or emotion, then we must not exact from *any one else* agreement with the aesthetic judgement passed by *us*. For in such matters each person rightly consults his own personal feeling alone. But in that case there is an end of all censorship of taste—unless the example afforded by others as the result of a contingent coincidence of their judgements is to be held over us as *commanding* our assent. But this principle we would presumably resent, and appeal to our natural right of submitting a judgement to our own sense, where it rests upon the immediate feeling of personal well-being, instead of submitting it to that of others. (*CJ*, 131–2, §29)

For Kant, the physiological aesthetic in its very principle undermines the possibility of a universally valid subjective accord, leaving judgement subject either to the despotic 'command' of an arbitrary standard of taste or to the potential anarchy of the assertion of individual idiosyncracy.

Kant here, if discreetly, acknowledges the political stakes of the aesthetic: the ideal republic that consists of autonomous subjects whose possibility is given by the common sense instantiated in the reflective formal subject of judgement is threatened by the immediacy of judgements predicated on sensations of gratification or pain. Burke's analysis of the sublime and the beautiful, being thus predicated on the sensations, undermines for Kant the *ethical* substrate of the judgement, its categorical form, which is crucial to the social function of taste. The 'psychological observations' that 'supply a wealth of material for the favourite investigations of empirical anthropology' (*CJ*, 131, §29) turn out not to be so easily relegated to the status of mere data, but actually pose a dangerous immediacy of *sensation* in place of the delight that for Kant is '*immediately* connected with a representation' (*CJ*, 132, §29): Burke's empirical laws 'only yield a knowledge of how we do judge, but they do not give us a command as to how we ought to judge, and what is more, such a command as is *unconditioned*' (*CJ*, 132, §29). The crucial term here is that of immediacy: on the one hand, Kant's aesthetic judgement must appear to take a delight *as if* it were immediately in the object itself, whereas it is actually, mediately, a delight in the disposition of the subject in relation to the representation of the object. Burke's aesthetic, on the other hand, is judged to be predicated all too empirically on the immediate sensation provoked by the object itself. The description of Burke's aesthetic as 'physio-logical' thus slips into its critique as *pathological*. It is, in the first place, literally pathological, being derived from what the subject undergoes or submits to (*pathein*). In the second place, the connotations of sickness or *pathology* are readily available, suggesting that Burke's aesthetic is one that is disordered or contaminated by its subjection to heteronomy, to forces that make the subject determined or conditioned rather than self-determining or autonomous.

The distinction between Kant's and Burke's aesthetics could not be clearer in the passages that Kant actually cites. On the one hand, the sublime is said by Burke to be 'grounded on the impulse towards self-preservation and on *fear*', while on the other, the beautiful he reduces to ' "the relaxing, slacken-ing, and enervating of the fibres of the body, and consequently a softening, a dissolving, a languor, and a fainting, dying, and melting away for pleasure" ' (*CJ*, 130–1, §29). In both cases, the aesthetic experience is one that approaches the dissolution rather than the affirmation of the subject, a dissolution that takes place by way of the intimacy of the subject and 'mere' sensation. In the case of the sublime, the distance that allows Burke's subject to survive the forces that threaten his 'self-preservation', and that permits 'a sort of tranquility tinged with terror', is merely contingent. It is the lucky accident of his location that allows the subject to be an observer of the storm rather than its victim and leaves him gasping at once with relief and fear, shock and awe. For Kant, on the contrary, the sublime is the effect of a quite different understanding of the subject's superiority to danger and is the product of its very opposition to the despotism of the senses, being precisely 'what pleases immediately by reason of its opposition to the interest of sense' (*CJ*, 118, §29). The sublime here is the pleasure taken by the subject in the recognition of its superiority as subject to the forces of nature, in its own triumph over mortality and limitation. This is equally true of the mathematical and the dynamical sublime:

In the immeasurableness of nature and the incompetence of our faculty for adopting a standard proportionate to the aesthetic estimation of the magnitude of its *realm*, we found our own limitation. But with this we found in our rational faculty another non-sensuous standard, one which has that infinity itself under it as unit, and in comparison with which everything in nature is small, and so found in our minds a pre-eminence over nature even in its immeasurability. Now in just the same way the irresistibility of the might of nature forces upon us the recognition of our physical helplessness as beings of nature, but at the same time reveals a faculty of estimating ourselves as independent of nature, and discovers a pre-eminence above nature that is the foundation of a self-preservation of quite another kind from that which may be assailed and brought into danger by external nature. This saves humanity in our own person from humiliation, even though as mortal men we have to submit to external violence. In this way external nature is not estimated in our aesthetic judgement as sublime so far as exciting fear, but rather because it challenges our power (one not of nature) to regard as small those things of which we are wont to be solicitous (worldly goods, health, and life), and hence to regard its might (to which in these matters we are no doubt subject) as exercising over us and our personality no such rude dominion that we should bow down before it, once the question becomes one of our highest principles and of our asserting or forsaking them. (*CJ*, 111, §28)

Nothing could be further from Burke's derivation of the sublime from the sensation of an overwhelming power which, though actually it threatens the life of the subject, does not destroy him. Kant's sublime is precisely one in which 'the interest of sense' is overcome by the mind's pre-eminence, freeing the subject into an autonomy predicated on its identity with all other humans as rational subjects.

We will return in a moment to Burke's physiology of the sublime. But let us note that what is implicit in Kant's aesthetic is profoundly political in its refusal of the despotism of sensation. Although, with self-preserving circumspection, he does not spell this out, the Kantian subject is both one that refuses the fear on which despotism is predicated, cleaving instead to the quasi-republican equivalence of moral and autonomous subjects, and one that grounds its political claim to autonomy discretely in a quite Protestant relation to the Godhead. That is, while fear of God is acknowledged to be a proper and customary relation to the divine power, it is by no means a source of the sublime. On the contrary, the sublime relation to the divine is one of the reflective judgement that opposes superstitious awe:

In religion, as a rule, prostration, adoration with bowed head, coupled with contrite, timorous posture and voice, seems to be the only becoming demeanour in presence of the Godhead, and accordingly most nations have assumed and still observe it. Yet this cast of mind is far from being intrinsically and necessarily involved in the idea of the *sublimity* of religion and of its object. The man that is actually in a state of fear, finding in himself good reason to be so, because he is conscious of offending with his evil disposition against a might directed by a will at once irresistible and just, is far from being in the frame of mind for admiring divine greatness, for which a temper of calm reflection and a quite free judgement are required. Only when he becomes conscious of having a disposition that is upright and acceptable to God, do those operations of might serve to stir within him the idea of the sublimity of this Being, so far as he recognizes the existence in himself of a sublimity of disposition consonant with His will, and is thus raised above the dread of such operations of nature, in which he no longer sees God pouring forth the vials of the wrath. (*CJ*, 113–14, §28)

Though Kant refrains from doing so, it is not difficult to extend this 'sublime' relation to God to secular authority and to read in it an enlightened refusal of submission to autocratic power entirely in keeping with his other writings, such as 'What is Enlightenment?' and *The Conflict of the Faculties*.[11] Kant's critique of Burke here manifests the political stakes of the third critique, posing an aesthetic and political claim for the autonomy and universality of the judgement against the heteronomy and arbitrariness that characterize the despotic.

In contradistinction to Kant's 'republican' aesthetics, with its disinterest towards the realm of the senses, Burke's essay presents the experience of the sublime and the beautiful as intimately linked to a dissolution of the subject in the face of powerful sensation. As Kant's paraphrase indicates, the feeling of beauty is closely linked to the effects of love, the subject 'being softened, relaxed, enervated, dissolved, melted away by pleasure'.[12] Furthermore, the effective cause of this pleasure lies in the qualities of the object itself and in the sensations they arouse in the subject rather than in the independent disposition of the

[11] For comments on Kant's response to the French Revolution and its very circumspect republicanism, as well as its place in his narrative of development, in *The Conflict of the Faculties*, see my 'Foundations of Diversity: Thinking the University in a Time of Multiculturalism', in John Carlos Rowe (ed.), *'Culture' and the Problem of the Disciplines* (New York: Columbia University Press, 1998), 32.

[12] Edmund Burke, *A Philosophical Enquiry into the Origin of our Ideas of the Sublime and Beautiful* (2nd edn, 1759; facs. edn, Menston: The Scolar Press, 1970) (cited in the text hereafter as *OSB*), 288.

subject himself. Burke is at pains to spell out the properties of the object that induce love or the feeling of beauty, properties like smallness, smoothness, sweetness, and variation, that are distinctly specific to the object rather than to any relation into which it enters, such that he explicitly excludes 'proportion' and 'fitness' as sources of beauty in so far as these have to do with comparative judgements rather than immediate sensations. If beauty, then, has to do with properties in the object that induce a relaxation of the subject, the sublime on the contrary induces a tension that is predicated on fear and the instinct of self-preservation. Again, however, the motive force of the sublime lies not in the subject's independence from the object but in his subordination to it. Several times, Burke emphasizes that in the experience of the sublime, sensation overwhelms the reason, hurrying it in a way that defies the act of reflection that for Kant is crucial to the judgement:

The passion caused by the great and the sublime in *nature*, when those causes operate most powerfully, is Astonishment; and astonishment is that state of the soul, in which all its motions are suspended, with some degree of horror. In this case the mind is so entirely filled with its object, that it cannot entertain any other, nor by consequence reason on that object which employs it. Hence arises the great power of the sublime, that far from being produced by them, it anticipates our reasonings, and hurries us on by an irresistible force. (*OSB*, 95–6)

Later, of Milton's portrait of Satan, he writes: 'The mind is hurried out of itself, by a croud of great and confused images; which affect because they are crouded and confused. For separate them, and you lose much of the greatness, and join them, and you infallibly lose the clearness' (*OSB*, 106). This displacement of the reason by poetic language is similarly induced by actual crowds and the violence of mobs: 'The shouting of multitudes has a similar effect; and by the sole strength of the sound, so amazes and con-founds the mind, the best established tempers can scarcely forbear being born down, and joining in the common cry, and common resolution of the croud' (*OSB*, 151). Ultimately, for Burke, the sublime is the effect of a power which comes close to overwhelming the subject, 'bearing it down', 'hurrying it out of itself', 'hurrying us on'. Indeed, he remarks, apart from terror itself, 'I know of nothing sublime which is not some modification of power' (*OSB*, 110). As he admits in the second edition of the essay, the archetypal figure of power is the Godhead and fear is a proper response to that power, fear that far overpowers the reflective judgement:

Some reflection, some comparing is necessary to satisfy us of his wisdom, his justice, and his goodness; to be struck with his power, it is only necessary that we should open our eyes. But whilst we contemplate so vast an object, under the arm, as it were, of almighty power, and invested upon every side with omnipresence, we shrink into the minuteness of our own nature, and are, in a manner, annihilated before him. And though a consideration of his other attributes may relieve in some measure our apprehensions; yet no conviction of the justice with which it is exercised, nor the mercy with which it is tempered, can wholly remove the terror that naturally arises from a force which nothing can withstand. (*OSB*, 119–20)

Far from deprecating this fear, Burke, unlike Kant, regards it as a 'salutary' and necessary element of 'true religion'.

The secular correlative of divine power is, as may be evident, the power of monarchy or of despotism, and its effect, like that of both natural and divine power, is to 'take away the free use of [the] faculties' (*OSB*, 116–17). Srinivas Aravamudan has finely demonstrated how Burke's invocation of despotism draws on and relates to the notion of Oriental despotism, in relation to both religious and secular power.[13] What I am interested in here is another aspect of Burke's analysis of terror, which is his extraordinary and fascinated intimacy with it. His derivation of the effects of both the sublime and the beautiful enters in minute detail into the modifications of the musculature of the body, from the straining of the eye in the face of darkness or obscurity, to the enervation or swooning-away of the bodily sinews in relation to the loved object, to the labour of the ear in attending to repeated or intermittent sounds. The essay registers, as Kant's critique never can, the thrill that affects the subject when it encounters objects that in one or other way threaten its autonomy, dissolving or overwhelming it in the passions of love and terror. Burke's is, as Kant seems to have realized, strictly speaking a pathological and not merely a physiological account of aesthetic pleasure. His subject undergoes or suffers the sensations that cause the terrors of the sublime or the pleasures provoked by beauty, a willing subjection to the heteronomy of sensations that would, for Kant, slip over into the other sense of a pathology, that of a subject distempered by its passions.

---

[13] Srinivas Aravamudan, *Tropicopolitans: Colonialism and Agency, 1688–1804* (Durham, NC: Duke University Press, 1999), 198–202.

But Burke insists that the universal claims of taste, as his introduction 'On Taste' makes clear, are derived from the physical rather than the formally subjective universality of the human. The human is an object that suffers its passions as much as it is a subject that reflects upon its objects. Accordingly, the senses are the foundation of any universal claims that can be made about human relations to the world:

All the natural powers in man, which I know, that are conversant about external objects, are the Senses; the Imagination; and the Judgement. We do and we must suppose, that as the conformation of their organs are nearly, or altogether the same in all men, so the manner of perceiving external objects is in all men the same, or with little difference. (*OSB*, 7)

Accordingly, the objects of the aesthetic, human pleasures and pains, are universally felt in the same way.[14] By the same token, the Imagination is also universal:

Now the imagination is the most extensive province of pleasure and pain, as it is the region of our fears and our hopes, and of all our passions that are connected to them; and whatever is calculated to affect the imagination with these commanding ideas, by force of any original natural impression, must have the same power pretty equally over all men. For since the imagination is only the representative of the senses, it can only be pleased or displeased with the images from the same principle on which the sense is pleased or displeased with the realities; and consequently there must be just as close an agreement in the imagination as in the senses of men. (*OSB*, 17)

The universality of taste, as a complex of the senses, the imagination and of reasoning thereon, is predicated upon this commonness of human sensation:

On the whole it appears to me, that what is called Taste, in its most general acceptation, is not a simple idea, but is partly made up of a perception of the primary pleasures of sense, of the secondary pleasures of the imagination, and of the conclusions of the reasoning faculty, concerning the various relations of these, and concerning the human passions, manners and actions. All this is requisite to form

---

[14] As Seamus Deane puts it, 'Burke's weakness, to others his strength, is his capacity to find in subjectivity a universal dimension.' *Foreign Affections: Essays on Edmund Burke* (Cork: Cork University Press, 2005), 5.

Taste, and the ground-work of all these is the same in the human mind; for as the senses are the great originals of all our ideas, and consequently of all our pleasures, if they are not uncertain and arbitrary, the whole ground-work of Taste is common to all, and therefore there is sufficient foundation for a conclusive reasoning on these matters. (OSB, 31)[15]

Far from regarding taste as the prerogative of the rational subject and as a yardstick that divides the cultivated subject of civilization from its savage or barbarian other, Burke's argument on the sensational foundation of taste seems almost radical in its inclusiveness, bringing the Oriental despot into community with the shoemaker:

On the subject of their dislike there is a difference between all these people, arising from the different kinds and degrees of their knowledge; but there is something in common to the painter, the shoemaker, the anatomist, and the Turkish emperor, in the pleasure arising from a natural object, so far as each perceives it justly imitated; the satisfaction in seeing an agreeable figure; the sympathy proceeding from a striking and affecting incident. So far as Taste is natural, it is nearly common to all. (OSB, 24)[16]

---

[15] If, as James Engell suggests, Burke is on the cusp at this point of endowing the Imagination with active creative powers, as opposed to regarding it merely as the faculty that bears images from the senses to the reason, the principal point of these passages is to assert that the *universality* of Taste is predicated on the universal conformity of the senses in humans. This is where Burke most profoundly differs from Kant, for whom that universality can be grounded only in a transcendental account of the subject. See James Engell, *The Creative Imagination: Enlightenment to Romanticism* (Cambridge, Mass.: Harvard University Press, 1981), 71–2.

[16] As Aravamudan points out, Burke does suppress the outcome of the anecdote that he tells here, as to the Turkish Emperor's superior empirical knowledge of the anatomical effects of execution: he demonstrates his point by actually having a slave beheaded. See *Tropicopolitans*, 202. However, the point remains that Burke introduces the anecdote to emphasize the common ground of aesthetic taste despite other differences. This of course places Burke at some distance from either of his immediate British forebears, Shaftesbury and Hutcheson. Shaftesbury's definition of the society that would be the community of taste where consensus is formed is that of 'polite society', that is, 'an elevated collective', as Carey puts it, but one that has 'something selective or restrictive about it'. Burke is closer to his countryman Hutcheson in the universalizing and more democratic streak that leads the latter to reject Shaftesbury's 'hierarchical notion of full access to the sociable and disinterested affections'. But even Hutcheson 'attempted to exclude from consideration those "unfortunates" . . . living in rude circumstances without the benefit of arts and proper human conditions. Hutcheson's traditional affiliations, based on innateness and a restrictive *consensus gentium*, become clearer in this context.' Carey, *Locke, Shaftesbury and Hutcheson*, 172; see also ibid. 127–8, 187. The limit on Burke's own capacity to include all human subjects will become clear later.

For such an analysis, differences in knowledge and in station are less important than the common element of pleasure in the object of judgement.

Such a 'naturalist' account of taste is far from the Kantian one.[17] Not only
is Kant's subject of judgement expressly indifferent to the gratification or
pain of the senses, focusing solely on the formal aspects of the representation, that subject emerges moreover only in consequence of a process of
cultivation. This is particularly true in relation to the sublime. For despite
the fact that Kant derives the capacity for taste from a 'common or public
sense' latent in all men, aesthetic judgement in the fullest sense, and a
capacity to appreciate sublimity in particular, is predicated on the development in the individual of a certain level of cultivation. Unlike the appreciation of the beautiful, in the case of the sublime 'a far higher degree of
culture, not merely of the aesthetic judgement, but also of the faculties of
cognition which lie at its basis, seems to be requisite to enable us to lay down
a judgement upon this high distinction of natural objects' (CJ, 115, §29). This
'degree of culture' is not merely based on a varied and extended acquaintance
with aesthetic objects, but has specifically to do with the development of the
mental capacity for ideas:

The proper mental mood for a feeling of the sublime postulates the mind's
susceptibility for ideas, since it is precisely in the failure of nature to attain to
these—and consequently under the presupposition of this susceptibility and of
the straining of the imagination to use nature as a schema for ideas—that there is
something forbidding to sensibility, but which, for all that, has an attraction for us,
arising from the fact of its being a dominion which reason exercises over sensibility
with a view to extending it to the requirements of its own realm (the practical) and
letting it look out beyond itself into the infinite, which for it is an abyss. In fact,
without the development of moral ideas, that which, thanks to preparatory culture,

---

[17] Cf. Zammito, *Kant, Herder and the Birth of Anthropology*, 256: 'Kant emphatically condemned the
impulses associated with empirical psychology as an obtuse "naturalism".' Although Zammito
is speaking here mostly of anthropology rather than aesthetics, in the broader sense, Burke's
analysis of taste is anthropological. Indeed, as Zammito elsewhere puts it, for Kant, aesthetics is
rather 'the key to anthropology' insofar as anthropology is thought not as the accumulation of
empirical data but as concerning the ends of man. See John H. Zammito, *The Genesis of Kant's
Critique of Judgment* (Chicago: University of Chicago Press, 1992), 292–305. For Kant, to project the
awe felt in the face of an object on to nature involves a 'subreption' that signals 'a misplacement
of the actual ground of the feeling, which authentically betokened the supersensible destination
in the subject' (ibid. 301).

we call sublime, merely strikes the untutored man [*dem rohen Menschen*] as terrifying. (*CJ*, 115, §29)

For Kant, the unmediated confrontation with the sublime leaves the savage or the peasant overwhelmed by the abysmal terror of the phenomenon that exceeds the imagination. As Spivak comments,

The raw man has not yet achieved or does not possess a subject whose *Anlage* [blueprint] or programming includes the structure of feeling for the moral. He is not yet the subject divided and perspectivized among the three critiques. In other words, he is not yet or simply not the subject as such, the hero of the *Critiques*, the only example of the concept of a natural yet rational being. This gap between the subject as such and the not-yet-subject can be bridged under propitious circumstances by culture.[18]

In a certain sense, it is precisely the requirement of mediation, the mediation of culture and of the ethical formation of the disposition of the subject, that enables the subject to partake of the public sense that the aesthetic both forms and instantiates. As I have argued more fully elsewhere, the pedagogical aims of the aesthetic that Schiller will draw out into a programme of education, transforming the 'raw man' into the citizen, are already deeply, if less evidently, inscribed in Kant's third critique.[19] Within such a pedagogy, the developmental history that separates the savage from the modern subject is spelled out more fully than it is in Kant's exposition, and the terms of the racializing judgement of culture are established in ways that are decisive for what we may call a liberal discourse of colonialism.[20] And yet, as Spivak remarks, it is only under 'propitious circumstances' that the bridge can be made by culture between the 'raw man', object of heteronomy, and the autonomous subject that is defined against that state. The differential example of the savage is a requirement of the thinking of autonomy itself and cannot therefore be cultivated out of the system: it is the threshold instance on which the narrative of development at once founds itself and founders.[21]

---

[18] Spivak, *Critique of Postcolonial Reason*, 14.
[19] Lloyd, 'Kant's Examples'.
[20] Lloyd, 'Race under Representation'.
[21] In this respect, the savage stands in Kant's third critique precisely as an example—that material remainder of particularity that cannot finally be formalized out of existence precisely because it is a requirement of the system. For an elaboration of this predicament of Kant's aesthetics, see my 'Kant's Examples'.

For Burke, in contradiction to Kant, the effects of the sublime are intimately bound up with the actual physical experience of the mind's incapacity to separate itself from the 'interest of sense'. The surety of self-preservation is not by any means the given of those endowed with cultural capital, like Kant's exemplary scientist de Saussure among the Savoyard peasants, but seems everywhere predicated on the exertions of human bodily labour. Even the work of theorizing the origins of taste becomes such a labour, one which 'exercises' the mind and strengthens it for future labours:

To conclude; whatever progress may be made towards the discovery of truth in this matter, I do not repent the pains I have taken in it. The use of such enquiries may be very considerable. Whatever turns the soul inward on itself, tends to concenter its forces, and to fit it for greater and stronger flights of science. (*OSB*, viii–ix)

Yet it is not my point here to suggest that the conservative Burke paradoxically offers on the basis of common labour a more democratic foundation for aesthetic thought than the proto-republican Kant. On the contrary, as is well known, the thrill which the younger Burke is able to entertain in the effects of the crowd, the transport which carries all along with it, will, in the face of the French Revolution and the seizure of Marie-Antoinette, become the basis of a reactionary critique of the immediacy of revolutionary violence.[22] That critique in turn feeds into the suspicion that informs British cultural discourse in its founding thinkers from Coleridge to Arnold as to the disturbing effects of radical politics and what is understood as the unmediated violence of 'terror'. Indeed, the discourse on culture that founds the humanities as we practise them could be understood precisely as an attempt to contain the potential for violence that is the spectre of radical democracy. Culture, which defines the work of pedagogy in the humanities

---

[22] Though, of course, in those celebrated passages, Burke seeks to counter the popular and immediate appeal of revolution with the no less immediately affecting spectacle of a tragedy befalling the French monarchs. Indeed, one could say that Burke has learned his own lesson well, as the *Reflections on the French Revolution* maintains the argument against the abstract theorizing of the radicals through the appeal of immediate affective rhetoric and through the invocation of familiar associations and the sublimity of power as the grounds for the legitimacy of monarchical government. On the theatrical rhetoric of the *Reflections* and other of his writings on the revolution, see Deane, *Foreign Affections*, 64–5 and 75–6.

since the Enlightenment, stems from the critique of revolutionary violence that it seeks to counter by forming the reflective subject on whom the possibility of representative democratic institutions is founded.[23]

But even as the convergence of a Kantian aesthetic with a Burkean reaction against revolution informs that cultural tradition, a counter-discourse that retains the traces of Burke's aesthetic sensationalism persists. It is, after all, the radical William Godwin who, in the wake of Burke's *Reflections on the Revolution in France*, derives the very grounds of human equality from the identity of the senses of pleasure and pain:

Justice has relation to beings endowed with perception, and capable of pleasure and pain. Now it immediately results from the nature of such beings, independently of any arbitrary constitution, that pleasure is agreeable and pain odious, pleasure to be desired and pain to be disapproved. It is therefore just and reasonable that such beings should contribute, so far as it lies in their power, to the pleasure and benefit of each other. Among pleasures, some are more exquisite, more unalloyed and less precarious than others. It is just that these should be preferred.

From these simple principles we may deduce the moral equality of mankind.[24]

Godwin's radical account of the grounds for human equality short-circuits the discourse of culture with an appeal to an aesthetic foundation for political justice that is located immediately in corporeal sensations. It could, I think, be argued that such a refusal of the separation of the subject from sensation is articulated throughout a radical counter-canonical discourse that insists, against and condemned by the canons of 'high culture', in working through the terrain of the corporeal pains and pleasures of the body in ways that vividly apprehend the workings of and resistance to what Foucault would come to term 'bio-power' in the emergence of industrial capitalism.[25]

---

[23] For a full version of this argument, see David Lloyd and Paul Thomas, *Culture and the State* (London: Routledge, 1997), ch. 1.

[24] William Godwin, *Enquiry Concerning Political Justice*, ed. Isaac Kramnick (Harmondsworth: Penguin Books, 1976), 183.

[25] See Shelley Streeby, *American Sensations: Class, Empire, and the Production of Popular Culture* (Berkeley: University of California Press, 2002) for one study of such a popular tradition rooted in sensationalism.

III The abyss of blackness

Although Foucault notoriously ignored the colonial sphere in his explorations of the genealogy of modern forms of power, there is probably no space in which the conjunction of power and violence more consistently and continuously impacted the body of humans declared to be not, or not yet, subjects. The distance that separates a 'physiological' from a 'transcendental exposition of the aesthetic', one predicated on the body from one that turns on the subject, may also serve to draw our critical reflections back to the intimate linking of violence and terror in the colonial project, an issue that postcolonial theory has notably veered away from addressing. Luke Gibbons has persuasively argued that Burke's intimacy with the corporeal sensations of violence and despotism, as well as his apprehension of the 'sublime' impact of mass politics in 'carrying away' the subject, derives from his experience in colonial Ireland.[26] Frantz Fanon, to whom the contemporary analysis of colonial discourse owes much of its impetus, was similarly familiar with the impact of colonial violence on the colonized body and with the denial of subjectivity or access to universality to the racialized. He was also in a position to critique the historical unfolding and colonial consequences of a discourse only emerging in the later eighteenth century.

In both *Black Skin, White Masks* and *The Wretched of the Earth* it is on the visceral, corporeal impact of colonialism and racism, as against the colonized intellectual's appeal to the universal values of Western culture and subjecthood, that Fanon places the weight of his analysis. Whether it is the black man's experience of racism as being transformed into 'an object in the midst of other objects', a sensation that causes him to encounter 'difficulties in the development of his bodily schema', or it is the peculiarly 'alert' and tensed 'tonicity of muscles' of the colonized that stems from the simultaneously 'inhibitory and stimulating' apparatus of colonial power, it is for Fanon always in the first place the body that registers the effects of a racialized culture.[27] It is the sensation of painful

[26] Luke Gibbons, *Edmund Burke and Ireland: Aesthetics, Politics and the Colonial Sublime* (Cambridge: Cambridge University Press, 2003), esp. chs 1, 2, and 5. See also Deane, *Foreign Affections*, 22–7.

[27] See Frantz Fanon, *Black Skin, White Masks*, foreword by Homi Bhabha, trans. Charles Lam Markham (London: Pluto Press, 1986), 109–10 (cited in the text hereafter as *BSWM*) and *The Wretched of the Earth*, pref. by Jean-Paul Sartre, trans. Constance Farrington (New York: Grove Press, 1968), 53.

terror that calls forth the colonized's violent resistance to a prior colonial violence. For the colonized, the developmental schema that underwrites the civilizational discourse of the colonizer and bars the colonized from recognition as a subject is apprehended as the collapse of the subject back into the body, a collapse in which the violence of the colonial state appears unmediated by the cultural apparatuses that undertake the formation of the white subject in the West. Precisely in so far as our own subjectivities as intellectuals are formed within those apparatuses, we risk, even in a postcolonial critique of the subject, occluding the corporeal terror and violence that still constitute the realm of colonial power.

For Fanon, it is in and on the racialized body that that violence—the violence of a negation that makes the raced body the very limit and other of the civilized—is registered. It is registered in the judgement that denies subjecthood to the racial other. If, for Spivak, Kant's *rohe Mensch*, 'untutored Man', is the 'not-yet-subject', for Fanon, 'the black is not a man' (*BSWM*, 10). For all that, the black man is not yet 'foreclosed' from the developmental structure, but rather caught at its threshold in the lethal mirror stage of racialization that he calls a 'dual narcissism' (*BSWM*, 12). In this specular domain, racialization itself prevents the white subject, let alone the black, from actually occupying the position of universality on which nonetheless the racial judgement itself is predicated. 'The black man wants to be white. The white man slaves to reach a human level' (*BSWM*, 11). As Fanon elsewhere puts it, the European declaration of its cultural 'normativity' is no more than 'unilateral'.[28] The continuing presence in the vision of the white of the black as an object denied full subjecthood thus constitutively prevents the white subject from realizing his representative universality: he has always already objectified another subject as mere body or matter in order to constitute the narrative of his own development, a narrative that, as Kant obliquely suggests, could not be anchored without that objectification.

---

[28] Frantz Fanon, 'Racism and Culture', in *Toward the African Revolution: Political Essays*, trans. Haakon Chevalier (New York: Grove Press, 1988), 31: 'The unilaterally decreed normative value of certain cultures deserves our careful attention.... There is first affirmed the existence of human groups having no culture; then of a hierarchy of cultures; and finally the concept of cultural relativity. We have here the whole range from overall negation to singular and specific recognition. It is precisely this fragmented and bloody history that we must sketch on the level of cultural anthropology.'

To read back into Burke from the perspective of Fanon is equally to throw open the racial blind spot of the corporeal schema of sensation on which the claims for the universality of taste are predicated. As we have seen, for Burke the aesthetic experiences of the sublime and the beautiful are registered in the first place on the sensitive body. Already, however, there is a fundamental asymmetry between the two spheres of taste, one of which regards self-preservation, the other love and sociability. The sublime, indeed, is an affect which derives its force from its anti-sociality: it is apprehended in the face of the wilderness or the stormy ocean, or in the face of a political or religious power that crushes the reciprocity on which any sociality is based. At the same time, however, it is the domain which calls forth labour, a mental labour that is the analogue of the physical labour by which the natural world is subdued and which counteracts the 'disorders' that result from overmuch 'relaxation' or inaction:

The best remedy for all these evils is exercise or *labour*; and labour is a surmounting of *difficulties*, an exertion of the contracting power of the muscles; and as such, resembles pain, which consists in tension, or contraction, in everything but degree. Labour is not only requisite to preserve the coarser organs in a state fit for their functions, but it is equally necessary to these finer organs, on which, and by which, the imagination, and perhaps the whole mental powers act. (*OSB*, 254–5)

In the economy of Burke's aesthetic, then, the sublime relates to the domain of *production* as the beautiful, the realm of love and society, does to that of *reproduction*. The sublime calls for the physical and mental exertions that extend men's domination over the natural world; the beautiful inhabits those domains that have already been reduced. In a certain sense, the sublime strengthens or forges the subject that it threatens to destroy, 'preparing it for further flights', while the beautiful relaxes it. But there is a further, more deeply implicit, asymmetry between the two domains. Where the objects of the sublime actually appear to produce their effects upon the subject, calling forth the counter-motion of a certain aesthetic labour, the objects that constitute domesticated nature appear as no more than the supports of the qualities that induce the sensation of the beautiful. Nowhere is this clearer than in the paradigmatic case of love, where the beloved woman who induces the passion in the male subject does not in fact appear: she is only the effect of her effects. Those effects are the remarkably powerful ones that Burke later paraphrases:

The head reclines something on one side; the eyelids are more closed than usual, and the eyes roll gently with an inclination to the object, the mouth is a little opened, and the breath drawn slowly, with now and then a low sigh: the whole body is composed, and the hands fall idly to the sides. All this is accompanied with an inward sense of melting and languor. (*OSB*, 287)

In a peculiar sense, beauty—which 'acts by relaxing the solids of the whole system' (*OSB*, 287)—works as powerfully to threaten the autonomy and integrity of the subject as do any of the objects of the sublime. It induces a 'fading' of the subject, a kind of powerful effect of dissolution. And the feminine, which never appears as the subject of taste, but only as its support, occupies the peculiar, non-symmetrical position of being at once outside the system of taste and the exciting object of both the beautiful and the sublime. Situated at the boundary of nature and culture, so to speak, the feminine takes on the ambiguous quality of nature 'herself', at once overwhelming power and nurturing servant. In this respect, indeed, woman occupies the same threshold as the savage or 'raw man', both belonging within the trajectory of culture and at the same time standing outside it as its counter-instance. Unable to recognize this parity, and caught perhaps in the dilemma of wishing neither to transform the woman into mere object nor to have her appear as having dominion over man, Burke allows her to fade into an uncanny metonymic absence that haunts the text.

At only one point, however, does woman appear and appear as an object with the effect of the sublime. That moment is when the already asymmetrically gendered subject is also racialized: the black woman appears as a kind of abyss in the text where the sublime and the beautiful collapse into one another. The passage comes in the course of the chapter entitled 'Darkness Terrible in its Own Nature', which endeavours to show 'that blackness and darkness are in some degree painful by their natural operation, independent of any associations whatsoever' (*OSB*, 275). Burke cites the case of a thirteen-year-old boy who was born blind but had recovered his sight after a cataract operation. We are informed 'That the first time the boy saw a black object, it gave him great uneasiness; and that some time after, upon accidentally seeing a negro woman, he was struck with great horror at the sight. The horror, in this case, can scarcely be supposed to arise from any association' (*OSB*, 276). What is striking in this passage is not only that blackness is held naturally to provoke uneasiness, but moreover that the blackness of a woman provokes, far more intensely, 'great horror'. Is it that the feminine, the support of the beautiful that relaxes and dissolves the subject, comes into conjunction with the dark mark of the racialized body, thus bringing about the collapse of the carefully maintained distinction between the domains of self-preservation and of reproduction, of the sublime and the beautiful, of subject and object, of the barred 'savage' and the civilized 'social'—in short, a foundering of the borders between death and life?

Certainly, and for the only time in the essay, Burke assimilates the sublime effects of blackness on the sensations with those of love, only to stage the subject as reacting to that affect with recoil rather than pleasure:

Black bodies, reflecting none, or but a few rays, with regard to sight, are but so many vacant spaces dispersed among the objects we view. When the eye lights on one of these vacuities, after having been kept in some degree of tension by the play of the adjacent colours upon it, it suddenly falls into a relaxation; out of which it as suddenly recovers by a convulsive spring. (OSB, 281)

The shock caused by the 'black body' is posed as an abysmal threat to the subject, operating as a 'vacuity' that causes a sudden fall. One is drawn to see here the play of the contradictory effects of attraction and repulsion—an ambivalence, indeed, that attends the thrill of the sublime throughout Burke's essay. Not for nothing, surely, do the three chapters on darkness and blackness (sections XVI–XVIII) abut the chapter entitled 'The Physical Cause of Love' (section XIX).[29]

But certainly we can read this moment, in which there converge the boundary marks of both the gendered and the raced objects that at once structure and threaten the white male subject, through Fanon's critical extension of the mirror stage into the terrain of racial subjecthood. The pathological phobia that constitutes racism derives for Fanon from the 'destructuration' of the white body image that the black body effects: 'At the extreme, I should say that the Negro, because of his body, impedes the closing of the postural schema of the white man—at the point, naturally, at

[29] Aravamudan comments extensively on this passage, remarking that 'the African woman seems in a strange structural equivalence to the despot'. See *Tropicopolitans*, 201 and, for the full discussion, 192–201. My point is rather that, while Burke as we have seen finds the source of the sublime to be some 'modification of power', in this singular case of blackness there is a convergence of the power of the sublime with the 'passive' power of the feminine/beautiful.

which the black man makes his entry into the phenomenal world of the white man' (*BSWM*, 160).[30] The very body of the black man functions as a kind of abyss that shatters the closed circuit of the white familial mirror stage. Fanon elaborates this point in an extended and complex footnote:

It would indeed be interesting, on the basis of Lacan's theory of the *mirror period* [*sic*], to investigate the extent to which the *imago* of his fellow built up in the young white at the usual age would undergo an imaginary aggression with the appearance of the Negro. When one has grasped the mechanism described by Lacan, one can have no further doubt that the real Other for the white man is and will continue to be the black man. And conversely. Only for the white man the Other is perceived on the level of the body image, absolutely as the not-self—that is, the unidentifiable, the unassimilable. For the black man, as we have shown, historical and economic realities come into the picture. (*BSWM*, 161 n.)

[30] It is important to note at this juncture that the black body that appears as an abyss to the white subject is, unlike in Burke, a black *male* body. For Burke, for reasons outlined above, it is structurally inevitable that the body be female, drawing together as it does a persistent anxiety in the text about the sublimity of the feminine with the anxiety provoked by blackness. For Fanon, the focus on the black male body is surely overdetermined. The passage is staged autobiographically and the analysis of the anecdote evidently draws on a very male-orientated body of psychoanalytic work. But beyond these contingencies, we can hypothesize within the terms of the larger argument of this essay more systematic reasons for the negation of the black female in Fanon's corpus. In the terms of the mirror stage, Fanon stands in the anecdote in the place of the image of the father. But rather than representing, as the white father would, the Name-of-the-Father, the Symbolic or the Law, he represents a terrifying abyss. He is not recognized as a subject who could represent the Subject: his existence is negated. Fanon's means to escape from that predicament is, throughout *BSWM*, to desire what, according to the Lacanian logic of heterosexually asymmetrical desire, the white man desires: the white woman. Pursuing that logic, it is the desire of the white woman that Fanon desires. This places him in the unenviable situation of desiring to become the male subject by way of a desiring of the other's desire, which places him back into the feminized position of the non-subject. He occupies in this relation the structural position therefore of the woman of colour who is the object of the white male's desire. The ineluctability of this contradictory outcome of his apparently simple desire to be recognized as subject may account for Fanon's often-remarked misogyny and his simultaneous recognition and denial of the homosociality and the homosexual desires that circulate through the scene of race and colonialism. For alternative readings of Fanon's misogyny and of his overdetermined 'infernal circle' (*BSWM*, 116), see Rey Chow, 'The Politics of Admittance: Female Sexual Agency, Miscegenation, and the Formation of Community in Frantz Fanon', in *Ethics after Idealism: Theory—Culture—Ethnicity—Reading* (Bloomington and Indianapolis: Indiana University Press, 1998), 55–73; Diana Fuss, 'Interior Colonies: Frantz Fanon and the Politics of Identification', in *Identification Papers* (New York: Routledge, 1995), 142–4 and 157–8; and Françoise Verges, *Monsters and Revolutionaries: Colonial Family Romance and Métissage* (Durham, NC: Duke University Press, 1999), 209–11.

The asymmetry is marked here: what for the white man takes place at the level of the ontological, as an ahistorical and immediate abyss, appears for him as such precisely because of the historical exclusion of the black from subjecthood and historicity. For the black man, on the contrary, the historical and the economic conditions of racialization become the means to an analysis of that exclusion and of the negation of subjectivity.[31] In the developmental schema of the West, for which the destiny of the racialized subject is to 'become white', as Fanon puts it, that subject will always remain the 'subject-yet-to-be': an object interpellated by historical judgement but never able to be fully in that history as its subject.

Reading Fanon's analysis in relation to the discourse on the aesthetic thus suggests that the body, which is for Kant a material to be transcended in the course of universalizing reflection and cultivation and which is for Burke the very foundation of aesthetic universality, is rather the locus of an ineradicable difference that, because it is constitutively inassimilable to the unilaterally declared norms of universality, necessarily evokes violence and objectification. What cannot simply be transcended must be destroyed, annihilated, in the sublime violence of colonialism. Burke, whose Irish background gave him an intimate acquaintance with the violence of colonialism towards what resists it, comes closer in his apprehension of the violence of power than Kant can to recognizing this, but his recognition necessarily falters when the universal eye of the white subject encounters the black body that embodies the difference that denies it universality. The black body becomes the abyss into which the claims of universality, founded as they are on its difference, inevitably founder.

In so far as both the transcendental and the physiological accounts of the aesthetic, and the political subject that they differently underwrite, remain inscribed within what we might call a precocious as well as a unilateral universalization of a singular conception of the human, the discourse of the aesthetic will remain a more or less discretely racialized as well as political

---

[31] For a related reading of Fanon's analysis, see Robert Gooding-Williams's essay on the Rodney King trial, 'Look, A Negro!', in *Look, A Negro! Philosophical Essays on Race, Culture, and Politics* (New York: Routledge, 2006), 1–16. The demythification of the deployment of the ahistorical figure of the black man as violent, threatening, and '[incarnating] a wilderness chaos inimical to civilization' (p. 11) can be countered only by strategies that invoke the 'economic and historical' realities of racist structures of power and violence that Fanon invokes.

discourse on the subject and on culture. Perhaps the convergence of post-colonial and eighteenth-century studies may succeed in provoking the work of a materialist counter-aesthetics—that is, one that engages with the historical emergence of the field of culture and with the transformation it effects in 'structures of feeling'—that would be fully informed by a race-critical account of the place of the body in that history.

Part Two

Enlightenment Categories and Postcolonial Classifications

3

Reading Contrapuntally

Robinson Crusoe, Slavery, and Postcolonial Theory

Daniel Carey

We need not look very far to locate the darker side of Enlightenment. Postcolonial scholarship in particular has been attuned to the disjunction in the period between a politics of liberation and autonomy, which coincides at the same time with imperial expansion and the subjugation of native peoples, and a new ethics of equality which nonetheless occurs in an era of slavery unprecedented in its scale and brutality. Sorting out our relationship to these historical events and injustices has led to alternative accounts of subjectivity, agency, and power, and new narratives redescribing the ostensible rise and progress of civilization and reason. What part literature has to play in these discussions remains contested. Although we are not prevented from contextualizing literary texts historically by the fact that they possess a

I am grateful to the Irish Research Council for the Humanities and Social Sciences for the award of a Government of Ireland Research Fellowship which made it possible to carry out research for this essay. For comments and suggestions I am indebted to Lynn Festa, Adrian Frazier, Susan Jones, James Kelly, Enrico Dal Lago, and Kim LoPrete.

distinctive *surplus* of meaning, their rhetorical construction inevitably complicates the task of treating them straightforwardly as representative of historical truths external to the text.

Among postcolonial critics perhaps the richest deliberation over these questions has come from Edward Said. In *Culture and Imperialism* (1993), Said provides a complex theoretical orientation on the relationship of literature to history and the expansion of empire. He describes his purpose as rejoining cultural forms with a 'worldly domain' of history, seeing them as 'quintessentially hybrid' entities that bear the trace, especially through their spatial construction, of an imperial moment.[1] According to Said's periodization, this development takes place in English fiction before the formal beginning of an age of empire around 1878 with the 'Scramble for Africa'. Indeed he asserts that a 'coherent, fully mobilized system of ideas' about European hegemony existed at the end of the eighteenth century.[2] As an example of what might be done to re-engage with literature in the period, Said focuses on Jane Austen's *Mansfield Park*. The passing references in the novel to the Antiguan estate of Sir Thomas Bertram, owner of Mansfield Park, take on a new significance when viewed in relation to a colonial system, as a locus of sugar production and slavery necessary to the stability and continuance of daily life at Mansfield. Yet Said remarked on the need to treat literature as a distinct form of source material. Critics should not generalize their readings in such a way as to 'efface the identity of a particular text'; even as they pursue the 'historical valences' of references to such places as Antigua, they must recognize that texts like Austen's do not merely reflect or repeat an experience but 'encode' it.[3]

These critical priorities require a new hermeneutic, which Said describes as 'contrapuntal reading'. Simply put, this mode of interpretation concentrates on understanding 'what is involved when an author shows, for instance, that a colonial sugar plantation is seen as important to the process of maintaining a particular style of life in England'. But in practice much more is at stake since Said stresses the need to 'draw out, extend, give emphasis and voice to what is silent or marginally present or ideologically represented'.[4] The significance of Said's position is that he articulates an emergent practice in

---

[1] Edward Said, *Culture and Imperialism* (New York: Alfred A. Knopf, 1993), 58.
[2] Ibid. 58.   [3] Ibid. 67, 89, 96.   [4] Ibid. 66.

postcolonial criticism at the same time as offering an influential statement on how such criticism should proceed.

In confronting the eighteenth-century literary canon, the question raised by Said's contrapuntal hermeneutic is that of what forms of reading it authorizes. This essay attempts to work through these issues in relation to one of the most important fictions of the period, Daniel Defoe's *Robinson Crusoe* (1719). The novel's basic mythos of shipwreck, survival, and self-sufficiency has been embedded at the deepest level of cultural imagination, yet the colonial dimension of the book is often elided from popular memory. Postcolonial scholars engaging with the text have not only re-established the centrality of colonialism for understanding Crusoe's aspirations,[5] but they have also emphasized the importance of the fact that the narrative includes Crusoe's enslavement of a native Carib Indian, Friday, which makes the need for a critique more urgent. Crusoe's ostensible ownership and domination of Friday take on a kind of inevitability in a story of Caribbean colonialism. The connection between them serves as the paradigm case of the master–slave relationship understood as inseparable from colonialism.

The most distinguished account of these textual dynamics has come from Peter Hulme,[6] but a fair consensus can be found among other postcolonial critics. For Syed Manzural Islam, Crusoe represents a 'petrified subject who not only possesses the island by obstinately digging his heels in but, predictably enough, installs himself as a master with a slave of his own'.[7] In Bill Overton's discussion, the novel provides an 'ideological blueprint for establishing colonies' which includes a 'narrative contrivance' naturalizing

---

[5] See e.g. Peter Hulme, *Colonial Encounters: Europe and the Native Caribbean, 1492–1797* (London: Methuen, 1986), ch. 5; Aparna Dharwadker, 'Nation, Race, and the Ideology of Commerce in Defoe', *The Eighteenth Century: Theory and Interpretation*, 39/1 (1998), 63–84; Brett C. McInelly, 'Expanding Empires, Expanding Selves: Colonialism, the Novel, and *Robinson Crusoe*', *Studies in the Novel*, 35/1 (2003), 1–21; Rajani Sudan, *Fair Exotics: Xenophobic Subjects in English Literature, 1720–1850* (Philadelphia: University of Pennsylvania Press, 2002), 1–7; Hans Turley, 'Protestant Evangelicalism, British Imperialism, and Crusonian Identity', in *A New Imperial History: Culture, Identity, and Modernity in Britain and the Empire, 1660–1840* (Cambridge: Cambridge University Press, 2004), 176–93. For Said, *Robinson Crusoe* is 'virtually unthinkable without the colonizing mission that permits him to create a new world of his own in the distant reaches of the African, Pacific, and Atlantic wilderness' (*Culture and Imperialism*, 64; see also 70).

[6] Hulme, *Colonial Encounters*, ch. 5. Hulme's work is commended by Said, *Culture and Imperialism*, 83.

[7] Syed Manzurul Islam, *The Ethics of Travel: From Marco Polo to Kafka* (Manchester: Manchester University Press, 1996), 3.

Friday's slavery.[8] For Hugh Ridley, the enslaved Friday and Crusoe have 'no actual relationship', which is no more than what we would expect in circumstances of 'colonial encounter'.[9] For other critics, Crusoe's wilful imposition of himself on a subjugated native becomes illustrative of an Enlightenment failure to imagine the Other.[10]

These readings receive a theoretical validation from Said's scheme of contrapuntal reading since his purpose is precisely to theorize the significance of neglected references to colonial experience in canonical literature.[11] His own account of *Mansfield Park* has a natural connection here, with its invocation of sugar and chattel slavery in the Caribbean. In the case of *Robinson Crusoe*, the importance of colonial possessions in the novel cannot be denied, whether we consider the island itself, which Crusoe transforms into personal property, or his earlier acquisition of a plantation in Brazil where he hopes to improve his status from a mere tobacco farmer to an owner of a lucrative sugar mill. The Brazilian interlude relates directly to slavery since he needs this source of labour to run his estate. Indeed his motive for undertaking the fateful journey that ends in shipwreck and his twenty-eight-year tenure on a deserted island is expressly to acquire African slaves to support the venture into sugar production.

What then should we make of Crusoe's encounter with Friday? Does it follow that this too is a master–slave relationship? This question is more difficult to determine than critics have allowed, as I will argue in this essay. An obvious way to proceed would be to return to the text itself in search of

---

[8] Bill Overton, 'Countering *Crusoe*: Two Colonial Narratives', *Critical Survey*, 4/3 (1992), 302–3.

[9] Hugh Ridley, *Images of Imperial Rule* (London: Croom Helm, 1983), 4. Ridley summarizes in part the position of O. Mannoni, *Prospero and Caliban: The Psychology of Colonization*, trans. Pamela Powesland (New York and Washington: Frederick A. Praeger, 1964), esp. 97–105.

[10] See Bernard McGrane, *Beyond Anthropology: Society and the Other* (New York: Columbia University Press, 1989), 43–55; Patrick Brantlinger, *Crusoe's Footprints: Cultural Studies in Britain and America* (London: Routledge, 1990), 1–3; Helen Tiffin, 'Post-Colonial Literature and Counter-Discourse', in Bill Ashcroft, Gareth Griffiths, and Helen Tiffin (eds), *The Post-Colonial Studies Reader* (London: Routledge, 1995), 98.

[11] In his extended review of *Culture and Imperialism*, Hulme recognizes the importance of Said's critical project, but regrets the absence of engagement by Said with Fernando Ortiz's *Cuban Counterpoint: Tobacco and Sugar* (1940). Hulme focuses on the central notion of contrapuntal reading before concluding that ' "counterpoint" is being given far too much work to do for an untheorised term . . . it is difficult to tell whether "counterpoint" is a description of Said's method or a description of the relationship between different sectors of a culture'. Peter Hulme, 'Imperial Counterpoint', *Wasafiri*, 18 (Autumn 1993), 60.

answers. But if we did, we might find that Friday is not a slave but a servant, not subjugated and possessed as property but someone who serves voluntarily on the basis of ongoing consent. Would such a conclusion constitute a new contrapuntal reading or one that required a contrapuntal reply? This issue exposes a central dilemma in Said's protocols. At a certain point it becomes valid to prioritize a historical truth external to the text itself, especially where the text is deemed silent or insufficiently explicit on the topic. In this case, the importance of chattel slavery as a historical phenomenon in the eighteenth century would take precedence over the text and therefore define, contrapuntally, the exchanges between Crusoe and Friday.

I call the latter mode of interpretation palimpsestic reading to draw attention to the fact that it superimposes one text on another. The justification for such a scheme derives from an imperative to redress historical injustices (like chattel slavery and racism) and to find in canonical texts a location for them. Yet it runs the risk of appropriating literature as a mere allegory of history while assigning to criticism the task of determining the ways in which such texts represent historical truths outside themselves. At the same time this arguably forecloses the possibilities of literary texts, their surplus of meaning, capacity for irony, and resistance to containment.

I Contrapuntal reading

Before addressing *Robinson Crusoe* we need a better sense of what is entailed in Said's conception of contrapuntal reading. The difficulty is that he provides several distinct accounts of what it constitutes. As we might expect from his naming of the practice, the first analysis comes from an analogy with music. Said remarks that in classical music, the theory of counterpoint depends on the relationship between multiple themes, none of which are dominant; together they create a polyphonic arrangement characterized by a tight structure in which an 'organized interplay' emerges from the themes themselves, 'not from a rigorous melodic or formal principle outside the work'.[12] This statement appears to guarantee that the identified themes remain integral to the piece itself rather than originating from an external source.

[12] Said, *Culture and Imperialism*, 51.

But Said quickly modifies the position. The analogy of 'various themes play-[ing] off one another' no longer applies to the musical composition itself, but rather to the manner of reading it: 'In the same way', he suggests, 'we can read and interpret English novels, for example, whose engagement (usually suppressed for the most part) with the West Indies or India, say, is shaped and perhaps even determined by the specific history of colonization, resistance, and finally native nationalism'.[13] For the moment, the statement that the shaping force comes from colonization, resistance, or native nationalism remains an assertion; what must be recognized is that for reading purposes, a contrapuntal approach does not confine itself to the text, but introduces themes from outside it to create the interplay. Thus, to reread the 'cultural archive' contrapuntally requires 'a simultaneous awareness both of the metropolitan history that is narrated and of those other histories against which (and together with which) the dominating discourse acts'.[14]

Said elaborates his position by maintaining that we must attend to the neglected category of space in order to shift our critical perspective. The 'inherent mode' of the form of reading he espouses is 'not temporal but spatial'.[15] On the whole, he points out, scholars have 'failed to remark the *geographical* notation, the theoretical mapping and charting of territory that underlies Western fiction, historical writing, and philosophical discourse of the time'.[16] By concentrating on the issue of space, we will recover the ways in which the metropole took precedence over the colony, and the parallel manipulation of space to relegate and confine the non-European to a 'secondary racial, cultural, ontological status'. More generally, the task remains one of establishing a counterpoint between 'overt patterns in British writing about Britain' and 'representations of the world beyond the British Isles'.[17]

Mansfield Park is exemplary in this respect for Said, with its narrative focus on the recovery of domestic stability. The privileging of 'home' in the novel depends on wealth generated by an Antiguan sugar plantation. Sir Thomas Bertram travels there to shore up his interests, leaving his English estate and

[13] Ibid.
[14] Ibid. This departs from the analogy with counterpoint in which, as he alerts us, no theme is dominant.
[15] Ibid. 81.
[16] Ibid. 58. He includes in this failure 'most cultural historians, and certainly all literary scholars'.
[17] Ibid. 59, 81.

family morally unprotected, but for all its utility as a plot device, Antigua (and its slave population) receives little mention in the text. The 'facts of empire' which leave their trace in the book thus reveal a deeper 'structure of attitude and reference' (and indifference), which is drawn out by contrapuntal reading.[18]

Yet we are entitled to do more than merely follow the narrative contours of the book in constructing a critical account of it. 'In reading a text, one must open it out both to what went into it and to what its author excluded', according to Said. This requires (as noted above) giving 'emphasis and voice to what is silent or marginally present or ideologically represented'.[19] In the case of *Robinson Crusoe*, this would mean articulating aspects of the English colonial system in operation in the period (for example the use of letters patent to secure title to private settlements)[20] but also the forms of slaveholding, indenture, and trafficking in slaves at the time. The merits of doing so are obvious and coincide with the patterns, in fact, of an established contextual criticism. But I would argue that a temptation accompanies this critical approach, in which it is not enough to describe what the text excludes; rather, a tendency exists to write what is excluded back into the text itself. At this stage, counterpoint gives way to palimpsest.

Although Said insists that, with his reading of *Mansfield Park*, there is 'no way of understanding the "structure of attitude and reference"' to empire 'except by working through the novel',[21] he in fact licenses a form of reading with palimpsestic implications. In his theory of interpretation, time ends up trumping space as the ultimate frame of reference. He argues that contrapuntal readings may legitimately take account of the fact that sites of British colonial power gave rise to later movements of resistance and eventually freed themselves from 'direct and indirect rule'. In this context, criticism juxtaposes the vision of a particular historical moment with 'the various revisions it later provoked', such as the nationalist experience of post-

---

[18] Ibid. 62.

[19] Ibid. 66, 67.

[20] On the use of letters patent, see Ken MacMillan, *Sovereignty and Possession in the English New World: The Legal Foundations of Empire, 1576–1640* (Cambridge: Cambridge University Press, 2006). For Crusoe's contemplation in the *Farther Adventures* of securing 'a patent for the possession', see Daniel Defoe, *Robinson Crusoe* (London: J. M. Dent & Sons, 1945), 230. This volume includes both *The Life and Strange Surprising Adventures of Robinson Crusoe* and *The Farther Adventures of Robinson Crusoe*. All further parenthetical citations in the text are to this volume.

[21] Said, *Culture and Imperialism*, 95.

independence India.[22] Slavery in *Mansfield Park*, mentioned after Sir Thomas's return home but then greeted with 'dead silence', is another case in point. Works of this kind must be seen as 'resisting or avoiding that other setting, which their formal inclusiveness, historical honesty, and prophetic suggestiveness cannot completely hide. In time there would no longer be a dead silence when slavery was spoken of, and the subject became central to a new understanding of what Europe was.'[23] Revisiting *Robinson Crusoe* and the subject of slavery provides an opportunity to evaluate the implications of Said's critical protocols and rereadings of the novel by postcolonial critics.

II *Robinson Crusoe* and the subject of slavery

In the vast body of his published work, Defoe's attention to the issue of slavery indicates a mixed record. Occasional comments in the *Review*, Defoe's periodical which appeared from 1704 to 1713, sometimes in connection with the future of the Royal African Company, indicate a pragmatic support for the slave trade as part of a mercantilist outlook on national economic interests. Yet he combined this, most notably in his long poem *Jure Divino: A Satyr* (1706) with disparagement of the political condition of slavery, associated with the exercise of and submission to despotic power.[24] Similar inconsistencies run through *Robinson Crusoe*, which is permeated by narrative

---

[22] Ibid. 66, 67.

[23] Ibid. 96.

[24] For Defoe's most extended discussion of slavery and the Royal African Company, see the *Review*, 5/147 (5 Mar. 1709), 585–8. For examples of Defoe's equation of existing under arbitrary rule with slavery, see *Jure Divino: A Satyr* (London, 1706); and the *Review*, 1/12 (15 Apr. 1704), 63a; *Review*, 1/47 (8 Aug. 1704), 202b; *Review*, 8/27 (26 May 1711), 111b; and esp. *Review*, 8/67 (23 Aug. 1711), 261–3 (all in *Defoe's Review*, 22 vols, ed. Arthur Wellesley Secord (New York: Columbia University Press, 1938). For secondary discussion of slavery and race in Defoe's journalism and economic, political, and fictional writing, see Eberhard Späth, 'Defoe and Slavery', in Wolfgang Binder (ed.), *Slavery in the Americas* (Würzburg: Königshausen & Neumann, 1993), 453–69; Richard Paul Kaplan, 'Daniel Defoe's Views on Slavery and Racial Prejudice', Ph.D. diss., New York University, 1970; John McVeagh, ' "The Blasted Race of Old *Cham*": Daniel Defoe and the African', *Ibadan Studies in English*, 1 (1969), 85–109; George E. Boulukos, *The Grateful Slave: The Emergence of Race in Eighteenth-Century British and American Culture* (Cambridge: Cambridge University Press, 2008), ch. 2; Patrick J. Keane, 'Slavery and the Slave Trade: Crusoe as Defoe's Representative', in Roger D. Lund (ed.), *Critical Essays on Daniel Defoe* (New York: G. K. Hall, 1997), 97–120.

interludes of and references to slavery. While postcolonial critics have focused on the relationship between Crusoe and Friday, several episodes earlier in the novel establish the importance of this theme. The first of these is Crusoe's own experience of enslavement. After rejecting his father's fateful advice to remain at home and adhere to the 'middle station' of life (p. 6), Crusoe travels to London and secures the patronage of a sea captain, who invites him to take part in a voyage to Africa. Crusoe participates in the mission as a private gentleman, not a sailor, with capital raised from his family, and he returns with a substantial profit, having traded trifles for gold on the African coast.[25] At the age of 19 he embarks on a second journey but on this occasion the trip ends in disaster. Corsairs intercept the ship and Crusoe finds himself held captive in the Moroccan port of Salé. There he is kept by the captain of the rover 'as his proper prize, and made his slave', performing the 'common drudgery of slaves about his house' (p. 16). Thus Crusoe cannot claim ignorance of the personal ordeal of slavery.[26]

The circumstances of Crusoe's escape from captivity raise different questions and confirm that in spite of his own experience he is willing to benefit from the slave trade himself and participate in it directly. After being held for two years in Morocco, Crusoe finds an opportunity to break free one day when his master appoints him to go out on the long boat to catch fish for a meal planned for his friends. Crusoe does so, accompanied by a young 'Maresco' named Xury and an adult Moor, Ishmael.[27] Once they make their way beyond the port, Crusoe tips Ishmael overboard, but he allows the boy to remain with him. Xury swears to be faithful to him and to 'go all over the world' with Crusoe (p. 19). In a famous transaction, Crusoe later

---

[25] Whether this is a slave-trading mission, as Roxann Wheeler asserts (*The Complexion of Race: Categories of Difference in Eighteenth-Century British Culture* (Philadelphia: University of Pennsylvania Press, 2000), 55, 56, 62), is difficult to determine. Crusoe does not indicate this explicitly while describing the journey itself. After his return he states, 'I was now set up for a Guiney trader' (p. 15) and while in Brazil he recounts his experience on the Guinea coast to his planter colleagues, explaining 'how easy it was' to trade trifles not only for 'gold dust, Guinea grains, elephants' teeth, &c., but negroes, for the service of the Brasils, in great numbers' (p. 30).

[26] For accounts of North African slavery at this time, see Linda Colley, *Captives: Britain, Empire and the World 1600–1850* (London: Jonathan Cape, 2002); Robert C. Davis, *Christian Slaves, Muslim Masters: White Slavery in the Mediterranean, the Barbary Coast, and Italy, 1500–1800* (New York: Palgrave, 2003).

[27] Wheeler, *Complexion of Race*, 56, 60, 61, may be correct in assuming that the term 'Maresco' identifies Xury as a Spanish Moor. The *OED* examples under 'Morisco' are less conclusive.

sells Xury to a Portuguese sea captain who rescues them both at sea (p. 27). This set of events has not received much attention from scholars, but it is worth looking at again. How is it that Xury becomes Crusoe's property? So far as I know, this question has not been asked by critics of the novel, and we merely assume Crusoe's entitlement to him. Yet they are both slaves in Salé and therefore share the same status. How does Crusoe escape from his captivity while Xury remains in bondage? Even if Crusoe regards Xury's condition as somehow justified while his own is not, this fails to explain how Crusoe acquires a financial right over him. The transfer of title appears to take place without question from either party, although Crusoe indicates that 'I was very loath to sell the boy's liberty who had assisted me so faithfully in procuring my own' (p. 27). This remark confirms that Xury's freedom is subject to sale but whether he had actually gained his liberty with Crusoe— only to lose it (by promising to follow him)—or whether he simply never made the transition out of slavery, remains unclear. The episode concludes with Crusoe accepting sixty pieces of eight for Xury from the Portuguese captain, who agrees to free him after a ten-year indenture if he converts to Christianity: 'upon this, and Xury saying he was willing to go to him, I let the captain have him' (p. 27).[28] The lack of protest from Xury, either on this occasion or at the end of the journey when Crusoe sells him, somehow naturalizes the exchange. The only mitigation is the promise that Xury will be liberated in ten years if he converts to Christianity (p. 27).

Crusoe confirms his readiness to engage in the slave trade in a number of ways during his four-year interlude in Salvador de Bahia in Brazil.[29] (The Portuguese captain deposits him there and assists him in setting up an estate.) Crusoe acquires a plantation and begins by growing tobacco with the intention of expanding into sugar cane. The mistake of parting with Xury strikes him forcefully at this point (p. 28), but he manages to acquire a Negro slave and two indentured servants by disposing of goods in London (the

---

[28] Wheeler, in *The Complexion of Race*, ch. 2, emphasizes the repetition of Crusoe's relationship with Xury in his dealings with Friday, but we also have to bear in mind that Crusoe in this early era of his life remains unregenerate. On this point see Catherine E. Moore, 'Robinson and Xury and Inkle and Yarico', *English Language Notes*, 19 (Sept. 1981), 24–9; G. A. Starr, *Defoe and Spiritual Autobiography* (Princeton: Princeton University Press, 1965), 85–7; and J. Paul Hunter, *The Reluctant Pilgrim* (Baltimore: Johns Hopkins University Press, 1966), 198 n.

[29] For some discussion of Crusoe's sojourn in Brazil, see Marcus Vinicius de Freitas, 'The Image of Brazil in *Robinson Crusoe*', *Portuguese Literary and Cultural Studies*, 4–5 (2000), 453–9.

proceeds from his first, successful African adventure). It would appear that he remains at this point a mere *lavrador de cana* with aspirations to become a wealthy *senhor de engenho*, owner of a sugar mill.[30] The problem for him, as for his fellow planters, is the lack of an adequate labour supply. Given his prior experience in Africa, Crusoe agrees to travel as supercargo on a private expedition to obtain slaves, and it is during this journey that the shipwreck occurs which leaves Crusoe alone on the deserted Caribbean island. However, at no point in Crusoe's burgeoning reflections on providence and religious duty does he connect his misfortune with divine judgement on slaving specifically. On the contrary, the lesson he should have learned, he tells us, was not to abandon the trade but to leave it for others whose proper business it was to 'fetch negroes' (p. 142). He ought to have stayed put in Brazil and waited for his fortunes to accumulate.[31]

Important though these episodes may be, there is no doubt that for postcolonial critics the crucial event regarding slavery happens in the novel when Crusoe encounters Friday and takes possession of him. Although this transpires in the twenty-fifth year of Crusoe's tenure on the island, it defines the narrative and shows the centrality of master–slave relations in a story of colonial occupation in the Caribbean. At the same time it invites a critique that refigures the book contrapuntally in relation to the contemporary trade in slaves. There is support for such a reading at a number of occasions in the novel, including the moment when Crusoe and Friday first meet.

Crusoe's first reference of note in this context appears when he relates a dream he had in his twenty-fourth year on the island, long after seeing the solitary footprint in the sand and his later discovery that the cannibals do indeed pay occasional visits to consume their victims. In the dream, Crusoe

---

[30] His intention to become a planter on arriving in Brazil arises from meeting the owner of 'an *ingenio* as they call it, that is, a plantation and a sugar-house' (p. 27). At the close of the novel Crusoe discovers that his plantation has indeed become a valuable '*ingenio*' (p. 204) during his long absence, courtesy of the efforts of his business partner. On the cane farmers and *engenhos* or mill owners in this region of Brazil, see Stuart B. Schwartz, *Sugar Plantations in the Formation of Brazilian Society: Bahia, 1550–1835* (Cambridge: Cambridge University Press, 1985), chs 10 and 11. See also Pedro de Almeida Vasconcelos, *Salvador de Bahia (Brésil): transformations et permanences (1549–2004)* (Paris: L'Harmattan, 2005), ch. 2.

[31] '[W]hat business had I to leave a settled fortune, a well stock'd plantation, improving and encreasing, to turn supra-cargo to Guinea, to fetch negroes, when patience and time would have so encreas'd our stock at home, that we could have bought them at our own door, from those whose business it was to fetch them?' (p. 142).

imagines escaping from the island with the aid of a native pilot who could navigate to the mainland. He has a preference for saving a prisoner condemned to be eaten and brought there for that purpose, but he recognizes that putting this plan into effect would require 'attacking a whole caravan of them, and killing them all' (p. 145), a desperate measure that might well miscarry. But he also admits to scruples over the 'lawfulness' of doing so. The duty of self-preservation, fundamental to the law of nature, offered a justification since he reasons that these men 'were enemies to my life, and would devour me, if they could' (p. 145). His action in attacking them would therefore be taken 'in my own defence as much as if they were actually assaulting me' (p. 145). He admits to perplexities over the matter, but the desire for liberation prevails over any misgivings at this point and he resolves to 'get one of those savages into my hands, cost what it would' (pp. 145–6), presumably in terms of human life.

Crusoe looks out for cannibal visitors for the next year and a half, intent on implementing such a plan. In his first explicit reference to slavery while on the island he states his conviction that he could manage as many as 'one, nay, two or three savages' and 'make them entirely slaves to me, to do whatever I should direct them, and to prevent their being able at any time to do me any hurt' (p. 146). On what legal basis would he enslave them? Although the text does not clarify whether they would come from the men awaiting imminent death and cannibalization or from those holding them as captives, it seems evident from the sequence of discussion that he has in mind the latter, in other words the same group of Carib assailants whom he understands as being bent on his destruction. If so, these individuals would constitute prisoners of Crusoe taken in a just war. In the natural-law tradition, slavery was given a justification in this set of circumstances. According to Lockean political theory, for example, a narrow basis existed for justifying slavery. If a certain group made war on an innocent people and the innocent people prevailed in the conflict, they would in turn be entitled to put those who offended against them to death. Alternatively, they could lawfully commute the sentence to slavery.[32] Crusoe has already imagined himself as an innocent, wronged party, and presumably feels he has a justification according to the law of nature not only to execute those

---

[32] See John Locke, *Two Treatises of Government*, ed. Peter Laslett (Cambridge: Cambridge University Press, 1988), 'Second Treatise', §23, §85.

who intend to kill him but furthermore to preserve the lives of a few of these offenders for his own use as slaves.

All of this remains at the level of fantasy until the day arrives when Crusoe sees five canoes approaching the island. The savages prepare a fire for their feast and pull two captives from the boats, one of whom is promptly killed and dismembered. The other victim breaks free and runs in the direction of Crusoe's domain, pursued by two men. Crusoe joins the fray and knocks down one of the pursuers with the stock of his gun and fires on the other as he prepares to shoot him with a bow and arrow (making Crusoe's act a lawful killing). In his fright at the sound of the gun, the fleeing native stands still until Crusoe beckons him to come forward with signs of encouragement. According to Crusoe, the man approached cautiously, kneeling down every 'ten or twelve steps in token of acknowledgement of my saving his life'. The narrative continues with significant detail: 'at length he came close to me, and then he kneel'd down again, kiss'd the ground, and laid his head upon the ground, and taking me by the foot, set my foot upon his head; this it seems was in token of swearing to be my slave for ever' (p. 148). The status of the man in question, soon to be renamed Friday, appears assured by this statement, confirming the enactment of a master–slave relationship at the heart of the eighteenth century's most powerful and widely disseminated fictional narrative.

Crusoe's hesitation in glossing the signification of the act—'this *it seems* was in token of swearing to be my slave for ever'—might give us pause, enough to suggest that the interpretation assigning him to the category of slave does not exhaust the possibilities of the text. In fact, evidence exists for an alternative conclusion about Friday, as I hope to show in a moment. Yet it is one of the paradoxes arising from Said's position that a contrapuntal reading of the novel which continued to define the relationship between Crusoe and Friday as that of master and slave would remain valid even if the text did *not* support it. The historical reality of slavery in the period would entitle us to give it priority in our interpretation of the text's ostensible silences or gaps.

To initiate an alternative account of the relationship between Crusoe and Friday, we can begin by looking again at the circumstances of the first encounter between them. Just before Friday abases himself, Crusoe informs us that he 'stood trembling, as if he had been taken prisoner, and had just been to be kill'd, as his two enemies were' (p. 148). Thus he imputes to Friday the belief that the armed Crusoe makes no distinction between Friday and his pursuers; far from effecting his rescue, Crusoe appears to Friday as if he now holds him as a prisoner and intends to execute him. The acknowledgement that Crusoe has spared his life comes, according to Crusoe, with Friday's kneeling down and approaching him on the ground. Whether Crusoe accepts him as a slave has not been established, however.

At this point, Crusoe tells us that he 'took him up, and made much of him and encourag'd him all I could' (p. 148), beckoning Friday to follow him and explaining through signs that more of his enemies might come after him (p. 149). Crusoe leads Friday not to his so-called 'castle' but rather to the refuge of his cave in a more remote part of the island. He gives him bread and raisins and water to drink for his refreshment, and then lays a bed for him, where Friday falls asleep. Such treatment appears to confirm that Friday now enjoys Crusoe's protection.

When Friday arises, a second set of exchanges occurs between them in which Friday enacts a parallel set of gestures, interpreted once more by Crusoe:

he came running to me, laying himself down again upon the ground, with all the possible signs of an humble thankful disposition. . . . At last he lays his head flat upon the ground, close to my foot, and sets my other foot upon his head, as he had done before; and after this, made all the signs to me of subjection, servitude, and submission imaginable, to let me know how he would serve me as long as he liv'd. (p. 150)

How should we interpret the new narrative? Apparently it takes place without a fear of death on Friday's part and does not result from a misunderstanding of Crusoe's intentions. On this occasion, Crusoe does not use the term 'slave' to gloss his semiotic performance. Rather, Friday seems to be making a kind of oath of loyalty, based no doubt on gratitude for the saving of his life, and one he intends to keep in perpetuity. Should we construe this as an enactment of chattel slavery? True, the first thing Crusoe teaches him, after giving him the name Friday, is to call him 'Master' (p. 150), but there were many forms of mastership and service in the period and we may run too quickly to the obvious one of slave-holding.[33] Friday's action

---

[33] Consistent with this passage, Crusoe subsequently never uses any word but 'servant' to refer to Friday's status.

may certify his subordination without placing him in the condition of a chattel slave lacking rights and civil status.

The contrary view, that Friday is a captive taken in a just war, runs into difficulties that critics have not acknowledged.[34] Such a conclusion depends on accepting not only that Crusoe is engaged in a just war against the cannibal Caribs, about which he himself entertains serious doubts, but more importantly that no distinction exists between Friday and the men trying to recapture him—in other words, that Friday also shares in their (hypothetical) desire to destroy Crusoe. But Friday is innocent towards him, not an enemy combatant engaged in unlawful conflict with Crusoe.[35] Throughout the story, Crusoe consistently understands his commission as that of being called 'plainly by Providence to save this poor creature's life' (p. 147).[36]

Crusoe has another motive, apart from this religious prompting, for the rescue of Friday, a sociable impulse with important implications that critics have neglected. To understand this other source of motivation we need to set his rescue of Friday in a somewhat wider narrative context. A year before their meeting, a significant event occurs on the island. One night, Crusoe hears the firing of a ship's gun, indicating that it is in distress. When he investigates in daylight he discovers that a Spanish frigate has foundered in the bay with no one left alive on board. Crusoe responds to this event with an unexpected reaction. He experiences a deep and painful longing for human company, breaking out into repeated invocations: ' "O that there had been.... one soul sav'd out of this ship, to have escap'd to me, that

---

[34] For critics who defend this view, see Wheeler, *The Complexion of Race*, 87; Hulme, *Colonial Encounters*, 206; Leonard Tennenhouse, 'The Case of the Resistant Captive', *South Atlantic Quarterly*, 95/4 (1996), 919–46, esp. 924–30; Sara Soncini, 'The Island as Social Experiment: A Reappraisal of Daniel Defoe's Political Discourse(s) in *Robinson Crusoe* and *The Farther Adventures*', in Marialuisa Bignami (ed.), *Wrestling with Defoe: Approaches from a Workshop on Defoe's Prose* (Bologna: Cisalpino, 1997), 13; Maximillian E. Novak, *Defoe and the Nature of Man* (Oxford: Oxford University Press, 1963), 52.

[35] The narrative might have made this distinction explicit had events developed differently. The 'savage' who chases Friday before being hit by the butt of Crusoe's gun survives the blow. He begins to sit up after Crusoe has shot his companion. Friday becomes afraid at this point and Crusoe responds by pointing one of his pistols at the man, as if to shoot him. Friday gestures to Crusoe for a loan of his sword, and to Crusoe's surprise he severs the man's head with one stroke. Had this individual not been killed, he would have occupied a different status from Friday, as an enemy of Crusoe and malefactor subject to enslavement.

[36] See also *Robinson Crusoe*, 160.

I might but have had one companion, one fellow-creature to have spoken to me, and to have convers'd with!" ' (p. 137).[37] The effect of contemplating his solitude so vividly leads Crusoe to consider escaping whatever the risk. Under the influence of these thoughts and aspirations, he has a prophetic dream prefiguring his encounter with Friday, which gives us an indication of the mixed motives surrounding his rescue of the native. In the dream, a captive Indian about to be cannibalized breaks free and makes his way towards Crusoe's habitation. Greeted by Crusoe with smiles and encouragement, the man 'kneel'd down to me, seeming to pray me to assist him'. Crusoe then takes him in, remarking, 'and he became my servant' (p. 145). Once this man is with him, Crusoe realizes that he can make an attempt for the mainland because he now has a pilot to direct him there. The dream galvanizes his intention to 'get a savage into my possession', preferably one of the prisoners who was 'condemned to be eaten' (p. 145).[38] He would be invaluable in securing Crusoe's escape from the island, and his loyal service would derive from gratitude in being saved from death.

Witnessing Friday's captivity and sudden escape in his direction, Crusoe recognizes that these events conform to his dream from the previous year. As Friday swims across the stream that separates the cannibals' landing point from Crusoe's habitation, chased by two men, Crusoe announces that 'It came now very warmly upon my thoughts, and indeed irresistibly, that now was the time to get me a servant, and perhaps a companion or assistant' (p. 147), a notion backed by a providential call to save his life. The double classification of servant and possible companion indicates Crusoe's mixed motivation. The first and most important consideration for him is the provision of a servant. How the role would be defined remains unclear at this point, but Crusoe already imagines a possible addition to it, that this person would provide companionship as well as assistance. Even at this crucial moment, Crusoe anticipates a sociable relationship with someone who would serve him, a figure to assist in his plans (whether for the island or

---

[37] He tells us his desire for company was so great that when he cried out 'my hands would clinch together, and my fingers press the palms of my hands, [such] that if I had had any soft thing in my hand, it would have crusht it involuntarily; and my teeth in my head wou'd strike together, and set against one another so strong, that for some time I could not part them again' (p. 137).

[38] See also *Robinson Crusoe*, 123, where he expresses a desire to save the impending victim of a cannibal attack.

his escape), who might at the same time remedy the social loss he has experienced.

As their relationship develops, Crusoe soon tells us that 'never man had a more faithful, loving, sincere servant, than Friday was to me . . . his very affections were ty'd to me, like those of a child to a father' (p. 152). The patriarchal self-conception consolidates a stratified social order composed of masters and servants tied by familial bonds. On this foundation a relationship of sociability emerges between the two and the urge for liberation from the island captivity felt by Crusoe begins to recede. The new-found satisfaction depends in no small measure on Friday's willingness to do him service, but Friday also remedies the social lack felt so acutely by Crusoe. 'I began now to have some use for my tongue again', he says, 'and I began really to love the creature' (p. 155), a love returned by Friday, we are told. Crusoe takes matters further by embarking on a process of evangelization. Heaven has made him an instrument not only to save Friday's life but also 'for ought I knew, the soul of a poor savage' (p. 160), and to bring him knowledge of Jesus Christ and the true religion. Indeed Friday excels him as a Christian, and Crusoe affirms, 'I have known few equal to him in my life' (p. 161). Later Crusoe confirms this account by describing him as a 'religious Christian' and 'grateful friend' (p. 163).[39] The conversation they share makes the period in which they live together 'perfectly and compleatly happy, if any such thing as compleat happiness can be form'd in a sublunary state' (p. 160).[40] Wherever he began, Friday has been transformed into a friend and trustworthy companion, fulfilling the mixed motivation of Crusoe. There are echoes in this portrait of the Puritan companionate marriage here—Friday is at once

---

[39] This comment comes after Crusoe allows himself to question Friday's affections at one point. They see Friday's homeland from the top of a hill on a clear day, and Friday responds joyfully at the sight. Crusoe experiences a spiral of doubt as a result, fearing that Friday will 'not only forget all his religion, but all his obligation to me'. If he made his way home he might return with one or two hundred of his countrymen and 'make a feast upon me'. But after some weeks he realizes that he 'wrong'd the poor creature very much', whose Christianity and friendship he acknowledges fully, together with his honesty and innocence: 'in spight of all my uneasiness [unperceived by Friday], he made me at last entirely his own again' (p. 163).

[40] Crusoe specifically uses the word 'conversation' to describe their interaction during the remaining three-year period on the island (p. 160). Compare Brantlinger, who suggests that Crusoe 'speaks to him mostly in commands, the imperative mode of imperialism' (*Crusoe's Footprints*, 2).

helpmeet, friend, and co-religionist in a relationship structured by paternal authority.[41]

Although this account helps to characterize their relationship more fully, we have not yet established Friday's 'legal' position. One of their early exchanges provides insight into the question. Crusoe raises the possibility of building a boat to travel over to Friday's homeland. Friday misunderstands this as Crusoe expressing a wish to send him there on his own, and he protests that he will go only if Crusoe joins him. Eventually he picks up a hatchet and presents it to Crusoe, saying that he would rather have Crusoe kill him than send him away. Crusoe concludes of this episode: 'I so plainly discover'd the utmost affection in him to me, and a firm resolution in him, that I told him then, *and often after*, that I would never send him away from me, if he was willing to stay with me' (p. 165; my emphasis). Their ongoing relationship depends on Friday's willingness to stay with Crusoe, and equally on Crusoe's often repeated resolution not to send him away. Each of them acts voluntarily. The story he tells simply does not make sense if Friday is enslaved.

But the clearest indication comes in a plot development involving Friday's father. The cannibals return to the island one day and make ready for a feast. Crusoe approaches warily, unsure of his authority to attack. At this point he sees a Christian captive about to be dispatched—one of the Spanish crew members who escaped to the mainland from the sinking ship four years before. Crusoe's duty becomes obvious. Together with Friday he launches an assault, and with the assistance of the liberated Spaniard they succeed in killing all but four of the enemy, the rest escaping in one of their canoes. This event reunites Friday with his father, who was also held captive and had the ill luck to be next on the cannibals' menu. The rescued Spaniard indicates his understanding of the debt he owes to Crusoe. Likewise, Crusoe receives from the 'old savage' 'all the tokens of gratitude and thankfulness that could appear in any countenance' (p. 174). The important point to note is that Friday's father is not enslaved, even though he is redeemed under the same

[41] Hulme interprets these exchanges as erotically charged, 'though this is not easy to separate from a master's joy in his well-proportioned and healthy slave' (*Colonial Encounters*, 212). See also Hans Turley, 'The Sublimation of Desire to Apocalyptic Passion in Defoe's Crusoe Trilogy', in Philip Holden and Richard J. Ruppel (eds), *Imperial Desire: Dissident Sexualities and Colonial Literature* (Minneapolis: University of Minnesota Press, 2003), 3–20.

circumstances as Friday. This fact offers crucial testimony about the legal position of Friday himself.

Shortly after this episode, Crusoe clarifies the status that he accords to these men. In a 'merry reflection', Crusoe reflects on how 'like a king I look'd' (p. 175). The aptness of the simile, for Crusoe, stems not only from the fact that he owns the island as private property, possessing a right of dominion over it, but that his 'people' were 'perfectly subjected' (each owes their lives to him and is ready to lay it down for him). In fashioning himself as a monarch, Crusoe establishes the role they occupy. He refers explicitly to Friday, the Spaniard, and Old Friday as his 'three subjects' (p. 175) and shortly thereafter to the Spaniard and Old Friday as 'my two new subjects', indicating that Friday already exists in this condition.[42] This statement finally tells us Friday's position. He is not a slave but a subject, under the authority of a master whose political power is absolute.[43] As a subject, he may owe his service but he is not held as property; his condition is voluntary since he is free to leave. While remaining dependent on Crusoe, he includes himself in the just commonwealth established by the man who saved him. As a subject he enjoys civil status incompatible with slavery. This is undoubtedly a patriarchal system of rule, with Crusoe substituting himself for Friday's actual father; the group as a whole becomes his 'family',[44] incorporated into an aristocratic household and receiving the benefits of his patronage.[45]

[42] The objection might be made that Crusoe only mockingly occupies the position of monarch. Long before he acquires these new subjects, including Friday, he has introduced this thought himself (p. 109). Nonetheless, there is a pattern in the book of moving from mock versions to the real thing: he begins as a mock penitent before becoming a real one, and changes from a mock possessor of estates on the island to the actual lord of this domain; even money or coin is mocked before being stored away and later redeemed as valuable.

[43] Crusoe states, 'my people were perfectly subjected: I was absolute lord and lawgiver' (p. 175).

[44] Crusoe discusses the additional husbandry required 'for my family, now it was encreas'd to four in number' (p. 179). For discussion of patriarchy and the family in *Robinson Crusoe*, see Richard Braverman, 'Crusoe's Legacy', *Studies in the Novel*, 18/1 (1986), 1–26.

[45] Friday's status as servant is reinforced when they return to Europe and plan an overland trip from Lisbon to Calais. Crusoe explains that he 'got an English sailor to travel with me as a servant, besides my man Friday, who was too much a stranger to be capable of supplying the place of a servant on the road' (p. 210). If Friday were a slave it would call for some comment on this occasion or during their extended time in England. See also the preface (ostensibly by Crusoe) to *Serious Reflections during the Life and Surprising Adventures of Robinson Crusoe* (London, 1720), A4r, which calls Friday his servant.

The question may be raised whether Friday perhaps exists in the anomalous condition of a voluntary slave.[46] The preceding discussion strongly suggests otherwise, but it would be difficult to rule out such a claim entirely. Settling the matter might take us in the contrapuntal direction of contemporary political theory. In early modern jurisprudence, opinion on the legality of self-enslavement was divided, with figures like the Spanish Dominican Francisco de Vitoria arguing against it on the basis of Thomist convictions, while some Jesuit authorities set out conditions in which it was allowable. Most famously, Locke rejected the possibility of self-enslavement on any terms in the second of the *Two Treatises of Government*.[47]

Yet compelling grounds for denying the claim that Friday is a voluntary slave can be found if we look at the continuation of the story in *The Farther Adventures of Robinson Crusoe* (1719). After a ten-year absence from the island, Crusoe returns to restock it with settlers and supplies. Much has happened in his absence. The existing inhabitants—consisting of a group of Spanish, Portuguese, and English mariners, with Old Friday, established there by Crusoe—have had fierce encounters with Carib invaders. After the most extensive of these battles with the colonists, a group of one hundred 'savages' remains behind on the island. They are not taken captive but reduced (through brutal measures) to dependence on the settlers, who grant them

[46] In the *Review*, 8/67 (23 Aug. 1711), 263, Defoe tells the story of a Barbadian planter who, 'being fill'd with Compassion for the Miseries of his poor *Negro* Slaves, and having a strong Regret upon his Mind at Oppressing Human Nature and his Fellow Creatures', decided to free them, only to find that they had 'no Tast' for liberty and returned to work for him. The parallel might be made with Friday by critics who wish to assert that he is a voluntary slave, but the anecdote in the *Review* is related by Defoe in the context of criticism of those who 'choose to be Slaves, when they may go free', which hardly coincides with the positive tone of his representation of Friday, whose voluntary service, as I suggest below, complements Crusoe's renewed relationship to divine authority.

[47] For some discussion, see Richard Tuck, *Natural Rights Theories: Their Origin and Development* (Cambridge: Cambridge University Press, 1979), 49, 54, 147. On the debate in sixteenth-century Jesuit circles, see José Eisenberg, 'Cultural Encounters, Theoretical Adventures: The Jesuit Missions to the New World and the Justification of Voluntary Slavery', *History of Political Thought*, 24/3 (2003), 375–96; on Locke, see Wayne Glausser, 'Three Approaches to Locke and the Slave Trade', *Journal of the History of Ideas*, 51 (1990), 199–216; James Farr, ' "So Vile and Miserable an Estate": The Problem of Slavery in Locke's Political Thought', *Political Theory*, 14/2 (1986), 263–89; Farr, 'Locke, Natural Law, and New World Slavery', *Political Theory*, 36/4 (2008), 495–522.

territory in a remote part of the island. When Crusoe arrives, he appears in the company of a French priest whom he rescued from a burning ship on the outward journey, a man whose piety and Christian zeal he admires. This individual admonishes Crusoe for neglecting the salvation of the native peoples, arguing that the failure to convert them puts Crusoe at risk of incurring divine displeasure. Crusoe accepts the rebuke, but he is taken aback when the priest adds a surprising request: he not only offers to take on the role of missionary but also asks that Crusoe leave Friday with him to serve as an interpreter and assistant.

Crusoe has several reasons for hesitating which merit attention and add significantly to our understanding of how he perceives his relationship with Friday. He cannot think of parting with Friday, he informs us, because he has been his companion during his travels, 'not only faithful to me, but sincerely affectionate to the last degree' (p. 309). What is more, Crusoe indicates that he 'resolv'd to do something considerable for him, if he out-liv'd me, as it was probable he would' (p. 309). If Friday were a slave, this would be the occasion to announce his intention to free him. But it is clear that he is a servant, not a slave, since the implication is that Crusoe intends to make a financial settlement on him out of his riches. His status as a servant bound by oath rather than an item of property, to be disposed as Crusoe sees fit, is confirmed as Crusoe continues:

I was persuaded that Friday would by no means consent to part with me, and I could not force him to it without his consent, without manifest injustice, because I had promised I would never put him away, and he had promis'd and engag'd to me that he would never leave me, unless I put him away. (p. 309)

Unlike a slave, Friday is asked for his consent, which is crucial, and Crusoe is governed by a promise to respect his wishes in the matter. (In the end, he finds an agreeable compromise, and Friday's father is allocated the role of interpreter to the French priest turned missionary.)

III Rereading *Robinson Crusoe*

One of the aims of contrapuntal reading on Said's account is to 'open up' novels like *Mansfield Park* through attention to spaces and places such as

Antigua,[48] but it may just as readily foreclose textual possibilities by privileging too narrow a criterion of analysis. In the case of *Robinson Crusoe*, how
should we interpret the relationship between the protagonist and Friday if
we do not designate it as one of slavery? Can we open the book out
(contrapuntally or otherwise) to another set of readings? I suggest that we
begin with Crusoe's recovery of an authentic relationship to the divine,
which reconfigures his own relationship to authority. Crusoe possesses a
perverse freedom to reject divine government, and he does so throughout
his life before recognizing the providential meaning of his shipwreck on the
island. He quickly becomes a strict enforcer of legitimate rule, with the
convenient addition that sovereignty is vested in himself. As his island is
populated, relations of service and duty become crucial. The number of
oaths, promises, and vows that appear throughout the book is quite startling;
they indicate that the stability of social and political relations depends on
trust and honesty more than on physical force, for all of Crusoe's weap-
onry.[49] At some level they must be freely given to have any value, and they
cannot be enforced realistically by threats of violence.

For example, Crusoe's redemption of the Spanish captive and Old Friday
galvanizes his intention to mount an escape from the island. Having learned
of the sixteen Spaniards and Portuguese who remain stranded on the
mainland in difficult conditions, Crusoe contemplates the prospect of making a rescue attempt and including them in his escape plans. But he
entertains doubts about their loyalty. His Spanish subject reassures him of
their gratitude, stating that he will secure a 'solemn oath' that they would be
entirely under Crusoe's direction 'as their commander and captain, and that
they should swear upon the holy sacraments and the Gospel, to be true to
me [Crusoe]... and to be directed wholly and absolutely by my orders'
(p. 178). The Spaniard makes an oath of loyalty of his own to Crusoe,
swearing never to stir from him as long as he lives and to pledge his blood
if his fellows breach their faith. Crusoe follows through with his intentions
when the Spaniard and Old Friday arrange to travel back to collect the
others. He directs that each man should swear before the Spaniard and Old

[48] Said, *Culture and Imperialism*, 93.
[49] In this respect I disagree with Tennenhouse, who only recognizes force as a means of
political stability. See also Christopher F. Loar, 'How to Say Things with Guns: Military
Technology and the Politics of *Robinson Crusoe*', *Eighteenth-Century Fiction*, 19/1–2 (2006), 1–20.

Friday his readiness to 'be entirely under and subjected' to Crusoe's command (p. 180).

The change of Crusoe's own social status over the course of the novel creates some tension in the story's moral demography. After all, the recommendation of his father was for Crusoe to adhere to the 'middle state' or the 'upper station of low life' (pp. 5–6). Yet we are confronted by his conspicuous advancement to the role of prince and governor.[50] What rescues this scenario from contradiction is the emergence of Crusoe into the role of father himself, with the authority to prescribe the conditions of others. This position is consolidated in his relationship with Friday, which involves an obvious substitution of himself for Friday's own father in the young man's affections. The struggle with the cannibals is in that sense a struggle over who is going to be incorporated into whom. He fears that they will absorb him, literally, into themselves, while he is bent on creating a state which will encompass those Indians worthy of redemption.[51]

The closing sequence of the island narrative consolidates this pattern. Crusoe awakens one day to find that an English ship has arrived near his island and sent a boat ashore. But it transpires that the ship has mutinied and the roguish mariners intend merely to abandon the captain on the island, along with his mate and a passenger. The condition of the three despairing captives reminds Crusoe of his own arrival twenty-eight years earlier. They too fail to realize how close at hand deliverance lies, and the reality of God's providential care for them (p. 183). Crusoe now has the opportunity, in this respect, to play the part of God by redeeming them.[52] His action provides a spiritual lesson, but above all one in which rightful, paternal authority is restored. Through a series of carefully worked manoeuvres, Crusoe—joined by his 'lieutenant-general' Friday (p. 194) and the captives—manages to reinstate the captain to his command. In the process, the captain receives promises of trust from some of those retaken on the island, who swear their

[50] Other terms for himself include 'emperor', 'generalissimo' (during the reprisal against the English mariners), and 'lord of a manor'.

[51] For a related reading, see Minaz Jooma, 'Robinson Crusoe Inc(corporates): Domestic Economy, Incest and the Trope of Cannibalism', *Literature, Interpretation, Theory*, 8/1 (1997), 61–81.

[52] On receiving Crusoe's unexpected aid, one of them says, 'He must be sent directly from heaven', while the captain exclaims, 'Am I talking to god or man! Is it a real man, or an angel!' (p. 185). Crusoe insists on his mere humanity, but by intervening to save them he literalizes the aid performed by divine providence in his own case.

loyalty and state 'that they would own him for a father to them as long as they liv'd' (p. 196), while Crusoe, having earned the captain's undying gratitude, becomes his commander in effect. Paternal authority is thus preserved, with the captain above his men, Crusoe above the captain, and God above them all. The lessons of obedience have at last been brought home.

Reading the novel in this way recharacterizes the relationship between Crusoe and Friday in several ways. No longer do they appear in the guise of master and slave but in a series of structurally related ways as father and son, master and servant, teacher and pupil, monarch and subject. The additions to the island in the form of Old Friday, the Spaniard, and the redeemed captain complement the pattern rather than disrupting it. Friendship, trust, loyalty, and service naturalize and humanize these structures of authority and bonds of duty. The question that needs answering is whether such a reading qualifies as contrapuntal. Provided that it meets Said's condition of seeking a connection with contemporary history outside the text, the answer appears to be yes. It would not be difficult to satisfy this requirement by considering the nature of royal power in the period, the role of 'favourites' in court culture, gently mocked in Crusoe's self-image,[53] or the existence of patriarchal hierarchy within domestic economies, and the impact of dissenting religious culture on education and spirituality. These are as much instances of ideological representation as any colonial forms present in the novel and in the era.[54]

Yet Said ties the purpose of his hermeneutic technique more exclusively to gaining insight into the nature of empire and its cultural articulations.[55] The privileging of this criterion exerts a kind of pressure on reading practices that becomes evident in postcolonial accounts of the relationship between Crusoe and Friday. For critics it is not enough to demonstrate the text's

[53] See *Robinson Crusoe*, 109, where he remarks self-mockingly that 'like a king I din'd too, all alone, attended by my servants [the animals he accumulates]. Poll, as if he had been my favourite, was the only person permitted to talk to me' (p. 109).

[54] Said, *Culture and Imperialism*, 66.

[55] George M. Wilson argues that it is relatively easy to take a contrapuntal reading such as Said's account of *Mansfield Park* and to devise plausible alternatives with 'equal force and epistemic value' which contradict it. The choice between readings becomes 'arbitrary and tendentious', suggesting that they derive not so much from 'responsible attention to the text' as they do from 'an adamantly insisted upon outside agenda'. George M. Wilson, 'Edward Said on Contrapuntal Reading', *Philosophy and Literature*, 18/2 (1994), 272–3.

ample engagement with colonialism and slavery elsewhere; the relationship between Crusoe and Friday must also be implicated and specifically defined as that of master and slave. If the text itself does not provide the desired evidence, Said has already covered the contingency, to some extent, by arguing that contrapuntal reading attends not only to what texts say but also to their silences.[56] Thus a missing or suppressed dimension to a given instance of canonical literature would not necessarily present an obstacle in interpreting the work as bound up with it. My point is not that such an approach is intrinsically wrong or misguided. On the contrary, enquiries of this kind may be very revealing.[57] However, there is a risk when attending to the importance of a historical truth like chattel slavery of writing it into the text and turning criticism into an occasion for palimpsest.

One of the subtlest treatments of these issues from a postcolonial perspective appears in Peter Hulme's long chapter on 'Robinson Crusoe and Friday' in *Colonial Encounters: Europe and the Native Caribbean, 1492–1797*. Through a series of insightful observations on Crusoe's construction of the self and his parabolic narrative, Hulme illuminates the ideological project of colonialism which is conditioned textually by engagements with the native Carib population and the rites of cannibalism. The centrepiece becomes the 'acquisition' of Friday. Hulme admits that 'Friday of course is never *called* a slave', but, he goes on, 'that absence is merely a symptom of the constant process of denial and renegotiation by which the text attempts to redraw the colonial encounter.'[58] Thus, Hulme maintains that 'it is not difficult to see in Crusoe's relationship with Friday a veiled and disavowed reference to the more pressing issue of black slavery'.[59] Disavowal is of course more than mere silence. It suggests an active or conscious effort of concealment or denial. The textual lacuna is remedied by making the very absence a form of proof of

[56] See Said, *Culture and Imperialism*, 66.

[57] To take an example from *Robinson Crusoe* outside the current context, it is at least interesting in the chronology of the novel that the protagonist comes of age during the Civil War period (he departs from his family home in 1651 at the age of 18), and yet no mention is made of his family's political leanings or experience.

[58] Hulme, *Colonial Encounters*, 205.

[59] Ibid. 205. Lydia H. Liu, 'Robinson Crusoe's Earthenware Pot', *Critical Inquiry*, 25/4 (1999), 728–57, pursues related hermeneutic possibilities. She argues that the humble earthenware pot fashioned by Crusoe 'evokes porcelain by metonymic association and calls up the existence of the latter by virtue of its absence', an instance of what she calls the 'poetics of colonial disavowal' (pp. 732–3; see also p. 741): see also Loar, 'How to Say Things with Guns'.

an effort to refigure colonial relationships. But it may be equally symptom-
atic of our own urge to refigure the text to coincide with a historical
narrative that takes priority over it.

To reinforce his point, Hulme argues that 'Friday is certainly a slave
inasmuch as he has no will of his own'. But he contradicts this assertion
by observing that 'within the fiction the term "slave" can be avoided because
Friday's servitude is voluntary, not forced'.[60] Yet an act of volition requires an
exercise of the will by definition. Hulme nonetheless maintains that Friday is
a 'subject with no will', even as the problem is deepened by allowing that
voluntary enslavement is 'not slavery at all'.[61] The text has been forced, in
some sense, to speak against itself because of its recalcitrance over an issue we
know must reside there. But 'slavery' may be true historically without a
fiction cooperatively instantiating it in precisely the terms that we require.
Crusoe, as we have seen, has no qualms about chattel slavery and happily
appropriates human beings as property, but something different is arguably
going on in his relationship with Friday. This is so even as slaves are all this
while contributing, unbeknownst to him, to his accumulating wealth in
Brazil.[62] In other words, the text provides more than enough evidence for a
contrapuntal reading of slavery based on the importance of Brazil to the
plot,[63] but its stubbornness in relation to Friday requires a critical intervention or adjustment in which we speak for its silences and disavowals.

The search for some kind of confirmation becomes more complicated
with Hulme's claim that Defoe has 'gone one better' than Locke,[64] who
justified slavery as a means of commuting a death sentence against a prisoner
whose life was forfeited because of performing an act worthy of death, a
standard legal position in the period. For Hulme, Friday's offer of perpetual
service absolves Crusoe of the need to enforce his right to enslave him with

---

[60] Hulme, *Colonial Encounters*, 205.

[61] Ibid. 206, 205.

[62] After his liberation from the island, Crusoe discovers that his plantation has indeed
prospered in his absence, having been transformed successfully into a sugar plantation or *engenho*,
run on the basis of imported slaves (p. 204) and yielding a return of £1,000 per annum. Crusoe's
'partner' writes a letter in which he first congratulates him on being alive and then reports on
the acreage of the plantation and the number of slaves who work it (p. 206).

[63] In this respect, the role of the plantation in Brazil parallels Antigua in Said's reading of
Mansfield Park.

[64] Hulme, *Colonial Encounters*, 205.

threats of violence, a 'brilliant negotiation' of the difficulty in hand.[65] Yet all of this presupposes that Friday is indeed a captive of Crusoe's, a point the text does not support, so the difficulty here may be of our own making. Hulme suggests that Friday's life has been surrendered as a result of Crusoe's effort to save him, and that this coincides with the Lockean justification for slavery. But if that were really Locke's position then anyone who saved someone from death—by drowning, fire, or other calamity—would thereby assume ownership of the individual. Locke's position is more narrow. The life is forfeit if someone has done something worthy of death in the midst of a just war. But Friday is not making war on Crusoe.[66] He is an innocent victim saved by Crusoe and he rewards his saviour with a voluntary promise of service. The crime of cannibalism, of which Friday is indeed guilty, is 'national' according to Crusoe, who decides, after lengthy consideration, that he cannot use it as just grounds to wage war (and therefore to take captives as slaves or to execute them as he sees fit).[67] The text naturalizes a host of actions and relations we may see as dubious, but at this point slavery is not one of them. It seems that our need for it to write our history has led us to override the text itself.

Hulme is not alone in reading the text this way.[68] Andrew Fleck places Friday at the centre of his postcolonial account of the novel, which concen-

[65] Ibid. 206.

[66] Crusoe's punctiliousness about these distinctions is evident in his deliberations over whether he has a right to attack the cannibals; he concludes that he does not, saying that they are 'innocent' towards him. Friday could justify it, however, 'because he was a declar'd enemy, and in a state of war with those very particular people; and it was lawful for him to attack them; but I could not say the same with respect to me' (p. 169).

[67] *Robinson Crusoe*, 126. To make war on them and kill the cannibals would 'justify the conduct of the Spaniards in all their barbarities practis'd in America, where they destroy'd millions of these people, who, however they were idolaters and barbarians, and had several bloody and barbarous rites in their customs, such as sacrificing human bodies to their idols, were yet, as to the Spaniards, very innocent people' (p. 125). This passage makes problematic Wheeler's conclusion that 'Eventually, of course, cannibalism justifies Crusoe's colonization project, which is instituted when he murders scores of island Caribees' (*The Complexion of Race*, 68). On Crusoe's implicit invocation of Las Casas and the 'Black Legend' of Spanish cruelty, see Diana de Armas Wilson, *Cervantes, the Novel, and the New World* (Oxford: Oxford University Press, 2000), 69–70, and on his attempts to distinguish his colonialism from the Spaniards', ibid. 75.

[68] His reading is endorsed by Boulukos, *Grateful Slave*, 1–2; in addition to the references discussed in nn. 6–10 above, see Loar, 'How to Say Things with Guns'; Gary Gautier, 'Slavery and the Fashioning of Race in *Oroonoko*, *Robinson Crusoe*, and Equiano's *Life*', *The Eighteenth Century: Theory and Interpretation*, 42/2 (2001), 161–79; Mary Louise Pratt, *Imperial Eyes: Travel Writing and*

trates on the representation of religion and religious conversion. He argues that Friday is subjugated by Crusoe and remains a slave who 'can approach but never attain the European standard of Christianity'.[69] Drawing on Abdul JanMohamed and Gayatri Spivak, he suggests that Friday is both part of a group constituting the Other from whom Crusoe is estranged and, as an individual, a source of identification; his renaming makes him another subaltern who cannot speak and he is doomed ultimately to serve Crusoe's own sense of self. These observations offer us some insight into the nature of Crusoe's mastery, but one may question the description of Friday's religion at the core of the argument. Fleck maintains that Crusoe turns Friday into 'a kind of palimpsest' on which he inscribes his own religion. The palimpsest at issue, I would suggest, may be of a different sort. There is no doubt that Crusoe engages in the evangelization of Friday, which constitutes the fulfilment of his own spiritual regeneration, a sign—within the text's shaping of itself as spiritual autobiography—that Crusoe has indeed transformed his religious outlook and now finds the wherewithal to instruct his charge in the faith. What is more, he acknowledges that in doing so he deepens his own faith and understanding of Scripture (pp. 160, 161). This process involves him in an enquiry into what he regards as the false beliefs that Friday and his tribe have held, including the embrace of their god Benamuckee and their clergy, who engage in what Crusoe diagnoses as priestcraft to enhance their power (a phenomenon, he notes, not merely apparent among the savage pagans as well as Roman Catholics but evident 'perhaps among all religions in the world' (p. 158)). Fleck is right to point out that Crusoe remains something of an arbiter as well as purveyor of divine revelation and that, as an instructor, he effectively substitutes himself for the natives' *oowocakee* or priestly caste.

But the argument becomes strained at this point in interesting ways as a critical imperative overtakes the analysis. Friday, we are told by Fleck, 'could never measure up to Crusoe's standards for conversion': 'There is no way for

Transculturation (London: Routledge, 1992), 97. McInelly argues that 'Friday is always Other, and Crusoe maintains the master–slave paradigm that underlies their relationship' ('Expanding Empires', 16–17). Wheeler sees Friday as initially 'enslaveable', and 'alternately' or 'interchangeably' a slave, servant, companion, and Christian (*The Complexion of Race*, 68, 78, 85).

[69] Andrew Fleck, 'Crusoe's Shadow: Christianity, Colonization and the Other', in John C. Hawley (ed.), *Historicizing Christian Encounters with the Other* (Basingstoke: Macmillan, 1998), 74.

Friday to pass the test; the system requires that he fail'.[70] One might reply that what requires him to fail is the system of interpretation, not Crusoe or Defoe. In fact Crusoe tells us that he finds Friday an apt and willing pupil, as he begins the process of laying 'a foundation of religious knowledge in his mind' (p. 157). He has already confirmed, beforehand, that when God offers occasion for such people to exercise reason and show their moral character, they have the same powers as others and 'are as ready, nay, more ready to apply them to the right uses for which they were bestowed, than we are' (p. 152). So it proves with Friday, who raises difficult points of theology from the start, especially regarding God's relative tolerance of the devil. As time goes on, Crusoe concludes, as we have seen, that 'the savage was now a good Christian, a much better than I',[71] and that he has become 'such a Christian, as I have known few equal to him in my life' (pp. 160–1).[72]

Before we conclude too rapidly that Crusoe engages in a wilful imposition of his belief system on Friday, we should remember that when he constitutes his commonwealth on the island Crusoe introduces a wide toleration, including the religion of Old Friday, whom he describes as a pagan—along with the Catholic Spaniard and the two Protestants (himself and Friday).[73] Thus Fleck's notion that Friday is pushed into 'a position of alterity from which he cannot escape' seems debatable.[74] If anything, the issue is not otherness but the assimilation of Friday. His line of argument leads to the conclusion that 'Friday's Christianity is really only an advanced version of the imitative speech of Crusoe's parrot, Poll, and he remains nothing more than an uncomprehending "savage"'.[75] We may recognize the parallel with Crusoe's parrot, who provides Crusoe with company, without accepting that the analogy is complete. To do so would consign Friday to the status of a

---

[70] Ibid. 83.

[71] Maximillian E. Novak observes: 'When Crusoe states that Friday was a "better Christian" than he, we should not take it lightly. Defoe could hardly imagine a higher compliment.' *Daniel Defoe: Master of Fictions: His Life and Ideas* (Oxford: Oxford University Press, 2001), 546.

[72] For further discussion, see Timothy C. Blackburn, 'Friday's Religion: Its Nature and Importance in *Robinson Crusoe*', *Eighteenth-Century Studies*, 18/3 (1985), 360–82.

[73] 'My man Friday was a Protestant, his father was a pagan and a cannibal, and the Spaniard was a Papist: however, I allow'd liberty of conscience throughout my dominions' (p. 175).

[74] Fleck, 'Crusoe's Shadow', 83.

[75] Ibid. 84. See also Brantlinger, for whom Friday is 'more parrot than man' (*Crusoe's Footprints*, 2).

domestic animal, which may be our own act of suppression, not the text's. The logic of Fleck's argument requires that the narrative deprive Friday of authentic speech, religion, and agency (as a slave); these points cooperate and reinforce one another to expose the practice of colonialism. To argue that the narrative does not support these readings, and indeed provides us with something very different, does not mean that colonialism is any more defensible, but simply that we have allowed a historical problem (colonialism) to override our ability to read the text and examine the forms which eighteenth-century fiction took in accommodating a colonial project to Christian and commercial priorities. In short, counterpoint has given way to palimpsest.

By adopting this approach we risk missing out entirely on something important about the story. Crusoe tells us in his description of Friday that he was a 'comely handsome fellow, perfectly well made', whom he reckoned to be 'about twenty six years of age' (p. 149). It is no coincidence that Crusoe himself was about 26 years of age when he arrived on the island. Just as the shipwreck and isolation on the island provide the occasion for Crusoe's spiritual transformation, so Friday's encounter with Crusoe and separation from his society become the moment for his own religious journey. Crusoe's conversion requires the recognition of divine mastery and the giving of thanks and service to God. Similarly, Friday acquires a new father and a new master in the person of Crusoe, who engages in his religious instruction. This relationship would not make sense if he were Crusoe's slave. Rather, Friday's elective and dedicated service parallels Crusoe's own change of outlook, however convenient it may be for Crusoe that he should find a helpmeet in the process. After all, Crusoe has confirmed his 'original sin' as that of disobedience in rejecting his father's advice (p. 142). Crusoe's difficulties in explaining points of theology lead him to conclude that divine knowledge depends, ultimately, on revelation. Just as Crusoe providentially recovered the text of Scripture from the wreck of his own ship, to aid in his conversion, so Friday receives the providential benefit of Scripture on the island: 'we had here the word of God to read, and no farther off from His spirit to instruct, than if we had been in England' (pp. 160–1). 'We had the sure guide to heaven, viz. the word of God; and we had, blessed be God, comfortable views of the spirit of God teaching and instructing us by His word, leading us into all truth, and making us both willing and obedient to the instruction of His word...' (p. 161).

Yet for Fleck, Friday must continue, it seems, a savage, a figure of difference assigned only a capacity for colonial mimicry which places him on the same level as the speaking bird who confirms Crusoe's identity. If it would be wrong simply to accept Crusoe's account of Friday on its own terms and to see Friday as liberated under Crusoe's care without critical comment, one may question at the same time the liberating effect of casting him, against the tenor of the text, as a passive and subhuman figure.

IV Conclusion

In the preface to the final volume in Defoe's Crusoe trilogy—*Serious Reflections on the Life and Surprising Adventures of Robinson Crusoe* (1720)—Defoe has his hero continue to insist on the authenticity of the tale. The story of being driven on shore by a huge wave, the footprint in the sand, Friday, and the rest 'are all real Facts in my History,' he proclaims. No distortion exists between the representation of Crusoe the subject of the narrative and Crusoe the historical figure; each episode 'chimes Part for Part, and Step for Step with the inimitable life of *Robinson Crusoe*'. Crusoe seems to feel as if the book's effect would be lost if it were unanchored to historical fact, a mere fiction (or 'Romance', to use his term).[76] Postcolonial critics have taken a similarly contrapuntal approach by making the history of chattel slavery outside the text a legitimating force in their interpretation of the relationship between Crusoe and Friday. Where gaps occur between text and history, the difficulty has been remedied by reshaping the narrative to conform to the known facts of history.

If palimpsest emerges at this point, a precedent can be found for it from the very beginning of the novel's reception, such as the accompanying illustrations in eighteenth- and nineteenth-century editions that transformed Friday into an African or the not infrequent slips by critics who refer to him as a black.[77] The most dramatic and self-conscious interventions have of course occurred in the context of fiction, poetry, and drama, in the many

---

[76] *Serious Reflections*, A3v, A5r, A2v. See also the preface by the 'editor' to the *Farther Adventures*.

[77] On the illustration of the novel, see Wheeler, *The Complexion of Race*, ch. 1; David Blewett, *The Illustration of Robinson Crusoe, 1719–1920* (Gerrard's Cross: Colin Smythe, 1995); Richard Phillips, *Mapping Men and Empire: A Geography of Adventure* (London: Routledge, 1997), ch. 2; on its narrative

rewritings of the tale from its appearance to the time of Coetzee, Tournier, Walcott, and beyond. And there is a sense in which history itself is simply a repeated process of palimpsest, so it may no longer be possible to distinguish the story of *Robinson Crusoe* from its paratexts and retellings. Said authorizes such a critical practice within the parameters of contrapuntal analysis. He encourages us to 'read what is there or not there' and to recognize 'the hybridizing intrusions of human history'. Time overcomes space as the ultimate frame of reference by seeing cultural works not just as the 'vision of a moment', but also by juxtaposing that vision 'with the various revisions it later provoked'.[78]

On this account, insofar as literature remains separable from history, its task is to represent it, to provide exemplary narratives that allegorize history. Contrapuntal reading arguably places an implicit limit, however, on what historical events may be allegorized, and in the process it restrains the signifying potential of literature and the surplus of meaning which consti- tutes its resourcefulness and political potential. The irony is that Defoe had already endorsed this practice. In the preface to the *Farther Adventures*, the 'editor' takes note of the reaction to the first volume and defends the book by insisting that the 'just application of every incident . . . must legitimate all the part that may be call'd invention or parable in the story' (p. 1). In the *Serious Reflections*, Crusoe consolidates this justification, describing the story of his life and adventures as an 'allusive allogorick History' in which 'the Fable is always made for the Moral, not the Moral for the Fable'.[79]

---

afterlife, see Lieve Spaas and Brian Stimpson (eds), *Robinson Crusoe: Myths and Metamorphoses* (Basingstoke: Macmillan, 1996); *Robinson, la robinsonnade et le monde des choses*, special issue of *Études françaises*, 35/1 (1999). For references to Friday as a black, see e.g. Martin Green, *The Robinson Crusoe Story* (University Park: Pennsylvania State University Press, 1990), 23; J. R. Hammond, *A Defoe Companion* (Lanham, Md.: Barnes & Noble, 1993), 49; Colley, *Captives*, 1; Keane, 'Slavery and the Slave Trade', 120.

[78] Said, *Culture and Imperialism*, 96, 67.

[79] *Serious Reflections*, 115, A2r. See Robert W. Ayers, '*Robinson Crusoe*: "Allusive Allegorick History"', *Publications of the Modern Language Association*, 82/5 (1967), 399–407.

4

Between 'Oriental' and 'Blacks So Called', 1688–1788

Felicity A. Nussbaum

Postcolonial theory in its application to eighteenth-century British literature usually separates 'Orientals' and 'blacks' into two distinct subjects of enquiry. The subject of abolition is, in large part, the Negro from sub-Saharan Africa, while the subject of Orientalism is the inhabitant of India, the Levant, the Barbary Coast, and the East Indies. The geographical regions usually serve different imaginative purposes for Europe: sub-Saharan Africa has often been represented as a wild zone that functions as a source for slaves rather as a threat to the polity of England and France, while the Islamic world, perceived as more potent even in decline, offers a menacing eschatology and a competing world-view. Yet the abolition movement and Orientalism are frequently linked as two roughly contemporaneous indicators of modernity. One historical impulse supplies legislation, the British Abolition Act and the Emancipation Act, to relinquish power in the name of human rights, while the other seeks sovereignty in the name of empire.

A troubled and contested term, 'Orientalism', as conceptualized by Edward Said, is an internally consistent discourse describing the metropole's construction of a marvellous East that was formulated for imperialist ends.[1]

[1] Edward W. Said, *Orientalism* (New York: Vintage, 1978). Though Said's book remains seminal, Ziauddin Sardar, *Orientalism* (Buckingham and Philadelphia: Open University Press, 1999) and others have elaborated upon Said's substantial intellectual debts to earlier thinkers regarding Islam and the West.

Said's version of Orientalism takes Napoleon's Egyptian expedition of 1798–1801 (on a ship appropriately named *L'Orient*) as its inaugural occasion.[2] During the same historical period, abolition was gathering force in 1772 after the Somerset case attracted support; abolition constituted a religious, philosophical, and economic movement that aimed first to halt the African Atlantic slave trade and eventually to emancipate African slaves in Europe and the New World. While Orientalism purports to be a discursive manifestation of Europe's attempt to interpret the East and to gain command over it, the rise of abolitionist sentiment has been variously attributed to the efforts of Evangelicalism, the alleged decline in African slavery's profits, excess sugar production, and the growing distaste for extracting forced labour from a captive population.[3] In this essay I argue that the conceptual borders that we have erected between the Oriental and black, between the 'East' and Africa, are often misleading dichotomies that significantly inhibit our interpretation of written and visual texts, and sometimes distort our understanding of the history of racial thinking.

Orientalism, then, has been conceptualized as a language of domination that undergirds colonization, while abolition promises a discourse of liberation leading to freedom, yet recent world events have reminded us that imperialist impulses have been and continue to be defended as advancing the expansion of human rights and liberty. There are, to be sure, moral imperatives in both Orientalist and abolitionist manifestations aimed at justifying conquest—especially sentimental, benevolent, humanitarian, and Christian ideals—but these imperatives have sometimes been at odds internally and have served conflicting purposes rather than congealing into positions that appear consistent to contemporary sensibilities. Of course, British imperialism was linked with the emancipation of slaves in that both involved the desire to 'civilize' and 'anglicize' Others.[4] As scholars have recently recognized, the abolitionist cause may have been manipulated as an imperialist

---

[2] Said, *Orientalism*, 122–3.

[3] David Brion Davis, 'Catching the Conquerors', reviewing Linda Colley's *Captives* in the *New York Review of Books*, 50/9 (29 May 2003), seems to discount these effects when he calls abolition a 'spontaneous upsurge' (p. 38). Among the most helpful discussions of the movement is Robin Blackburn, *The Overthrow of Colonial Slavery, 1776–1848* (New York: Verso, 1988).

[4] Debbie Lee (ed.), *Slavery, Abolition and Emancipation: Writings in the British Romantic Period*, iii: *The Emancipation Debate* (London: Pickering and Chatto, 1999). See also Niall Ferguson, *Empire: How Britain Made the Modern World* (London: Allen Lane, 2003), who commends such an impulse.

weapon in the case of England's employing anti-slavery arguments in the West Indies as a ploy against France to heighten their own opportunities for expansion. In another example, the East India Company interests joined forces with the anti-slavery lobby late in the century to improve profits in sugar. Others have pointed towards England's anti-slavery imperialism, which established the freed slave colonies of Sierra Leone and Liberia, in part as a means to penetrate Africa and encourage trade. Similarly, recent investigations into Edmund Burke's political theory have suggested that his policies regarding India and the Americas were anti-imperialist, but his views on the 'Negro question'—the status of slaves, abolition, and racial equality— were less reputable by progressive standards. At the same time as Burke opposed the British imperial goals in India, most famously during the Warren Hastings trial, he apparently supported an 'expansionist' position in the Americas to civilize the savages of the West Indies and the Americas.[5] The will to control territory may sometimes be deeply embedded and veiled within emancipatory efforts.[6]

It is rare that analyses of Oriental subject and African slave are held in close conjunction in the early modern periods, though Montesquieu's *L'Esprit des lois* (1748) argued that slavery in its broadest interpretation squelched liberty: both Oriental despotism and chattel slavery offended principles of law and justice. 'Slavery' in common parlance is most often assumed to be almost exclusively associated with the Atlantic slave trade after the Society for Effecting the Abolition of the Slave Trade in Britain began in 1787, and the focus on the West African slavery of the Atlantic slave trade increased slavery's racialization in distinguishing it from other kinds of captivity. Literary and historical critics have become accustomed, since Paul Gilroy's important book on the Black Atlantic, to re-conceptualizing slavery through its intercultural and transnational formation—that circulating intermixture of African, American, Caribbean, and British ideas defined by

[5] See Margaret Kohn and Daniel I. O'Neill, 'A Tale of Two Indias: Burke and Mill on Empire and Slavery in the West Indies and America', *Political Theory*, 34/2 (2006), 192–228.

[6] Peter J. Kitson, introduction in Peter J. Kitson (ed.), *Slavery, Abolition and Emancipation: Writings in the British Romantic Period*, ii: *The Abolition Debate* (London: Pickering and Chatto, 1999), p. xix: 'The defenders of the [slave] trade in the debates of 1792 repeatedly blamed the St Domingue uprising on the activities of the French and British abolitionists', resulting in increased fear that abolition would unsettle the relations between French and British in the colonies. Abolitionists were thus accused of encouraging Jacobin sympathies and antimonarchical stances. The Atlantic slave trade was abolished on 1 May 1807.

oceanic commerce and exchange.[7] Gilroy and others have expanded the concept of the black subject to include Creolization in the wider circum-Atlantic and diaspora.[8] But blackness also circulated in the eighteenth century in another domain that has not been much discussed. That conceptual territory is what I am describing as the unassimilated space between 'Oriental' and '*Blacks* so called'.[9] Geographical divisions are sometimes silently allied with racial categorizations to organize discussions about the costs and benefits of such designations, including the right to enslave, but recent attempts at mapping them have been inadequate because of the failure to consider several directions at once. If Orientalism privileges looking towards the East then, assuming a perspective from a location in England, abolition studies are shaped by a 'tyranny of continents' that has privileged looking towards the West and South.[10] The directional axes commonly applied are often skewed: the 'East' turns out to be, frequently, the North (as in the North of Africa) or, if one takes Europe as the compass, the South; and West Africa is at once black and Islamic, south of Europe *and* North Africa.

Even if we assume that Orientalism had become an internally consistent discourse by the first decades of the nineteenth century, its earlier eighteenth-century formulations are geographically, religiously, and historically diffuse as applied respectively to China, Persia, Turkey, North Africa, and India. Attitudes and descriptions of the Orient—particularly North Africa and the Ottoman Empire—were disjointed and various until at least the 1750s, when, as Linda Colley has most recently argued, Britain's fear of Islamic capture yielded to a new confidence in its ability to subdue not only the Barbary Coast but India as well, bolstered by a presumption of

---

[7] Paul Gilroy, *The Black Atlantic: Modernity and Double Consciousness* (Cambridge, Mass: Harvard University Press, 1993).

[8] See e.g. Joseph Roach, *Cities of the Dead: Circum-Atlantic Performance* (New York: Columbia University Press, 1996).

[9] Betty Joseph, 'Re(playing) Crusoe/Pocahontas: Circum-Atlantic Stagings in *The Female American*', *Criticism*, 42/3 (Summer 2000), 317–35, suggests the usefulness of this term for postcolonial theory (though in another context), by examining the way in which texts escape into 'unassimilated spaces within national narratives', and finds that Homi Bhabha's concept of liminality facilitates a ' "cross-roads" for imagining a new transnational culture' (p. 320, 329).

[10] The term appears in Peter A. Coclanis, review of Ira Berlin, *Generations of Captivity: A History of African-American Slaves* (Cambridge, Mass.: Belknap Press of Harvard University Press, 2003), in *William and Mary Quarterly*, 3rd ser., 61/3 (July 2004), 544–55.

Christianity's moral superiority.[11] As a number of critics have shown, 'Orientalism is already . . . a divided and flexible construct . . . , not a monolith of otherness.'[12] Most relevant for my purposes here, Lisa Lowe and Sara Suleri are among those who have reminded us that there are 'Easts' rather than an 'East'; and Srinivas Aravamudan has offered the useful neologism 'Levantinization' to 'name the multiple uses—some utopian, others repressive—that orientalisms were put to in the eighteenth century'.[13] We might also point to the crux of Orientalisms arising from Asia Minor, Mediterranean, and North African sources as particularly relevant to an understanding of the late seventeenth and early eighteenth centuries.

Building on these insights, my purpose here is to show that attitudes towards the Orient and its Eastern subjects overlap and are deeply enmeshed in attitudes towards abolition and the transport of African slaves in the eighteenth century. We need, I think, an alternative approach to the period of the late seventeenth and early eighteenth centuries that would incorporate these interminglings of Orientalism and anti-slavery in their proto-stages.[14] Here I want to ask, in a very limited way, what it would mean to re-examine the century's texts of culture from *Oroonoko* (1688) to Olaudah Equiano's *Life* (1789), before Orientalist and abolitionist discourses fully cohere, first to explore the inadequacy of this division to represent what goes before them, and second to begin to reassess early traces of Oriental and

[11] Linda Colley, *Captives: Britain, Empire and the World, 1600–1850* (London: Jonathan Cape, 2002). Nabil Matar, *Turks, Moors, and Englishmen in the Age of Discovery* (New York: Columbia University Press, 1999), writes, 'By the end of the seventeenth century the Muslim "savage" and the Indian "savage" became completely superimposable in English thought and ideology. But it was only in the eighteenth century that this superimposition was transferred into the colonial discourse; in that century a colonial discourse against Islam in the full sense of the term evolved' (p. 170).

[12] Laura Chrisman, 'The Imperial Unconscious? Representations of Imperial Discourse', *Critical Quarterly*, 32/3 (Autumn 1990), 50.

[13] See Lisa Lowe, *Immigrant Acts: On Asian American Cultural Politics* (Durham, NC: Duke University Press, 1996); Sara Suleri, *The Rhetoric of English India* (Chicago: University of Chicago Press, 1992); and Srinivas Aravamudan, *Tropicopolitans: Colonialism and Agency, 1688–1804* (Durham, NC: Duke University Press, 1999).

[14] Matar remarks in *Turks, Moors, and Englishmen* on the 'imprecision with which North African Muslims and sub-Saharan Africans have been conflated and identified' in the earlier period. He continues, 'England's relations with sub-Saharan Africans were relations of power, domination, and slavery, while relations with the Muslims of North Africa and the Levant were of anxious equality and grudging emulation' (p. 6).

black subjects before the British Abolition Act. If, as Stuart Hall reminds us, racism 'operates by constructing impassable symbolic boundaries between racially constituted categories, and its typically binary system of representation constantly marks and attempts to fix and naturalize the difference between belongingness and otherness',[15] then it is clearly counterproductive to reduce Others to Oriental and African, or to any other binary, as somehow representing racially, culturally, or geographically separate groups. In other words, we might instead think *across* these two powerful ways of making sense of the period, between 'Oriental' and 'Black so called', making use of postcolonial thinking but also critiquing it, in order to reread texts that have been located and interpreted principally within one or the other discourse, and to think of them instead as occupying unarticulated and unabsorbed spaces that fall in between these partial histories and systems. Straddling these categories reveals a literary and cultural borderland which is, to borrow from Saskia Sassen, 'constituted in terms of discontinuities [that] are *given a terrain* rather than reduced to a dividing line' (my emphasis).[16] These two strains—though also joined together as Othering—might encourage investigations in terms of thickening entanglements rather than discrete spaces. Negrified sub-Saharan African subjects and Orientalized figures, instead of being fixed and knowable subjects, may then themselves be characterized in terms of ambiguities and affinities as well as oppositions.

I Shades of blackness

As critics have recently demonstrated, reading the eighteenth century poses a threat to the stability, coherence, and purity of the racial self that is paralleled

---

[15] Stuart Hall, 'New Ethnicities', in David Morley and Kuan-Hsing Chen (eds), *Critical Dialogues in Cultural Studies* (London: Routledge, 1996), 445. Ter Ellingson, *The Myth of the Noble Savage* (Berkeley: University of California Press, 2001) states that 'the "savage" and the "Oriental" were the two great ethnographic paradigms developed by European writers during the age of exploration and colonialism'. As I attempt to show here, these two paradigms are inadequate for explicating eighteenth-century texts of culture.

[16] See Saskia Sassen, *Globalization and its Discontents* (New York: The New Press, 1998), 102 n. 19. Doreen Massey speaks similarly of a 'sphere of co-existing multiplicity' in *Space, Place, and Gender* (Minneapolis: University of Minnesota Press, 2001).

only by the circumstances of the twenty-first century. As we are increasingly coming to recognize, representations of people of colour in the eighteenth century mutate through the spectrum of tawny, sallow, olive, mulatto, sooty, and ebony—of East Indian, West Indian, American Indian, Pacific Islander, and North and sub-Saharan African, all of whom are at times designated in British (if not American) parlance as 'black'. In some cases we can assign the muddles to historical accident, and in others to geographical confusion. The shadings of blackness convey discernable variations that constitute crucial hierarchies for many eighteenth-century European travellers.[17] For example, Edward Ives on his mid-century visit to the Coramandel Coast in India remarks on the association between slavery and Negritude to locate race, as is commonly done, in skin colour and hair texture: 'The natives on this coast are black, but of different shades. Both men and women have long shining black hair, which has not the least tendency to wool, like that of the *Guinea Negroes*. You cannot affront them more, than to call them by the name of *negroe*, as they conceive it implies an idea of slavery.'[18] Seeking to make a distinction between varied hues of black, these natives of India confirm that the term 'Negro' clearly signifies a sub-Saharan African who is subject to enslavement. Similarly, the female adventurer Jemima Kindersley, having travelled through Bahia, Brazil, the Cape of Good Hope, and several regions of India in the 1760s and 1770s, produces an incomplete but telling global racial taxonomy. The scarified black slaves in Brazil are 'of the Negro kind', 'by nature disagreeable, but often rendered still more so, by frightful marks on their faces'.[19] At the Cape of Good Hope, she observes Malaccan servants transported from the Malay peninsula in the Dutch East Indies who speak a kind of Portuguese. She notes that they are 'less black' than the indigenous South Africans (p. 68). The darker native 'Hottentot' slaves, as she calls them, 'are by nature tolerably white, and not unhandsome, but as soon as a child is born, they rub it all over with oil, and lay it in the sun; this they repeat till it becomes brown . . . as they grow up, they continue constantly to rub themselves with oil or grease, and by degrees become almost a jet black' (p. 68).

[17] Coramantien constituted the first English settlement in West Africa in 1631; the Royal African Company was chartered in 1672 and ended its monopoly in 1698.

[18] Edward Ives, *A Voyage from England to India, in the Year MDCCLIV and an Historical Narrative of the Operations of the Squadron and Army in India, under . . . Watson . . . and Colonel Clive* (London, 1773), 22.

[19] Jemima Kindersley, *Letters from the Island of Teneriffe, Brazil, the Cape of Good Hope, and the East Indies* (London, 1777), 50. Subsequent references appear in parentheses.

Moving on to India and remarking on the differences among regions, she distinguishes a racial hierarchy between light-skinned men in Allahabad and darker Indians elsewhere. There the Persians and Tartars 'have so little title to the appellation we give them of black, that if they were dressed as Europeans, they would differ from such as have been long exposed to this climate, rather as being paler than darker. They do not like to be called black men, and those of the highest rank are in general least so' (pp. 249–50).

The resonant phrase '*Blacks* so called' that Aphra Behn uses to describe the Coramantien people of West Africa suggests some scepticism about the label's applicability to her hero Oroonoko (though she does not suggest an alternative), and the uneasiness about its accuracy persists throughout the century as European encounters with peoples of colour multiply. These kinds of gradation of complexion in the wider eighteenth-century world complicate and transform the calibrations more familiar to students of the greater Caribbean—including Moreau de Saint-Méry's elaborate classification of degrees of black ancestry based on fractions of 'blood' transmitted through seven generations—and extend well beyond the increasingly rigid categorizations of early anthropology to sketch out an intricate racial atlas.[20] The abolition movement parallels the evolution of racial phenotypes, combined with particular character traits, into categories of human difference that are identified with given geographical origins and locations. Linnaeus, Prichard, and Blumenbach among others created schemes of racial varieties. For Blumenbach the Ethiopian is distinguished from the Malay and the Mongolian. The Caucasian category includes Europeans but, less predictably, Northern Africans and Eastern Asians as well as those living near the river Obi, the Caspian Sea, and the Ganges. Mongolians include Asians (except Malays), and Finns, Lapps, and Esquimaux, while Ethiopian encompasses 'all the Africans, except those of the north'.[21] Linnaeus categorizes the Asiatic as sooty, melancholic, and rigid, and the African as black, phlegmatic, and

---

[20] See Joan Dayan, *Haiti, History, and the Gods* (Berkeley: University of California Press, 1995); and Werner Sollors, *Neither Black nor White yet Both: Thematic Explorations of Interracial Literature* (New York: Oxford University Press, 1997). In private correspondence Dayan has helpfully noted that Behn's '*Blacks, so called*' resonates with Jean Genet's phrase, 'Un noir, mais de quelle couleur?'

[21] Johann Friedrich Blumenbach, *De generis humani varietate nativa* (1775; 3rd edn, Göttingen, 1795), trans. as 'On the Natural Variety of Mankind', in *The Anthropological Treatises of Johann Friedrich Blumenbach*, trans. Thomas Bendyshe (London: Published for the Anthropological Society by Longman, Green, Longman, Roberts, & Green, 1865), 266.

capricious, though Prichard separates humans into the Indo-European, the Syrian Arabian, and the African.[22] In none of these groupings is there a racial type that closely corresponds to a nineteenth-century 'Oriental' category, though the darkest black in all of these instances is most consistently associated with the African. Negotiating through an often unintelligible racial calculus, the arguments for abolition ironically attempted to locate a more exactly fixable and knowable identity in order to name the subject who would be emancipated. In that very naming, in addition to inadvertently enabling racism, I suggest, a more coherent discourse around Islam and the Orient begins to assume the discursive place of abolition; by excluding the 'Oriental' subaltern from the subject of abolitionist emancipation, the necessity to identify an Oriental subject as distinct from the African justified itself. Once abolition legislation was enacted, the concept of the subject of despotism was largely reserved for the 'Oriental' who needed to be freed from political tyranny, not through abolition but through the liberation of imperial expansion.

In the century I am considering here—roughly the 100 years between 1688 and the British Abolition Act—we might first of all remind ourselves to avoid collapsing the differences between North and sub-Saharan Africa, first identified as such in Leo Africanus's writings from the early sixteenth century, translated into English by John Pory as *A Geographical Historie of Africa* (1600). Samuel Purchas popularized Africanus's work by including it in his travelogue collection *Hakluytus Posthumus or Purchas His Pilgrimes* (1625). According to Oumelbanine Zhiri,

From the point of view of the population, the Berbers of North Africa, mixed with their Semite Arab invaders, are distinguished from the Black population of sub-Saharan Africa. Culturally, North Africa, almost totally islamized and largely Arabized, seems to belong to a different history, despite the links, attested since centuries, between the two regions.[23]

[22] See Peter J. Kitson, introduction in Peter J. Kitson (ed.), *Slavery, Abolition and Emancipation: Writings in the British Romantic Period*, viii: *Theories of Race* (London: Pickering and Chatto, 1999), p. x; James Cowles Prichard, 'Of the Causes which have Produced the Diversities of the Human Species', 1813, in Kitson (ed.), *Theories of Race*, 269–308.

[23] Oumelbanine Zhiri, 'Fractured Africa: Space, Time and Intelligibility in the European Conception of Africa', paper presented at conference 'Race in the Early Modern Period', University of California, Santa Cruz, spring 1997, 2, quoted with permission of the author. Leo Africanus's original name was Al-Hassan Ibn Mohammed Al-Wezâz Al-Fâsi.

North Africa attaches itself both to Europe and the 'East' rather than to the continent of Africa—an intellectual distinction that has been naturalized—while Egypt stands separate from both. According to this way of thinking, both Egypt and Mediterranean Africa are not really Africa. If the sub-Saharan Africa of the sixteenth century appears to the postcolonial reader to be an 'undifferentiated' and unintelligible space, then Africa appears to be most 'itself only in its sub-Saharan part' as it awaits its revelation as an economic benefit.[24] While the Orient revels in history as an emblem of an antiquated past, the eighteenth-century concept of sub-Saharan 'Africa' seems to run counter to the very idea of history, yet it paradoxically represents the less phantasmagoric, the more real, corporeal, and essential part of the continent.

Second, blackness in its linkages with the bestial is principally associated with the Gold Coast slavery of sub-Saharan Africa rather than with North or even East Africa; as a result, in postcolonial discussions of slavery the slippage in terms means that eighteenth-century blacks are most often assumed to be chattel slaves traded around the Atlantic whether they are of noble or lesser status, slaves awarded to other Africans as the spoils of war, Indian slaves, slaves with limited tenures, or indentured servants. Metonymic signs of unexpected continuity appear, for example, in the omnipresent turban that migrates—in pictorial representations and on the stage—across the apparent divide between Oriental and black, across East and West Indian, symbolizing a generalized exotic, and thus suggesting that thinking of the Orient and the Black Atlantic as consistently separate is not characteristic of this early period.[25] For example, Moors could be considered white, dusky, or black, and were often described generically as 'Ethiopian'.[26] For the Renaissance and much of the eighteenth century, the Moorish prince, often

---

[24] Ibid. 3–10.

[25] John Locke referred to Muslims as the 'turbanned Nations' in *Two Tracts on Government*, ed. and introd. by Philip Abrams (Cambridge: Cambridge University Press, 1967), 146. For an influential text that travels between these discourses and asserts that one Indies was discovered while looking for the other, see Guillaume-Thomas-François Raynal, *A Philosophical and Political History of the Settlements and Trade of the Europeans in the East and West Indies. 2nd ed. Revised and Corrected. With Maps Adapted to the Work, and a Copious Index*, 5 vols, trans. J. Justamond (London, 1776).

[26] For earlier definitions of 'Moor' see Anthony Barthelemy, *Black Face, Maligned Race: The Representation of Blacks in English Drama from Shakespeare to Southerne* (Baton Rouge: Louisiana State University Press, 1987), 13–17; Emily Bartels, 'Making More of the Moor: Aaron, Othello and Renaissance Refashionings of Race', *Shakespeare Quarterly*, 41/4 (Winter 1990), 437–9; and Kim Hall,

turbaned, who is fixed in rank but subject to enslavement, represents a kind of swing figure between sexualities, skin colours, and sometimes religions. What was originally held together in the word 'Moor' (Eastern, North African, Muslim, and sometimes black) is frequently broken apart during the eighteenth century into its component and more rigidly classified bits by the century's end.

The 'Moorish fancy' that Lord Shaftesbury found to prevail in the early decades of the century may have arisen in part from the Grub Street publication in English translation of Antoine Galland's *Les Mille et une nuits* or *Arabian Nights' Entertainments* (1704–17). The fascination with things Moorish may also have sparked the near-constant presentation of dramatic versions of *Oroonoko* throughout the century. One reason why the characters of Oroonoko and his precursor Othello were so central in helping to consolidate a national identity at a time of emerging empire may well have been that they blended together the Eastern subject and the African black, unlike Samuel Johnson's Prince Rasselas (1759), who represented the ersatz Moor, Abyssinian and vaguely non-European, but who was clearly not Negrified, Islamized, or Arabized.[27] This surrogation arises as an Orient increasingly imagined as coherent becomes a more efficient organizer for imperialist impulses, and as abolition legislation in England becomes the central force for freeing black sub-Saharan Africans wherever they were located around the world. As translators and editors told and retold *Arabian Nights* in its various renderings in the eighteenth and nineteenth centuries, the captive genie harboured in the lamp in 'The Story of Aladdin', one of the orphan tales incorporated by Galland, curiously transforms from an Orientalized figure, pictured as Chinese or 'Arab', into a more fully racialized caricature of an African slave as abolitionists made use of the motif of the spellbound genie who

---

'"Troubling Doubles": Apes, Africans, and Blackface in *Mr. Moore's Revels*', in Joyce Green MacDonald (ed.), *Race, Ethnicity, and Power in the Renaissance* (Madison, NJ: Fairleigh Dickinson University Press, 1997), 120–44.

[27] I argue for the centrality of *Oroonoko* in shaping English identity in *The Limits of the Human: Fictions of Anomaly, Race, and Gender in the Long Eighteenth Century* (Cambridge: Cambridge University Press, 2003). Roxann Wheeler, *The Complexion of Race: Categories of Difference in Eighteenth-Century British Culture* (Philadelphia: University of Pennsylvania Press, 2000), believes that the 'absence of black Africans in intermarriage plots [of the novel] suggests a narrative avoidance' (p. 141). Wheeler appropriately applies 'black' to sub-Saharan Africans, and only occasionally lapses, as when Moroccan men and women seem excluded from possessing African heritage (p. 175).

was subject to the will of his master. In eighteenth-century versions of the tale, the Chinese Aladdin at first believes that the African magician is his father's brother, his physiognomic features apparently not registering differences sufficient to arouse Aladdin's suspicions of a ruse. But in later nineteenth-century versions the gigantic and monstrous genie in the lamp is beneficent yet terrifying and is clearly racialized.[28]

A third consideration defying a resort to sharp divisions and distinct histories of the Orientalized subject and the Negrified sub-Saharan subject is that geographical mixtures critical to the scheme such as the Maghreb, a place of contending economic, imperial, and racial interests, are largely unaccounted for within descriptions of either Eastern despotism or the Atlantic slave trade. Ann Thomson writes of the Maghreb of the 1830s that 'as it became more barbaric and ripe for "civilisation" by the Europeans, so it became more African'.[29] The new interest in Barbary was sparked because it was believed to be a gateway to the gold of sub-Saharan Africa. The Maghreb serves as 'a geohistorical location that is constructed as a crossing instead of a grounding'—or, one might say, as a terrain of discontinuity rather than a fixed place—'between Orient, Occident, and Africa, of Turks, Christians, Jews, Moors, Arabs, Bedouins, Berbers, and Kabyles'.[30] Although Catherine Gallagher's Bedford teaching edition of Aphra Behn's *Oroonoko* is rich with documents about the slave trade and the Black Atlantic, its 'literary contexts' section has little to do with Islam, the Orient, the Sahara, the Barbary Coast, or the Levant.[31] On the other hand, neither does the helpful source study in

---

[28] See Marina Warner's *Fantastic Metamorphoses, Other Worlds: Ways of Telling the Self* (New York: Oxford University Press, 2002) for an African-inflected illustration.

[29] Ann Thomson, *Barbary and Enlightenment: European Attitudes towards the Maghreb in the Eighteenth Century* (Leiden: E. J. Brill, 1987), 8. For a discussion of 'Aladdin', see Felicity Nussbaum, 'Slavery, Blackness, and Islam: *The Arabian Nights* in the Eighteenth Century', in Brycchan Carey and Peter J. Kitson (eds), *Slavery and the Cultures of Abolition: Essays Marking the Bicentennial of the British Abolition Act of 1807* (Woodbridge, Suffolk: Boydell & Brewer, 2007), 150–72. A few sentences derive from that essay and the introduction to Saree Makdisi and Felicity Nussbaum (eds), *The Arabian Nights in Historical Context: Between East and West* (Oxford: Oxford University Press, 2008), 1–24, and appear in altered form here.

[30] Thomson, *Barbary and Enlightenment*, 102.

[31] Aphra Behn, *Oroonoko; or, The Royal Slave*, ed. Catherine Gallagher with Simon Sterne (Boston and New York: Bedford/St Martin's, 2000). Subsequent references to this text appear in parentheses. Behn's precise phrasing is '*Blacks* so called', but I have sometimes silently altered it to omit the italics and employ the singular noun or the adjectival form.

the introduction to the Yale Samuel Johnson edition of *Rasselas* make mention of black Africans, of sub-Saharan Africa, or of abolition in spite of the Happy Valley's location in Abyssinia (or modern-day Ethiopia). These omissions and slippages may be perhaps partly explained as a function of the different streams of criticism emanating from the United States where 'black' does not usually include subcontinental Indians or Middle Easterners as opposed to common usage in the United Kingdom, where 'black' may include bodies that are Levantine in origin as well as sub-Saharan African. In the imaginative geography of the eighteenth century, Ethiopia (often a synonym for Africa) seems to migrate from Africa to Arabia and back again. It is sometimes contiguous to Egypt and sometimes depicted on the western side of the continent, though Ethiopia eventually comes to represent a lost and unrecoverable premodern glory in the later Ethiopianism movement.[32] Job Ludolphus (Hiob Ludolf), seeking the genealogy of the Queen of Sheba, declares in *A New History of Ethiopia* (1682) that Ethiopia was earlier perceived to be both Asiatic and African. 'But these different Opinions are easily recon-cil'd', he writes,

if as many of the Old Writers held, the ancient Ethiopia extended it self into Arabia. They assert the Sabeans and Homerites to have bin [*sic*] Nations of Ethiopia, which without question were formerly seated in Arabia the Happy.... Therefore was the Ethiopia of the Ancients two-fold, Asiatic and African, or Oriental and Western. For the Ancients did not limit the principal Parts of the World as we do now; while they extended India into Africa, and brought Ethiopia into Asia, and believed that the Indians inhabited beyond the Ethiopians. Nor did they think that Asia and Africa were distinct parts of the Orbe of the Earth, but onely particular Regions. Egypt seemed to belong sometimes to Asia, sometimes to Africa; and others made Nilus to be the bounds between those two Continents.[33]

This portability of geographical location persists, however, into the eighteenth century, and it is made graphic in Daniel Defoe's 'A Map of the World, on wch is Delineated the Voyages of Robinson Cruso [*sic*]'. That map shows

[32] Zhiri, 'Fractured Africa', mentions Ethiopia's 'movement' (p. 7). Blumenbach refers to 'the head of an Ethiop from the southern part of Africa' in 'Of the Natural Variety of Mankind' (p. 120).

[33] Job Ludolphus [Hiob Ludolf], *A New History of Ethiopia. Being a Full and Accurate Description of the Kingdom of Abessinia, Vulgarly, though Erroneously called the Empire of Prester John. In Four Books ... Made English by J. P. Gent* (London, 1682), 160. I am grateful to Wendy Belcher for calling this passage to my attention.

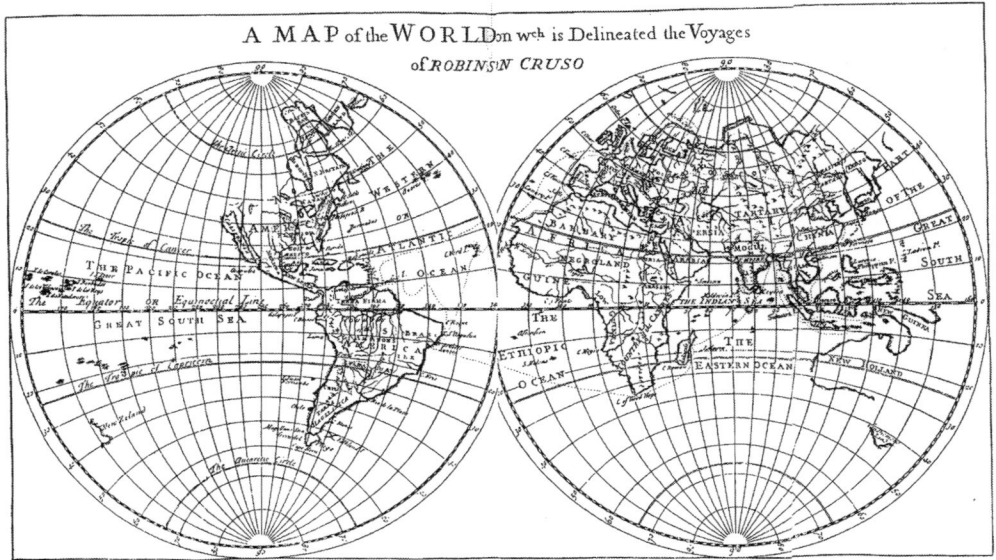

Figure 4.1 'A Map of the World, on wch is Delineated the Voyages of Robinson Cruso [sic]', in Daniel Defoe, *The Farther Adventures of Robinson Crusoe; Being the Second and Last Part of His Life, and of the Strange Surprising Account of his Travels Round Three Parts of the Globe. Written by Himself*, 7th edn (London, 1747). By permission of the William Andrews Clark Memorial Library, University of California, Los Angeles.

Barbary, Negroland, Guinea, Low Guinea, and the country of the Cafres, with Nubia to the East and below that Abassia (*sic*) and Arabia, Persia, Tartary, Mogul [North India], and China. The body of water near Guinea is 'The Ethiopic Ocean', and below the Indian Sea, 'The Eastern Ocean' (see Figure 4.1). As Ethiopia migrates from East to West and back again, these confusions complicate any simple division between the Orient and Africa.

In *Rasselas* Johnson drew heavily upon European sources—various French, Spanish, and German histories of Ethiopia—for the opening portions of the book that include the imprisonment of the Abyssinian prince and princess in the Happy Valley, and their harem-like confinement in the terrestrial paradise. Rasselas, suggests Srinivas Aravamudan, 'is a living parody of the enlightened despot, the Enlightenment's benevolent counterpart to the Oriental antitype'.[34] At the same time Rasselas is also an African prince

---

[34] Aravamudan, *Tropicopolitans*.

who radically departs from the popular noble native prototype familiar from Behn's or Southerne's Oroonoko. His character is evacuated of any specifically African or Eastern reference system, though the Bedouin abduction of Pekuah, Nekayah's servant, is identifiably a Turkish incident reminiscent of Richard Knolles's *Generall Historie of the Turkes* (1603), John Greaves's *Description of the Grand Seignor's Seraglio* (1650), Alexander Russell's *Natural History of Aleppo* (1756), and Aaron Hill's *Full and Just Account of the Present State of the Ottoman Empire* (1709).[35] In short, reading *Rasselas* is enhanced by contrasting it with other contemporaneous African renderings or situating it within the context of Johnson's views on slavery, while, in a point I shall return to, *Oroonoko* is enriched by recognizing that it draws on representations of a pseudo-East.

A fourth point I am making is that re-examining the relationship among the various Easts, the 'Orient', North Africa, and sub-Saharan Africa provokes new and significant questions germane to the way in which gender helps to constitute these divisions. For example, very different representations of manliness appear in the two sets of discourses. While black slave men appear as noble princes, Oriental men are regularly stereotyped as Muslim despots or Hindu ascetics in eighteenth-century novels and plays. The sentimental genre in its colonial setting seems largely reserved for sub-Saharan Africans and Europeans and is less applicable to 'Oriental' subjects. The native sub-Saharan African prince is depicted with a fierceness that is sometimes ameliorated by a sentimental undertone, while the native prince of the East is most often a tyrannical usurper of liberty rather than the object of sweet pity. While African slave women may be eroticized and degraded, abandoned or ignored, or represented as objects of terrifying sublimity in a combination of both, native Eastern women usually appear as sultanesses, nautch dancers, veiled harem women, or Hindu widows participating in suttee. Neither Orientalist nor Black Atlantic tropes explain, for example, the dramatic figure of the Black Sultaness (Figure 4.2). What are we to make of an Islamic woman of rank, a woman both Eastern and black, whose representation stands in bold contrast to the more conventional pictures of bare-breasted African slave women? Yet perhaps because of their shared asymmetrical positions in power relations, literary and visual depictions of sub-Saharan African women and North African or Oriental women may

[35] Gwin J. Kolb (ed.), *Rasselas and Other Tales*, The Yale Edition of the Works of Samuel Johnson, 16 (New Haven: Yale University Press, 1990), p. xxxiii.

Figure 4.2 'Habit of the Black Sultaness in 1749'. This image appears in a book of costumes designed for the British theatre: *A Collection of the Dresses of Different Nations, Antient and Modern. Particularly Old English Dresses. . . . To which are added the Habits of the Principal Characters on the English Theatre*, i (London, 1757). By permission of the William Andrews Clark Memorial Library, University of California, Los Angeles.

resemble each other more than those of their male counterparts, structurally linked as women are within patriarchy and racism.

In Jonathan Richardson's well-known portrait of Lady Mary Wortley Montagu in Turkish costume (c.1726), her queenly authority derives from her rich exotic dress and statuesque deportment. In that picture Turquerie reveals itself in feminine luxury, while African slavery appears in the shadows as a compromised masculinity held captive. This trope of an elegant European woman of rank accompanied by a slave carrying exotic fruits, a pet, or a parasol was a relatively common convention of such portraits, and Montagu's erotic power is underscored by the admiring, and perhaps even sensual, gaze of the black page.[36] Montagu's Oriental impersonation, class status, and feminine appeal depend in some measure upon her display of the page as a possession even though African child slaves, as opposed to adult male eunuchs, were virtually unknown in Turkey. The complex relationship between masquerade and authenticity, superiority and dependency, femininity and masculinity, represented by the figures in the painting offers another nuanced linkage between 'Oriental' and 'Blacks so called'.

II Africa Orientalized

In the remainder of this essay I will offer three examples that suggest the range of differences that result from re-examining the relationship between Eastern subjects and '*Blacks* so called'. These examples derive from three different periods of the eighteenth century and three different genres (a novel, a picture, and a play) and span a spectrum of Oriental and black subjects. They have been chosen in order to reflect the diversity of Othering as well as its progression: Aphra Behn's 1688 novella set in the Gold Coast and Surinam, Plate 4 of William Hogarth's 1745 *Marriage A-la-Mode*, picturing two '*Blacks* so called', and Mariana Starke's dramatic comedy *The Sword of Peace*

---

[36] Though it is not known whether Montagu was a slave-owner, she may have travelled with attending child slaves. The metal collar encircling the neck of Montagu's black page identifies him as a slave rather than a domestic servant. See Isobel Grundy, *Lady Mary Wortley Montagu: Comet of the Enlightenment* (Oxford: Oxford University Press, 1999), 301–3, and Marcia Pointon, *Hanging the Head: Portraiture and Social Formation in Eighteenth-Century England* (New Haven: Yale University Press, 1993), 140–57.

(1788), which portrays the English in India. Juxtaposing Oriental and black, the play opened just six months after the Warren Hastings trial began and in the same year as Pitt the Younger called for debates on the slave trade.

As I have argued, the making of a consistent, coherent, and legible literary African Negro in the eighteenth century is critical to shaping a subject of abolition. This may be one reason why critics return again and again to *Oroonoko* to locate that subject, while at the same time largely ignoring the untidy aspects of his story that associate him with an Oriental subject. The novella is often taken to be typical of anti-slavery literature,[37] but in *Oroonoko* the West Africa of the hero's origins, in spite of its being identified as Coramantien, is not at all geographically specific, but ultimately both pseudo-African and the stuff of Oriental romance. Behn's Orientalized *Oroonoko* begins by avoiding a Negrified 'African' dimension, aligning the story more closely with Islamic culture in order to focus on a part of Africa that may have seemed accessible to an English audience who could only conjure up Africa's interiors in their imaginations before significant European exploration began. Although Oroonoko is yoked together in radical contemporaneity with Charles I and with the Roman Caesar after whom he is named, as Laura Brown has persuasively argued, he is also bound up with a more generalized Eastern exoticism that brings to mind Restoration stagings of popular Eastern themes.[38]

In the first half of the novella an Orientalized Africa, inhabited as it is by '*Blacks* so called', predominates, while in the second half the New World is a land where slaves contest the legitimacy of slavery. The Orientalized romance in a generic Africa transmogrifies into a tale of slavery's abolition when it moves out of Africa to another continent. Oroonoko, though he is called a 'gallant *Moor*', comes from 'Coramantien, a Country of *Blacks* so called' (p. 41). Coramantien was in reality a port on the Gold Coast of Africa in the larger territory of Guinea, but Behn renders it as an imagined territory, a romantic place that is more in-between than located. That liminal terrain bears a palpable

---

[37] See Laura Brown, 'The Romance of Empire: *Oroonoko* and the Trade in Slaves', in Felicity Nussbaum and Laura Brown (eds), *The New Eighteenth Century: Theory, Politics, English Literature* (New York: Methuen, 1987), 42. David Brion Davis, *The Problem of Slavery in the Age of Revolution 1770–1823* (Ithaca: Cornell University Press, 1975), 479, traces the confusion between 'Negro' and 'slave' in the early eighteenth century.

[38] Brown, 'The Romance of Empire', 41–61. See also Brown's discussion of the native prince in *Fables of Modernity: Literature and Culture in the English Eighteenth Century* (Ithaca: Cornell University Press, 2001), 177–220.

resemblance to an Islamized and Arabized North Africa—in short, Oroonoko is African but not; he is in between European, North African, and sub-Saharan African. He does not resemble a sub-Saharan African because he is purportedly 'more civilized, according to the *European* Mode'; his classical physiognomy lacks a Negrified flat nose, or large lips, or even the brown, rusty black of his countrymen. Part of the 'noble Negro tradition' but much more,[39] Oroonoko's characterization initially offers an alternative to the abject position of the male slave by adding Oriental aspects.

Both Oroonoko and Imoinda are themselves slave-owners in their Orientalized West Africa.[40] Oroonoko's aged grandfather, the polygamous, despotic, and vindictive King of Coramantien, possesses numerous beautiful black wives and concubines: he is characterized as both Oriental despot and native African prince. His grandson Oroonoko, 'ador'd as the Wonder of all that World' (p. 42), is a modern man, a self-taught cosmopolitan or more exactly a transculturated tropicolitan who has learned French, Spanish, and English, and he insists on monogamous devotion to one woman.[41] Although Behn's polytheistic Coramantiens (whose supreme god is rendered as 'Captain of the clouds') are not portrayed as Muslim, the early sections of *Oroonoko* are riddled throughout with the tropes of Oriental romance. Other predictable signs of the Orient in the Coramantien sections include the paradisal citrus groves, the violent and sensual nature of the court, the despotic old king's giving Imoinda a royal veil to command her to his bed, Imoinda's captivity, and the '*Otan*' as it is called, or seraglio, furnished with couch, carpets, and baths (Figure 4.3).[42]

[39] Sypher, *Guinea's Captive Kings: British Anti-Slavery Literature of the XVIIIth Century* (Chapel Hill: University of North Carolina Press, 1942). In Thomas Southerne's transformation of Behn's novella into a play (1695), Oroonoko's origins are moved to Angola, the Portuguese colony, and Imoinda is European.

[40] Among the growing number of studies of African slavery, see Humphrey J. Fisher, *Slavery in the History of Muslim Black Africa* (London: Hurst and Company, 2001); Patrick Manning, *Slavery and African Life: Occidental, Oriental, and African Slave Trades* (Cambridge: Cambridge University Press, 1990); Paul Lovejoy, *Transformations in Slavery: A History of Slavery in Africa* (Cambridge: Cambridge University Press, 1983); and John R. Willis, *Slaves and Slavery in Muslim Africa* (London: Frank Cass, 1985).

[41] For this conceptualization as an 'object of representation *and* agent of resistance', see Aravamudan, *Tropicopolitans*, 4.

[42] *Oroonoko*, ed. Gallagher with Stern, 49, indicates that the word probably comes from the Persian *otagh*, meaning tent or pavilion. A connection between Mohammed and the Jacobite pretender Charles Edward (though in a negative sense) extended into the eighteenth century in, for example, James Miller's *Mahomet, the Imposter* (1744).

Figure 4.3 *Oronoko [sic], Ou Le Prince Négre. Imitation de l'Anglois. Nouvelle Édition, par M. de la Place* (London, 1769), 45. By permission of the Newberry Library, Chicago, IL.

Illustrations of *Oroonoko* throughout the eighteenth century reflect both 'Oriental' and 'African' derivations. In the early portions of the novella, Imoinda is held captive in the seraglio but later becomes an African slave in the New World. In the Otan she begs to be excused from the old king's sexual command. Betrothed to Oroonoko, Imoinda (monogamously inclined like her beloved) begs for mercy; but finally the virginal maiden is commanded to lay aside her mantle and accept the elder man's caresses. The lovesick prince Oroonoko, despairing over her plight, anticipates the language of enchantment and captivity in the Oriental tales familiar to English audiences from the *Arabian Nights*. Oroonoko laments, '*Were she in wall'd Cities, or confin'd from me in Fortifications of the greatest Strength; did Inchantments or Monsters detain her from me, I wou'd venture through any Hazard to free her: But here, in the Arms of a feeble old Man, my Youth, my violent Love, my Trade in Arms, and all my vast Desire of Glory, avail me nothing*' (p. 48). Being counselled that he himself, not his grandfather, is the injured party, advisers urge him to rescue her from the king's seraglio. Their romance involves soul-probing sighs and furtive glances, a trusted go-between, dancing women engaged in 'antick Postures', and the former mistress's coaching Imoinda in 'those Wanton Arts of Love'. Other standard romance fare made steamier in its harem location includes Imoinda's fortuitous fall into Oroonoko's arms, exchanges of gifts, the hot sexual tension of double-plotting, and transporting consummation, as well as surprise attack, alleged rape, and exotic laws.

In the novella, then, blackness carries with it both an Eastern romance element and a raw corporeality, united in Negritude. When the grandfather allows Oroonoko entrance to the women's quarters, the young prince suddenly becomes Negrified by negation. The narrator identifies Oroonoko as a Negro in claiming that 'A Negro *can change Colour.*' That change, that blush on a Negro face, is the visible sign confirming for Imoinda that his love is secured—their love being based on that involuntary manifestation of an interior emotion on the body, the blush, that simultaneously associates him with white feminine virtue and at the same time, in being a feature asserted to be characteristic of Negroes, realigns him with sub-Saharan Africans, rather than with Levantines. The Oriental, European, and sub-Saharan African Oroonoko is 'Negro', but he is not confined and limited to its conventions. Surinam, 'the [Romantic] other World' to which Oroonoko travels, extends in Behn's words from the East to the West, 'one Way as far as *China*, and another to *Peru*' (p. 76), in a phrase that anticipates Samuel

Johnson's poem *The Vanity of Human Wishes*. In the transition to the New World, Oroonoko, regarded as a divine oracle, king of the slaves, and a Caesar, paradoxically gains stature. Becoming 'more like a Governor, than a Slave', he 'endur'd no more of the Slave but the Name . . . without stirring toward that part of the Plantation where the *Negroes* were' (p. 69).

But in the second half of the novella, the black male subject becomes more tightly tethered to 'Africa' and the contest over slavery's legitimacy, rather than to Islamic culture or a vaguely located romantic exoticism. Once the cosmopolitan Oroonoko sheds his European clothing and travels away from his Orientalized home, he is more fully aligned with the real, material body that evokes a residue of the black Africa of slavery.[43] Oroonoko is increasingly Negrified, his learning and linguistic facility forgotten; and as he sheds his Oriental customs, the focus turns more and more to his tortured, mutilated body. Oroonoko's slow, painful death erases the Eastern tropes that dominated the first half of the book; he comes to inhabit not at all an Islamized or Arabized body, but the body of a prototypical noble native slave whose blackness, so-called, defines him in the eyes of his persecutors.

To look at the intersections and discontinuities between Oriental and black, between Easts and Africas, is thus to learn something more about the complexities of racial thinking in eighteenth-century texts of culture, and of the trajectory that seems to lead towards more distinctly 'Oriental' or 'Negrified' subjects. In another example, this time from mid century, in Plate 4 of Hogarth's *Marriage A-La-Mode*, 'The Toilette', commentators often draw parallels between the two black servants attending the lady's levée (Figure 4.4). They apply conventions about Africans and slaves to both figures without distinguishing between them or contextualizing the younger page within Eastern conventions. If we assume that both figures may be interpreted solely through the Black Atlantic triangle, rather than incorporating 'the East' within their blackness, we miss important metaphoric connections and differences.

Of the two black servants, both of whom seem amused at the adulterous scene, one is a corpulent adult dressed as an English servant who,

[43] Madhu Dubey, 'Racial Difference in Postmodern Theory', paper presented at University of California at Los Angeles, Nov. 2002, has discussed the association of African Americans (though not, of course, Oroonoko) with the real. See her *Signs and Cities: Black Literary Postmodernism* (Chicago: University of Chicago Press, 2003).

Figure 4.4 Simon François Ravenet after William Hogarth, *Marriage A-la-Mode*, Plate 4, 'The Toilette'. Engraving. By permission of the Hood Museum of Art, Dartmouth College.

yoking black and Oriental materials, offers hot chocolate in a china cup to a white-frocked and ghostly complexioned young lady swooning at the castrato's singing. The other black figure is a small turbaned low-grade servant, who mockingly points at the horns of Actaeon he holds. The horns are emblematic of the cuckoldry that transpires behind him between the philandering Lady Squander and her paramour Silvertongue, the lawyer. The auction from which the lovers have returned has yielded miscellaneous exotic curios that spill out of the page's basket, including a tray, porcelain china, pottery, and wooden figures. The younger servant, turbaned and feathered, wears white clothing that is vaguely reminiscent of East Indian dress; his slim graceful hands contrast to those of the older wide-eyed footman attired in bright green, whose plumper hands inspire thoughts of actual labour and of unaesthetic connections with the bestial;[44] they also contrast with the leaner hands of the castrato. The East or West Indian boy, his skin a noticeably lighter brown than that of the central figure in the colour painting, is linked with the illicit desire signified by the renderings of Correggio's 'Jupiter and Io', and Cavallino's picture of an intoxicated Lot seduced by his daughters on the wall above the Countess and the lawyer.[45] 'Jupiter and Io', underscoring the racial implications of chiaroscuro, may also be interpreted as a 'rape' of whiteness (Io was the mother of the founder of Egypt, Epaphus) whom Jupiter, figured as dark smoke, seduces and caresses. The boy sitting on the floor mimics the position of the hunting dogs in the other pictures on the wall. But in addition, the phallic feather on the page's headdress appears to caress Silvertongue's knee, suggesting a homoerotic register, for same-sex fears were typically aroused in the British more often by Turks and North Africans than by sub-Saharan slaves. The boy's figure aligns both with the screen behind it, upon which features a masker in Turkish costume, and with the red sofa, where Crébillon fils's book *Le Sopha*, an erotic parody of the *Arabian Nights*, is tucked into the crevices.[46] (In a later picture in the series, the Countess and her lover will also be discovered *in flagrante* in a brothel called the 'Turk's Head'.) *Le Sopha* describes the erotic pleasures that black pages or eunuchs purportedly provided for their white mistresses on sofas.[47] Further, the older, darker black figure seems especially significant because he divides the picture in half, turning away from the cuckolded pair towards the musical group and the swooning lady, his eyes leering at the white maiden's bodice and following her hand, which gestures towards the crotch of the effeminate cross-legged fop. The homoerotic elements of the young page contrast with the more specifically heterosexual

---

[44] David Dabydeen, *Hogarth's Blacks: Images of Blacks in Eighteenth-Century English Art* (Kingston-on-Thames, Surrey: Dangeroo Press, 1985).

[45] See Robert L. S. Cowley, *Hogarth's 'Marriage A-la-Mode'* (Ithaca: Cornell University Press, 1983), 101–21, for an illuminating discussion from which I have drawn. Cowley assumes that both figures are African and implicitly sub-Saharan.

[46] The book, published in defiance of a 1740 French royal decree, appeared in English as *The Sopha: A Moral Tale. Translated from the French Original of Monsieur Crebillon*, 2 vols (London, 1742). Galland, translator of the *Arabian Nights* into French, liberally inserts lounging sofas into the exotic interiors and exteriors described in the tales, according to R. Hawari, 'Antoine Galland's Translation of the *Arabian Nights*', *Revue de littérature comparée*, 54 (1980), 154.

[47] Dabydeen, *Hogarth's Blacks*, 79. I am extremely grateful to Angela Rosenthal and Dian Kriz for expert suggestions in interpreting these images.

placement of the central servant, emerging as he does from the pink vaginal-like opening to the mistress's bedchamber. The two servants conjure up different notions of illicit sexuality, drenched in excess, associated with 'the East', with Africa, and with both at once. In short, interpreting the 'black' servants beyond the context of the transatlantic African slave trade offers new revelations for the reader who recognizes the iconographical mixture.

Near the end of the century, in Mariana Starke's play *The Sword of Peace* (1788), we have, I think, a sign of both the increasing distinctions developing between the language applied to Oriental and black African subjects, and the dependency of the two discourses upon each other for their formulation. Starke capitalizes in the play upon the audience's interest in the Warren Hastings trial and his eventual replacement as Governor of Bengal by Cornwallis, which forecasts a new day in India, but the play is also, surprisingly, about abolition.[48] In its Orientalist vein, it is characterized by the display of uneven—and unacknowledged—power relations in the marriage between India and England. The Moreton sisters disingenuously claim to be superior to other Englishwomen who travel to India to 'barter [their] charms for Eastern gold', and they actively oppose the advances of the Resident, who is tainted by his stint in administering India's Cormandel Coast:[49] 'I declare I wou'd as soon marry Tippoo Saib', scoffs Eliza Moreton in Act 4 (p. 182), referring to the notorious son of Hyder Ali.[50] Usurping the place of an

[48] Mariana Starke, *The Sword of Peace* (Dublin, 1790), repr. in Jeffrey N. Cox (ed.), *Slavery, Abolition and Emancipation: Writings in the British Romantic Period*, v: *Drama* (London: Pickering and Chatto, 1999). In another dramatic example from the same decade, in Elizabeth Inchbald's farce *The Mogul Tale; or, the Descent of the Balloon* (1784), three English people (a doctor, a cobbler, and his wife) drift into a Great Mogul's harem. Among the exotic characters in addition to the Mogul and his three women are two eunuchs, whom the English enlist as allies. They are called by racial epithets such as 'blackamoor', 'blacky', and 'black dog' throughout the play, but they manage to exercise subaltern agency in preventing the wife's abduction into the seraglio.

[49] In spite of this ironic tone, Jeanne Moskal, 'English National Identity in Mariana Starke's "The Sword of Peace": India, Abolition, and the Rights of Women', in Catherine Burroughs (ed.), *Women in British Romantic Theatre: Drama, Performance, and Society, 1790–1840* (Cambridge: Cambridge University Press, 2000), 102–31, believes these women to be 'trustworthy representatives of English national identity'. More persuasive is her argument that Starke combines allegiance to Burke's aristocratic sentiments with sympathy for enslaved blacks, who, like the English married women with whom they are compared, are oppressed.

[50] Eliza Fay's *Original Letters from India (1779–1815)*, ed. E. M. Forster (New York: Harcourt Brace and Company, 1925) describes her captivity under Hyder Ali in Calicut. Cornwallis defeated Tipu Sultan of Mysore in 1792.

Oriental despot, the half-caste Mrs Tartar (her name signifying the chalky acidic residue of potassium bitartrate deposits on wine casks) rules the reigning Resident, who is 'under petticoat-government' but who is finally replaced with the more beneficent and worthy Northcote. Instigator of a plot to poison the two Englishwomen, Mrs Tartar is the daughter of a tallow chandler and a 'black' Indian merchant's daughter, as well as the wealthy widow of an English basket-maker's son. Her mixed-race status and trans-culturation as a kind of female nabob call to mind both the East and West Indies, especially because she owns a slave.

Complicating the Orientalism of the plot, then, is the abolitionist subplot. Mrs Tartar, labelled 'a vixen' and a 'hag', is both a womanly counterpart to the nabob, as I have suggested, and the dramatic equivalent to the creolized plantation-owning women of the Caribbean such as Mrs Ellison in Sarah Scott's novel *The History of Sir George Ellison* (1766), who cares more for her lapdog than her slaves. Like Mrs Ellison, Mrs Tartar owns a black slave, Caesar, as well as at least two female slaves, but Jeffreys, the servant to the Misses Moreton, generously purchases Caesar in order to free him. The half-caste Indian woman clarifies the compromised status of the 'Oriental' in relation to the English even as she makes clear her superiority to her Negro slave, but she also personifies and parallels the mixed-race status typical of another area of the British Empire, the Caribbean.

In the Indian Ocean slave trade, as distinct from the Atlantic trade, East African and Arab traders transported slaves to India through Mada-gascar, often from Mozambique, in the eighteenth and nineteenth cen-turies.[51] In fact, the numbers of slaves in India from Mozambique were accorded a special name, 'mosses', a shortened form of the name of their place of geographical origin; and slavery remained part of Anglo-Indian life because the English resisted outlawing forced captivity in their colo-nial territories even after the Abolition Act.[52] Just after the Napoleonic

[51] Peter J. Kitson and Debbie Lee, 'General Introduction', in Peter J. Kitson and Debbie Lee (general eds), *Slavery, Abolition and Emancipation: Writings in the British Romantic Period* (London: Pickering and Chatto, 1999), i, p. xi.

[52] In their 'General Introduction' to *Slavery, Abolition and Emancipation*, Kitson and Lee note that ' "Slavery" thus had *everything* to do with where the act of slavery took place—on British soil, or somewhere else' (p. xv).

Wars, the Third Ceylon Regiment constituted itself completely of former slaves,[53] and in 1840 the number of slaves in British India exceeded the number that had been emancipated in the British Caribbean.[54] Eighteenth-century women travelling abroad often carried domestic slaves with them. Elizabeth Marsh Crisp indicates that she possessed three slave girls in India in 1788. Eliza Fay in her travels to India confesses to having treated her female slave cruelly. Such abuses on the island of St Helena prompted regulations that required slave-owners such as Fay to teach their slaves a trade and also required slaves on the island to attend church services at least once every fortnight.[55]

I have argued, then, that the tropes surrounding Eastern and Oriental subjects and '*Blacks* so called', so often confined in postcolonial theory to the East or to the Atlantic respectively, are significantly linked in literary representations in the century before the 1780s. In Starke's play, placing a black African Negro slave, whether noble or not, in India makes him a magnet for sentiment that, typically, does not rest easily on Oriental characters. When Caesar learns that he is freed, Jeffreys offers to teach him to be an Englishman with whom, as an equal, he may dare to quarrel. Jeffreys attempts to disentangle chattel slavery from national identity and to align it with liberty:

An Englishman . . . lives *where* he likes—*goes* where he likes—*stays* where he likes— *works* if he likes—lets it *alone*, if he likes—starves, if he likes—abuses who he likes— boxes who he likes—thinks what he likes—speaks what he *thinks*—for, damme, he fears nothing, and will face the devil . . . for a true-born Englishman, if he provokes

[53] Richard Hall, *Empires of the Monsoon: A History of the Indian Ocean and its Invaders* (London: HarperCollins, 1998), 297, 368, 537 n. 7. 'The term "Sidi", from the Arabic *seyyid* (Lord), was used from the sixteenth century to describe the Janjira community of Africans in India; in 1668 the Janjira had captured Bombay from the British and were paid a ransom to leave. . . . Later the expression was applied to all Africans in India, and is still used in Pakistan for people descended from black slaves' (p. 334).

[54] Kitson, introduction in Kitson (ed.), *The Abolition Debate*, p. ix. See Davis, *The Problem of Slavery in the Age of Revolution*, 57, and Hugh Thomas, *The Slave Trade: The Story of the Atlantic Slave Trade 1440–1870* (New York: Simon and Schuster, 1997), 559–785.

[55] E. M. Forster offers these remarks in his edition of Eliza Fay, *Original Letters from India*, 303 n. 47. For Elizabeth Marsh Crisp, see the MS 'Journal of a Voyage by Sea from Calcutta to Madras, and of a Journey from thence back to Dacca, was written by my deceased Sister Elizabeth Crisp, and given to me by her Daughter Elizabeth Maria Shee, on her arrival in England from Bengal in the Year 1788', University of California at Los Angeles Library, Special Collections, MS 170/604.

him, damme, he'd knock his best friend's teeth down his throat,—[*to be spoken quick*]—but never lifts his hand against the oppress'd.[56]

The newly freed slave Caesar longs for the liberty that he is led to believe will attach to him in England, though the fact that his blackness may limit that freedom goes unmentioned. 'I like you!' declares Caesar to the white servant Jeffreys, meaning that he resembles him as if to say, 'I am like you'—as well as to indicate that he cares for him; but he follows with the critical question, inflected with his alterity, that is meant to be rhetorical: 'Am I Englishman?' The English nation portrayed on stage in *The Sword of Peace* affects to be the home of liberty welcoming the freed Negro slave, even as he returns from an Eastern space that will increasingly substitute an imperial subjugation of East Indians for enslaving sub-Subharan Africans. In the texts of culture that I have discussed here, characters from the 'East' and sub-Saharan Africans complicate a more generalized alterity. In *Oroonoko*, Moor and sub-Saharan, Oriental and black, are held together in one character, the Oriental linked to African, and blackness linked to the greater Caribbean; in Hogarth the subtle sexual connections between effete English people of 'quality', East Indian page, and sub-Saharan servant enhance and complicate the satire; and in *The Sword of Peace* the shifting relations among English servants, Indian and Anglo-Indian merchants, and black slaves shed new light on national identity. These texts provide indices by which we can gauge the formation of racial thinking during the English emancipation of African slaves and the growth of empire.

III Postcolonial theory and the eighteenth century

So what, then, can the eighteenth century add to postcolonial theory, or postcolonial theory to the eighteenth century? Caution, I'd suggest, in writing a postcolonial genealogy of the present that incorporates the eighteenth century as we historicize, refine, and contest postcolonial narratives

---

[56] Starke, *The Sword of Peace*, in Cox (ed.) *Slavery, Abolition and Emancipation*, v, pp. 165–6. The play ran for six performances in the same season that George Colman the Younger's *Inkle and Yarico* was popular, and productions continued until as late as 1809. Colman the Younger wrote the epilogue, and Starke thanked Colman the Elder as manager of the Haymarket. John Burton played the black slave.

relating to Orientalism or to black Atlantic slavery. 'Is such critical work,' Suvir Kaul has asked, 'no matter how revisionist, inevitably going to expand the ambit of English literature and of English literary studies without being able to prise these texts away from the ideological implication within nationalist and imperialist discourse?'[57] Perhaps one step towards attempting the monumental and perhaps impossible task of disentangling these texts from imperialist discourse, I have argued, is to attempt not only to extricate the eighteenth century from the dominant discourses of nineteenth-century colonialism, but also to encourage twenty-first-century readers to consider cross-theoretical approaches that require their own terms and that draw on but also differ from theories of transculturation, *métissage*, *mestizaje*, or hybridity which lend themselves to romanticizing and elide power differentials. If 'Orientals' and '*Blacks* so called' sometimes share the 'romance of the residual', the magnificently horrific and the sublime, and even on occasion the abject, the two discourses also diverge to merge again in ways that postcolonial studies has largely ignored.[58] In sum, I have suggested that we might become more alert to the ties between slavery imposed by Eastern despots and the Atlantic slave trade; to the manipulation of abolitionist impulses to advance imperialism in India and other Eastern territories; to the assumptions regarding the temporal distancing in play in parts of Africa and Asia; and especially to the cultural, geographical, and literary terrain that does not fit the expected critical categories. In recognizing that the eighteenth century may provide not only more pliable terms and languages than the nineteenth or the twentieth centuries, but also moments of interconnection, we need not lapse into nostalgia. My reading of several representative texts argues that Orientalist and abolitionist discourses arise in marked relation to each other, and that—if I may be permitted a relatively large claim suggested by this modest amount of evidence—Orientalist discourse in England becomes more coherent and legible when the British slave trade ends and the focus moves away from African slaves as abject persons. Sub-Saharan Africans

---

[57] Suvir Kaul, 'Provincials and Tropicopolitans: Eighteenth-Century Literary Studies and the Un-Making of "Great Britain"', *Diaspora*, 9/3 (2000), 421–37.

[58] Madhu Dubey, 'Racial Difference in Postmodern Theory', drawing on Cornel West's memorable phrase 'ragged edges of the Real', speaks of 'the romance of the residual that characterizes contemporary approaches to African-American experience in the postmodern era'.

become more clearly recognizable as prototypical subjects of slavery through the process necessary to identify them as eligible for freedom, a process that also, ironically, increasingly racializes them. Locating and naming a racially inflected sub-Saharan African black contributes to enabling a certain kind of Oriental 'so-called' to cohere in the cultural imagination. Recognizing these terrains that 'Orientals' and '*Blacks* so called' traverse in the eighteenth century may begin to modulate the cognitive and spatial structures by which we make sense of the literary history of British attitudes towards the East, and of the history of blackness, before the turn into the nineteenth century.

5

Orientalism and the Permanent Fix of War

Siraj Ahmed

Scholars of eighteenth-century British Orientalism have often taken issue with Edward Said's sweeping generalization that the scholarly discipline of Orientalism made the Orient available for rule.[1] Looking further back than Said did, at a period to which he only alluded but which nonetheless constitutes the first coincidence of Oriental studies and colonial rule, these scholars emphasize the extraordinary respect that the East India Company's initial generation of Orientalists evinced for the native cultures they studied.

I would like to thank the editors, Daniel Carey and Lynn Festa, for their comments on this essay, which improved it immeasurably.

[1] See e.g. A. L. Macfie, *Orientalism* (New York: Longman, 2002), 57–8: 'the accusation that the British orientalists concerned were "orientalist," in the critical sense . . . cannot for the most part be sustained . . . As children of the eighteenth-century Enlightenment, . . . they were inclined to believe that man, though culturally different, was basically the same everywhere. . . . Rather, many Orientalists formed enduring relations with Indians, in particular members of the Bengali intelligentsia. . . . Were such men . . . afflicted by the narrow racialism, nationalism and paro-chialism attributed to them by the critics of orientalism? It would seem improbable.' For J. J. Clarke, *Oriental Enlightenment: The Encounter between Asian and Western Thought* (London: Routledge, 1997), 26, 'The Saidian mode of explanation . . . is . . . too broad because, even if we allow for its cogency within the "high" colonial period of roughly 1800 to 1950, it becomes fragile when stretched beyond those limits.' According to John M. MacKenzie, *Orientalism: History, Theory, and*

Their explicit premises—that India and Europe were part of a common civilization whose roots stretched to the furthest reaches of antiquity; that Hindu theology was in many respects superior to Christian practice; and that the Company should base colonial law on native jurisprudence—do not easily fit Said's model, in which Orientalism silences the Orient, enabling colonial rule to undertake 'projects that involved but were never directly responsible to the native inhabitants' and to claim, subsequently, that Europe therefore 'made the Orient what it was now'.[2] The Company's early Orientalists confound our received ideas about 'the imperial project', suggesting that eighteenth-century British India contained possibilities different from those of the centuries that followed, whose peculiar histories have determined our theories of empire. In short, Said's argument and the voluminous body of scholarly work it has spawned appear simply not to apply to the eighteenth century.

the Arts (Manchester: Manchester University Press, 1995), 26, 'the description applied to the activities of a group of eighteenth-century scholars who sought to rediscover the languages, arts, and laws of India comes to be identified with an ideological faction constituted of their sworn enemies.... Nothing could better illustrate the problems of Said's conception of a continuous oriental discourse.' See also David Smith, 'Orientalism and Hinduism', in Gavid Flood (ed.), *The Blackwell Companion to Hinduism* (Oxford: Blackwell, 2003): 'This perverse sleight-of-hand [by Said] magics away into thin air the editions, translations, and dictionaries of the true and original Orientalists who devoted their lives to understanding the meaning of instances of Oriental culture and civilization' (p. 46). Smith adds, 'Orientalist indologists... were not "making a career of the East"... the goal... was purely intellectual' (p. 60). See also J. L. Brockington, 'Warren Hastings and Orientalism', in Geoffrey Carnall and Colin Nicholson (eds), *The Impeachment of Warren Hastings* (Edinburgh: Edinburgh University Press, 1989), 91–108; S. N. Mukherjee, 'European Jones and Asiatic Pandits', *Journal of the Asiatic Society*, 27/1 (1985), 43–58; P. J. Marshall and Glyndwr Williams, *The Great Map of Mankind: British Perceptions of the World in the Age of Enlightenment* (London: Dent, 1982), 156–7; and David Kopf, 'The Historiography of British Orientalism, 1772–1992', in Garland Cannon and Kevin R. Brine (eds), *Objects of Enquiry: The Life, Contributions, and Influences of Sir William Jones (1746–1794)* (New York: New York University Press, 1995), 141–60. See Carol Breckenridge and Peter van der Veer (eds), *Orientalism and the Postcolonial Predicament: Perspectives on South Asia* (Philadelphia: University of Pennsylvania Press, 1993) for essays that treat or touch on eighteenth-century British colonial Orientalism, generally sympathetic to but not completely in agreement with *Orientalism*. The essay by David Ludden, 'Orientalist Empiricism: Transformations of Colonial Knowledge', in Breckenridge and van der Veer (eds), *Orientalism and the Postcolonial Predicament*, 251–2, criticizes the lack of specificity in Said's use of the term 'Orientalism'.

[2] Edward Said, *Orientalism* (New York: Vintage, 1978), 94 and 221.

If we want, then, to reconsider the initial relationship between Oriental-ism and colonial rule, we need to return to the 1772 'Plan for the Admin-istration of Justice' by Warren Hastings, Governor of Bengal, which Parliament would eventually enact as the Administration of Justice Regula-tion of 1781.[3] During its sessions of 1772, Parliament broached the question of what form the East India Company's nascent sovereignty in Bengal should take, because the Company had, it appeared, already failed so badly in its primary sovereign obligation—to manage the collection of property rent—that it had precipitated a famine in which an estimated one-third of Bengal's native population had starved to death and which threw the Company into deep financial crisis.[4] Hastings formulated his 'Plan' to pre-empt parliamen-tary control: the plan insisted that only a state modelled on India's ancient traditions could protect native rights. Hence, revenue appropriation was at the origins of colonial Orientalism: it was Hastings's attempt to legitimize the Company's methods of revenue appropriation by making it refer to native law that first turned select Company servants into Orientalists who needed to master the prestige languages—Sanskrit and Persian in particular—in which the law was written.[5]

The most influential of these Orientalists was Sir William Jones (1746–1794), arguably the most commanding scholar whom Oriental studies has yet produced, the master of more languages and the supposed origin of more tendencies and even disciplines in the comparative study of culture than there is space here to name.[6] While heading Bengal Presidency's Supreme

[3] G. W. Forrest (ed.), *Selections from the State Papers of the Governors-General of India*, 4 vols (Oxford: B. H. Blackwell; London: Constable & Co. Ltd, 1910–26), ii: *Warren Hastings Documents*; Javed Majeed, *Ungoverned Imaginings: James Mill's 'The History of British India' and Orientalism* (Oxford: Clarendon Press, 1992), 17 and 26; and Michael John Franklin, introduction in William Jones, *Institutes of Hindu Law, or The Ordinances of Menu, According to the Gloss of Cullúca, Comprising the Indian System of Duties, Religious and Civil*, in Michael John Franklin (ed.), *Representing India: Indian Culture and Imperial Control in Eighteenth-Century British Orientalist Discourse*, 9 vols (New York: Routledge, 2000), ix, p. v.

[4] Bernard S. Cohn, 'Law and the Colonial State in History', in June Starr and Jane F. Collier (eds), *History and Power in the Study of Law: New Directions in Legal Anthropology* (Ithaca: Cornell University Press, 1989), 133.

[5] Bernard S. Cohn, 'The Command of Language and the Language of Command', in Ranajit Guha (ed.), *Subaltern Studies IV* (Delhi: Oxford University Press, 1985), 282.

[6] Before he arrived in India, Jones is thought to have already learned Greek, Latin, Hebrew, French, Italian, Spanish, Portuguese, Arabic, Persian, and Chinese; subsequently, he became the second modern European to learn Sanskrit. He applied these linguistic skills in diverse forms, each of which would subsequently be identified as an origin of a distinct discipline or disciplinary

Court during the last decade of his brief life, Jones also managed to compile from native-language originals the monumental codifications—*Al Sirajiyyah: or The Mohamedan Law of Inheritance* (1792), *Institutes of Hindu Law; or, The Ordinances of Menu* (1794), and *A Digest of Hindu Law* (1797)—that provided the historic 1793 Act of Permanent Settlement with its legal architecture.[7] Responding to Parliament's determination in 1784 that Hastings's policy of short-term leases had failed to make colonial property profitable, the Permanent Settlement entitled a native property-owning class to rent fixed in perpetuity. Its stated aim was to encourage the development of agricultural commerce by protecting the rights of native aristocrats, thereby turning them into improving landlords who, supposedly like European aristocrats, would form moral communities with their tenants. Spreading from its colonial origins in Bengal across the empire, the theory of property behind the Permanent

---

method, including (*a*) his six-volume work of literary criticism in Latin, *Poesos Asiaticae Commentariorum* (1774), which analysed numerous Asian literary traditions in the context of Latin, Greek, and Hebrew literature, the precedent for comparative literature; (*b*) *A Persian Grammar* (1771), the model for subsequent grammars of Arabic, Hindi, and Bengali; (*c*) his translation of the classical Arabic poem *The Moallakát* (1783), the precedent for the modern translation of Arabic literature into European languages; (*d*) after he reached India, his essays 'On the Gods of Greece, Italy, and India' (1784) and 'On the Hindus' (1786), the first statement of the Indo-European or Aryan thesis, pioneering the study of the historical connection between Oriental and Occidental religions and cultures (see Frank Manuel, *The Eighteenth Century Confronts the Gods* (Cambridge, Mass.: Harvard University Press, 1959), 114); (*e*) across these works, the modern origin of linguistics, revolutionizing its study on historical, comparative, and structural lines (see Hans Aarsleff, *The Study of Language in England, 1780–1860* (Princeton: Princeton University Press, 1967), 134); and (*f*) his translations from Sanskrit literature and his own poetry in a supposedly Oriental style, the roots of Romanticism. (As M. H. Abrams puts it, 'It was Jones's distinction to be the first writer in England to weave these threads into an explicit and orderly reformulation of the nature and criteria of poetry and the poetic genres.' Abrams, *The Mirror and the Lamp: Romantic Theory and the Critical Tradition* (New York: Oxford University Press, 1953), 87–8.) See Michael John Franklin, introduction in *Sir William Jones: Selected Poetical and Prose Works*, ed. Michael John Franklin (Cardiff: University of Wales Press, 1995), pp. xix, xxiii, xxvi, and headnotes 104–5, 337, 348, 355, and Rosane Rocher, foreword in *Sir William Jones: A Reader*, ed. Satya S. Pachori (New York: Oxford University Press, 1993), 3–7.

[7] Ibid. 10; S. N. Mukherjee, *Sir William Jones: A Study in Eighteenth-Century British Attitudes to India* (Cambridge: Cambridge University Press, 1968), 4 and 132. See Majeed, *Ungoverned Imaginings*, 29. H. T. Colebrooke, Jones's successor on the Supreme Court of Bengal, completed *The Digest* after Jones's death, but according to Franklin, Jones had spent the final six years of his life on it (Franklin, introduction in Jones, *Institutes of Hindu Law*, in Franklin (ed.), *Representing India*, ix, p. xi).

Settlement would subsequently form the ideological basis of the British Empire's progressive claims.[8] It is no coincidence, then, that the Permanent Settlement provided the subject of what is often taken to be the urtext of *Subaltern Studies*, Ranajit Guha's *A Rule of Property for Bengal* (1963). And it was with the Permanent Settlement—whose legitimacy lay wholly in Jones's Islamic and Hindu legal codes—that Orientalism first achieved global significance.

But in stark contrast to eighteenth-century British Orientalism itself, the scholarship about it has generally been unconcerned with the history of colonial property: scholars of eighteenth-century Orientalism have made arguments about its political implications, in other words, without attending to the specific realm of its political efficacy. Those who take issue with *Orientalism* tend to invoke Jones in particular—the embodiment of the deep respect for Indian culture and traditions supposedly characteristic of eighteenth-century British Orientalism—as a counter-example to Said's argument, but without reference to the motives and consequences of his colonial jurisprudence.[9] Ironically, Said also avoided questioning the material relationship of Orientalism to colonial history—but he did so in contrast

[8] C. A. Bayly, *Imperial Meridian: The British Empire and the World, 1780–1830* (New York: Longman, 1989), 155–7.

[9] 'Jones's actions and ideas', Cannon tells us, 'stand for themselves and show that he always resisted any political aspects of his scholarship' (Garland Cannon, *The Life and Mind of Oriental Jones: Sir William Jones, the Father of Modern Linguistics* (Cambridge: Cambridge University Press, 1990), p. xv). Franklin contends that 'Said's definition of Orientalism as "a Western style for dominating, restructuring and having authority over the Orient" proves totally inadequate to describe the work of the Asiatic Society and its president; Jones's Anniversary Discourses have as little in common with Said's notion of Foucauldian discourse as Jones's Orientalism has in common with Eurocentric imperialism.' He continues, '[Jones] had established a cultural link between East and West wherein the colonized appeared in a superior light to the colonizer' (Franklin, introduction in *Sir William Jones: Selected Poetical and Prose Works*, ed. Franklin, pp. xxiii–xiv, and headnote 355); Cannon notes, 'If all colonial European administrators had been like Jones and his most productive followers, the unsavory quality of European political and cultural exploitation might never have developed' (Garland Cannon, 'Oriental Jones: Scholarship, Literature, Multiculturalism, and Humankind', in Cannon and Brine (eds), *Objects of Enquiry*, 48). See also Macfie, *Orientalism*, 58; Robert Irwin, *For Lust of Knowing: The Orientalists and their Enemies* (London: Allen Lane, 2006), 293; and even Gyan Prakash: 'the genuine respect and love for the Orient of William Jones gave way to the cold utilitarian scrutiny of James Mill' (Prakash, 'Writing Post-Orientalist Histories of the Third World: Perspectives from Indian Historiography', *Comparative Studies in Society and History*, 32/2 (1990), 386).

by presupposing that the two terms were effectively identical. For Said, Orientalism and colonial history form what he ingeniously described as 'a *preposterous* transition': that is, what should have come before only came after. Colonialism should have produced Orientalist knowledge, but was according to Said produced by it.[10] For Said, Orientalist discourse is not only prior to colonial praxis, but is precisely *what* was put into practice.[11] Hence, the history of colonial property does not and *cannot* exist in Said's narrative either.[12] When Said alludes to the motive behind Orientalism, he does so generally in terms of an ultimately mysterious 'will to power' or 'will to govern'; in the specific case of Jones's Orientalist scholarship, the will to govern resurfaces in the form of an equally mysterious 'impulse to codify'.[13] To the extent that he provided immaterial explanations of Orientalism, Said shared what he called Orientalism's 'textual attitude'.[14] Said unwittingly drew attention to the reductive quality of his own textualism when he observed, tellingly, that '[o]nce we begin to think of Orientalism as a kind of Western projection onto and will to govern over the Orient, we will encounter few surprises'.[15]

In fact, when we return Orientalism to its original context within the construction of a colonial rule of property, we will find that it still contains an extraordinary capacity to surprise. Indeed, in this context, it forces us out of the aporia that confronts 'postcolonial theory' between the equally forbidden paths of 'textualism' or 'culturalism' on the one hand

[10] Said, *Orientalism* (1978), 96.

[11] By '*preposterous* transition', Said refers in particular to 'the transition from a merely textual apprehension, formulation, or definition of the Orient to the putting all this into practice in the Orient' (ibid. 96).

[12] While Said acknowledged Jones as Orientalism's 'undisputed founder' (ibid. 78), it is not the history of British India, but rather the moment of Napoleonic Egypt that provides the origin and serves as the exemplary type of Said's model of colonial Orientalism. For Said, Jones's colonial career does not exist in any material sense: he dates the onset of the Orient being 'made and remade' by Europe to Napoleon's 1798 invasion of Egypt, not the previous decades of East India Company rule in India (Said, *Orientalism* (25th anniversary edn, New York: Vintage, 2003), p. xvii). And he locates the origin of this invasion in turn, remarkably, in Napoleon's adolescent *reading* of Orientalist histories, which supposedly 'proposed' to him 'the idea of reconquering Egypt as a new Alexander' (*Orientalism* (1978), 80).

[13] Said, *Orientalism* (1978), 94 and 78.

[14] Ibid. 92–3.

[15] Ibid. 94.

and 'economism' on the other.[16] To make sense of eighteenth-century British Orientalism, we will need to leave behind not only textual attitudes of all stripes, but also the hoary materialism that sees 'the logic of capital' behind all things. Here, remarkably, such materialism fails to explain even the establishment of modern property relations.

Eighteenth-century British Orientalism's chief aim and achievement was to provide a textual basis for Indian law, property law in particular—indeed in a form that would become absolutely seminal for the subsequent development of Indian history *and* historiography.[17] In doing so, Orientalism helped the East India Company simplify India's otherwise profoundly complicated, heterotopic, and fluid system of property ownership and sovereignty. In other words, Orientalism used its putative authority on all subjects Indian to legitimize the Company's attempts to fix, to control, and so to centralize revenue appropriation—which the Permanent Settlement brought to logical culmination. But though it established modern property relations in Bengal, the Permanent Settlement nonetheless famously *failed* to improve colonial property; the Bengali countryside became in fact only *less* productive after the Permanent Settlement. In itself, then, the logic of capital does not explain the Permanent Settlement or Orientalism's involvement in it; to explain this, we must look elsewhere.

What is rarely acknowledged is that the Permanent Settlement succeeded according to a different logic. When it fixed Bengali rent, the Permanent Settlement gave the East India Company—if not what it should have wanted in the long term, a more productive economy—what it absolutely demanded in the short term, a *fixed* source of capital that would serve as collateral in global financial networks. The Permanent Settlement enabled the Company to use debt to finance its conquest economy, whose cost always exceeded its revenue and hence bankrupted it. But in relying on

[16] See Sumit Sarkar, 'The Decline of the Subaltern in *Subaltern Studies*', in Sumit Sarkar (ed.), *Writing Social History* (Delhi: Oxford University Press, 1997), 84, and Nicholas Dirks, 'From Little King to Landlord: Colonial Discourse and Colonial Rule', in Nicholas Dirks (ed.), *Colonialism and Culture* (Ann Arbor: University of Michigan Press, 1992), 175 for criticisms of the former; and Ranajit Guha, preface and 'On Some Aspects of the Historiography of Colonial India', in Ranajit Guha (ed.), *Subaltern Studies I* (Delhi: Oxford University Press, 1982), pp. vii and 1, and Gyan Prakash, 'Postcolonial Criticism and Indian Historiography', *Social Text*, 31–2 (1992), 13 for criticisms of the latter.

[17] Cohn, 'Law and the Colonial State', esp. 146, 147, and 150.

debt-financing to pay for its wars and war-making capacity, the Company merely adopted the military-fiscal logic that already shaped European states, whose domestic productivity was generally insufficient for the unprecedented costs of modern warfare.[18] We could say, then, that when the Permanent Settlement fixed Bengal within a system of property relations that was less productive but more capable of underwriting war than pre-colonial property had been, it brought to the colony not a failed version of modernity, but rather its still largely undisclosed essence. Regardless, it is only this military-fiscal logic—states, concerned above all to augment their war-making capacity, redirecting profit ultimately *not* towards productive re-investment, but rather towards the cost of war—that can explain how colonial rule could afford to ruin native economies and, by extension, how ruined colonial and postcolonial economies are not aberrations within, but in fact constitutive of modernity's trajectory.

So when it helped make Indian history and law textual, eighteenth-century Orientalism did not reflect either the abstract imperatives of the supposed Enlightenment will to govern nor the material ones of capital accumulation. This Orientalism instead articulated the political economy of modern war. As we shall see, such an economy is in diametric opposition not only to agricultural improvement, but also to the reconstruction of native traditions. Hence, *pace* those who claim that it was more conciliatory than Said gave it credit for, eighteenth-century British Orientalism was in fact instrumental—if anything only more directly than Said was in a position to appreciate—in the historical rupture that eighteenth-century colonial rule wrought. The original function of colonial Orientalism—the most troubling and perhaps precisely for that reason the most overlooked—was to facilitate the construction of a radically different form of property ownership whose end was not to encourage capitalism, but rather to make possible a political economy founded in war.

The first part of this essay explores Orientalism's little-studied precolonial genealogy—a different history that is particularly hard for us to appreciate in the wake of Said's work—in which Orientalism formed an essential, if admittedly bizarre, chapter in the Enlightenment's ongoing critique of

---

[18] See P. J. Cain and A. G. Hopkins, *British Imperialism, 1688–2000* (London: Longman, 2002), 73 f. on 'the evolution of the military-fiscal state'.

governmental reason. In particular, Orientalism promised to recover the ancient esoteric thought that was understood to be the antithesis of modern political degeneration. As we shall see, it was precisely Orientalism's supposed potential to reverse the slide towards despotism that would empower early colonial Orientalism. Where the widespread metropolitan criticism of the Company (aired during Parliament's investigations of the Company's fiscal mismanagement during not only 1772–3 but also 1767–8) held that the property relations in force in its territories were essentially despotic, colonial Orientalism under Hastings promised instead to re-establish property on ancient Indian traditions that were supposed to be naturally anti-despotic.

The second part notes that by the 1790s, when Jones's Orientalist publications became a Europe-wide phenomenon, intellectuals across the Continent believed that Jones had realized Orientalism's potential—that is, to rediscover an ancient esotericism that could interrupt the main lines of European philosophical and literary development. Not coincidentally, Jones claimed that the Orientalist jurisprudence that underwrote the Permanent Settlement unified an ancient, practically universal, mythic system with modern political economy. By doing so, he ensured that the Permanent Settlement could serve, like the Company's earlier rules of property but more effectively, as a defence against metropolitan accusations of colonial despotism.

The third part of the essay then returns to the origins of colonial rule to reconsider more carefully the first Company Orientalists' actual proposals in regard to colonial property. These proposals betray the Orientalist premise that the Company must base property on native traditions. The structures of property that the first Orientalists envisioned were aligned neither with ancient traditions nor with capitalist production, but on the contrary with the Company's military-fiscal needs. Here, the function of Orientalism will begin to become clear: it helped fix a rule of property that could turn territorial revenue towards the costs of war and it buried that rule so deeply in what appeared to be India's ancient traditions that its modern logic was no longer visible.

The fourth and final part of the essay argues that we need to see the Permanent Settlement as the cutting edge of this logic—not, as we have conventionally seen it, as an addendum to capitalist modernity. It was the fiscal imperatives of modern war that Jones's juridical scholarship enshrouded in a mystified past for which European intellectuals had long pined. The essay's overarching argument is that it is only within the structure of military-fiscalism that late eighteenth-century colonial Orientalism regains its historical significance. When we replace Orientalism within this original logic and structure—which in fact remain with us now more powerfully than ever—we will see that the aims of the Enlightenment, of Said's life-work, and of contemporary postcolonial studies come suddenly into a startling convergence around their shared desire to exile themselves from the modern state-form, an alignment that is particularly compelling now.

I Precolonial and early colonial Orientalism

While Orientalism had come to serve colonial rule with Hastings's plan, its own history was in fact older. In its precolonial genealogy, Orientalism was not yet the instrument of historical progress and of the expansion of the European state-form that it would subsequently become; it was on the contrary above all a critique of 'history' as such and of European history in particular. Orientalism's roots in fact lie in the debate between the Christian Church and its deist critics that had been under way since the late seventeenth century and which aimed to settle, once and for all, the original form of natural reason.[19] The official Christian line was that Judaism was the origin of religion as such and hence the cradle of civilization. In other words, all religious practice outside the Judaeo-Christian tradition was a corrupt version of that tradition, and Hinduism merely a particularly bizarre perversion of it. Hence in its increasingly global practice of conversion, the Christian Church could claim that its aim was merely to bring lapsed Jews back into the Judaeo-Christian fold. In diametric opposition, the deists argued that it was not religions outside the Judaeo-Christian tradition that were corruptions of it, but rather the reverse: it was only the belated rise of a Hebraic priestly caste—which arrogated all religious authority to itself, turned what had once been an original 'natural religion' into esoteric and mysterious rites it alone controlled, and hence colluded with the rise of despotism—that was responsible for the Judaeo-Christian tradition. In deism, the Enlightenment

---

[19] For thorough discussions of this debate, see Peter Byrne, *Natural Religion and the Nature of Religion: The Legacy of Deism* (New York: Routledge, 1989); and P. J. Marshall (ed.), *The British Discovery of Hinduism in the Eighteenth Century* (Cambridge: Cambridge University Press, 1970).

offered the most radical disavowal of European history imaginable, since deism claimed that the very origin and essence of European development were corrupt.

But to prove that the Judaeo-Christian tradition was merely a corruption of a precedent natural religion, the deists needed evidence of that religion.[20] Once the East India Company gained de facto sovereignty over Bengal in the middle of the eighteenth century, Hinduism became the deists' primary weapon in their attack on the Christian Church's religious authority.[21] The original context of colonial Orientalism, then, was a practically all-encompassing drive to recover textual versions of the original form of natural reason as an antidote to the degeneration that now characterized European and world history. From Orientalism's perspective, if history was not to surrender to despotism altogether, it had little choice but to turn (back) to Hinduism.

Like most of the Company Orientalists who followed in their immediate wake, the two earliest Company servants to enter the field of Orientalism, J. Z. Holwell and Alexander Dow, were indeed deists.[22] Reviewed by major British periodicals and translated into multiple languages, the works within which their Orientalist research was included, *Interesting Historical Events, Relative to the Provinces of Bengal, and the Empire of Indostan* and *The History of Hindostan* respectively, attracted Europe-wide readerships far greater than previous Orientalist works had acquired, in large part because they appeared to resolve the long-standing argument between Christianity and deism.[23]

---

[20] Byrne, *Natural Religion and the Nature of Religion*, 86–7.

[21] Marshall, *The British Discovery of Hinduism*, 3. See also Raymond Schwab, *Oriental Renaissance: Europe's Rediscovery of India and the East, 1680–1880* (New York: Columbia University Press, 1984), 47.

[22] See Rosane Rocher, 'British Orientalism in the Eighteenth Century: The Dialectic of Knowledge and Government', in Breckenridge and van der Veer (eds), *Orientalism and the Postcolonial Predicament*, 219.

[23] Marshall, *The British Discovery of Hinduism*, 5. The second volume of Holwell's *Interesting Historical Events, Relative to the Provinces of Bengal, and the Empire of Indostan* (London, 1765–71) contains extracts from and analysis of texts that Holwell claims are *vedas*. Dow's *History of Hindostan*, 2 vols (London, 1st edn., 1768; 2nd, rev. edn., 1770) contains his 'Dissertation concerning the Customs, Manners, Religion and Philosophy of the Hindoos', which includes, according to Dow, two extracts from the *Vedanta* school of Hindu philosophy, one from the *Nyaya*, and a fourth from the *Dharma Sastras*. (A third volume of *The History of Hindostan* was published in 1772.) Referring to the first Company servants to write about India after the establishment of colonialism, Ranajit Guha notes: 'We owe the beginnings of Indological studies to this body of literature, with all its curious mixture of the erudite and the polemical, which still must be recognized as being among

Moses Mendelssohn, for one, commented with strange confidence that Holwell's texts displayed a capacity 'mit den Augen eines eingeborenen Braminen zu sehen' ('to see through the eyes of a native Brahmin').[24] Mendelssohn's epithet has the virtue at least of capturing Holwell's and Dow's essential ambition precisely: to convince a European readership that they saw with the eyes of the natural-born Brahman, that they had recovered natural reason before its corruption at the hands of political history, and hence that they had reproduced it textually.

Accordingly, prefiguring the professional Orientalists who would follow immediately in their wake, Holwell and Dow each claim to be the first European to have returned to civilization's 'fountainhead'—a term that, we shall see, becomes increasingly resonant as the period under study here develops—thereby making Hinduism's now esoteric truths once again public. Holwell writes: 'it is . . . to be regretted, that in place of drinking at the fountain head, [previous authors] have swallowed the muddy streams which flowed from [corrupt commentaries on the *vedas*]'.[25] Similarly, Dow comments: 'They took their accounts from any common Brahmin, with whom they chanced to meet, and never had the curiosity or industry to go to the fountain head'.[26] If the term 'fountainhead' refers generally to the object of a quest that possesses the power to rejuvenate, here it refers particularly to a set of supposedly ancient Hindu scriptures that articulate the original form of natural reason. The term implies that Europeans must study these

---

the first intellectual attempts in modern times to explore the East.' See *A Rule of Property for Bengal: An Essay on the Idea of Permanent Settlement* (1963; Durham, NC: Duke University Press, 1996), 25. Both Holwell and Dow were read widely in Europe. Holwell's *Interesting Historical Events* was translated into German in 1767 and into French in 1768, while Dow's *History of Hindostan* was published in French in 1769, with an expanded Swiss edition in 1771.

[24] Quoted in John Michael Franklin, introduction in John Zephaniah Holwell, *Interesting Historical Events, Relative to the Provinces of Bengal, and the Empire of Indostan Parts I and II*, in Franklin (ed.), *Representing India*, i, p. xii.

[25] John Zephaniah Holwell, *Interesting Historical Events, Relative to the Provinces of Bengal, and the Empire of Indostan. With A Seasonable Hint and Perswasive To the Honourable The Court of Directors of the East India Company. As Also The Mythology and Cosmogony, Fasts and Festivals of the Gentoo's, followers of the Shastah. And A Dissertation on the Metempsychosis, commonly, though erroneously, called the Pythagorean Doctrine*, 3 vols (London, 1765–71), ii, 63.

[26] Alexander Dow, *The History of Hindostan, second revised, corrected and enlarged edition with a prefix on Ancient India based on Sanskrit Writings, translated from Persian*, 3 vols (London, 1770–2; repr. New Delhi: Today & Tomorrow's Printers & Publishers, 1973), i, p. lxxiii.

scriptures if they are to reverse the process of decay that has shaped their history.[27] The fountainhead alone stems from the time that existed before, and against, the historical rise of despotic power.[28]

Holwell and Dow both published their Orientalist studies during the 1767–8 parliamentary hearings that investigated the fiscal crisis that had beset the East India Company immediately on its assumption of de facto sovereignty in Bengal. Reluctant before Hastings's 1772 'Plan' to formulate its own policy of property management, the Company had to an extent merely grafted itself on to a pre-existing Mughal economy.[29] Typical of tributary systems, the ground rent that peasants paid in this economy trickled up through many layers of sovereignty, from themselves through the landlords' agents to regional sovereigns and ultimately to the Mughal emperor—the primary producer's labour supporting, then, an elaborately shared system of sovereignty. From the perspective of British property, where enclosure had greatly simplified the structure of property ownership, the multiple expropriations to which Indian peasants were subject appeared to be corrupt.[30] Hence Company officials blamed its fiscal crisis on the nature of 'Asiatic despotism'.

Both Holwell and Dow were in fact centrally involved in these debates. Before Parliament in 1767, Holwell argued that the Company must dispossess Bengali landlords—who he claimed expropriated a disproportionate share of the agricultural surplus, thereby simultaneously impoverishing peasants and the Company—and auction their property to the highest bidder.[31] But Holwell's position on colonial property was far from merely theoretical. While still in Bengal, he had been Calcutta's Chief Magistrate.[32] In 1759, when in the aftermath of the Battle of Plassey the Company had first wrested Bengali sovereignty from the Nawab, it faced the question of how it would manage the exceedingly complex function of collecting rent from the

[27] Byrne, *Natural Religion and the Nature of Religion*, 68.

[28] When Herder argued that India was the cradle of humanity, he cited Holwell as his source (Franklin, introduction in Holwell, *Interesting Historical Events*, in Franklin (ed.), *Representing India*, i, p. xvii).

[29] Robert Travers, 'Ideology and British Expansion in Bengal, 1757–72', *Journal of Imperial and Commonwealth History*, 33/1 (2005), 15.

[30] Ibid. 16.

[31] Ibid. 15; Robert Travers, ' "The Real Value of the Lands": The Nawabs, the British and the Land Tax in Bengal', *Modern Asian Studies*, 38/3 (2004), 525.

[32] Franklin, introduction in Holwell, *Interesting Historical Events*, in Franklin (ed.), *Representing India*, i, p. xiii.

expansive territories it had recently acquired, which were larger than England. The options included assuming the function itself or auctioning it to, in effect, speculative capitalists. Under Holwell's influence, the Company chose the latter; not coincidentally, Holwell then became one of the original speculative capitalists who bought the rights to collect rent from its territories.[33] After speculating on Bengali rent, Holwell himself served as Governor of Bengal (1760).[34] In *India Tracts* (1764), he would subsequently argue that a 'chain of frauds runs through the revenues of the whole [Mughal] empire' and that if the Company reformed its entire rule of property in line with his proposals 'the Emperor would regularly receive more than double what these provinces ever produced him, and that the East India Company would become, in a short time, the richest body of subjects in the world'.[35]

Dow's position was, on the other hand, strictly opposed to Holwell's. While also considering Bengal's problem to be Asiatic despotism, Dow insisted that it was the Company's own servants in their private expropriation of the Company's monopoly trading privileges and the Company itself in its 'ruinous policy of farming out the lands annually' that exemplified it.[36] He noted that under Nawabi rule, '[c]ommerce, manufactures, and agriculture, were encouraged; for it was not then the maxim to take honey, by destroying the swarm'.[37] In contrast, Company servants '[w]ith a peculiar want of foresight . . . began to drain the reservoir without turning it into any stream to prevent it from being exhausted'.[38] Guha notes that Dow's analysis of the Company's 'drain' of Bengal's wealth has precedence by a full century over Romesh Chandra Dutt's much more famous one in *The Cambridge Economic History of India*.[39] Regarding Bengal's

---

[33] Subhas Chandra Mukhopadhyay, *The Agrarian Policy of the British in Bengal: The Formative Period, 1698–1772* (Allahabad: Chugh Publications, 1987), 26–7.

[34] Franklin, introduction in Holwell, *Interesting Historical Events*, in Franklin (ed.), *Representing India*, i, p. xiii.

[35] Quoted in Travers, 'Ideology and British Expansion in Bengal', 15.

[36] Ibid. 16. The quotation, from *The History of Hindostan*, iii, p. xcv, is cited by Guha, *A Rule of Property for Bengal*, 34; see also *The History of Hindostan*, iii, pp. xcii–xcix.

[37] Quoted in John Michael Franklin, introduction in Alexander Dow, *The History of Hindostan translated from the Persian*, in Franklin (ed.), *Representing India*, ii, p. viii (the quotation is from *The History of Hindostan*, iii (1772), p. lxviii).

[38] Quoted ibid. xi.

[39] Guha, *A Rule of Property for Bengal*, 24 and 27. See also the discussion in Franklin, introduction in Dow, *The History of Hindostan*, in Franklin (ed.), *Representing India*, ii, p. xi.

suddenly decreasing population and productivity, Dow claims, 'We may date the commencement of decline from the day on which Bengal fell under the dominion of foreigners; who were more anxious to improve the present moment to their own emolument, than, by providing against waste, to secure permanent advantage to the British nation.'[40] In response to the Company's method of auctioning its land rents to the highest bidder, thereby rendering colonial property radically unstable, Dow offered a detailed plan for a different colonial rule of property, beginning with the proposal that the Company fix the rent of 'all the lands in Bengal and Behar, in perpetuity'.[41] Dow's idea of a colonial rule of property founded on rent fixed in perpetuity to a great extent prefigured the Permanent Settlement, which would follow two decades later.

Holwell's and Dow's analyses of the colonial rule of property, then, were not only contemporaneous with their Orientalist publications, but indeed inflect their function. They both presupposed that colonial rule gains legitimacy to the extent that it *appears* to emerge out of the Orientalist study of native traditions, a premise that would of course be a constant throughout the subsequent period studied in this essay. Dow offered *The History of Hindostan*, his translation of a Persian-language narrative of the rise and decline of ancient and medieval Indian empires, to the British as an object lesson in the fate of despots: 'The history now given to the public, presents us with a striking picture of the deplorable condition of a people subjected to arbitrary sway; and of the instability of empire itself, when it is founded neither upon laws, nor upon the opinions and attachments of mankind.'[42] In his *Interesting Historical Events, Relative to the Provinces of Bengal, and the Empire of Indostan*, Holwell likewise called on the Company to replace Asiatic despotism with a sovereign power organically linked to its subject population: 'the [Hindus]... now labouring under *Mahometan* tyranny, [are] fated I hope, soon to feel the blessings of a mild *British* government'.[43]

Holwell's and Dow's works not only criticized the Company, but also recognized, presciently, that the Company's sovereign legitimacy would

---

[40] Dow, *The History of Hindostan*, iii, p. lxxvii.
[41] Ibid., p. cxix.   [42] Ibid., i, p. xi.
[43] Holwell, *Interesting Historical Events... Part 1*, 2nd ed. (London, 1766), 5n.

depend in the future on Orientalism.[44] And to the extent that they imagined a colonial rule legitimized by Orientalism, Holwell and Dow also activated Orientalism's prior genealogy, in which India's ancient esoteric traditions were supposed to contain an antidote to the despotism that had come to shape European and Indian history alike. Hence, within this vision, if the conqueror is to resist despotism, he has little choice but to turn—counter-intuitively for us—towards Orientalism. Explaining the importance of Orientalism, Dow comments: 'Posterity will perhaps...find fault with the British for not investigating the learning and religious opinions, which prevail in those countries in Asia, into which either their commerce or their arms have penetrated.'[45] Dow implies that without Orientalism, the only logic that can underpin colonial rule is 'commerce' and 'arms'; with it, colonial rule activated another history altogether.

Accordingly, Hastings forwarded instalments of the first Orientalist work that his 1772 'Plan' spawned—Nathaniel Brassey Halhed's *A Code of Gentoo Laws* (1776)—to London even before it was complete and sponsored its publication in London afterwards.[46] Where metropolitan criticism argued that, un-leashed from any sovereign principle other than the dubious one the Company embodied, its servants had monopolized and hence ruined previ-ously flourishing trading networks, Hastings claimed that the Orientalists' scrupulous regard for Indian civilization was precisely what placed a limit on the Company's potentially degenerative tendencies:

the service has at no period more abounded with men of cultivated talents, of capacity for business, and liberal knowledge; qualities which reflect the greater lustre on their possessors, by having been the fruit of long and laboured application, at a season of life, and with a licence of conduct, more apt to produce dissipation than excite the desire of improvement.[47]

---

[44] Franklin, introduction in Holwell, *The History of Hindostan*, in Franklin (ed.), *Representing India*, i, p. xiii; Thomas Trautmann, *Aryans and British India* (Berkeley: University of California Press, 1997), 30–7.

[45] Dow, *The History of Hindostan*, i, p. xix.

[46] Rocher, 'British Orientalism in the Eighteenth Century', 224; Franklin, introduction in Nathaniel Brassey Halhed, *A Code of Gentoo Laws, or, Ordinations of the Pundits*, in Franklin (ed.), *Representing India*, iv, p. vii. See also Marilyn Butler, 'Orientalism', in David Pirie (ed.), *The Romantic Period* (New York: Penguin, 1994), 403.

[47] The quotation comes from a letter to the Chairman of the Company's directors that served also as the foreword to the London edition of Wilkins's *Bhagvat-Geeta*: Warren Hastings, 'Letter to Nathaniel Smith, from *The Bhagvat-Geeta*', in Marshall (ed.), *The British Discovery of Hinduism in the Eighteenth Century*, 189.

Hastings sponsored the dual publication in Calcutta and London not only of the *Code* but also of Charles Wilkins's translation of the *Bhagavad Gita*—exemplary of Hindu esoteric knowledge, but irrelevant to the Company's administrative exigencies. In doing so, he advertised the claim that the Company had initiated a new relationship in India between sovereignty and the natives' mysteries, making them once again public.[48] In his foreword to the *Bhagvat-Geeta* (1785), Hastings echoed Dow, arguing that in its Orientalist studies the Company would leave a legacy, simultaneously political and literary, much more valuable than the wealth it incidentally extracted from its colonies:

Every instance which brings [the natives'] real character home to observation will impress us with a more generous sense of feeling for their natural rights.... But such instances can only be obtained in their writings: and these will survive when the British dominion in India shall have long ceased to exist, and when the sources which it once yielded of wealth and power are lost to remembrance.[49]

At its origins, Orientalism had a profoundly critical attitude towards European history, a feature that is, though typical of the Enlightenment in general, no longer consistent with our received ideas about Orientalism. It was, ironically, precisely this attitude that allowed it to serve the East India Company: we must note that the defence of eighteenth-century British colonial rule by reference to its Oriental studies, which persists to this day, originated with the East India Company itself, in response to the widespread metropolitan charge that colonial rule was already a profoundly degenerative force. For Orientalism's fundamental critique of European history in no sense amounted to a genuine openness to Indian history. On the contrary, for Orientalism the value of that history was wholly textual, in scripture

---

[48] Rocher, 'British Orientalism in the Eighteenth Century', 228; Brockington, 'Warren Hastings and Orientalism', 94.

[49] Hastings, 'Letter to Nathaniel Smith', 189. The 1790s metropolitan press adopted Hastings's and Hamilton's rhetoric: 'After the contingent circumstances to which we owe our present preponderance in that country shall have ceased to operate, and the channels of Indian knowledge and Indian wealth shall have again become impervious to the western world, the Asiatic Researches will furnish a proof to our posterity, that the acquisition of the latter did not absorb the attention of their countrymen to the exclusion of the former; and that the English laws and English government, in those distant regions, have sometimes been administered by men of extensive capacity, erudition, and application' (*Monthly Review* (1797), 408; quoted by Trautmann, *Aryans and British India*, 24–5).

whose origins supposedly lay outside despotism. Orientalism's textual biases—that contemporary Indian culture was corrupt, that its truths lay wholly in ancient scriptures, and hence that ancient scriptures had priority over social practice—coincided only too neatly with the exigencies of colonial rule and enabled Orientalism to transform itself from Europe's tireless critic to empire's faultless servant. The scholarly discipline that deists had devised within Europe as a form of critique was instead quickly reinvented by Orientalists in the colony as a form of propaganda. While Orientalism considered European politics and history despotic in essence, it advertised their colonial projection, remarkably, as despotism's very *antithesis*. Orientalism claimed to found an anti-despotic colonial rule, making religious mysteries effectively the basis of state and property. We could say, in other words, that Orientalism enabled the Company to claim that it had brought myth and history—which are of course categorically disjunct—paradoxically together, making possible an altogether different world history, one which would become associated with the Orientalist work of Sir William Jones.

II Jones and mythic law

Soon after arriving in Bengal, Jones echoed the claim—of having reached the Hindu fountainhead—that both Holwell and Dow had already made almost two decades before. Introducing himself in the 'Hymn to Surya' (1786) as one of the first Europeans to have learned Sanskrit, he described it as the 'celestial tongue' that 'Draws orient knowledge from its fountains pure'.[50] Jones agreed with Holwell and Dow that ancient Hinduism contained manifestations of the original form of natural reason.[51] In his seminal essay 'On the

---

[50] *Sir William Jones: Selected Poetical and Prose Works*, ed. Franklin, 152. See the discussion of the idea of the fountainhead in Majeed, *Ungoverned Imaginings*, 37–8.

[51] But Jones disagreed with Holwell that Hinduism necessarily predated Judaism. He was in fact concerned to use 'Orientalist research into India's ancient past to provide a . . . "scientific" substantiation of the Mosaic account of creation as it appears in the Book of Genesis'. Michael Dodson, *Orientalism, Empire, and National Culture: India, 1770–1880* (New York: Palgrave Macmillan, 2007), 28.

Gods of Greece, Italy, and India' (1788), he claimed that 'we may infer a general union or affinity between the most distinguished inhabitants of the primitive world, at the time when they deviated, as they did too early deviate, from the rational adoration of the only true God'. He claimed moreover that this original civilization had the most global influence imaginable: 'we shall, perhaps, agree...that Egyptians, Indians, Greeks and Italians, proceeded originally from one central place, and that the same people carried their religion and sciences into China and Japan: may we not add, even to Mexico and Peru?'[52] Reversing centuries of Islamic tyranny and millennia of Brahman priestcraft, Jones's supposed recovery of the pure source of 'orient knowledge' claimed to make once again public in both India and Europe the spiritually integrated reason that was supposedly natural to 'prehistoric' humanity (in Hegel's sense).

Much of the Romantic generation accepted Jones's claims without hesitation. Offering the possibility of a different world-historical origin, Jones's Orientalism authorized their ambition to create a radically new aesthetic. His 1789 translation of Kalidasa's Sanskrit play *Sakuntala*, dating from about the fourth century, heralded what Raymond Schwab refers to in *Oriental Renaissance* as 'A *Sakuntala* Era'.[53] For Herder, it was further proof that India was humanity's fatherland.[54] Herder recommended it to Goethe, who in turn passed his love of it down to Schiller.[55] Contemporary scholars have hailed Jones's 'A Hymn to Náráyana' and the 'argument' that prefaces it in particular as seminal for the subsequent history of Romanticism.[56]

---

[52] Sir William Jones, 'On the Gods of Greece, Italy, and India', *Asiatick Researches*, i (Calcutta, 1788), ch. 9.

[53] Schwab, *Oriental Renaissance*, 57–64; John Michael Franklin, 'General Introduction', in Franklin (ed.), *Representing India*, i, p. x. The first edition of *Sacontala* was published in Calcutta (1789), the second in London (1790). German (1791), French (1803), and Italian (1815) translations soon followed (Trautmann, *Aryans and British India*, 29).

[54] Schwab, *Oriental Renaissance*, 58–9.

[55] Rocher, foreword, in Pachori (ed.), *Sir William Jones: A Reader*, 8.

[56] Franklin, headnote to 'A Hymn to Náráyana', in *Sir William Jones: Selected Poetical and Prose Works*, ed. Franklin, 104–5. 'A Hymn to Náráyana' is the opening text of Jerome McGann (ed.), *New Oxford Book of Romantic Period Verse* (Oxford: Oxford University Press, 1993). It was first published in the *Asiatic Miscellany* of 1785 and reprinted in *Gentleman's Magazine*, 57 (Feb. 1787) as well as *Dissertations and Miscellaneous Pieces* (1792).

It is no coincidence, then, that 'A Hymn to Náráyana' became in its own way no less central to the colonial rule of property.[57] Jones reused the creation myth with which he began it to preface his translation of *Institutes of Hindu Law; or, The Ordinances of Menu* (Calcutta and London, 1796; German translation, 1797). In importing his own creation myth into the *Manavadharmasastra* (or *The Laws of Manu*), he aimed ironically to give his translation of what is generally considered the oldest text of Hindu law the *appearance* of antiquity and hence greater authority.[58] In the preface to *The Mahomedan Law of Succession to Property of Intestates* (1782)—a translation from Arabic, which he had published in order to prove his qualifications for Bengal's Supreme Court— Jones had already explicitly insisted that, no less than his subsequent Orientalist poetry, his colonial jurisprudence returned to the 'fountain head'.[59] But with the publication of *The Laws of Manu*, Jones's argument in this regard became much more elaborate. He not only accepted the general belief that Manu was 'not the oldest only, but the holiest of legislators' in India, but suggested furthermore that his laws were 'one of oldest compositions existing' as such.[60] Much more imaginatively, he submitted the possibility that Manu ('Menu or Menus in the nominative and Menos in an oblique case') might in fact have been linked to Minos of Crete: 'though perhaps he was never in *Crete*, yet some of his institutions may well have been adopted in that Island, whence Lycurgus, a century or two afterwards, may have imported them to *Sparta*'.[61] In that case, the publication of *The Laws of Manu* restored not only the original Hindu law, but in a sense original law as such: 'If Minos, the son of Jupiter, . . . was really the same person as Menu, the son of Brahma, we have the good fortune to restore, by means of *Indian* literature, the most celebrated system of heathen jurisprudence, and this work might have been entitled *The Laws of* Minos'.[62] The Romantic generation was of course only too ready to embrace Jones's mythic dissimulations and far-fetched etymologies:

---

[57] Schwab, *Oriental Renaissance*, 195. On the hymns generally, see also Majeed, *Ungoverned Imaginings*, 21–4, who notes their concern to legitimize British rule.

[58] Rosane Rocher, 'Weaving Knowledge: Sir William Jones and Indian Pandits', in Cannon and Brine (eds), *Objects of Enquiry*, 54.

[59] Sir William Jones, *The Works of Sir William Jones*, ed. Lord Teignmouth, 13 vols (London, 1807), viii, 163.

[60] Sir William Jones, *Institutes of Hindu Law: or, the Ordinances of Menu, according to the Gloss of Cullúca. Comprising the Indian System of Duties, Religious and Civil* (Calcutta and London, 1796), pp. iv, v.

[61] Ibid., p. viii.

[62] Ibid., p. ix.

Goethe, Herder, Fichte, Schelling, Novalis, the Schlegels, Blake, Coleridge, Shelley, and Emerson, among many others, were fascinated by the apparently unprecedented capacity of *The Laws* to unite mythic with practical functions.[63]

If the point of the creation myth was to authorize Jones's translation of the law, the point of the translation was in turn, as mentioned, to provide the 1793 Permanent Settlement—the new and in fact revolutionary rule of property the Company instituted in Bengal—with its legal architecture.[64] And in Jones's own view, it was the legal codes on which he laboured tirelessly during the final years of his life that were his most valuable contributions to history, not his many other Orientalist works nor the Indo-Aryan thesis, for which he has in fact become much more famous; Jones aspired to be 'the Justinian . . . of the East'.[65] Hence Jones's Orientalism followed the imperatives of colonial property; as Holwell and Dow had foreseen it must, Orientalism in Jones's hands served to fold British colonial law into the sphere of an ancient esoteric knowledge and in particular into the Sakuntala era, at least as far as his European reading public was concerned. *The Laws of Manu* simultaneously authorized the colonial rule

---

[63] Franklin, introduction in Jones, *Institutes of Hindu Law*, in Franklin (ed.), *Representing India*, ix, p. x; see also Schwab, *Oriental Renaissance*, 53.

[64] On the employment of the creation myth, see Franklin, introduction in Jones, *Institutes of Hindu Law*, in Franklin (ed.), *Representing India*, ix, p. x. It was also included in Jones's 'On the Gods of Greece, Italy, and India', first published in *Asiatick Researches*, i (1788). On the relationship between *A Digest of Hindu Law* and the Permanent Settlement, see Franklin, introduction in Jones, *Institutes of Hindu Law*, in Franklin (ed.), *Representing India*, ix, p. viii; see also Jones's letter of 19 Mar. 1788 to Cornwallis on the need for digests of Hindu and Islamic law 'confined to the laws of contracts and inheritances': *The Letters of Sir William Jones*, ed. Garland Cannon, 2 vols (Oxford: Clarendon Press, 1970), ii, 796.

[65] The quotation 'the Justinian of . . . the East' is drawn from *Sir William Jones: Selected Poetical and Prose Works*, ed. Franklin, p. xxvii; Sir William Jones himself discusses being the 'Justinian of India': see *The Letters of Sir William Jones*, ii, 699 (see also p. 902). Majeed notes that '*Al Sirajiyyah: or the Mohamedan Law of Inheritance* . . . and the *Institutes of Hindu Law, or the ordinances of Menu* . . . remain the basis on which all juridical interpretation of this branch of law in India has been built' (p. 16), though he also notes that '[it] was H.T. Colebrooke's rigorous work, however, starting with his *Digest of Hindu Law* (1798), which commanded the development of Hindu law as we know it'; see Majeed, *Ungoverned Imaginings*, 16, 17; see also p. 29. For confirmation of Jones's importance for subsequent Indian legal history, see David Ibbetson, 'Sir William Jones as a Comparative Lawyer', in Alexander Murray (ed.), *Sir William Jones, 1746–1794. A Commemoration* (Oxford: Oxford University Press, 1998), 17–42. *Al Sirajiyyah* was Jones's translation of a Persian-language code of Islamic law on which the administration of civil law for Muslims was based during this period.

of property and drew attention away from its material context and consequences. With it, colonial property gained a mythic aspect; its logic seemed
to be dictated by the ancient esoteric foundation on which it apparently
was built.

In fact, the Orientalist return to the fountainhead served always to replace
the fluid processes that had shaped Indian history with the rigid structures
that colonial political economy required. According to the Orientalists, the
essence of India was necessarily religious, and religion emanated only from
certain original texts, which themselves had no history—except for their
subsequent corruption at the hands of priestcraft. And this history was anyway
reversible, since Orientalists could recover the scriptures in their original
form and give them back their proper signification. But while Orientalism
and Company rule presumed to rescue Hinduism's ancient scriptures from
their corruption at the hands of Brahman priestcraft and hence to undermine its power, they actually colluded with Brahmanism's deeply partisan
narrative of Indian history, because they all relied, inevitably, on Brahman
informants.[66] Contrary to their premises, the *vedas* and *sastras* were not created
at some originary moment. They were instead transmitted orally across
generations. They were, it is true, written and rewritten as they were
transmitted, but the writing was only an aid to memory. It in no way
stabilized their form, but on the contrary incorporated into them the
historical traces of their infinitely layered composition.[67]

These circumstances include the Brahmans' continual exchange with and
adaptation to the local and regional cultures that preceded and surrounded
them: their desire to maintain their priestly function required them to

---

[66] Cohn, 'The Command of Language', 293–4; see also Rosane Rocher, 'Weaving Knowledge:
Sir William Jones and Indian Pandits', in Cannon and Brine (eds), *Objects of Enquiry*, 51–79, and
Kate Teltscher, *India Inscribed: European and British Writing on India 1600–1800* (Delhi: Oxford University
Press, 1995), 197 and 200. Dodson, *Orientalism, Empire, and National Culture*, 49 f. carefully explains that
the relationship between the colonial state and Brahman pandits enabled both the Company to
replace prior sovereigns' patronage of Brahman priestly groups with its own and natives to help
fashion the Orientalist knowledge that shaped Indian politics in the colonial period and after.
On the latter point, see also Gauri Viswanathan, 'Colonialism and the Construction of
Hinduism', in Flood (ed.), *The Blackwell Companion to Hinduism*, 23–44, esp. 26–7 and 37.
[67] See Peter van der Veer, 'Sati and Sanskrit: The Move from Orientalism to Hinduism', in
Mieke Bal and Inge Boer (eds), *The Point of Theory: Practices of Cultural Analysis* (Amsterdam:
Amsterdam University Press, 1994), 255.

compromise with other sects, often introducing the gods of independent religions into the Brahman pantheon. Ancient Indian religion, then, needs to be seen as the religions—with an absolutely necessary emphasis on plurality—of autonomous sects or social segments, who in no sense saw themselves as part of a whole.[68] The history of *vedas* and the *sastras* includes, furthermore, the Brahmans' gradual rise to hegemony, gained in part as a consequence of their royal appointment as landowners during the first millennium AD. From this position, they built institutions of religious learning that ascribed to their beliefs the status of divine revelations obtaining from the origins of time. In sum, then, a Brahman priestly caste presented the scriptures as the embodiment of the reason that supposedly precedes history, but precisely in this design they in fact contain, on the contrary, an infinitely complex genealogy, a history of endless corruption.

The attributes of scripture that made them amenable to Brahmanic efforts at self-authorization and hence essential to Brahmanic hegemony—their capacity to dehistoricize and delocalize what were in fact only particular religious practices—also enabled them to satisfy the Orientalist desire to locate the supposed origins of Indo-European civilization. More to the point, the Orientalists' interest in Sanskrit texts reflected as well their appreciation of the hegemonic functions that the texts had served and the new ones towards which the Company could turn them.[69] But the crucial difference between Brahmanic and Company authority was that in the former case the transmission of texts remained perforce largely oral and hence open to endless contextual variability. In contrast, the Company brought the printing press to India. Print effectively codified the *Manavadharmasastra*, turning it from the customary law of a single caste into the universal law of all Hindus, as the Company hoped.[70] Whether in the case of the *sastras* or *sha'ria*, the Company's legal codifications made the interpretation of law *more* orthodox than it had previously been.[71] It was of course only after 'Hindu

[68] Romila Thapar, 'Imagined Religious Communities? Ancient History and the Modern Search for a Hindu Identity', *Modern Asian Studies*, 23/2 (1989), 222.

[69] Van der Veer, 'Sati and Sanskrit', 257–8 and 259.

[70] Cohn, 'The Command of Language', 328; Thapar, 'Imagined Religious Communities', 218; C. A. Bayly, 'The British and Indigenous Peoples, 1760–1860: Power, Perception and Identity', in Martin Daunton and Rick Halpern (eds), *Empire and Others: British Encounters with Indigenous Peoples, 1600–1850* (London: UCL Press, 1999), 35.

[71] Majeed, *Ungoverned Imaginings*, 26–7.

civilization'—which, to the extent that it could be said to have existed at all, had been shaped by radically heterogeneous and conflicting forces—became identical with a set of supposedly timeless scriptures that colonial rule could begin to fix it both temporally and spatially, in the process making it appear intrinsically static, rather than susceptible to development through historical time.[72]

We could note, in an aside, that the Indian nationalism that emerged during the course of the nineteenth century in opposition to colonial rule derived, ironically if inevitably, in large part from the Orientalist construction of Hinduism and in particular its central tenets of a sacred book and the theological sovereignty of one sect over all.[73] Insisting on its antiquity and hence authority, this new Hinduism attempted to dictate which practices and groups belonged to the essence of India and which were mere corruptions to be excluded or marginalized. It in effect transformed into a far-reaching ideology what the British Orientalists first recovered as a supposedly authentic theology.[74] Or, more precisely, the Orientalist quest for the origins of civilization disseminated a Brahman ideology that in the precolonial period had only had a local or regional function through the centralized structures that colonialism had introduced to India: not only printing presses, but also educational institutions and, not least of all, the judicial system. In the process, colonial rule made Brahmanism's claim to be the

[72] Bernard S. Cohn, 'Notes on the History of the Study of Indian Society and Culture', in Milton Singer and Bernard S. Cohn (eds), *Structure and Change in Indian Society* (Chicago: Aldine, 1968), 7.

[73] Thapar, 'Imagined Religious Communities', 228–9. See also John Hutchinson and Anthony Smith (eds), *Nationalism* (New York: Oxford University Press, 1994), 7–8; and Uma Chakravarti, 'Whatever Happened to the Vedic Dasi? Orientalism, Nationalism and a Script for the Past', in Kumkum Sangari and Sudesh Vaid (eds), *Recasting Women: Essays in Indian Colonial History* (New Brunswick: Rutgers University Press, 1990), 27–87. For a discussion of the relationship of Orientalist scholarship and twentieth-century Indian nationalism, see Gyan Prakash, 'Writing Post-Orientalist Histories of the Third World: Perspectives from Indian Historiography', *Comparative Studies in Society and History*, 32/2 (1990), 383–408. See also Majeed, *Ungoverned Imaginings*, 36; and Romila Thapar, 'Communalism and the Writing of Ancient Indian History', in Romila Thapar, Harbans Mukhia, and Bipan Chandra, *Communalism and the Writing of Indian History* (Delhi: People's Publishing House, 1969), 1–21.

[74] 'Ideas Gandhi used to conjure the essential India—with its ageless rural simplicity and moral continuity—came from the treasure chest of Orientalism. . . . Nehru's *Discovery of India* is a more systematic use of Orientalism to craft a charter for nationhood. In nationalism we find the vitality of Orientalism today.' Ludden, 'Orientalist Empiricism', 271.

origin of Hinduism a self-fulfilling prophecy.[75] Regardless of the subsequent scholarship that has delineated the constantly changing legal culture of precolonial India, the mistaken priority that Jones gave to the *Manavadharma-sastra* has still not been reversed.[76] The separate civil codes that apply to Hindus and Muslims in the postcolonial Indian state attest to the enduring significance of the Orientalists' supposed reconstruction of Hindu and Muslim legal traditions.[77] 'Indian history' became the effect of the deist attempt to refute the Judaeo-Christian claim on world history and ultimately, as we shall see, of the radically centralizing pressure of the British state's and the East India Company's military-fiscalism. When it claimed to uncover the pure waters of the fountainhead, the early Orientalist construction of ancient Indian history inevitably concealed the dirty history that actually gave it rise.

III Precolonial and early colonial sovereignty

Let us consider the peculiar form of sovereignty and hence of property in which colonial Orientalism first emerged. Early modern innovations in the practice of war—which have come to be known as the 'military revolution'—had increased the cost of war far in excess of what royal treasuries had conventionally afforded, forcing European sovereigns to revolutionize correspondingly their fiscal systems, which began now to depend increasingly on, for example, piracy, monopoly trade, colonial rule, and ultimately debt-financing.[78] Despite the quasi-sovereign status and military powers that its

---

[75] On educational institutions, see David Kopf, *British Orientalism and the Bengal Renaissance: The Dynamics of Indian Modernization, 1773–1835* (Berkeley: University of California Press, 1969), esp. 180–7; and Cohn, 'The Command of Language', esp. 317–19. On the judicial system, see Thapar, 'Imagined Religious Communities', 218.

[76] According to Rocher, 'British Orientalism in the Eighteenth Century', 229: 'Later scholarship was unable to reverse, either in the West or in India that accepted British view, the privileging of the *Manusmrti* as the premier book of Hindu law.' Quoted in Franklin, introduction in Jones, *Institutes of Hindu Law*, in Franklin (ed.), *Representing India*, ix, p. ix.

[77] Tejaswini Niranjana, *Siting Translation: History, Post-Structuralism, and the Colonial Context* (Berkeley: University of California Press, 1992), 18.

[78] Geoffrey Parker, *The Military Revolution: Military Innovation and the Rise of the West, 1500–1800* (Cambridge: Cambridge University Press, 1996), 174.

original royal charter had granted it, the East India Company had purposefully avoided this military-fiscal logic, attempting instead to reap the profits
of trade—however militarized and monopolistic—without incurring the
costs of war and conquest. But with its victory in the Battle of Plassey
(1757), the Company was finally and irrevocably pulled directly into military-fiscalism: from this point forward, its military expenditures always
exceeded its revenue, and in response it ceaselessly attempted to expand
the territory from which it drew rent and over which it imposed monopoly
trade.[79] Trapped in this vicious cycle of war debt and war as an economic
strategy to escape debt, the East India Company became a type of sovereignty
categorically different from those that had hitherto occupied Indian soil.
And while the Company's largest financial drain by far was the cost of war, it
had other demands on its revenue absolutely unknown to prior forms of
Indian sovereignty: for example, its obligations, as a joint-stock company, to
pay investors a regular dividend and, as a monopoly trader, to buy all of
Bengal's export commodities.[80] Furthermore, since the British state in turn
depended on the Company as a source of finance capital, Bengali property
was hostage not only to the Company's own military-fiscal exigencies, but
also to the British state's, to wars it had fought and would fight continents
away.

These pressures led the Company to extract wealth from Bengali property
in a way that was historically unprecedented: Hastings himself concluded
that where the British state extracted a fifth of the profits of British property
in rent, the Company extracted nine-tenths of the profits of Bengali property in rent.[81] It was not the precolonial system, but rather the Company,
precisely because of its own insatiability, that always extracted more than the
peasant—and the economy in general—could bear. Even during its initial
period of sovereignty, when the Company partially engrafted itself on the
Mughal economy, it had introduced a number of rather drastic innovations.
The Company brought in speculative capitalists to collect rent; monetized
rent; ascribed the ownership of property not to communities, but rather
to private individuals, whom it thus made responsible for the rent; and

[79] See Cain and Hopkins, *British Imperialism*, 91–4.
[80] C. A. Bayly, *Origins of Nationality in South Asia: Patriotism and Ethical Government in the Making of Modern India* (Oxford: Oxford University Press, 1998), 259 (from ch. 8, 'The British Military-Fiscal State and Indigenous Resistance: India 1750–1820').
[81] Travers, 'The Real Value of the Lands', 524 and 539.

incorporated previously rent-free lands as well.[82] Hence regardless of what its Orientalist scholarship explicitly advertised, the Company could *not* in fact afford actually to base its rule of property on native traditions.

As Company servants, Holwell and Dow experienced these transformations directly. Like the official Orientalists who followed in their wake, they understood intuitively what the Company's revenue demands entailed. Hence, while their Orientalist publications called for the reconstruction of native traditions as the basis of colonial rule, their own concepts of property demanded a wholly new political economy; the function of the former then was to obscure the radical nature of the latter. Holwell designed his own plan of auctioning the collection of Bengali land rent to speculative capitalists 'to appeal to cash-hungry British MPs'.[83] He testified before Parliament that '[i]f [Bengali rent] now amounts to Three Millions Sterling, the real produce is three or four times as much' and that to obtain something approximating the latter sum, the Company must lease Bengali land 'to the best Bidders': 'there would be few Persons to account with, and much therefore saved in the Collections'.[84] Though Hastings opposed Holwell's plan precisely because it did *not* respect pre-existing traditions of property, it eventually became the orthodox approach, and Hastings himself instituted it when he became Governor in 1772.[85]

While Dow criticized not only Holwell's policy of auctioning the collection of Bengali rents, but also the various political revolutions that the Company engineered in the wake of Plassey and in which Holwell had assumed a central role, his alternative proposal that the Company protect the rights of native property owners by permanently fixing rent demanded, nonetheless, that it undertake the 'military conquest of the whole subcontinent' and reform all its sovereign institutions accordingly.[86] Dow's intention in fixing rent was, decidedly, *not* to return to ancient traditions, but again on the contrary to *create* a native class of comprador property owners to whom the Company could turn to pacify its subjects: 'To give them property

[82] Mukhopadhyay, *The Agrarian Policy of the British in Bengal*, 13.

[83] Travers, 'The Real Value of the Lands', 525.

[84] Evidence of Zephaniah Holwell, 30 Mar. 1767, British Library, Add. MS 18,469, fols 13 and 14. Travers, 'The Real Value of the Lands', first drew my attention to this manuscript.

[85] Ibid. 'The Real Value of the Lands', 526 and 527.

[86] Franklin, introduction in Dow, *The History of Hindostan*, in Franklin (ed.), *Representing India*, ii, pp. ix and xi n. 6.

would only bind them with stronger ties to our interest; and make them more our subjects; or, if the British nation prefers the name—more our slaves'.[87] Once Holwell's plan of auctioning rent had run its course in Company policy, Dow's proposal for fixing rent would take over. But in either case, these diametrically opposed plans both fundamentally reimagined the structure of Indian property ownership, by formulating a rule of property in which—in short—all forms of intermediate property ownership and hence sovereignty across the Subcontinent's radically heterotopic territory would be eliminated.

So in their concepts of territorial sovereignty, Holwell and Dow set the pattern for all subsequent Company reforms: as its economic and hence territorial ambitions became infinite, the Company, like the European state, progressively reconceptualized the very idea of sovereignty in terms of absolute power, as the absence of any other sovereign or extractive entity. It is this stark reconceptualization that characterizes the actual transformation in the Company's imperial logic from Clive's victory at Plassey in 1757, when it ceased to be a primarily seaborne power and, rapidly militarizing itself, began to expand its territorial possessions, to Hastings's plan in 1772, when it effectively declared its territorial autonomy from the Mughal Empire.[88] At that time, in response to the Company's fiscal crisis, Hastings not only generalized the dispossession of Bengal's *zamindars*, or property-owning class, and the auctioning-off of their rent across Bengal, but also rejected the very idea of power sharing, arresting native governors and stopping the Company's stipulated payment to the Mughal Emperor.[89] Soon thereafter, Hastings would proclaim, confidently if much too optimistically: 'every intermediate power is removed, and the sovereignty of the country wholly and absolutely vested in the Company'.[90]

---

[87] The quotation is from Dow, *The History of Hindostan*, iii, p. cxx; quoted by Guha, *A Rule of Property for Bengal*, 34. Franklin, introduction in Dow, *The History of Hindostan*, in Franklin (ed.), *Representing India*, ii, p. xi, notes that this argument 'was the chief justification used by Lord Cornwallis for the Permanent Settlement of 1793'.

[88] Travers, 'Ideology and British Expansion in Bengal', 15.

[89] Travers, 'The Real Value of the Lands', 529; Travers, 'Ideology and British Expansion in Bengal', 17–18.

[90] Letter of Mar. 1773 to the chairman of the directors, in *Memoirs of the Life of the Right Hon. Warren Hastings, First Governor-General of Bengal*, ed. G. R. Gleig, 3 vols (London: R. Bentley, 1841), i, 293 (quoted in Travers, 'Ideology and British Expansion in Bengal', 17).

In other words, from the very origins of colonial rule, British Orientalists were concerned not to preserve ancient Indian civilization, but rather in diametric opposition to replace its present form with a European absolutist model. And it was precisely for this reason that they recognized that the Company would need Orientalism to mystify the utterly *modern* structure of property and sovereignty that its military-fiscal structure demanded. Behind the façade of ancient traditions was a process definitive of colonial history generally: the colonial state aimed, by reifying formerly fluid legal practices, to exert greater control over its territory than precolonial sovereigns had done.[91] In the process, it created a sovereign form that was 'singular', existing 'not alongside other legal and political authorities but above them'.[92]

While Company officials referred to the precolonial multi-layered expropriation of the peasants' labour as the 'fraud' and 'corruption' of 'middlemen', sovereign ruthlessness—though no doubt actual—had been of necessity circumscribed, precisely because there had been so many levels of sovereignty, each administering a relatively few subalterns.[93] Gift economies obtained at every level, enforcing a delicate balance of extraction and reciprocation in the exercise of sovereignty. Hence the shared sovereignty that characterized precolonial India differed essentially from the absolute sovereignty for which the Company ceaselessly aimed: the Company could hardly afford to return the wealth it extracted from peasants in the form of gifts or in the generous laying-out of funds to buy what they produced, because the costs of modern warfare had always already laid claim to it. It was the Company itself, then, that created the economic crises—precisely by undoing the circumscribed nature of precolonial sovereignty—in which it repeatedly found itself and which it typically blamed on the structure of that sovereignty. It was to these crises—manifestations of the historical rupture in property and sovereignty that colonial rule had induced—that the rule of property claimed to be the ultimate response.

---

[91] Lauren Benton, *Law and Colonial Cultures: Legal Regimes in World History, 1400–1900* (Cambridge: Cambridge University Press, 2002), 128–9.

[92] Ibid. 131, referring to the colonial state in 1924.

[93] Sugata Bose, 'Space and Time on the Indian Ocean Rim: Theory and History', in Leila Tarazi Fawaz and C. A. Bayly (eds), *Modernity & Culture: From the Mediterranean to the Indian Ocean* (New York: Columbia University Press, 2002), 377.

IV A spatio-temporal fix for Bengal

In the wake of the 1784 India Act's rejection of Hastings's policy of short-term leases, the 1793 Permanent Settlement entitled the *zamindars* to rent fixed in perpetuity. The Permanent Settlement's claim was that if the *zamindar* knew that the rent he collected would remain largely in his own hands, he would have no need to rack-rent his tenants and would instead have the incentive to improve his property. Improvement would in turn lead to a market in land which, alongside the Company's renewed efforts to protect commerce, would liberate native capital and enable it to circulate freely. In the process, the *zamindars* would theoretically have transformed organically into a capitalist class, and the Permanent Settlement would apparently have brought traditional property rights in line with modern political economy. And as mentioned, in the years that followed the establishment of the Permanent Settlement in Bengal, the principle of aristocratic capitalism that lay behind it spread from its colonial origins in Bengal across the British Empire.[94] By claiming to transform native elites across its colonies into gentlemen farmers, the British Empire finally separated itself—at least symbolically—from the associations with mercantile degeneration that had characterized it throughout its past and attached itself instead to the idea of progress.[95]

But contrary to its claims, the Permanent Settlement turned out to be one more stage in the history of colonial enfeudalization, forcing Bengal, for instance, gradually to revert to preindustrial modes of production and ultimately rendering it a non-competitive sphere from which the British Empire's industrial economy could extract primary goods and devalued labour.[96] Rather than improving their property, the *zamindars* chose instead to use their state-protected status precisely to rack-rent tenants, whose rights

[94] Cf. Peter Gray, 'The Peculiarities of Irish Land Tenure, 1800–1914: From Agent of Impoverishment to Agent of Pacification', in Donald Winch and Patrick O'Brien (eds), *The Political Economy of British Historical Experience, 1688–1914* (Oxford University Press, 2002), 142.

[95] Travers, 'The Real Value of the Lands', 550. On 'gentlemanly capitalism', see Cain and Hopkins, *British Imperialism*, 14 f., and for the claim that the imperial mission was to export this form, ibid. 34–5 and 45.

[96] Guha, *A Rule of Property for Bengal*, 200; Dirks, 'From Little King to Landlord', 199; C. A. Bayly, *Indian Society and the Making of the British Empire* (Cambridge: Cambridge University Press, 1988), 2.

the colonial government did not protect in supposed deference to the traditional belief that aristocrats habitually form moral economies with their tenants.[97] The *zamindars* instead used their tenants' surplus to underwrite their urbane lives as absentee landlords in Calcutta, comfortably removed from the source of their income. These facts constitute a history that we now know rather too well, recounted from *A Rule of Property for Bengal* to the volumes of *The New Cambridge History of India* and beyond.[98] What our histories do not explain is the logic behind the Permanent Settlement's construction of an unproductive colonial economy. From the perspective of a *capitalist* modernity, such an economy appears merely as an aberration and hence ultimately a mistake—Guha eloquently encapsulates this perspective: 'Capitalism which had built up its hegemony in Europe by using the sharp end of Reason found it convenient to subjugate the peoples of the East by wielding the blunt head'.[99]

In fact, the explanation of the Permanent Settlement lies not in capitalism, but rather, as Robert Travers's recent studies make clear, in military-fiscalism. Despite its stated aim to ensure that the *zamindars* would keep enough rent to be able comfortably to reinvest part of it in improvement of their property, the Permanent Settlement did *not* in fact significantly lower the Company's revenue demands. Rather it kept them more or less at the high levels of the preceding decades, in proportion to its military costs.[100] The Company did *not* need to increase its territorial revenue—at least in the short term—because it came to rely, no less than European states, on debt-financing. It needed only to show potential creditors that it had a *fixed* source of revenue that could function as collateral against which it could borrow capital in the global financial networks emerging all around it; it needed to impose a 'spatio-temporal fix' on Bengal—to extract, in other words, a quantity of rent from the colony that would remain fixed over a given time.[101]

---

[97] Guha calls this—the belief that if the owners of the land know that their land is secure, they will improve it—'The classic illusion of the Permanent Settlement'. *A Rule of Property for Bengal*, 175.

[98] Besides Guha, see e.g. Thomas Metcalf, *Ideologies of the Raj* (Cambridge: Cambridge University Press, 1994), 20–1.

[99] Guha, *A Rule of Property for Bengal*, p. xiv.

[100] Travers, 'The Real Value of the Lands', 548.

[101] See Immanuel Wallerstein, 'Bourgeois(ie) as Concept and Reality', in Étienne Balibar and Immanuel Wallerstein, *Race, Nation, Class: Ambiguous Identities* (London: Verso, 1991), 146–7, and

Accordingly, then, the Permanent Settlement not only fixed the Company's revenue demand in principle, but also insisted on the collection of this fixed demand in practice. Where the Mughal Empire accepted that there would be discrepancies between the amount at which it assessed its lands and the always variable amount that the *zamindars* would be able to pay in any given season, the Permanent Settlement insisted that its demand always be paid in full, even if such a demand forced the landlord to sell his lands.[102] As a consequence, the *majority* of the *zamindars* did in fact have to sell their lands.[103] In the process, the Permanent Settlement imposed on Bengali property the tripartite structure of landlord-tenant-labour—famously at the origins of capitalist waged labour—that already characterized British property relations, thereby pulling Bengal into modernity; when the principles behind the Permanent Settlement were subsequently disseminated globally across the British Empire, modernity would drag many other colonies behind.[104] But we cannot repeat this truism without emphasizing the colonial difference that attended it: in the colonies, with the rent that was supposed to be reinvested in improvement mortgaged in fact to war, capitalism's original tripartite structure led not to productive dynamism, but on the contrary to economic sclerosis. And perhaps we need to see this colonial difference not as an aberration within modernity, but rather as the essence of the modernity that we still inhabit clearly revealed: not the endless increase of production, but on the contrary its sacrifice to the exigencies of war.[105] At the very least, it

David Harvey, *The New Imperialism* (New York: Oxford University Press, 2003), 43–4 and 115–24, for the argument that the essentially non-competitive or monopoly imposition of 'spatio-temporal control' or a 'spatio-temporal fix' is fundamental to actually existing capitalism and imperialism respectively.

[102] Bayly, *Origins of Nationality in South Asia*, 250; Travers, 'The Real Value of the Lands', 549.

[103] Bayly, *Origins of Nationality in South Asia*, 258; Travers, 'The Real Value of the Lands', cites Sirajul Islam, *The Permanent Settlement in Bengal: A Study of its Operation, 1790–1819* (Dacca: Bangla Academy, 1979), 144–57; in addition, see John R. McLane, *Land and Local Kingship in Eighteenth-Century Bengal* (Cambridge: Cambridge University Press, 1993), 267–70; and P. J. Marshall, *Bengal. The British Bridgehead: Eastern India, 1740–1828* (Cambridge: Cambridge University Press, 1987), 147.

[104] Guha, *A Rule of Property for Bengal*, 130. See also F. M. L. Thompson, 'Changing Perceptions of Land Tenures in Britain, 1750–1914', in Winch and O'Brien (eds), *The Political Economy of British Historical Experience*, 121.

[105] Cf. Wallerstein, 'Bourgeois(ie) as Concept and Reality', 139: 'the number of national bourgeoisies that are said to have "betrayed" their historic roles turns out not to be small but very large—indeed, the vast majority'; see also ibid. 146.

was absolutely no coincidence that the main period of the British Empire's territorial expansion, from 1795 to 1805, occurred immediately after the establishment of the Permanent Settlement, even as Bengali agriculture was being ruined.[106] Like the British state, using debt to finance war, the Company could afford, at least in the short term, to become oblivious to the actual condition of its property.[107]

An obvious and primary intent of Jones's Orientalist legal codes was to support the fiction that in establishing this peculiar form of private property, the Company was only returning its native subjects to their ancient traditions. Insisting that 'the old Hindus most assuredly were absolute proprietors of their land' and that according to the Muslim legal theorist Sharif, 'freedom established [man's] right of property, which chiefly distinguishes [him] from other animals and from things inanimate', Jones's codes advertised the Company's supposedly exceptional recognition of and respect for indigenous traditions of private property.[108] But in the context of indigenous tax systems, the Permanent Settlement was in fact an absolute oddity, in which colonial officials effectively threw up their hands at the diversity and fluidity of local arrangements and in their stead imposed a universal principle.[109] For example, the supposedly ancient aristocracy that the Permanent Settlement entitled had in fact been, far from nobility, the Mughal Empire's tax collectors. It was only as Mughal authority declined that these tax collectors insisted they had a hereditary right to the land, turned their vocations into landlordship, and began to extract as much as they could, confronting peasant hostility in the process.[110] When it fixed their property rights, the Permanent Settlement effectively turned these sometime tax collectors into a comprador class that depended on the Company to

[106] Butler, 'Orientalism', 401.

[107] 'By the 1790s, the company's capacity for waging war was much strengthened, not as yet by any major enlargement of territorial revenues, but above all through the greater ease with which it borrowed'. J. R. Ward, 'The Industrial Revolution and British Imperialism, 1750–1850', *Economic History Review*, 47/1 (1994), 48; quoted by Travers, 'The Real Value of the Lands', 555. 'The Permanent Settlement, with its promises of stable revenues, enforced by land sales, had a clear logic. The "real value of the lands" may have become … the security that these collections provided for debt-financing in Calcutta". Ibid. 556.

[108] Sir William Jones, *Al Sirajiyyah; or, the Mohammedan Law of Inheritance* (1792), in Jones, *Works*, ed. Lord Teignmouth, viii, 208 and 207.

[109] Travers, 'The Real Value of the Lands', 521.

[110] Mukhopadhyay, *The Agrarian Policy of the British in Bengal*, 10, 12.

protect it in its ruthless exactions; at the same time, the Permanent Settlement stripped them of the sovereign powers that they had begun to exert over tenant farmers and local markets.[111] In doing so, the Permanent Settlement radically simplified the structure of Bengali sovereignty, re-routing all revenue streams towards the Company. It was, in short, the Company's most thorough attempt to date to replace the heterotopia that had characterized native property with a British model of absolute sovereignty.

But more subtly, Jones's codes claimed that the Company's ultimate aim was in fact to join 'the old jurisprudence of this country' with 'the improvement of a commercial age'.[112] Jones insisted that by fixing the rent it demanded from its native subjects, the Company would ensure that colonial rule would be a 'blessing' to them as well as 'a durable benefit' to the British.[113] From this avowedly capitalist perspective, then, the value of the codes lay wholly in the fact that, whatever 'defects' they possessed, they 'are actually revered, as the word of the Most High, by nations of great importance to the political and commercial interests of *Europe* . . . whose well directed industry would add largely to the wealth of *Britain*'; the publication of the codes, then, purposefully laid the groundwork for a subsequent capitalist development.[114] However convincing, Jones's argument is scarcely less false than the previous one was. The Permanent Settlement served its function—within the British state's and the East India Company's global financial networks—*without* in fact providing a durable source of revenue, much less

---

[111] Travers, 'The Real Value of the Lands', 549. Ultimately, the Orientalist codification of native law and the comprador aristocracy that it created played a role essential to colonial history: the replacement of the sacerdotal caste with, or its subordination to, the very different type of sovereignty that governs the modern national community. See Majeed, *Ungoverned Imaginings*, 20; Majeed in turn cites Ranajit Guha, *An Indian Historiography of India: A Nineteenth-Century Agenda and its Implications* (Calcutta: Published for Centre for Studies in Social Sciences, Calcutta, by K. P. Bagchi & Co., 1988), 6; Ernest Gellner, *Nations and Nationalism* (Oxford: Blackwell, 1983), 141–2; and Benedict Anderson, *Imagined Communities: Reflections on the Origin and Spread of Nationalism* (London: Verso, 1991), 47.

[112] Jones, *Institutes of Hindu Law*, p. iv.

[113] Jones, *Al Sirajiyyah*, in *Works*, ed. Lord Teignmouth, viii, 209. See also: 'Our nation, in the name of the king, has *twenty three millions* of black subjects in these two provinces; but nine tenths of their property are taken from them, and it has even been publickly insisted, that they have no landed property at all: if my Digest of Indian Law should give stability to their property, real and personal, and security to their persons, it will be the greatest benefit they ever received from us'. Letter to Lady Spencer, 24 Oct. 1791, *The Letters of Sir William Jones*, ii, 902–3.

[114] Jones, *Institutes of Hindu Law*, pp. xvi, iv.

serving Europe's 'commercial interests': as short-term collateral, colonial property was more valuable when it was fixed than when it was productive. The historical significance of Jones's legal codes lay in their capacity to authorize this fixed structure, in which colonial property acquired its value. Jones unwittingly acknowledged that value; he noted that the 'resources of *Bengal*' will 'continually increase' only 'when [our *Asiatick* subjects] shall have well grounded confidence, that the proportion of [the land-tax] will never be raised, *except for a time on some great emergency, which may endanger all they possess*' (my emphasis).[115] Colonial property *never* ceased to be mortgaged to the Company's state of emergency, because this was not an exceptional time, but rather a permanent rule. We could say, then, that the Orientalists' scholarly-textual tendency to reify Indian history matched perfectly the Company's military-fiscal need to 'fix' the Indian economy. When colonial Orientalism and the colonial rule of property are placed, as they in fact occurred, side by side, their underlying logic reappears: that logic involves neither a will to know nor the rise of a capitalist modernity, but rather the reorientation of property towards war, the fundamental historical shift that Orientalism served to faciliate and—then as now—to obscure.

A few months before his death, Said wrote the foreword to the twenty-fifth anniversary edition of *Orientalism*, in the immediate aftermath of the US invasion of Iraq: he drew attention to the essay's historical context by concluding it, simply, with a date ('May 2003'). Within the foreword proper, both at its outset and its end, Said repeatedly made clear that he considered *Orientalism* in particular and the intellectual vocation in general to be part of the project of Enlightenment.[116] His references to Enlightenment evoke Kant's definition of *Aufklärung*: 'the public use of reason' or, in other words, a type of thought that steps outside state and professional rationality and subjects them to criticism.[117] This 'attitude of Enlightenment'—an

---

[115] Jones, *Al Sirajiyyah*, in *Works*, ed. Lord Teignmouth, viii, 209–10.

[116] See Said: ' the ongoing and literally unending process of emancipation and enlightenment that, in my opinion, frames and gives direction to the intellectual vocation'; '[t]he human, and humanistic, desire for enlightenment and emancipation is not easily deferred, despite the incredible strength of the opposition to it.... I would like to believe that *Orientalism* has had a place in the long and often interrupted road to human freedom.' *Orientalism* (2003), p. xvi.

[117] Kant, 'An Answer to the Question: What is Enlightenment?', in James Schmidt (ed.), *What is Enlightenment?: Eighteenth-Century Answers and Twentieth-Century Questions* (Berkeley: University of California Press, 1996), 59–60.

open-ended critique meant to lead not to a new synthesis or sovereign form, but rather in Kant's terms to 'an exit from one's self-incurred immaturity' or in Said's to 'liberation'—describes precisely the intellectual and political stance that Said assumed throughout his public life.[118] An irony of post-colonial studies over the past two decades, when it has increasingly come to focus its own critique on what it refers to as Enlightenment or post-Enlightenment reason in the name of a non-statist politics, is that in doing so it only extends this Enlightenment project.[119] Those who disavow this tendency within postcolonial studies place the responsibility for it squarely on Said's shoulders.[120] He at least realized that exile from the state-form was, in a real sense, the telos of the Enlightenment's own critical method. In Said's exilic demand for a ceaselessly critical orientation towards one's own time and place—an untimeliness or what he would call, in his final work, 'lateness'—the Enlightenment returns in its most intransigent form.[121] Though this is rarely acknowledged, it was the Enlightenment itself that bequeathed to postcolonial studies the critique of governmental reason.

It was first in the late eighteenth century that, hired by the nascent colonial state, Orientalism started its own professional career. But what state interests did this new type of professional reason serve? Until we consider this question, we cannot even begin to work through the specific relationship of Orientalism to imperialism 'analytically and historically', as Said insisted we must.[122] Until we answer it, we cannot know the substance of the modernity from which our critical method must exile itself. Said's own temperament and training, if not his critical ideals, colluded in avoiding the question: willy-nilly, *Orientalism* turned colonial history into a textual process; if 'Orientalism overrode the Orient', the study of Orientalism has equally

[118] Ibid. 58; Edward Said, *Culture and Imperialism* (New York: Alfred A. Knopf, 1993), 214, 268, 273, and 276.
[119] See Dipesh Chakrabarty, *Provincializing Europe: Postcolonial Thought and Historical Difference* (Princeton: Princeton University Press, 2000), 107; Dipesh Chakrabarty, *Habitations of Modernity: Essays in the Wake of Subaltern Studies* (Chicago: University of Chicago Press, 2002), 34–6; Ranajit Guha, *History at the Limit of World-History* (New York: Columbia University Press, 2002), 5, 14–23, 34–47; Gyan Prakash, 'Who's Afraid of Postcoloniality?', *Social Text*, 49 (Winter 1996), 187–203.
[120] Sarkar, 'The Decline of the Subaltern', 84.
[121] Edward Said, *On Late Style: Music and Literature against the Grain* (New York: Vintage, 2007).
[122] As Said puts it, 'it is not enough to say [that modern Orientalism has been an aspect of both imperialism and colonialism]; it needs to be worked through analytically and historically.' *Orientalism* (1978), 123.

overridden the material specificities of colonial history.[123] However schemat-ically, this essay has attempted to account for that history. It reveals at the essence of the modern state-form neither the stereotypically capitalist im-perative to turn the colony into a space of always increasing production *nor* the stereotypically imperialist imperative to let it remain a source of tribute, a feudal aberration trapped within a modern trajectory. The history in which Orientalism and colonial property became conjoined fits neither of these narratives.[124] That history foregrounds instead the anti-productive exigencies of war, which depend above all on the European state's capacity to *fix* the colonial economy spatially and temporally, an endeavour that depends for its legitimacy on the textual protocols of Orientalism. It is this now unneces-sarily obscure history that troubles both that era's sovereign claims to have aligned ancient property rights with modern political economy and our own scholarly premises that it must be either an Enlightenment will to know and govern or the logic of capital that is at the heart of modernity. Attention to this colonial history, since it interrupts all such narratives, is part of a simultaneously Enlightenment and postcolonial project, every bit as pertin-ent to our own hyper-armed and indebted present as it is to the colonial past.

---

[123] Ibid. 96. For Said's insistence on the importance of analyses in terms of 'socio-economic reality', see *Orientalism* (2003), p. xxiii.

[124] Gayatri Spivak, *A Critique of Postcolonial Reason: Toward a History of the Vanishing Present* (Cambridge, Mass.: Harvard University Press, 1999), 89, 220, and 222, rejects the traditional view that the colony—and the East India Company colony in particular—was 'a not quite correct transitional space from semi-feudalism to capitalism' or, in other words, 'failed capitalism'. But following Samir Amin, she sees it as 'successful imperialism' *only* in virtue of the fact that it was a 'tribute-paying economic formation'.

Part Three
Nation, Colony,
and Enlightenment
Universality

6

Of Speaking Natives and Hybrid Philosophers

Lahontan, Diderot, and the French Enlightenment Critique of Colonialism

Doris L. Garraway

For all the debate that postcolonial theory has generated about what it calls 'colonial discourse', there has emerged in the field of postcolonial studies a significant degree of consensus about its ideological function. In the work of Edward Said, Gayatri Spivak, and Homi Bhabha, 'colonial discourse' has been described as the epistemological corollary to colonial violence, a system of knowledge and representation through which Europeans produced, defined, and contained non-European difference and, in the process, developed ideological justifications of colonialism.[1] This discursive apparatus of power is said to have relied in many instances on a structure of binary opposition that posited the racial, cultural, and linguistic inferiority of the colonized as compared with Europeans. According to this view, dominant traditions of

---

[1] My discussion of colonial discourse draws upon the following works: Edward Said, *Orientalism* (New York: Vintage, 1978); Homi Bhabha, *The Location of Culture* (London: Routledge, 1994); Gayatri Spivak, *A Critique of Postcolonial Reason: Toward a History of the Vanishing Present* (Cambridge, Mass.: Harvard University Press, 1999); Gayatri Spivak, 'Can the Subaltern Speak?', in Patrick

European literature, art, historiography, and the human sciences have been complicit in constructing non-European or colonial subjects as objects of European colonial authority, who are, as such, unable to represent a counter-hegemonic discourse in order to challenge colonial rule or the presumed cultural superiority of the colonizer. In an early elaboration of this view, Spivak famously claimed that the subaltern woman could not speak at all because she was silenced by both colonialist and patriarchal power structures.[2] Bhabha, though less absolute in his position, nonetheless considers the 'originary myth of colonialist power' to rely on 'the demand that the space it occupies be unbounded, its reality *coincident* with the emergence of an imperialist narrative and history, its discourse *non-dialogic*, its enunciation unitary, unmarked by the trace of difference'.[3]

While theorists of colonialism have continued to refine their terms and critical theories of colonial discourse over time, many scholars within and outside the field of postcolonial studies have challenged postcolonial theorists to consider the ways in which such broad, totalizing claims confuse discourses of representation with regimes of governmentality, thus discounting the violent struggles of anticolonial resistance movements, the historical development and variability of European writings on the colonial world, and the various ways in which European literary texts have resisted or problematized colonialist discourses and power structures.[4] Just as importantly, the

Williams and Laura Chrisman (eds), *Colonial Discourse and Postcolonial Theory: A Reader* (New York: Columbia University Press, 1994), 66–112. On the historical emergence, theoretical imperatives, and debates in colonial discourse analysis, see Nicholas Thomas, *Colonialism's Culture: Anthropology, Travel, and Government* (Cambridge: Polity Press, 1994), 33–65; Benita Parry, 'Problems in Current Theories of Colonial Discourse', *Oxford Literary Review*, 9/1–2 (1987), 27–58; and Benita Parry, 'Signs of Our Times: Discussion of Homi Bhabha's *The Location of Culture*', *Third Text*, 28–9 (1994), 5–24; Francis Barker, Peter Hulme, and Margaret Iversen, introduction in *Colonial Discourse / Postcolonial Theory* (Manchester: Manchester University Press, 1994), 1–23.

[2] As Spivak explains, 'Between patriarchy and imperialism, subject-constitution and object-formation, the figure of the woman disappears . . . into a violent shuttling which is the displaced figuration of the "third-world woman" caught between tradition and modernization . . . There is no space from which the subaltern can speak.' 'Can the Subaltern Speak?', 102–3.

[3] Homi Bhabha, 'Signs Taken for Wonders', in *The Location of Culture*, 115.

[4] For a critique of postcolonial theorists' functionalist tendency to equate discourse with governmentality, see Thomas, *Colonialism's Culture*, 38–41. On postcolonial theory's erasure of native resistance, see Parry, 'Problems in Current Theories', 34; Ania Loomba, 'Overworlding the Third World', *Oxford Literary Review*, 13/1–2 (1991), 164–91; Abdul JanMohamed, 'The Economy of Manichean Allegory: The Function of Racial Difference in Colonialist Literature', *Critical Inquiry*,

dominant, nearly stereotypical understanding of 'colonial discourse' prevalent in postcolonial studies has arguably downplayed the extent to which European writers willingly configured the colonized as speaking subjects in an oppositional, critical position with respect to European rule. Rather than investigating subversive contestations of colonial discourse within European texts, critics have arrogated to themselves the role of rupturing binaries, exposing colonial hybridities, and even partially recovering the voice of the subaltern, all the while propagating a critical theory that tends to deny that such critical operations were present in dominant European literary or philosophical traditions produced during the period of European expansion. Spivak, for one, has affirmed the necessity of representing the voiceless subaltern of imperialist oppression through the rigorous exposure of the conditions of her silencing.[5] Closer examination of the French Enlightenment, however, would have revealed a discourse that liberally invokes the figure of the speaking native to articulate a complex rhetorical attack on colonialism abroad, as well as on French politics, morality, and the *ancien régime* social order. Writers such as baron de Lahontan and Denis Diderot imagined the colonial encounter as fundamentally dialogical in that the native spoke back to colonial power at the scene of its enunciation in the non-European world, ridiculing its pretensions, exposing its discontinuities, and unsettling its binaries. Ironically, as I shall argue, French Enlightenment writers used these figures to thematize something very much like the 'hybridization' of colonial discourse theorized in postcolonial criticism.

In this essay, I examine the obsession of two French Enlightenment *philosophes* with representing anticolonial resistance, as well as a radical critique of European culture and society, through the figure of the speaking native. In particular, I explore the ideological implications of deconstructing,

---

12 (1985), 59–87; and Arif Dirlik, 'The Postcolonial Aura: Third World Criticism in the Age of Global Capitalism', *Critical Inquiry*, 20/2 (1994), 328–56.

[5] Rejecting what she considers to be the anti-intellectualism of post-structuralists such as Michel Foucault and Gilles Deleuze, who have abandoned the task of representing marginalized or oppressed people in favour of efforts to create the conditions for them to speak for themselves, Spivak aligns herself with the methods and assumptions of the subaltern studies historian Ranajit Guha, for whom 'there is no unrepresentable subaltern subject that can know and speak itself'. 'Can the Subaltern Speak?', 80–1.

in a fictional medium, the contradictions, fallacies, and ethnocentrism of early modern colonial discourses. Looking at two philosophical dialogues, each written at a critical juncture in the history of French colonial expansion—Lahontan's *Dialogues de Monsieur le baron de Lahontan et d'un Sauvage dans l'Amérique* (1704) and Diderot's *Supplément au voyage de Bougainville* (written c.1772–84)—I argue that these works represent the subversion of colonial discourses by the putative object of colonial command, thus anticipating and rigorously illustrating some of the most influential critiques of colonial discourse in late twentieth-century postcolonial theory. In so doing, I address the ways in which Enlightenment writers' appropriation of the native voice and subject position may in fact contribute to the silencing of the Other, thus potentially nullifying the anticolonial implications of their discourse. However, I propose that careful attention to the ironies of eighteenth-century philosophical dialogues compels the critic to move beyond that position. Through a close reading of the representational strategies and aporias of Diderot's *Supplément*, I argue that the author in fact thematizes the very impossibility of recovering the voice of the Other, thus parodying the trope of the enlightened native as well as the project of speaking for and through non-Europeans.

Yet in exploring the ways in which Enlightenment dialogues instantiate and in some cases surpass the critical acumen and degree of self-reflexivity exhibited in postcolonial theory, I nonetheless reject the idea, most recently set forth by Sankar Muthu, that either of these works constitutes an anti-colonial or anti-imperialist discourse.[6] Rather than accepting at face value the *philosophes*' rhetorical opposition to colonialism, I propose that the dialogue was instead the essential device whereby Enlightenment philosophers simulated the kinds of contestation and debate that were absent from the metropolitan public sphere and that they deemed necessary to the reform of French colonial policies and ideology. In this respect, I argue, the eighteenth-century critique of colonialism ultimately contributed to a new colonial discourse based on Enlightenment conceptions of universal reason, individual freedom, and commercial globalization. By figuring a critique of French colonial power through fictionalized colonized subjects, Enlightenment thinkers anticipated as well the consent of those imagined colonized peoples to the reform proposals implied within the critique itself.

---

[6] Sankar Muthu, *Enlightenment against Empire* (Princeton: Princeton University Press, 2003).

I Mimicry and hybridity in Lahontan's
Dialogues avec un sauvage

Dialogues avec un sauvage by Louis-Armand de Lom d'Arce, baron de Lahontan,[7] is remarkable not merely for having established the trope of the savage critic in French literature and philosophy, but also for articulating many of the most radical principles of early Enlightenment thought.[8] First published in 1704, the work quickly became an enormous popular success, appearing in over twenty editions by the middle of the eighteenth century. A synthesis of the anticlerical rationalism of Bayle and Fontenelle, the *Dialogues* also contained scathing critiques of French civil society, absolute monarchy, and morals, and the work was read by the major philosophers of the French Enlightenment. Yet it was inspired as much by the author's experience among indigenous groups in colonial Canada, or 'New France', as it was known, as by the intellectual ferment of *libertinage érudit*.

An impoverished nobleman from south-western France, Lahontan travelled to Canada in 1683 with a contingent of sailors from the Royal Navy sent to reinforce the French governor's defences against the Iroquois nation, and remained there for ten years. In the late seventeenth century, Canada was riddled with ethnic tension and rivalry between European powers for influence among several groups of Indians who were partners in the fur trade. In the mid seventeenth century, a massive war had led to the massacre of the Huron, allies of the French, by the Iroquois, who were associated with English and Dutch colonial interests. Shortly thereafter, the French found a new ally in the Algonquian, with whom they waged a brutal war against the

---

[7] I have used the short form *Dialogues avec un sauvage*, by convention, to refer to Lahontan's text, which has a complicated bibliographical history. The *Dialogues de Monsieur le Baron de Lahontan et d'un Sauvage dans l'Amerique* appeared as part of Lahontan's *Suite du Voyage de l'Amérique* (Amsterdam, 1704). Quotations in this essay are taken from *Oeuvres complètes*, ed. Réal Ouellet with Alain Beaulieu (Montreal: Presses Universitaires de Montréal, 1990), with page numbers provided in the text. It should be noted, however, that the dialogues first appeared in 1703. Réal Ouellet points out that the *Suite du Voyage* was published in September of 1703 despite having been dated 1704 (p. 791 n. 1), and the work also appeared in The Hague as a separate volume dated 1703 with the title *Supplément aux voyages du Baron de Lahontan, Où l'on trouve des Dialogues curieux entre l'auteur et un Sauvage*.

[8] I borrow the term 'savage critic' from Anthony Pagden's essay 'The Savage Critic: Some European Images of the Primitive', *Yearbook of English Studies*, 13 (1983), 32–45.

Iroquois that lasted until the end of the century. Lahontan was critical of French cruelties towards the Iroquois, as well as of the role of the evangelical mission in inflaming ethnic hostilities and aiding French colonial interests. In addition to developing close relationships with Indians of various nations, he took part in commercial hunting, exploration, and military operations in Canada until his differences with the French leadership finally led him to seek exile in England.[9]

Within a decade following his departure from New France, Lahontan published a two-volume travel relation entitled *Nouveaux Voyages de M. Le Baron de Lahontan*. These volumes, published in Amsterdam in 1703, comprised epistolary and narrative accounts of the author's experience in Canada as a soldier and explorer in the southern Great Lakes region. Subsequently he published his *Suite du voyage de l'Amérique* as a supplement, which was divided into two sections, the 'Dialogues de Monsieur le Baron de Lahontan et d'un Sauvage de l'Amerique' and the 'Voyages de Portugal et de Danemarc'.[10] According to Lahontan, the *Dialogues* were based on a series of exchanges between himself and a Huron chief named Kondiaronk, nicknamed 'Le Rat' by the French. This chief had suffered the defeat of his nation at the hands of the Iroquois, but was reputedly a long-time ally of the French, extolled for his skills in oratory.[11] The highly satirical dialogue transpires between a Huron by the name of Adario, arguably a partial anagram of 'Kondiaronk', and a Frenchman who bears the author's name in the text.[12]

[9] On Lahontan's experience in colonial North America, see Réal Ouellet and Alain Beaulieu, introduction in Louis Armand de Lom d'Arce, baron de Lahontan, *Oeuvres complètes*, ed. Réal Ouellet, 2 vols (Montreal: Presses Universitaires de Montréal, 1990), 13–14; Gordon Sayre, *Les Sauvages Américains: Representations of Native Americans in French and English Colonial Literature* (Chapel Hill: University of North Carolina Press, 1997); Maurice Roelens, introduction in Louis Armand de Lom d'Arce, baron de Lahontan, *Dialogues avec un Sauvage* (Paris: Éditions Sociales, 1973).

[10] The complete title of the third volume is as follows: *Suite du Voyage, de l'Amérique, ou Dialogues de Monsieur le Baron de Lahontan et d'un Sauvage, dans l'Amerique. Contenant une description exacte des moeurs et des coutumes de ces Peuples Sauvages. Avec les voyages du même en Portugal et en Danemarc, dans lesquels on trouve des particularitez trés curieuses, et qu'on n'avoit point encore remarquées* (Amsterdam, 1704).

[11] This impression is recorded in the *Mémoires de l'Amérique Septentrionale*, the second volume of Lahontan's relation, and in Charlevoix's *Histoire et description générale de la Nouvelle-France*, 6 vols (Paris, 1744) ii, bk 18, quoted in Roelens, introduction, 44–5.

[12] Ouellet and Beaulieu, introduction, 25.

By the time Lahontan was writing, the theme of Amerindian eloquence had appeared in numerous early modern travel relations and histories containing the harangues of native subjects critical of the colonial crimes of conquering Europeans as well as of their putatively 'savage' culture and manners, and the dialogue form in particular had been incorporated into the travel accounts of Jean de Léry, Samuel de Champlain, and Paul Le Jeune.[13] Yet Lahontan's transposition of the speaking 'savage' trope into a semi-autonomous philosophical dialogue represented a significant innovation in the French literary tradition. Although Montaigne was the first to incorporate the figure of the indigenous American savage critic into French literary writing and philosophy, he eschewed the dialogic encounter in favour of an extended reflection on second-hand information about New World natives, supposedly divulged by a European traveller informant with first-hand experience of their ways. Only in the concluding paragraphs of his famous essay 'Des cannibales' does a putatively native American character—whom Montaigne claims to have met in Rouen—speak his own impressions of European society. Even then, the non-European voice is doubly mediated, first by a bad translator, and second by the author's admittedly faulty memory and indirect style.[14]

In contrast, Lahontan elevates the native Other into a speaking subject engaging in extended dialogue with a European representative of the French colonial project. What Lahontan retains from Montaigne's 'savage' figure is the idea of travel; Adario, a Huron in war-torn Canada, is an experienced

---

[13] Jean de Léry, *Histoire d'un voyage faict en la terre du Bresil (1578)*, ed. Frank Lestringant (Paris: Librairie Générale Française, 1994); Samuel de Champlain, *Des Sauvages, ou, Voyage de Samuel Champlain, de Brouage, fait en la France nouvelle, l'an mil six cens trois: contenant les moeurs, façon de vivre, mariages, guerres, & habitations des Sauvages de Canadas* [sic] (Paris, 1604); Paul Le Jeune, *Relation de ce qui s'est passé en la Nouvelle France* (Paris, 1634).

[14] Summarizing the natives' response when asked what they found most admirable about French society, Montaigne explains, 'ils repondirent trois choses, d'où j'ai perdu la troisième, et en suis bien marri, mais j'en ai encore deux en mémoire...' ('they replied three things, the third of which I forgot, and am quite upset about, but I still have two of them in memory...'). On his discussions with one native in particular, the author complains, 'Je parlai à l'un d'eux fort longtemps, mais j'avais un truchement qui me suivait si mal, et qui était si empêché à recevoir mes imaginations par sa bêtise, que je n'en pus tirer guère de plaisir.' ('I spoke to one of them for a long time but I had a translator who followed me badly and was so busy receiving my thoughts by his ignorance that I could hardly take any pleasure from it.') Michel de Montaigne, 'Des cannibales', in *Les Essais*, ed. André Tournon, 3 vols (Paris: Imprimerie Nationale Éditions, 1998), i, 357–8 (my translation).

traveller, having seen not only France, but also French Québec and the English colony of New York. Yet, unlike Montaigne's 'cannibal', Adario is fully conversant in the French language and uses it to resist European authority in the colonies. Indeed, his character is founded on his refusal to submit to the colonialist strategy described by Homi Bhabha as 'mimicry', or the desire to produce a 'reformed, recognizable Other', Europeanized in tastes and opinion, yet native in appearance and language, through whom colonial power may be administered, represented, and legitimated before the native population.[15] According to Bhabha, this strategy has an ironically disturbing effect on colonial discourse, for it exposes colonialism's tendency to produce, under the guise of Enlightenment, salvation, and 'civilization', modes of subjection and discipline, thus alienating these projects from their prior meaning and function. What is more, as is demonstrated by Lahontan's text, the project of mimicry opens the colonizer up to ridicule and mockery by the colonized. As Adario explains, the Jesuit priest, in addition to proselytizing to him incessantly, has tried to make him into a translator and go-between to advance the Christian evangelical campaign:

il me persécute à tout moment de les expliquer [ses raisonnements] mot pour mot au gens de ma Nation, parce que, dit-il, ayant de l'esprit, je puis trouver des termes assez expressifs dans ma Langue pour rendre le sens de ses paroles plus intelligible que luy, à qui le langage Huron n'est pas assez bien connu. (p. 829)

he importunes me at every moment to explain [his reasoning] word for word to the people of my nation because, he says, having imagination, I can find terms in my language that are sufficiently expressive to render the meaning of his words better than he, who does not know the Huron language well enough.[16]

Instead, much like Shakespeare's Caliban, Adario exploits his eloquence in the colonizer's language to express a scathing critique of Christianity, colonialism, and French society. He is thus the ideal adversary for Lahontan's character, a soldier and enthusiastic representative of French colonialism and the Christian mission. Displaying an intransigent and naive belief in the moral superiority of the French over the Huron, Lahontan provokes Adario into a series of ironic refutations of European religious ideas and social practices.

[15] Bhabha, 'Of Mimicry and Man', in *The Location of Culture*, 86.
[16] All translations in the text are mine.

Lahontan's text is thus a parody of a didactic dialogue. Not only is Adario already familiar with and thoroughly perturbed by the 'truths' that Lahontan professes to him, but Lahontan himself soon proves woefully inept in defending them, thus losing ground to a much more eloquent and rationally sophisticated interlocutor. Yet if the text appears to valorize Huron society and cultural values over the European, it is just as significant as an exploration of the subversive effects of an encounter with difference on a discourse of power, a phenomenon theorized in Homi Bhabha's postcolonial criticism as 'hybridization'. Bhabha's notion of 'hybridity' is based in part on his interpretation of a missionary registrar's account of a discussion that took place in 1817 between the Indian catechist Anund Messeh and a group of Indians reading a translation of the Gospels. Drawing on their own beliefs and opposition to English dietary practices, they pose challenging questions to the catechist and refuse to take the sacrament. Bhabha interprets the scene as a moment of the 'disturbing questioning of the images and presences of authority' that allows 'other "denied" knowledges [to] enter upon the dominant discourse and estrange its authority', an idea which he develops further into a metacritical theory for reading postcolonial cultural representations.[17]

This process of contestation and subversion by the subaltern is arguably what is thematized in Lahontan's *Dialogues*. It is no accident that the discussion begins with religion, the legitimating discourse of colonialism in New France. Like that of Anund Messeh in Bhabha's narrative, Lahontan's evangelical position stresses the centrality of Scripture as the basis for Christian belief; the Bible is the fetishized source of colonial authority, signifying both the 'truth' of Christianity and the putative superiority of the European technology of writing. For Adario, however, the Christian book is but a collection of dangerous fables and chimerical notions that contradict human experience and threaten the exercise of reason. When Lahontan evokes the biblical image of heaven and hell, Adario baulks:

Ces saintes Ecritures que tu cites à tout moment, comme les Jésuites font, demandent cette grande foy, dont ces bons Pères nous rompent les oreilles.... Comment donc aurois-je cette foy, puisque tu ne sçaurois ni me prouver, ni me faire voir la moindre chose de ce que tu dis? Croy-moy, ne jette pas ton esprit dans des obscurités, cesse de soûtenir les visions des Ecritures saintes, ou bien finissons nos Entretiens. (p. 804)

[17] Bhabha, 'Signs Taken for Wonders', 113.

These holy Scriptures that you, like the Jesuits, are quoting at every moment demand that great faith those good Fathers burst our ears with.... How would I have that faith when you are able neither to prove to me nor to let me see the least of the things that you are telling me? Believe me, thrust not your mind into obscurities, stop upholding the visions of the holy Scriptures or we'll have to finish our conversations.

Adario's objections arise from his own cultural belief system, which blends reverence towards a Creator God with a form of materialist rationalism. According to him, the Huron lead their lives in conformity with principles gleaned from experience in the material world, since, as he puts it, 'la portée de nôtre esprit ne pouvant s'étendre un pouce au dessus de la superficie de la terre, nous ne devons pas le gâter ni le corrompre en essayant de pénétrer les choses invisibles et improbables' (p. 803) ('as the scope of our imagination cannot extend one thumb's length beyond the earth's surface, we must not spoil nor corrupt it by trying to discern invisible and improbable things'). Yet in refusing to believe the Scripture, Adario rejects not only its presumption of supernatural knowledge, but also the very practice of writing itself, which purports to fix past events, impressions, and spoken words so as to preserve them as truths for all time. In particular, the Huron critiques the Jesuits' ethnographic accounts of native cultures, which in his view grossly misrepresent his people:

Or, si nous voïons de nos propres yeux des faussetez imprimées et des choses diférentes de ce qu'elles sont sur le papier; comment veux-tu que je croïe la sincerité de ces Bibles écrites depuis tant de siécles, traduites de plusieurs langues par des ignorans ... ou par des menteurs ... (pp. 806–7)

However, if we see with our own eyes printed falsities and things that are different from how they are on paper, how do you expect me to believe the sincerity of these Bibles written so many centuries ago and translated from several languages by ignorant people ... or liars?

Furthermore, remarking upon the violent antagonism and religious hatred between the French and the English, the Huron laments that the literal spoken words of the Christian God were either completely lost, or were meant to bring 'la guerre dans ce monde au lieu de la paix; ce qui ne sçauroit estre' (p. 808) ('war in this world instead of peace, which should not be'). Adario's analytic and rationalist approach to religion leads to some rather humorous interpretations of the Scriptures. His greatest frustration concerns the centrepiece of the Christian faith, the story of the Incarnation and Crucifixion of Jesus Christ:

Quoy! ce grand et incomprehensible Etre et Createur des Terres, des Mers et du vaste Firmament, auroit pû s'avilir à demeurer neuf mois prisonnier dans les entrailles d'une Femme, à s'exposer à la miserable vie de ses camarades pécheurs, qui ont écrit vos Livres d'Evangiles, à Estre batu, foüetté et crucifié comme un malheureux? C'est ce que mon esprit ne peut s'imaginer. (pp. 812–13)

What? This great and incomprehensible Being and Creator of the Earth, the Sea, and the vast Firmament could have so debased himself as to remain nine months imprisoned in the entrails of a woman, expose himself to the miserable life of his fellow sinners who wrote your Books of the Gospels, be beaten, whipped and crucified like a wretch? That is what my mind cannot imagine.

If the Christians can believe such things, they do so, argues Adario, because they have been conditioned since youth to override their reason. Of course, belief does not necessarily compel obedience to Christian law. Though he praises the justice of the Ten Commandments, Adario attributes much of the violence of colonialism in the New World, including rape, theft, murder, and dishonesty, to Europeans' systematic disregard for these laws. Exhibiting the subversive power of the would-be mimic, he thus concludes, 'les Européans ... ne songent jamais à leur Créateur, que lors qu'ils en parlent avec les Hurons' (p. 828) ('Europeans ... never think of their creator except when they speak to Hurons about him'). Christianity is thus exposed as other to itself; no longer a discourse of truth and salvation, it is merely the justification for French colonialist hegemony. In the words of Bhabha, colonialism has 'produce[d] a knowledge of Christianity as a form of social control', one that conflicts with and thus makes a mockery of the original it imitates.[18]

Adario therefore takes advantage of the dialogic colonial encounter to deconstruct the discourse of colonial authority, destabilizing at the same time the binary between savagery and civilization. If on one hand the dialogue demonstrates the French need to make the Other 'almost the same'[19] through conversion and assimilation, Adario's 'savage' discourse points up the radical incommensurability of the beliefs of the characters Lahontan and Adario, and hence the absurdity of founding colonial power on a pretension to higher truth. Ironically, it is Adario's ethnocentricity that

---

[18] Bhabha, *The Location of Culture*, 87.

[19] The reference is to Bhabha's characterization of the ambivalence of mimicry: 'almost the same, but not quite'. See *The Location of Culture*, 86.

ultimately dooms what begins as an amicable conversation. Whereas initially Adario professes his tolerance of Lahontan's character's views, wishing only that he might be allowed to doubt them (p. 814), he gradually shows himself to be intolerant of Christianity. Ultimately, the author sets up a striking parallelism between his character and Adario as the latter adopts a proselytizing discourse, beseeching Lahontan to save himself by *becoming* Huron. Convinced that the 'grand Esprit' ('great spirit') sent the French to Canada to 'corriger [leurs] défauts et suivre nostre exemple' ('correct their faults and follow our example'), Adario exclaims, 'Ainsi, mon Frére, croi tout ce que tu voudras, aïe tant de foy qu'il te plaira, tu n'iras jamais dans le bon pais des Ames si tu ne te fais Huron' (p. 828) ('So, my brother, believe all that you want, have as much faith as you wish, you will never go to the good country of the Souls if you do not make yourself Huron'). In this respect, the characters Lahontan and Adario are each the other's double; identical in their refusal of the other's difference, they differ only in the means by which they wish to impose sameness. Whereas Adario chooses dialogue, only war— the profession that Lahontan's character actually practises—will ensure the subjugation of the Indians to French religion and colonial rule. Adario thus exposes the illegitimacy of French colonialism among the Huron:

Il y a cinquante ans que les Gouverneurs du Canada prétendent que nous soyons sous les Loix de leur grand Capitaine. Nous nous contentons de nier nostre dépendance de tout autre que du grand Esprit...Car sur quel droit et sur quelle autorité fondent-ils cette prétention? Qui vous a donné tous les pays que vous habitez?...Ils apartiénent aux *Algonkins* depuis toujours. (p. 831)

For fifty years the governors of Canada have claimed that we are under the laws of their Great Captain. We content ourselves with denying our dependence on anyone other than the Great Spirit...For on what right and on what authority do they found this pretence?... Who gave you all the lands you are living on?...They have always belonged to the Algonquians.

Although Lahontan the author effectively illustrates Adario's resistance to colonial discourse and missionary mimicry, the anticolonial theme is arguably undermined by his own shaping of the Huron's cultural difference in the mould of Enlightenment philosophy. In the preface, Lahontan indicates that the thoughts of his 'savage' character will be 'habillées à l'Européane' ('dressed in the European manner') so as, ironically, to enhance their verisimilitude in the eyes of his correspondent. Rehearsing a common

European characterization of Native American speech, the author attests that the latter implored him to 'ne plus traduire à la lettre un langage si rempli de fictions et d'hiberboles sauvages' ('no longer translate literally a language so full of fictions and savage hyperbole').[20] While here Lahontan asserts that modifications pertain only to style and diction, the preface elsewhere suggests that Adario becomes the vehicle for a full-blown critique of established religion and society in France. Defiantly addressing his critics, Lahontan defends the incendiary nature of the work:

On m'avertit aussi que j'ay tout lieu de craindre le ressentiment de plusieurs Eclésiastiques, qui prétendent que j'ay insulté Dieu, en insultant leur conduite.... Ce qui me console, c'est que je n'ay rien écrit que je ne puisse prouver autentiquement; outre que je n'ay pû moins dire à leur égard que ce que j'ai dit. (p. 796)

I was also warned that I would have reason to fear the resentment of several Ecclesiastics who claim that I insulted God by attacking their conduct... What consoles me is that I have not written anything that I cannot prove authentically; especially since I could not have said less in regard to them than what I have said.

In the dialogues, Lahontan elaborates on a number of contemporary polemics, evoking the deism, materialism, and natural law theory of early French Enlightenment philosophy. In Adario's discourse, Huron society appears as a thought-experiment in materialist utopia, the diametrical opposite to Catholic, absolutist France. Lacking private property and money and their attendant social hierarchies maintained by the law, the Huron social order is guaranteed by the natural harmony of 'free' individuals. The fictional Adario thus attacks a range of abuses in French society including the venality of office, the indiscretions of the clergy, the oppression of women, the persecution of witches, and laws of inheritance that had left Lahontan himself virtually impoverished. In these respects, then, Lahontan himself places Adario in the position of a mimic, not of the colonial missionary, but rather of the European philosopher. Under his pen, the author reforms, remakes, and Europeanizes the native, one of those he calls 'Philosophes nuds' (p. 795) ('nude philosophers'), such that Adario becomes an articulate representative of early Enlightenment thought, a critical mediator between the radical libertine philosopher and the contemporary European lectorate. Almost

---

[20] Lahontan, preface in *Suite du Voyage*, in *Oeuvres complètes*, ii, 794–5. On European colonial stereotypes of Amerindian eloquence, see David Murray, *Forked Tongues: Speech, Writing, and Representation in American Indian Texts* (Bloomington: Indiana University Press, 1991).

the same as the philosopher in the intellectual sense, Adario is critically different in his culture, his ethnicity, and, most importantly, his opposition to colonial domination, all of which function to legitimate his radical critique for a European readership. Indeed, what provokes the reader's sympathy and identification with Adario is the suffering that he and his people have experienced at the hands of the French and their position as an unjustly colonized nation, from which a counter-discourse to colonialism is both credible and warranted. Ironically, however, the author's reliance on Adario as his mimic further subverts his character's critique of European hegemony, for insofar as the authority of his Enlightenment polemic is staked on the anticolonial stance of the defeated Huron, the success of colonialism is its primary condition of possibility.

II Parodic mimicry and utopia in Diderot's
Supplément au voyage de Bougainville

To a certain extent, the same is true of Diderot's *Supplément au voyage de Bougainville*, drafted in the 1770s and 1780s and published posthumously in 1796, almost a century after Lahontan's *Dialogues* and more than two decades after Bougainville's travel relation, *Voyage autour du monde* (1771).[21] Like Lahontan, whom he reputedly admired greatly,[22] Diderot depicts a native speaking subject who contests the European colonial presence, hybridizes its discourse, and exposes the corruption of European social and moral values. Yet Diderot was as interested in subverting the philosopher's strategy of mimeticism as he was in exposing the ills of French society and sexual mores, and the violence of colonialism. The result is a structurally complex, highly self-referential, polyphonic text that questions both the unity and the authenticity of mediated speech. Read together with Lahontan's dialogues, Diderot's text forces a reappraisal of the ideological function of the 'savage critic' in French Enlightenment discourse, as well as of the notion that Enlightenment dialogues necessarily colonize native subject

---

[21] Parenthetical references to the *Supplément* in the text are to the version printed in Denis Diderot, *Oeuvres philosophiques*, ed. Paul Vernière (Paris: Bordas, 1990).

[22] Gilbert Chinard, introduction in Denis Diderot, *Supplément au voyage de Bougainville*, ed. Gilbert Chinard (Paris: Librairie E. Droz, 1935), 67.

positions, thus reinscribing colonial power. Diderot's text demands that we consider instead the ways in which the Enlightenment dialogues illuminate the strategies and pitfalls of postcolonial theorists' own desire to represent the colonized subject, while at the same time promoting a revision of colonialism based on Enlightenment ideals.

The theme of the indeterminacy of authorship and representation is first suggested by the very title of the work: *Supplément au voyage de Bougainville, ou Dialogue entre A et B* ('Supplement to the voyage of Bougainville, or dialogue between A and B'). The undecidability posed by the doubleness of the title is compounded by the fact that each of these places Diderot in the position of impostor. In the first case, Diderot appears paradoxically to usurp the authority of another author, Bougainville, by claiming to complete his text. On the other hand, the dialogue between two unnamed subjects, A and B, raises the question of the hidden identity of the speakers, one or both of whom may not be identical to the author. What becomes clear is that the *Supplément* is a text within the text, which contains another dialogue and a prosopopoeia, to which the reader of Diderot's text will gain access only through the dialogue of A and B. In this dialogue, the two figures, who are themselves already familiar with Bougainville's *Voyage*, engage in the act of reading and interpreting the *Supplément*, which B quotes and appears to read from at length, though often with no textual indication of the shift from his own speech to the quoted text. By structuring the work around the *mise-en-abyme* of the act of mediation, Diderot thus requires that the reader constantly track and question the shifting boundaries in the text between author, narrator, and speaking subject.

The interpretive challenges posed by multiple mediations are suggestively foreshadowed in the conversation between A and B, for the dialogue turns around the problem of deception, untruth, and inauthenticity. A opens the discussion with a remark about the inconstancy of the weather: 'Cette superbe voûte étoilée, sous laquelle nous revînmes hier, et qui semblait nous garantir un beau jour, ne nous a pas tenu parole ... Le brouillard est si épais qu'il nous dérobe la vue des arbes voisins' (pp. 455–6) ('That superb starry sky under which we came back yesterday, and which seemed to promise a beautiful day, has failed to keep its word ... the fog is so thick that it conceals our view of those nearby trees').[23] The metaphor of 'not

---

[23] English translations of quotations from the *Supplément* are my own. Anglophone readers may otherwise refer to the following English edition: Denis Diderot, *Political Writings*, trans. and ed. John Hope Mason and Robert Wokler (Cambridge: Cambridge University Press, 1992), 35–75.

keeping one's word' suggestively poses the problem of misrepresentation, a theme that returns more explicitly in the speakers' subsequent discussion of Bougainville himself. For A, Bougainville is a man of contradictions, displaying a troubling inauthenticity in his new occupation as traveller. Having abandoned a former sedentary life as a mathematician, Bougainville the world traveller also suppresses his insatiable love of society, entertainment, and women. While A takes such changeability to be incomprehensible, B accepts it as human nature: 'Il fait comme tout le monde: il se dissipe après s'être appliqué, et s'applique après s'être dissipé' (p. 457) ('He's no different from anyone else. After he has applied himself he looks for distraction, and after distraction he applies himself'). Yet A and B's reading of the *Supplément* is prefaced by another case of misrepresentation which is much more difficult to resolve, for it has to do with the perils of cross-cultural communication. A and B recall the story of the Tahitian named Aotourou who had accompanied Bougainville on his return voyage to France only to languish in a state of disorientation and mutism. In addition to entirely misreading the cultural difference of Europeans, he never learned to speak French, which B maintains was too sophisticated for his savage tongue. For B, this linguistic inadequacy renders Aotourou mute not only in France, but also at home, for in attempting to describe to his countrymen what he saw there, 'il ne trouvera dans sa langue aucun terme correspondant [aux choses] dont il a quelques idées' (p. 464) ('he . . . will find no terms in his language corresponding [to the things] of which he formed some impressions'). Even if he could express the cultural difference of Europeans, he would not be believed, for 'en comparant leurs moeurs aux nôtres, ils aimeront mieux prendre Aotourou pour un menteur, que de nous croire si fous' (p. 464) ('in comparing their own ways with ours, they will rather take Aotourou for a liar than think us so mad'). While B implies that cross-cultural understanding can take place only in the language of the 'higher' culture, he also asserts that radical difference is fundamentally incommunicable when reported by a mere observer. Behind the ironic critique of French culture is the suggestion that the credibility of travellers' tales of other lands is subject to question and denial by readers unwilling or unable to accept the cultural differences they expose.

This remark is suggestive of the ambiguous relationship between Bougainville's *Voyage* and the text of the *Supplément*. As B explains to A, 'vous n'auriez aucun doute sur la sincérité de Bougainville, si vous connaissiez le Supplément de son voyage' (p. 464) ('you would have no doubt about Bougainville's sincerity if you knew the Supplement to his voyage'). If the *Supplément* vouches for the truth of the travel relation, it is presumably because it contains the discourse of the Tahitians themselves. Yet, in presenting the point of view of the 'savage' in French, Diderot directly contradicts Bougainville's idyllic portrait of his visit to 'La Nouvelle Cythère' ('New Cythera'), and departs significantly from the representational model of Lahontan's dialogues by refusing to accord to one native figure the privilege of speaking for his or her entire society. Instead, the representation of Tahitian society is splintered into a discontinuous set of impressions offered by two speaking subjects, whose views on Bougainville's visit and on Tahitian society do not always coincide. What is more, the problem of translation is brought to the fore, thus disrupting the illusion of mimesis and communicability represented by the forms of prosopopoeia and dialogue.

Of Diderot's two native informants, the *vieillard* ('old man') figure comes closest to articulating a counter-discourse to European colonialism. His eloquent harangue is announced upon the departure of Bougainville's expedition from Tahiti, and comprises a passionate denunciation of the European incursion. As his fellow Tahitians rush to bid Bougainville farewell with an emotional display of affection and sorrow, the *vieillard* admonishes them for falling prey to the deceptions of possessive Europeans, not knowing that they have become complicit in their own destruction. His critique revolves around issues of property and theft, which he claims were unknown to Tahitians before Bougainville's arrival. If colonization itself is the purest act of theft, signified by Bougainville's inscription '*Ce pays est à nous*' (p. 467) ('This country is ours'), the European presence has, he contends, propagated among Tahitians themselves a kind of possessiveness leading to criminality, violence, and jealousy in love relationships:

Ici tout est à tous; et tu nous as prêché je ne sais quelle distinction du *tien* et du *mien*. Nos filles et nos femmes nous sont communes; tu as partagé ce privilège avec nous; et tu es venu allumer en elles des fureurs inconnues. Elles sont devenues folles dans tes bras; tu es devenu féroce entre les leurs. Elles ont commencé à se haïr; vous vous êtes égorgés pour elles; et elles nous sont revenues teintes de votre sang. (pp. 466–7)

Here, everything belongs to everyone, and you preached to us I don't know what distinction between 'yours' and 'mine'. Our daughters and our wives are held in common by all of us. You shared that privilege with us, and you came to enflame them with a frenzy they had never known before. They became wild in your arms, and you became ferocious in theirs. They began to hate each other. You butchered one another for them, and they came back stained with your blood.

Women are the exploited site of contact in the colonial encounter; powerless themselves, they mediate the relationship between European and Tahitian men. The tainting of their blood through miscegenation adds a further dimension to the theft of colonization, for it irremediably destroys the two hallmarks of the Tahitian state of nature: excellent health and bountiful reproduction. Whereas a policy of unrestricted procreative sexuality had allowed Tahitians to 'se reproduire sans honte' ('reproduce without shame'), sex between Tahitian women and European men has had precisely the opposite effect, leading to sickness, infection, and the death of women and mixed-race children. In the *vieillard*'s account, Bougainville's voyage precipitates a genocidal disaster in which Tahitians may be forced to exterminate infected persons in order to save their race:

tu as infecté notre sang. Il nous faudra peut-être exterminer de nos propres mains nos filles, nos femmes, nos enfants. . . . Malheureux! tu seras coupable, ou des ravages qui suivront les funestes caresses des tiens, ou des meurtres que nous commettrons pour en arrêter le poison (p. 469)

You have infected our blood. We will perhaps be forced to wipe out, with our own hands, our daughters, our wives, our children. . . . Wretched man! You will bear guilt, either for the ravages that will follow the deadly caresses of your people, or for the murders we shall commit to stop the poison.

If the *vieillard* presents the French expedition as literally sowing the seeds of death and destruction in Tahiti, the dialogue between Orou and the French chaplain offers a very different view of the power dynamics and effects of the colonial encounter. Orou's account is the inverse of the *vieillard*'s; it recounts a scene of arrival and the momentary prohibition of sexual contact due to the resistant morals of the French chaplain, who blushes before Orou's invitation to sleep with his wife or one of his daughters. In one of the most famous exchanges, Orou questions the chaplain's hesitation:

Je ne sais ce que c'est que la chose que tu appelles religion; mais je ne puis qu'en penser mal, puisqu'elle t'empêche de goûter un plaisir innocent, auquel nature, la souveraine maîtresse, nous invite tous; de donner l'existence à un de tes semblables; de rendre un service que le père, la mère et les enfants te demandent; de t'acquitter envers un hôte qui t'a fait un bon accueil, et d'enrichir une nation, en l'accroissant d'un sujet de plus. (p. 476)

I don't know what you mean by religion, but I can only think ill of it, since it prevents you from enjoying an innocent pleasure to which Nature, that sovereign mistress, invites all of us: that is, of bringing into the world one of our own kind; rendering a service which the father, mother, and children ask of you, repaying a gracious host, and enriching a nation by adding one more subject to it.

The passage suggests that reproduction is the fundamental objective of the Tahitian sexual and social order. Sexual promiscuity of women and men is encouraged as long as both partners are fit to reproduce, and children enhance a woman's desirability in marriage. What is fascinating is that Orou embraces the arrival of Europeans as a procreative opportunity. In offering his daughters to the chaplain, Orou suggests that a demand is being made on the European male body to enrich the Tahitian nation. Later, Orou reveals the 'secret' of the Tahitian response to the Europeans as the deliberate manipulation of the European libido to service the demographic needs of Tahitian society. Rather than being a mere gift, the Tahitians' hospitality is the means by which they may profit from the colonial encounter: 'Nous ne t'avons point demandé d'argent; nous ne nous sommes point jetés sur tes marchandises . . . mais nos femmes et nos filles sont venues exprimer le sang de tes veines. Quand tu t'éloigneras, tu nous auras laissé des enfants' (p. 500) ('We did not ask you for money; we did not loot your goods . . . but our wives and daughters drew blood from your veins. When you've gone you will have left us children'). Directly contradicting the *vieillard*'s story of a colonialist assault on natural innocence, Orou evokes a premeditated plot to exploit European desire in order to produce soldiers and men to work the fields, replace the population lost to disease, and settle a debt with a neighbouring nation. The moral of the story is simple; the Tahitians are neither innocent, nor easily duped, and nature demands reciprocity: 'Va où tu voudras; et tu trouveras presque toujours l'homme aussi fin que toi. Il ne te donnera jamais que ce qui ne lui est bon à rien, et te demandera toujours ce qui lui est utile' (p. 501) ('Go wherever you will, and you'll almost always find a man as shrewd as yourself. He will never give you anything but what is worthless to him, and will always ask you for what he finds useful').

It is possible to read Orou's discourse of *métissage* as a fantasy whereby French colonial desire is displaced onto the Other and colonial coercion suppressed. The Tahitian strategy of harnessing European reproductive power is based on a eugenic notion of a 'good' *métissage* which combines European intelligence with non-European physicality, thus reinscribing European stereotypes of racial superiority. As Orou explains, 'Plus robustes, plus sains que vous, nous nous sommes aperçus au premier coup d'oeil que vous nous surpassiez en intelligence; et, sur-le-champ, nous avons destiné quelques-unes de nos femmes et de nos filles les plus belles à recueillir la semance d'une race meilleure que la nôtre' (p. 500) ('While more robust and healthy than you, we noticed at first glance that you surpassed us in intelligence, and we immediately destined some of our most beautiful women and girls to receive the seed of a race superior to ours'). For Pamela Cheek, this programme makes a fetish of colonial hybridity while repressing the violence of mis-cegenous sexual union: 'In the *Supplément*, the French fantasy of the savage's fantasy is that the savage wishes to be marked by French identity because it can ameliorate the race.'[24] Yet, as Lahontan's dialogue attests, by the time Diderot was writing the idea of sexual innocence and promiscuity had already become a stereotype through which European writers imagined newly 'discovered' lands as a vulnerable site of rape and plunder at the hands of European conquistadors or as a fantasized porno-tropics for European male travellers.[25] Countering this image of savage vulnerability to sexual and territorial incursion and political dissolution, Diderot transforms the fabled Tahitian 'hospitality' into a means by which Tahitian men exploit the repressed libidinal energies arising from the gap that Orou identifies in European society between civil and natural laws. Already in Bougainville's account, Tahitian men appear in one case to use nude women as a lure to bring European men on land where they would be forcibly strip-searched and their bodies examined.[26] Radicalizing this narrative of native sexual

---

[24] Pamela Cheek, *Sexual Antipodes: Enlightenment Globalization and the Placing of Sex* (Stanford: Stanford University Press, 2003), 182.

[25] Anne McClintock characterizes the eroticized non-European continents as a 'porno-tropics', 'a fantastic magic lantern of the mind onto which Europe projected its forbidden sexual desires and fears'. McClintock, *Imperial Leather: Race, Gender, and Sexuality in the Colonial Context* (New York: Routledge, 1995), 21.

[26] Bougainville offers the anecdote of his cook who defied the captain's orders not to fornicate with the natives, only to be terrorized by the stripping ritual: 'A peine eut-il mis pied à terre, avec la belle qu'il avait choisie, qu'il se vit entouré par une foule d'Indiens qui le déshabillèrent dans un instant, et le mirent nu de la tête aux pieds. Il se crut perdu mille fois, ne sachant où aboutiraient les exclamations de ce peuple, qui examinait en tumulte toutes les parties de son corps. . . . Il fallut que les insulaires ramenassent à bord le pauvre cuisinier, qui me dit que j'aurais beau le réprimander, que ne je lui ferais jamais autant de peur qu'il venait d'en avoir à la terre.' ('No sooner had he put his feet on land with the beauty he had chosen, than he was surrounded by a crowd of Indians who instantly undressed him and made him naked from head to toe. He thought himself lost a thousand times, not knowing what the exclamations of these people, who rigorously examined all the parts of his body, would lead to. . . . The islanders had to take the poor cook back on board the ship, and he told me that no matter how much I reprimanded him, I could never scare him as much as he had just been scared on land.') Louis Antoine, comte de Bougainville, *Voyage autour du monde par la frégate du Roi, la Boudeuse et la flûte l'Étoile*, ed. Jacques Proust (Paris: Gallimard, 1982), 226–7.

manipulation, Diderot suggests that in so freely pursuing their libidinal urges in the tropics, Frenchmen essentially subjugate themselves to the procreative programme of Tahitian men, the hidden agents of the colonial sexual encounter.

A more powerful and comprehensive attack on Diderot's attempted subversion of certain colonialist discourses and assumptions maintains that such a critique is fatally flawed by the author's insistence on speaking for others. As Mira Kamdar has argued, the paradox of the representation of the other in Diderot's *Supplément* and in the *Histoire des Deux Indes* is that in benevolently 'supplementing' the mutism of the colonized and representing them as speaking subjects voicing their own contestation of colonization, the author only further silences them and speaks only for himself. Extending Spivak's critique of the Eurocentrism inherent in post-structuralist notions of subjectivity to the Enlightenment fashion of speaking for non-Europeans, Kamdar maintains that this act of representation reinforces the West's privilege of the word and of mimetic superiority over the Other. The construction of the universal, global subject of European Enlightenment thus depends fundamentally on what Kamdar calls the desubjectification of the sovereign subject, and on the assimilation of the colonized voice to that of the colonizer who speaks in everybody's name, even as the colonized voices remain entirely unrepresented in the political sense. As Kamdar writes,

the purpose of the desubjectification of the sovereign Subject is, purportedly, to create a register where all on the world stage may be represented, that is to say, may speak in their own particular voices.... In each instance, these mimed voices tell their oppression as absence of *vertreten*, political representation, in the domination of their colonizers.... The subaltern cannot speak on the stage of European world history. Her enunciation is already colonized by the Enlightenment project of assimilation that seeks to benevolently represent her voice and thus mutes it.[27]

The notion that Diderot exploits the 'savage' subject position to speak for himself would appear to be supported by the text's genesis as a review essay written for Grimm's *Correspondance littéraire*. Though unpublished, the review includes a harangue that interpellates both the silent *vieillard* of Bougainville's account, imputing to him a stoic indignation before the imminent destruction of the Tahitian utopia, and Bougainville himself, whom he attacks for

[27] Mira Kamdar, 'Subjectification and Mimesis: Colonizing History', *American Journal of Semiotics*, 7/3 (1990), 99. See also Mira Kamdar, 'Poétique et politique: le paradoxe de la représentation de l'autre dans le *Supplément au voyage de Bougainville*', *Qui parle*, 1 (1985), 71–86.

unjustly taking possession of Tahiti and ravaging its state of nature.[28] It is this same discourse that Diderot proceeded to place into the mouth of the *vieillard* in the text of the *Supplément*. Yet to reduce automatically such an operation to a discursive recolonization of the Other is to misread much of the irony that makes Diderot's text strikingly complex and highly self-referential. Critics commonly recognize that the most distinctive feature of the work is its irreducible polyphony, which, combined with the multiple mediations, raises the hermeneutic problem of determining if any of those voices represent that of the author. Whereas for Georges Van Den Abbeele the device of enunciative undecidability leads to the 'loss of the philosopher's voice as unitary, authoritative and objective',[29] in the case of the speaking native it arguably has the opposite effect, which is to question the degree to which an apparently mimetic voice can represent anything but the discourse and ideas of the European philosopher. As I will show in the remainder of this essay, Diderot appears in several instances deliberately to posit the mediated enunciation of spoken discourse as inauthentic and unrepresentative of Tahiti. More than merely signalling the fictionality of the representation, therefore, Diderot's text may be seen as itself posing a radical challenge to the very strategy of mimetically speaking for non-Europeans, thereby placing the author in a critical position with respect to the tradition of 'savage critic' within which he writes. His insistence on playing games with his speaking subjects, multiplying the degrees of mediation of each voice, and openly subverting the authority of the voices that he ventriloquizes, amounts to so many attempts to mock the Enlightenment fashion of fictive prosopopoeia.

One of the most problematic instances of reported speech is the story of Polly Baker, which is abruptly inserted into the dialogue between Orou and

[28] Diderot's review is reproduced in Gilbert Chinard's edition of the *Supplément* (1935), 203–11. On the genesis of the text, see Gilbert Chinard's introduction to the above edition, and Herbert Dieckmann's introduction in his subsequent edition of the *Supplément* (Geneva: Droz, 1955), esp. p. lxxi.

[29] Georges Van Den Abbeele, 'Utopian Sexuality and its Discontents: Exoticism and Colonialism in *Le Supplément au Voyage de Bougainville*', *L'Esprit créateur*, 24/1 (1984), 52. On the polyphony and authorial indeterminacy of Diderot's text, see also Julie Candler Hayes, *Reading the French Enlightenment: System and Subversion* (Cambridge: Cambridge University Press, 1999), 178–9; Georges Benrekassa, 'Le Dit et le non-dit idéologique: à propos du *Supplément au voyage de Bougainville*', in *Le Concentrique et l'excentrique: marges des Lumières* (Paris: Payot, 1980), 213–24; and Michèle Mat, 'Le *Supplément au voyage de Bougainville*: une aporie polyphonique', *Revue internationale de philosophie*, 38/148–9 (1984), 159–70.

the chaplain. On A's request, B tells the story of a single mother from New England who was convicted for having children out of wedlock, but succeeded in avoiding punishment by eloquently denouncing the laws as unjust. The figure seems uncannily familiar; healthy and fecund, Polly Baker is the persecuted Western counterpart of the Tahitian ideal woman. At the same time, she is the *vieillard*'s double, a subaltern without access to the means of representation, whose resistance to power is primarily oral. Yet the authenticity and reliability of her narrative are critically in doubt. In recounting her story in the third person, B speaks as though from memory, and then inexplicably proceeds to quote in its entirety what he represents as Polly Baker's courtroom testimony. When he finishes, A poses the question invariably in the reader's mind: 'Et ce n'est pas là un conte de votre invention?' (p. 491) ('Isn't this just a tale of your own invention?'). B wonders if Raynal had not reported the same speech in his *Histoire des Deux Indes*. Immediately, however, the authorship of that work is called into question, as A remarks that the work is 'excellent', but 'd'un ton si différent des précédents qu'on a soupçonné l'abbé d'y avoir employé des mains étrangères' (p. 492) ('one so different in tone from his previous writings that the abbé is suspected of having used other hands'). Given that Diderot himself worked on that volume and that the story is otherwise traceable to Benjamin Franklin,[30] the author seems deliberately to be mocking both the repeated mediations of Polly Baker's testimony and his own practice of hiding himself behind the name of another, an admission which calls into question the authenticity of all quoted speech in the story.

The theme of misrepresentation is especially pronounced where the discourse of Tahitians is concerned, for Diderot all but declares it to be a fabrication, constantly providing clues to the unrepresentability of the native voice in the European text. Nowhere is this more apparent than in the *vieillard*'s harangue. Already in the dialogue leading up to the passage, A introduces the problem of translation, asking, 'Comment Bougainville a-t-il compris ces adieux prononcés dans une langue qu'il ignorait?' (p. 465) ('How could Bougainville understand farewells pronounced in a language he didn't know?'). During his eloquent harangue, it becomes clear that the *vieillard* could only be speaking in his native tongue, for he calls upon Orou—'toi qui

[30] Max Hall, *Benjamin Franklin and Polly Baker: The History of a Literary Deception* (Chapel Hill: University of North Carolina Press, 1960).

entends la langue de ces hommes-là' ('you who understand the language of these men')—to translate the territorial claims of the French. At the end of the passage, A questions further the authenticity of the speech: 'Ce discours me paraît véhément; mais à travers je ne sais quoi d'abrupt et de sauvage, il me semble retrouver des idées et des tournures européennes' (p. 472) ('This speech seems vehement to me, but in spite of what I find abrupt and savage, I seem to detect European ideas and turns of phrase'). The author persists in ridiculing the implausibility of the prosopopoeia by providing a highly nonsensical account of its translation. As B explains,

Pensez donc que c'est une traduction du tahitien en espagnol, et de l'espagnol en français. [Le vieillard] s'était rendu, la nuit, chez cet Orou qu'il a interpellé, et dans la case duquel l'usage de la langue espagnole s'était conservé de temps immémorial. Orou avait écrit en espagnol la harangue du vieillard; et Bougainville en avait une copie à la main, tandis que le Tahitien la prononçait. (pp. 472–3)

Bear in mind that it's a translation from Tahitian into Spanish, and from Spanish into French. That night the old man had made a visit to that same Orou to whom he called out and in whose home knowledge of the Spanish language had been preserved for generations. Orou had written down the speech of the old man in Spanish, and Bougainville had a copy of it in his hand while the old man delivered it.

Here B represents an absurd scenario in which the *vieillard*'s speech is both translated and transcribed after the fact, and paradoxically available to Bougainville in written form at the site of its first enunciation. Several critics have read this subversion as a distancing device through which Diderot signals to the reader that his solution to the problem of cross-cultural communication—a problem addressed openly in the case of Aotourou—is a fictional one.[31] In a larger sense, however, the effect of the deliberately perturbed mediation is to undermine the very idea of cross-cultural representation and, furthermore, to parody the tradition of making non-Europeans the putative subjects of European philosophical ideas. As the reader loses track of the manoeuvres of deferral, translation, and inscription which

---

[31] Dena Goodman, *Criticism in Action: Enlightenment Experiments in Political Writing* (Ithaca: Cornell University Press, 1989), 189. Several other critics have called attention to the ways in which Diderot's ludic subversion of the Tahitians' discourse proclaims its fictionality. See Henri Coulet, 'Deux confrontations du sauvage et du civilisé: les *Dialogues de Lahontan* et le *Supplément au voyage de Bougainville* de Diderot', *Man and Nature, Proceedings of the Canadian Society for Eighteenth-Century Studies*, 9 (1990), 122–7; Peter France, *Rhetoric and Truth in France: Descartes to Diderot* (Oxford: Clarendon Press, 1972), 227.

only end in aporia, the point of Diderot's provocation becomes clear: the voice of the Other can never be reproduced in the European account. The device of prosopopoeia relies on the fantasy of reported speech, which Diderot suggests is completely implausible in a cross-cultural context. There can be no referentiality for the speaking native subject outside the European philosophical imagination. All quoted speech is the invention of the author, and the subaltern cannot speak.

As in other works by Diderot, the subversion of mimesis in the *Supplément* serves to foreground the very textuality of writing—that is, the material process and structures through which a literary text mediates its relation to the 'real', only to construct rather than to represent it—and, as importantly, to parody the putative literary genre or fashion that the text at first appears to resemble.[32] In many ways, Diderot's Tahitian characters are overdrawn imitations of the *bon sauvage*. They play the role not of real or even imagined Tahitians, but of the stereotypical savage critic. At one point, Orou's discourse parodies the hackneyed reversal of the binary between civilization and savagery in Europeans' idealized representations of non-Europeans: 'Oh! le vilain pays! Si tout y est ordonné comme ce que tu m'en dis, vous êtes bien plus barbares que nous' (p. 503) ('Oh, what a wretched country! If everything there is set up the way you say it is, you are much more barbarous than we are'). Similarly, B's comment above makes light of the tendency in primitivist discourse to degrade European civilization as 'corrupt' and 'superficial'. The effect of such ironic remarks is both to call into question the pious binaries of primitivism and to point out their functionality in European discourse as a means of legitimating social critique. Georges Benrekassa has argued that in the *Supplément* Tahiti is a space of absence, because it exists only to enable the European's (i.e. Diderot's) discourse.[33] I would contend that through his overt subversion of mimesis, Diderot himself demonstrates that point, repeatedly undermining all external referentiality for his imaginary Tahiti and alerting the reader to the fact that the 'savage' in his text is nothing more than a constructed subject of alterity meant to spur readers' critical reflection on their own society. Diderot's Tahiti is therefore a 'utopia' in Michel Foucault's sense of the term; that is, a fundamentally 'other' space with no

[32] See e.g. Daniel Brewer's provocative reading of *Jacques le fataliste* in *The Discourse of Enlightenment in Eighteenth-Century France: Diderot and the Art of Philosophizing* (Cambridge: Cambridge University Press, 1993), 10–11, 214–35.

[33] Benrekassa, 'Le Dit et le non-dit idéologique', 222.

real place, a perfected or inverted vision of 'real' society that ultimately remains unreal and unlocalizable.[34] Tahiti thus emerges as a fantasm through which Diderot hypothesizes a subversive sexual ideology, a radical inversion of French customs and beliefs, and a critique of European colonial practices.

In this respect, the anticolonial rhetoric in French Enlightenment texts cannot be discounted simply because it is not moored in native subjectivity, or because it colonizes native subject positions. If we avoid idealizing 'the colonized' as a particular subject being spoken for or silenced, we find that what these Enlightenment dialogues offer is a counter-discourse to colonialism articulated from the centre of European imperial power. By dialogizing the cultural encounter in a fictional medium, both Lahontan and Diderot question the univocal pretensions of colonial discourses and place the colonizing power in the position of object. Like the postcolonial critics of our time, they illustrate the enunciative ruptures and ambivalences of colonial discourse and expose the potential hybridizations enacted by a subject on the receiving end of this discourse. What is fascinating is that the Enlightenment *philosophes* proved able not only to anticipate many of the central contentions of late twentieth-century postcolonial theory, notably by exposing the pitfalls of colonial mimicry for the colonized and the subversive effects of both mimicry and hybridity on colonial power, but also to do so in a form and fashion that arguably evades some of the methodological drawbacks of more recent analyses of colonial discourse. As Daniel Brewer argues in his study of Diderot, by so relentlessly calling attention to the materiality of writing and foregrounding the constructedness of narratives, their telling, and their interpretation, Diderot's self-reflexive critical discourse anticipates many of the concerns of postmodernism, notably its anti-foundationalism and refusal to ground knowledge in truths outside texts themselves. He writes, 'Diderot repeatedly stages the impossibility of moving beyond or outside representation. His texts play out innumerable situations in which there can be no end to interpretation, suggesting that what must be judged instead are interpretation's ends and its practical effects.'[35] The same feat is clearly at work in the *Supplément*, where it is ironically by appearing to represent the Other that Diderot proclaims the

---

[34] Michel Foucault, 'Of Other Spaces', trans. Jay Miskowiec, *Diacritics*, 16/1 (Spring 1986), 24.
[35] Brewer, *The Discourse of Enlightenment*, 253.

impossibility of doing so, thus prompting the reader to interpret, with and against his textual interlocutors, the meanings and implications of a critique of European society and colonialism voiced by invented non-European subjects. In this respect, Diderot arguably avoids the trap, encountered by many postcolonial scholars, of attempting to speak for or recover the voice of 'the subaltern'. Even Homi Bhabha, in his recourse to a colonial missionary registrar for his account of hybridity, rather uncritically reads this text as a transparent, reliable representation of historical native speech, thereby neglecting to examine the conditions of its production or the ways in which the representation of Indian resistance to colonial discourses could have worked within rather than against colonial ideologies.[36] In contrast, through their construction of fictionalized and at times parodic caricatures of the subalterns they could in many cases only imagine, the eighteenth-century *philosophes* refused mimesis, even as they appeared to instantiate it.

III Dialogue, critique, and the imagined consent of the colonized

The question nonetheless arises of why the French Enlightenment philosophers felt they needed to indulge so frequently in the fantasy of mimicking, even in parodic fashion, non-European speaking subjects, and, in particular, the ideological significance of this gesture. I would contend that to acknowledge the ways in which French Enlightenment writers create figures of otherness in order to contest discourses of colonial power is not to identify them with a counter-hegemonic, anti-imperialist project. Michèle Duchet has argued at length against the notion that French *philosophes* were anticolonial or abolitionist by pointing out the reformism at the heart of most philosophical contestations of the colonial system. According to Duchet, 'Quand on y regarde de près, et qu'on compare leur position à celle des responsables de la politique coloniale, on ne peut s'empêcher de conclure qu'en accord avec ceux-ci ils ont surtout cherché à remédier aux abus, et par là contribué au maintien de l'ordre établi.' ('If we look closely and compare their position to that of colonial policy makers, we can't help but conclude that like them they

---

[36] Bhabha, 'Signs Taken for Wonders', in *The Location of Culture*.

tried first and foremost to remedy abuses, and in so doing contributed to the maintenance of the established order.')[37] If the philosophers and the policy makers differed little in the kinds of reforms they proposed, they diverged significantly in the means by which they intervened discursively, and it is the dialogic form that suggests the particular function of the French Enlightenment critique within contemporary discourses on colonialism. I would maintain that by voicing the resistance of the colonized in the language of 'universal' reason, Enlightenment philosophers sought not to repudiate European colonialism, but on the contrary to enact an imaginary process of dissent and contestation through which colonial hegemony, in the Gramscian sense, could be consolidated and secured through negotiation, compromise, and reform.[38] In this respect, the Enlightenment literary critique of colonialism was fundamental to the 'progress' of colonialism itself. By invoking fictionalized subalterns as their surrogates in a debate that was largely absent from the European public sphere, Enlightenment philosophers modelled the kinds of criticism that would galvanize support among the European readership for a new, 'enlightened' colonialism, one that would accommodate the views and criticisms of the imagined subjects of empire.

The reformist implications of dialogue are most apparent in the closing passages of the *Supplément*, where A and B reflect on the moral consequences of the chaplain's encounter with the Tahitian state of nature. Rather than advocating that the French simply go native, patterning themselves on the Tahitian social and sexual order, B chooses to examine critically the relation between moral ideas, social laws, and natural instincts in French society:

Nous parlerons contre les lois insensées jusqu'à ce qu'on les réforme; et, en attendant, nous nous y soumettrons.... Disons-nous à nous-mêmes, crions incessamment qu'on a attaché la honte, le châtiment et l'ignonomie à des actions innocentes en elles-mêmes; mais ne les commettons pas, parce que la honte, le châtiment et l'ignominie sont les plus grands de tous les maux. (p. 515)

We'll speak out against senseless laws until they are reformed, and in the meantime, we'll abide by them.... Let us tell ourselves and cry out incessantly that shame,

---

[37] Michèle Duchet, *Anthropologie et histoire au siècle des Lumières* (Paris: F. Maspero, 1971), 18.

[38] Here I cite Gramsci's notion of hegemony, which refers to the process by which a ruling group or ideological formation gains influence through a continuous process of contestation and negotiation with subordinate or resistant groups. See Antonio Gramsci, *Selections from the Prison Notebooks*, ed. and trans. Quintin Hoare and Geoffrey Nowell Smith (New York: International Publishers, 1971), 181–2.

punishment, and dishonour have for too long been associated with actions that are quite innocent in themselves; but let us not perform such actions, because shame, punishment, and dishonour are the worst evils of all.

In the passage, oppositional speech and dialogue, either with others or with the self, become the means by which to effect the reform of unjust laws. Whereas transgression will only lead to repression, active questioning and critique such as that modelled in the *Supplément* will presumably compel a response from the system itself.[39] With this conclusion in mind, the *vieillard*'s spirited apostrophe to Bougainville may be read as the author's literal enactment of a dialogue necessary for the eventual reform of the colonial system. Yet what the *vieillard* attacks are not merely the excesses of colonialism, such as Bougainville's proclamation that '*ce pays est à nous*' ('this land is ours') and his putative future plans to chain, slit the throats of (*égorger*), and enslave the Tahitians, but any contact at all with the French:

nous sommes innocents, nous sommes heureux, et tu ne peux que nuire à notre bonheur.... Laisse-nous nos moeurs; elles sont plus sages et plus honnêtes que les tiennes; nous ne voulons point troquer ce que tu appelles notre ignorance, contre tes inutiles lumières. Tout ce qui nous est nécessaire et bon, nous le possédons. (pp. 466–8)

We are innocent, we are happy, and you can only spoil our happiness.... Leave us to our ways; they are wiser and more honest than yours. We have no wish to exchange what you call our ignorance for your useless knowledge. We already possess all that is necessary and good for us.

Such passionate entreaties, coming as they do after the moment of colonial contact, and after the ironic corruption of Tahitian blood by means of 'Tahitian hospitality', strike a tone of nostalgia and futility, and serve only to confirm that Tahitians have in fact suffered a definitive fall from their putative prior innocence. There is no turning back from the colonial encounter, the text seems to say, a message that is all the more symbolic in the case of Tahiti, situated as it was in the South Seas, the last frontier of European discovery and exploration in the eighteenth century. Through the representation of anticolonial contestation in a dialogic form, what the *Supplément* implicitly argues for therefore is not an end to colonialism, but

[39] For an extended argument on the ways in which the *Supplément* models criticism as responsible action, see Goodman, *Criticism in Action*, 219–20.

rather a revision of its precepts, an idea that comes through clearly in Diderot's admonishment to Bougainville in his unpublished review: 'Commercez avec eux, prenez leurs denrées, portez-leur les vôtres, mais ne les enchaînez pas.' ('Trade with them, take their goods, bring them yours, but do not place them in chains.')[40]

I will conclude by briefly comparing the *Supplément* with the *Histoire des Deux Indes*, the multi-volume compilation to which Diderot contributed while working on revisions to the *Supplément*, so as to suggest some of the ideological dimensions of Lahontan's and Diderot's philosophical critiques of colonialism.[41] Sankar Muthu has argued that many of Diderot's own insertions into the *Histoire* represent passionate critiques of imperial savagery and favour a model of non-exploitative commercial relations that respects the plurality of human cultural values.[42] Yet to characterize these arguments as anti-imperialist is to downplay the implications of their appearance in a work that elsewhere defends colonialism and advocates the imposition of European conceptions of agriculture, commerce, and culture abroad. Whereas in the *Supplément*, Bougainville appears in the mould of the conquistador sowing death and destruction among innocent, 'savage' races, in the *Histoire*, Diderot and Raynal abandon older evangelical, mercantilist, and territorial colonial ideologies in favour of one based on Enlightenment ideas about commerce, individual freedom, and what Raynal and Diderot call the 'general will of humanity'. This is initially apparent from the rhetorical stance and figuration of the historian-philosopher, an omniscient, ahistorical, first-person narrator hovering above mankind and ready to judge ruler and ruled, masters and slaves alike with a mix of rationalism, sentimentality, and moral indignation. In many of the passages written by Diderot, the speaker occupies multiple and at times paradoxical functions; in addition to recounting a global history of European expansion and ascertaining its consequences for all peoples who have thus come into contact, he speaks for the oppressed,

---

[40] Diderot, *Supplément au voyage de Bougainville*, ed. Chinard, 207.

[41] As early as 1771–2, Diderot composed fragments for Raynal's work, some of which were published in Grimm's correspondence. His most significant contributions were to the 1780 edition: Guillaume-Thomas Raynal, *Histoire philosophique et politique des Etablissements et du Commerce des Européens dans les deux Indes* (Neuchâtel and Geneva, 1780). On the precise extent and duration of Diderot's collaboration with Raynal, see Michèle Duchet, *Diderot et 'L'Histoire des deux Indes', ou l'écriture fragmentaire* (Paris: Éditions A.-G. Niget, 1987), 13–47; Yves Bénot, *Diderot, de l'athéisme à l'anticolonialisme* (Paris: François Maspero, 1981), 138–55.

[42] Muthu, *Enlightenment against Empire*.

denounces all forms of tyranny, and even calls on the enslaved and the colonized to take up arms against their European 'despots'. Yet although the oppressors are castigated and the victims bemoaned, the history of colonial tyranny is nonetheless redeemed as a singular revolution in commerce, which is defined as the motor of civilization:

C'est là enfin que, voyant à mes pieds ces belles contrées où fleurissent les sciences et les arts, et que les ténèbres de la barbarie avaient si longtemps occupées, je me suis demandé: qui est-ce qui a rassemblé, vêtu, civilisé ces peuples? et qu'alors toutes les voix des hommes éclairés qui sont parmi elles m'ont répondu: c'est le commerce, c'est le commerce.[43]

It was there, after all, where, seeing stretched out below my feet those beautiful lands where sciences and arts flourish but where previously the darkness of barbarism had for so long abided, that I asked myself: who brought together, clothed, and civilized these people? And all the voices of the enlightened men among us responded: commerce, commerce.

By identifying commerce as the primary agent of the global civilizing mission, the philosopher-historian distances himself from any particular nation's imperialist agenda, even as the text repeatedly defends colonial rule, advocates the European takeover of parts of Africa, and lends support to the reform rather than the abolition of slavery in the West Indies.[44]

Michèle Duchet and others have been keen to identify these contradictions in the *Histoire des Deux Indes*, pointing out that calls for the insurrection of the colonized (penned mainly by Diderot) served either to frighten policy makers into enacting the reforms necessary to keep colonial hierarchies intact or to inspire resistance among the masses in France, the other 'slaves' subject to arbitrary, authoritarian, and hence illegitimate rule at home.[45] In

[43] Raynal, *Histoire philosophique et politique des Deux Indes*, ed. Yves Bénot (Paris: François Maspero, 1981), 15.

[44] Note, for example, the section entitled 'Contre la traite des Noirs', to which Diderot contributed and which juxtaposes prescriptions for a 'softened' practice of slavery as a means of achieving colonial productivity and profit, proposals for gradual abolition, and emotional calls for the slaves themselves to rise up for the cause of freedom. Raynal, *Histoire*, 173–202.

[45] On the reformist agenda of the *Histoire*, see Duchet, *Diderot et 'L'Histoire des deux Indes'*, 160–76. On the self-referentiality of Raynal's and Diderot's global humanitarianism, see Hans Wolpe, *Raynal et sa machine de guerre* (Paris: Librairie de Médicis, 1956). On the narration, structure, and rhetoric of the text, see Duchet, *'L'Histoire des deux Indes*: sources et structure d'un texte polyphonique' and Michel Delon, 'L'Appel au lecteur dans l'*Histoire des deux Indes*', in Hans-Jürgen Lüsebrink and Manfred Tietz (eds), *Lectures de Raynal: 'L'Histoire des deux Indes' en Europe et en Amérique au XVIIIe siècle* (Oxford: Voltaire Foundation, 1991), 9–16, 53–66.

this case, the *Histoire des Deux Indes* would follow the convention of Montesquieu's *Lettres persanes* (1721) and Voltaire's *Zadig* (1747) and *Micromégas* (1752), works in which the imagined non-European world became the terrain on to which Enlightenment writers transposed domestic class conflicts, political dissent, and revolutionary challenges to the *ancien régime* social and moral order.[46] Yet, more than these texts, Lahontan's *Dialogues*, Diderot's *Supplément*, and the *Histoire des Deux Indes* suggest the centrality of a rhetorical defence of the colonized to the Enlightenment's self-conception as a movement in the interests of universal human rights, a conception that relied on the voicing of domestic concerns in the guise of cosmopolitan humanitarianism. This point recalls Louis Althusser's Marxian critique of the myth of bourgeois liberalism, according to which Enlightenment claims about the universality of humanist values such as equality, freedom, and reason served to legitimate a class-specific programme of political change: '[the bourgeoisie] hoped thereby to enroll at its side, by their education to this end, the very men it would liberate only for their exploitation'.[47] Similarly, the dominant Marxian reading of the French Revolution identifies the paradox of universalism in its constitutive particularism, since only a portion of society emancipates itself by equating its own interests with that of the entire community.[48]

I would contend that the French Enlightenment portrayal of imaginary colonial speaking subjects as allies of both metropolitan subalterns and the *philosophes* themselves functioned to enhance the legitimacy of liberal philosophical thought at home while also publicizing a programme of reforms for the colonial mission abroad. Through the tradition of the savage critic and the impassioned defence of all of humanity, French Enlightenment writers such as Lahontan, Diderot, and Raynal grounded the ethical validity of their theories of universal reason, individual freedom, and commercial exchange in their sympathy towards oppressed foreign peoples and in their willingness to condemn the excesses and cruelties of European colonialism. While deflecting onto non-European speakers arguments that were politically dangerous or morally scandalous at home, the *philosophes* succeeded in

---

[46] On the self-referential dimension of Montesquieu's *Lettres persanes*, see Lisa Lowe, *Critical Terrains: French and British Orientalisms* (Ithaca: Cornell University Press, 1991), 52–74.

[47] Louis Althusser, *For Marx*, trans. Ben Brewster (London: Allen Lane, 1969), 234.

[48] See e.g. Ernesto Laclau, 'Identity and Hegemony: The Role of Universality in the Constitution of Political Logics', in Judith Butler, Ernesto Laclau, and Slavoj Žižek, *Contingency, Hegemony, Universality: Contemporary Dialogues on the Left* (London: Verso, 2000), 44–89.

making accessible their core ideals, initiating a discourse of contestation against colonial abuses, and proposing to their readership a new relation to the non-European world based on Enlightenment values. In so doing, they consolidated the philosophical foundations for a battle to be waged at home against the forces of religious and political conservatism, and reimagined colonialism under the guise of commerce and individual freedom. Implicit, however, in such expressions of imaginary global solidarity was the knowledge, variously avowed or suppressed, that the full realization of this vision would require the reshaping of the rest of the world in the Enlightenment's image through continued European dominance. Taken together, the representation of enlightened 'savages', the insistence on the power of reason to liberate peoples around the world from tyranny, and the assumed analogy between the political struggles of domestic and global subalterns served as an ideology that obfuscated the more exclusionary or imperialist implications of certain Enlightenment ideas about reason, progress, property, citizenship, and free trade, many of which were nonetheless clearly exposed in the pages of the *Histoire* and in Lahontan's travelogues. What the French *philosophes* offered, therefore, was a new discourse of empire that derived legitimacy from the presumed compliance of fictive subalterns such as Adario and Orou, because it incorporated the rationalist critique of colonialism that they had been made to speak.

7

Universalism, Diversity, and the Postcolonial Enlightenment

Daniel Carey and Sven Trakulhun

Among the many features of Enlightenment thought that have come under contemporary critical scrutiny, universalism remains perhaps the most contentious. The impulse in the period to universalize the claims of reason, to articulate the category of a shared human nature, or to fashion history in a grand narrative of social progress has been subject to widespread critique from an array of sources. Far from representing an inclusive and liberating force, the universalizing tendency is said to mask exclusion and appropriation, shaping the history and future of native peoples in pernicious ways that became apparent in the nineteenth century. Enlightenment ostensibly allows no place for cultural diversity, or rather, diversity exists only in order to be overcome.

Postcolonial scholars have been at the forefront of this critique, although they are not alone in advancing it. In *White Mythologies*, for example, Robert Young questions the use of 'man' as an explanatory category, 'an assumed

The authors are grateful for comments and suggestions from Angelica Nuzzo, Luciana Villas Bôas, and Markus Wörner. Daniel Carey wishes to thank the Irish Research Council for the Humanities and Social Sciences for the award of a Government of Ireland Fellowship which made his research possible. Sven Trakulhun thanks the European Research Council for the award of a Marie Curie Intra-European Fellowship that enabled him to conduct research on this chapter.

universal predicated on the exclusion and marginalization of his Others, such as "woman" or "the native"'. In a discussion of Roland Barthes's famous essay 'The Great Family of Man', Young emphasizes the way in which 'diversity is only introduced so that it can be taken away again in the name of an underlying unity . . . underneath there is one human nature and therefore a common human essence'.[1] The most searching and significant discussion of these questions has come from Dipesh Chakrabarty. Near the outset of *Provincializing Europe*, he identifies a common purpose among post-colonial scholars who are 'committed, almost by definition, to engaging the universals—such as the abstract figure of the human or that of Reason—that were forged in eighteenth-century Europe and that underlie the human sciences'.[2] Political modernity, he argues, found expression in the abstract and universal categories that formed the basis for social scientific conceptualization of historical, social, and economic phenomena in a secular vein. The power of this legacy of the Enlightenment—realized in different ways, for Chakrabarty, in Marxism and liberal thought—translated heterogeneity into a narrative of implicit progress, assimilating difference into sameness over time.

Yet the complexity of Chakrabarty's position derives from his decision not to repudiate this Enlightenment tradition, unlike many of his peers, but to hold it in balance within another possibility. On the one hand, universalized concepts of citizenship, human rights, the public sphere, civil society, democracy, and popular sovereignty are constitutive of political modernity and remain indispensable to social science concerned with issues of social justice. On the other hand, these features of Enlightened thought were preached by European colonizers in the nineteenth century, as he points out. The challenge this poses is to retain these notions while making room for alternative ways of life and practice, to admit diversity into the narrative.

The purpose of this essay is to question the assumption that the Enlightenment had no place for diversity or no account of it. Consideration of the centrality of religious toleration within Enlightenment debates is enough to establish this point. But our discussion is undertaken not in order to defend or rehabilitate the Enlightenment against its accusers. The case does not

---

[1] Robert Young, *White Mythologies: Writing History and the West* (London: Routledge, 1990), 122.

[2] Dipesh Chakrabarty, *Provincializing Europe: Postcolonial Thought and Historical Difference* (Princeton: Princeton University Press, 2000), 5.

admit of such simple conclusions. As Chakrabarty's caution in the matter suggests, diversity is not an automatic good and universalism an evil.[3] Rather, we need to recognize the dialectical relationship between the two. This is true not only logically, in so far as the formation of abstract universals depends on the existence of particulars, but also at the level of practice and politics, where a critical balance is necessary between them. Neither contains an answer in itself. For this reason we require a richer account of the methods and conclusions of Enlightenment thinking about difference before attempting a more definitive statement on the merits or deficiencies of this inheritance. To this end we look at the question of diversity in an array of Enlightenment contexts, focusing particularly on British and German traditions.[4]

What emerges is an inevitably mixed record which complicates the simple view of Enlightenment as committed to a shared narrative of universal reason and human nature. To begin with, we discuss religion, 'stadial' history, and national character as contexts in which Enlightenment thinkers confronted the question of diversity. Race appears as a category in this milieu, deployed in various ways to explain and ossify difference. We move on in the second half of the essay to consider the ways in which Kant, Herder, and others in eighteenth-century Germany confronted the same questions. Yet there is no correlation—despite the assumptions of some postcolonial critics—between the adoption of what may be characterized as a universalizing account of human history allied to the progress of reason and a *pro*-colonial position. In fact a widespread consensus existed in Germany criticizing colonial expansion in the period.

---

[3] For an example of the postcolonial valorization of difference over universalism, see Luke Gibbons's recovery of Burke in *Edmund Burke and Ireland: Aesthetics, Politics, and the Colonial Sublime* (Cambridge: Cambridge University Press, 2003), ch. 6.

[4] The separation into national traditions is a convenience which allows for the indication of certain chronological developments, but these discussions did not occur separately from one another. Voltaire's position and polemicizing were inspired by his time in England; later, Montesquieu had a huge impact on Scottish historiography (as elsewhere), while Scottish Enlightenment texts were avidly read in Germany. On the latter, see Fania Oz-Salzberger, *Translating the Enlightenment: Scottish Civic Discourse in Eighteenth-Century Germany* (Oxford: Clarendon Press, 1995). Some of the flavour of German encounters with British Enlightenment texts can be gleaned from Herder's letter to Kant of November 1768. See Immanuel Kant, *Correspondence*, trans. and ed. Arnulf Zweig (Cambridge: Cambridge University Press, 1999), 96–9.

The exploration of Enlightened thought leaves us with a serious question—can Enlightenment ideals of human rights and democratic association survive in tandem with diversity? Do they merely naturalize one particular political model or trajectory as a universal telos or can they be reconciled with the preservation of differences among cultures and peoples? Much of postcolonial criticism has tended to shy away from posing the matter in quite so pointed a fashion, and has concentrated for the most part on the work of addressing historical injustices and ingrained sources of prejudice while disparaging universalism and upholding diversity. Chakrabarty is something of an exception in this respect. But a radical choice between the two alternatives may not be necessary. We therefore turn at the end of the essay to a different locus of discussion—contemporary political theories of multiculturalism—in which an explicit attempt has been made to combine a liberal theory of the state (with strong Enlightenment affinities) with the inclusion and acceptance of cultural variation, in the wake of centuries of colonial domination.

I Enlightenment and diversity: three contexts

In the range of Enlightenment engagements with diversity, the most conspicuous context overlooked by postcolonial critics is surely that of religious toleration, despite the centrality of this theme to that era's preoccupations. The importance of these debates should give us pause before we suggest that the defining feature of Enlightenment is a relentless universalism. The Enlightenment investment in tolerance of religious difference stemmed on the Continent from the seventeenth-century experience of the Thirty Years War; in England, from the Civil War and the Restoration Acts of Uniformity suppressing religious difference; and in France, from the revocation of the Edict of Nantes (1685). These events represent the most significant episodes in an era of struggle over the entitlement of states to regulate belief and impose religious uniformity in their territories. Among the many contributions to this debate, John Locke's *Letter concerning Toleration* (1689) occupies a central place. One of the notable features of the *Letter* is the emphasis that Locke places on the irreducibility of difference. The *Letter* makes this point explicitly: 'It is not the diversity of Opinions, (which cannot be avoided)', according to Locke, 'but the refusal of Toleration to those that are of different Opinions, (which might have been granted), that has produced all the Bustles and Wars that have been in the Christian World, upon account of Religion'.[5] For Locke, diversity in this context is inescapable. We have, in that sense, no choice in the matter. But we do have choices when it comes to how we respond to the existence of diversity. The answer is not to oppress and penalize difference in order to achieve uniformity and consensus; rather we should support toleration. The 'Bustles and Wars', as he puts it, have been the result of the failure to appreciate the impossibility of overcoming difference. Although Christians of different denominations remain entitled to make efforts to persuade others of the error of their ways, they have no justification for using force against those who dissent from them. The nature of belief and persuasion, so central to Locke's conception of religion, make any such attempt impertinent as well as impossible. Yet Locke's position was not without its limits, as he excluded Catholics from toleration as well as atheists on different grounds.[6]

Pierre Bayle—after Locke, perhaps the most famous exponent of toleration in the period, and himself an exile in the Netherlands from persecution in his native France—provided a wide-ranging defence of religious toleration, presented in various rhetorical guises. In opposition to the familiar view that a multiplicity of religions threatened the political stability of states, he argued that it was the failure to tolerate such differences that was the source of difficulty. In a characteristically wry fashion, he declined to take advantage in his *Philosophical Commentary* (1686–8) of the fact that the 'odd Variety of Worship in the World' was apparently not unbecoming to the Divinity, 'who has left such a vast Diversity in Nature as an Image of his Character of Infinite'. Instead, he conceded for the moment the invaluable blessing of 'Unity and Agreement' and merely lamented that such a condition was 'more to be wish'd than hop'd for'. As he put it, 'Difference seems to

---

[5] John Locke, *A Letter concerning Toleration* [1689], trans. William Popple, ed. James H. Tully (Indianapolis: Hackett, 1983), 55.

[6] For further discussion, see John Marshall, *John Locke, Toleration and Early Enlightenment Culture: Religious Intolerance and Arguments for Religious Toleration in Early Modern and 'Early Enlightenment' Europe* (Cambridge: Cambridge University Press, 2006).

be Man's inseparable Infelicity'.[7] He concluded, more seriously, that the only remedy was to engage in mutual toleration.[8]

The role of the Netherlands in fostering toleration and providing a place of refuge for numerous figures connected to the Enlightenment is well known, from Bayle to Spinoza and Locke (who composed the *Letter* while in exile there). In France, as Robert Wokler observes, 'the institutionalization of political and theological intolerance coincides with the whole history of the French Enlightenment itself, as opposition to the Revocation united *philosophes* of all denominations.'[9] Montesquieu's critique of religious controversy in the *Lettres persanes* (1721) or Voltaire's anticlericalism are familiar enough, but if we understand them only as directed against the Catholic Church we miss their objection to the enforcement of religious orthodoxy more generally, which springs from a tolerationist source.[10]

Toleration of religious diversity also plays an important if little recognized part in the work of some figures in the period better known for defending a unified human nature and insisting on moral agreement. The third Earl of Shaftesbury, to take an influential example, attempted to establish a terrain of consensus in moral and aesthetic judgements, grounded in nature, but he adopted this strategy precisely in order to accommodate an area of difference in religion. His appeals to uniformity in the former context must therefore

[7] Pierre Bayle, *A Philosophical Commentary on These Words of the Gospel, Luke 14.23, 'Compel Them to Come In, That My House May be Full'*, ed. John Kilcullen and Chandran Kukathas (Indianapolis: Liberty Fund, 2005), 208. This edition is based on the anonymous 1708 translation of the text. The original French reads: 'toutes les religions du monde, bizarres et diversifiées comme elles le sont, ne conviennent pas mal à la grandeur infinie de l'Être souverainement parfait, qui a voulu qu'en matière de diversité toute la nature le prêchât par le caractère de l'infini. Non, j'aime mieux dire que ce serait une belle chose que l'accord de tous les hommes . . . c'est une chose plus à souhaiter qu'à espérer, comme la diversité d'opinions semble être un apanage inséparable de l'homme . . .'. Pierre Bayle, *De la tolérance: commentaire philosophique sur ces paroles de Jésus-Christ 'Contrains-les-d'entrer'*, ed. Jean-Michel Gros (n.p.: Presses Pocket, 1992), 267.

[8] Bayle endorsed Locke's *Letter* in the *Dictionary*, and Locke purchased Bayle's *Philosophical Commentary* for his friend Sir Walter Yonge, who sought help in compiling an intellectual library. Marshall, *John Locke*, 490, 491. On Bayle and toleration, see Walter E. Rex, *Essays on Pierre Bayle and Religious Controversy* (The Hague: M. Nijhoff, 1965).

[9] Robert Wokler, 'The Enlightenment Project as Betrayed by Modernity', *History of European Ideas*, 24/4–5 (1998), 304.

[10] On Montesquieu, see Tzvetan Todorov, *On Human Diversity: Nationalism, Racism, and Exoticism in French Thought*, trans. Catherine Porter (Cambridge, Mass.: Harvard University Press, 1993), 359–61. For Voltaire, see especially his *Traité sur la tolérance* ([Geneva], 1763). For discussion of Voltaire and tolerance, see Graham Gargett, *Voltaire and Protestantism* (Oxford: Voltaire Foundation, 1980).

be read in relation to his pronouncements in the latter. In the closing text of the *Characteristicks* (1711), he addressed the subject of religious difference, noting that 'the variety of opinions was not to be cured' and that it is 'impossible all should be of one mind'.[11] Elsewhere he mocked the insistence on religious uniformity as 'a hopeful project!' No government should have the authority to 'settle wit'.[12] Francis Hutcheson, who defended Shaftesbury's principles, was a beneficiary of extended toleration in eighteenth-century Dublin, where he wrote his most important philosophical work. His account of human nature stressed what mankind had in common, namely a shared moral sense and consensus over the virtue of benevolence, rather than differences over points of religion.

If the emphasis on irreducible diversity in the context of early Enlightenment defences of toleration has proved an inheritance that can be built upon, another strand of Enlightenment discussion of difference remains more problematic, in the context of what is variously called stadial or conjectural history.[13] Philosophers and historians offered a theoretical account, based on conjecture, of the origins of government, the emergence of civil society, and a progression towards an ever more polite and commercial social condition through a series of historical stages. The complex strands that fed into this eighteenth-century enquiry can only be indicated here: one tradition derived from reflection by jurists on the transition from a state of nature to one of government. Grotius, Pufendorf, and Locke developed their own versions of this account, which extended, in Locke, to an analysis of the role of property, accumulation, and money in transforming social and political relations.[14] The anthropological dimension of the argument called for a certain amount of empirical testimony from those positioned to describe the conditions of savage and barbarian peoples, who ostensibly existed in conditions that offered insight into the past of more advanced and polite

[11] Anthony Ashley Cooper, third Earl of Shaftesbury, *Characteristics of Men, Manners, Opinions, Times*, ed. Lawrence E. Klein (Cambridge: Cambridge University Press, 1999), 472.

[12] Ibid. 11–12.

[13] Dugald Stewart referred to '*Theoretical* or *Conjectural History*' in his 'Account of the Life and Writings of Adam Smith, LL.D.', in Sir William Hamilton (ed.), *The Collected Works of Dugald Stewart*, 10 vols (Edinburgh: T. Constable, 1854–8), x, 34. Quoted in Ronald L. Meek, *Social Science and the Noble Savage* (Cambridge: Cambridge University Press, 1976), 113.

[14] See Istvan Hont, *Jealousy of Trade: International Competition and the Nation-State in Historical Perspective* (Cambridge, Mass.: Harvard University Press, 2005), ch. 1; and James Tully, *An Approach to Political Philosophy: Locke in Contexts* (Cambridge: Cambridge University Press, 1993), ch. 5.

societies.[15] (Locke drew on such figures as José de Acosta, Gabriel Sagard, and the Inca Garcilaso de la Vega.) Locke's famous positing of the world as existing, originally, in a condition akin to America[16] had an important corollary in a colonial setting: it followed that European contact accelerated Amerindian societies on a course that was already predetermined for them.

The scheme that became formalized in Scottish conjectural history identified four different stages of development: hunting, fishing, and gathering constituted the first stage, which was usually characterized as a specifically 'savage' condition; this in turn gave way to pasturage, transhumance, and shepherding, an ostensibly more dynamic social system, often described as properly 'barbarian'; the third stage was that of agriculture and settlement, which laid the groundwork for more advanced social and political forms, terminating in a fourth stage of trade and commerce.[17] Different inflections can of course be found, from the shared interests of Sir John Dalrymple, Lord Kames, and Adam Smith in the role of property and law in effecting and reflecting social change[18] to Adam Ferguson's rather different analysis, in which social progression from the savage to the polite required a reconciliation of the virtues that existed in rude societies.[19]

The implications of this account were far-reaching. The narrative reconciled social difference with a unified conception of human nature. The

[15] See esp. Meek, *Social Science and the Ignoble Savage* on the representation of American Indians in this context.

[16] John Locke, *Two Treatises of Government*, ed. Peter Laslett (Cambridge: Cambridge University Press, 1988), Second Treatise, §49: 'Thus in the beginning all the World was *America*'.

[17] There was dissent from this of course, not merely from Rousseau but from those who, like David Doig, regarded corruption, not progress, as the narrative of human nature. See David Doig, *Two Letters on the Savage State* (London, 1792), written in response to Lord Kames between 1774 and 1776 but not published until after Kames's death.

[18] Sir John Dalrymple, *An Essay towards a General History of Feudal Property in Great Britain* (London, 1757); Henry Home, Lord Kames, *Essays on the Principles of Morality and Natural Religion* (2nd edn, London, 1758); Henry Home, Lord Kames, *Historical Law-Tracts*, 2 vols (Edinburgh, 1758).

[19] Without this, the threat of corruption remained. See Adam Ferguson, *An Essay on the History of Civil Society*, ed. Duncan Forbes (Edinburgh: Edinburgh University Press, 1966), 71. Noted in James Moore, 'Montesquieu and the Scottish Enlightenment', in Rebecca Kingston (ed.), *The Legacy of Montesquieu* (Albany: SUNY Press, forthcoming). Ferguson acknowledged the influence and inspiration of Montesquieu. His account of social progress was complicated by his attachment to Highland culture: he had been born in 1723 on the border of the Lowlands and Highlands in the village of Logierait, Perthshire. The Ossianic controversy drew out the primitivist leanings of some philosophers, but this inclination was usually offset by an acknowledgement of the benefits of progress.

determining factors in creating difference were social, political, and economic, while human nature itself remained consistent. Agreement of moral sense or sentiments was thus unthreatened, even as mankind was differentiated by historical circumstance. Those peoples whose customs failed to coincide with British or more widely European modes of economy and society did not constitute unassimilable figures of dissent from consensus; rather they existed at a different stage of development. History was thus the answer to difference and would comfortingly transform the other into the same. There was a kind of consistency in the argument worth noting, in so far as some commentators, such as the third Earl of Shaftesbury, recognized the course of British history in the same narrative (from brutish Picts to polite members of society; or Anglo-Saxons accelerated, by the Norman conquest, into a more civil condition).[20] Conquest and colonization, from this perspective, had resulted in an entirely positive social outcome.

At the same time, the argument lent itself to two other troubling (and related) conclusions. It became possible to maintain that certain peoples were locked in a savage or barbarous condition, unable to advance, and therefore

---

[20] Shaftesbury, *Characteristics*, 403. At the end of the eighteenth century, the narrative was already being sentimentalized in Europe, as we see in Friedrich von Schiller's reflections, composed in his capacity as professor of history at Jena in 1789: 'The discoveries which our European mariners have made in faraway oceans and on distant coasts give us a spectacle both instructive and entertaining. They show us peoples who are spread around us at the most diverse levels of development, as children of different ages stand around an adult and by their example remind him of what he used to be and where he originated. A wise hand seems to have preserved these crude tribes till the point in time where we would be advanced enough in our own culture in order to utilize this discovery in a practical application to ourselves and to restore from this mirror the forgotten origin of our species.' ('Die Entdeckungen, welche unsere europäischen Seefahrer in fernen Meeren und auf entlegenen Küsten gemacht haben, geben uns ein ebenso lehrreiches als unterhaltendes Schauspiel. Sie zeigen uns Völkerschaften, die auf den mannigfaltigsten Stufen der Bildung um uns herum gelagert sind, wie Kinder verschiednen Alters um einen Erwachsenen herumstehen, und durch ihr Beispiel ihm in Erinnerung bringen, was er selbst vormals gewesen, und wovon er ausgegangen ist. Eine weise Hand scheint uns diese rohen Völkerstämme bis auf den Zeitpunkt aufgespart zu haben, wo wir in unsrer eignen Kultur weit genug würden fortgeschritten sein, um von dieser Entdeckung eine nützliche Anwendung auf uns selbst zu machen, und den verlornen Anfang unsers Geschlechts aus diesem Spiegel wiederherzustellen.') 'Was heißt und zu welchem Ende studiert man Universalgeschichte?' (1789), in Friedrich von Schiller, *Werke in drei Bänden*, ed. Herbert G. Göpfert (Munich: Hanser, 1966), ii, 13. This account would be realized more fully in his *Über naive und sentimentalische Dichtung* (1795).

in a perpetual state of inferiority.[21] In tandem with this, as J. G. A. Pocock points out, the stadial analysis of progressive civilization could be read as an account exclusively of *Europe's* historical development, becoming thereby 'a means of proclaiming European uniqueness and ascendancy' and supplying the rationale (for the Scots and others) for seeing Europe, in its progressive advancement, as enjoying the destiny of 'world empire'.[22]

Chakrabarty's critique of historicism in *Provincializing Europe* is directed against precisely this kind of historical narrative. He advocates 'unlearning', as he puts it, the conception of history 'as a developmental process in which that which is possible becomes actual by tending to a future that is singular'. The diversity for which he speaks requires a recognition of the present as 'irreducibly not-one',[23] identifying futures that are not in the process of becoming but exist already, in plural forms. Marxism represents, in this respect, one more scripted account of history, based on its own particular stadial narrative. At the same time, Chakrabarty emphasizes that narratives of capital are necessary in order to critique 'capitalist imperialism'. The 'Enlightenment promise' of an abstract and universal humanity creates a political modernity that he wants to keep in dialogue with the 'diverse ways of being human, the infinite incommensurabilities'.[24]

These two Enlightenment accounts of diversity—toleration and stadial history—have survived in different ways, the first as a continued aspiration to allow for and respect religious difference, and the second as expressed in ongoing imperatives of modernization. A third account of difference has been superseded and discredited to a large extent, after reaching a kind of zenith in the nineteenth century. We may call this for convenience the eighteenth-century conception of race and racism, which really represents a complex of interacting assumptions and ideologies. Some of the variants of this form of thought emerged specifically from a deliberation over the issue

---

[21] J. G. A. Pocock, *Barbarism and Religion*, ii: *Narratives of Civil Government* (Cambridge: Cambridge University Press, 1999), 323, 327. In the case of 'Orientals', they were excluded for different reasons, 'by the premise that they were the servile subjects of despotism' (ibid. 317). See on this, more generally, Joan-Pau Rubiés, 'Oriental Despotism and European Orientalism: Botero to Montesquieu', *Journal of Early Modern History*, 9/1–2 (2005), 109–80.

[22] Pocock, *Narratives of Civil Government*, 317. See also Karen O'Brien, *Narratives of Enlightenment: Cosmopolitan History from Voltaire to Gibbon* (Cambridge: Cambridge University Press, 1997), ch. 5.

[23] Chakrabarty, *Provincializing Europe*, 249.

[24] Ibid. 254.

of social progress; others arose from reflection on cultural and national diversity, and, indebted to a method of natural history as practised in the period, diversified mankind in different species or races; and still others offered polygenesis as an explanatory scheme, introducing a separate creation to account for racial variation. While broaching these traditions, it is important not to assume that they somehow constitute inevitable or consensual conclusions of Enlightenment. It was perfectly possible to be committed to the notion of social progress without endorsing racism; for that matter, the supposition that different species or varieties of man existed did not automatically create a rank order among them, even if those with racist convictions capitalized on this possibility.[25] Some of the talk of species and races appeared among natural historians intent on organizing and classifying the diversity of the natural world, a project with implications realized or exploited only later.[26] In a number of cases the polygenist argument was motivated by a polemical desire to disrupt orthodox accounts of creation and biblical history, as we see in Voltaire. Many of the pernicious uses of these narratives of difference, meanwhile, were answered with precisely the kind of Enlightenment universalism about human nature that some critics have found so objectionable, as we see in the responses to racist polemic of, for example, James Beattie and Anthony Benezet.

The Scottish jurist Lord Kames provides an illustration of the complex and rather contradictory impulses in the period. His *Sketches of the History of Man* (1774), published when he was 80, constituted the outcome of long years of historical and legal research, which he conducted while a judge in Scotland's Court of Session and later in the High Court of Judiciary. Like Adam Smith and John

---

[25] Giuliano Gliozzi emphasizes the differences between a theory of distinct races and racism in 'Poligenismo e razzismo agli albori del secolo dei lumi', *Rivista di filosofia*, 70 (1979), 1–31, repr. in Gliozzi, *Differenze e uguaglianza nella cultura europea moderna* (Naples: Vivarium, 1993), 255–87.

[26] Linnaeus's account of human races appeared in his *Systema naturae, sive regna tria naturae systematice proposita per classes, ordines, genera et species* (Leiden, 1735). Johann Friedrich Blumenbach's rejection of a 'chain of being' was so great that he classified man in a separate order from that of the other primates. In the first edition of his *De generis humani varietate nativa* (Göttingen, 1770) he classified man into four races (a total increased to five in the second edition of 1781). He explained the morphological differences to be found in the races of man and concluded: '[This investigation] brings us to that conclusion, which seems to flow spontaneously from physiological principles applied by the aid of critical zoology to the natural history of mankind; which is, *That no doubt can any longer remain but that we are with great probability right in referring all and singular as many varieties of man as at are present known to one and the same species*'. James S. Slotkin (ed.), *Readings in Early Anthropology* (Chicago: Aldine Publishing, 1965), 190–1 (emphasis in original).

Millar, both of whom he supported, Kames adopted a stadial account of social development which was consistent with a unified human nature. Yet he found anomalies which required some explanation: there were savage peoples in the world who failed to progress, and in order to account for this phenomenon he had recourse to a notion of polygenesis. God had evidently performed separate acts of creation.[27] As Colin Kidd has pointed out, Kames was more concerned by the need to explain the origins of native peoples in the New World and Australasia than by the problem of African difference. Furthermore, his position was complicated by his Presbyterian principles and the wish to reconcile his theory with divine history described in Genesis.[28]

While Kames's deliberations emerged from the stadial scheme, his kinsman David Hume approached the question of diversity and race from Montesquieu's point of departure, namely the variety apparent in national characters (nor was he burdened, one might add, by Kames's attempt to maintain a degree of Presbyterian orthodoxy). Inherited accounts of this subject allocated to climate an often decisive explanatory role, in a tradition derived from antiquity and recirculated, influentially, by Bodin and Montesquieu in France. Hume took issue by emphasizing the formative influence of social, political, and economic factors rather than physical environment. In his essay 'Of National Characters' (1748), for example, he asserted the effect of what he called 'moral causes' in the form of a country's mode of government, its founding figures, economic circumstances, and political situation vis à vis its neighbours, among other considerations determining character. Differences of this kind could not be mapped on to climate, a point he proved by noting disparities between the French and Spanish or English and Scots, despite the fact that they lived in comparable climates. The Chinese, meanwhile, exhibited a remarkable sameness of character according to Hume, even though the vast extent of the empire meant that it embraced a great variety of distinct climates.[29]

Yet Hume's analysis did not end there, and in a revision of the essay in 1753 he added a now notorious footnote addressing the subject of

---

[27] For discussion, see Silvia Sebastiani, 'Race and National Characters in Eighteenth-Century Scotland: The Polygenetic Discourses of Kames and Pinkerton', *Cromohs*, 8 (2003), 1–14.

[28] Colin Kidd, *The Forging of Races: Race and Scripture in the Protestant Atlantic World, 1600–2000* (Cambridge: Cambridge University Press, 2006), 95.

[29] David Hume, 'Of National Characters', in *Essays Moral, Political, and Literary*, rev. edn, ed. Eugene F. Miller (Indianapolis: Liberty Fund, 1987), 197–215.

Africans.[30] Although variety marked national character elsewhere, Hume alleged that Africans exhibited uniformity. On this basis he remarked, 'I am apt to suspect the negroes...to be naturally inferior to the whites'. No dark-skinned peoples could be counted among the civilized nations, nor had anyone of distinction in 'action' or intellect arisen from their ranks. 'No ingenious manufactures amongst them, no arts, no sciences.' By contrast, even the rudest of white nations, whether the ancient Germans or modern-day Tartars, could lay claim to some eminence, in martial valour, mode of government, or in some other respect. Hume emphasizes the absence of exceptions: 'Such a constant difference could not happen, in so many countries and ages, if nature had not made an original distinction betwixt these breeds of men'. He discounted talk of a Jamaican who had been described as a man of 'parts and learning': 'he is likely admired for very slender accomplishments, like a parrot, who speaks a few words plainly'.[31] In other words, the difference here is founded in nature rather than in moral or for that matter climatological causes. Hume does not aim, in the essay form, for a systematic statement but writes in a more casual mode of suggestion and observation; nonetheless, his argument depends, ultimately, on the assumption of the 'natural inferiority' of 'all the other species of men'—not merely blacks—to whites. His undeveloped suggestion that there 'are four or five different kinds' into which humanity has been distinguished constitutes a significant emergence of a concept of species variation into the discussion of racial difference.[32] Thus the polygenetic thesis implicit in his account was tied to a racist assessment of human difference.

[30] There is an extensive secondary literature on this question. See Aaron Garrett, 'Hume's "Original Difference": Race, National Character and the Human Sciences', *Eighteenth-Century Thought*, 2 (2004), 127–52; Robert Palter, 'Hume and Prejudice', *Hume Studies*, 21 (1995), 3–23; Richard H. Popkin, 'Hume's Racism', *Philosophical Forum*, 9 (1977–8), 211–26; Emmanuel Chukwudi Eze, 'Hume, Race, and Human Nature', *Journal of the History of Ideas*, 61/4 (2000), 691–8; John Immerwahr, 'Hume's Revised Racism', *Journal of the History of Ideas*, 53/3 (1992), 481–6.

[31] Hume, 'Of National Characters', 629–30. Hume did not name him, but the person in question was Francis Williams (c.1690–1762), the son of free blacks in Jamaica, who received patronage from the island's governor, the Duke of Montagu, and was sent to Cambridge. He returned to the island and set up a school, gaining celebrity as a Latin poet.

[32] In the 1777 version of the essay, Hume altered the passage to read 'I am apt to suspect the negroes to be naturally inferior to the whites', deleting the clause 'and in general all the other species of men (for there are four or five different kinds)'. *Essays*, 208 n.

The transition from such an argument to a defence of slavery was not automatic—Hume rejected the institution of slavery in another essay while Kames remarked on its ill effects on the character of West Indian planters and quoted Raynal's *Histoire des deux Indes* in support of this conclusion.[33] Yet the potential for linking a theory of race to slavery was certainly recognized in the period. The Scottish philosopher John Dunbar foresaw that 'According to this theory [of specific differences of species and European superiority], the oppression or extermination of a meaner race, will no longer be so shocking to humanity. Their distresses will not call upon us so loudly for relief. And public morality, and the laws of nations, will be confined to a few regions peopled with this more exalted species of mankind'.[34] Two of the most prominent defenders of slavery in the later eighteenth century, Samuel Estwick and Edward Long, both invoked Hume in support of their position and made use of the argument from distinct species,[35] while Christoph Meiners, the notorious Göttingen professor and proponent of racism, made use of their work in *Ueber die Natur der afrikanischen Neger* (1790).[36] Back in Scotland, James Beattie replied to Hume in *An Essay on the Nature and Immutability of Truth* (1770), and made an explicit link between Hume's position

---

[33] In his essay 'Of the Populousness of Ancient Nations', Hume remarked: 'The remains which are found of domestic slavery, in the American colonies, and among some European nations, would never surely create a desire of rendering it more universal. The little humanity, commonly observed in persons, accustomed, from their infancy, to exercise so great authority over their fellow-creatures, and to trample upon human nature, were sufficient alone to disgust us with that unbounded dominion'. *Essays*, 383–4. See Henry Home, Lord Kames, *Sketches of the History of Man*, 3 vols, ed. James A. Harris (Indianapolis: Liberty Fund, 2007), i, 188–9. He described the Spartan treatment of Helots as 'a reproach to the human species' (i, 188). Elsewhere, Kames stated that the difference of colour led him to conclude that Negroes were of a different species but that he had abandoned the notion that this theory was supported, as Hume held, by their 'inferiority of understanding' (i, 41). Where inferiority was evident, he now believed that this was probably the result of the condition of enslavement. There was no telling what might be possible in a 'state of freedom'. Some African nations showed 'great improvements' in government and manners, others a good judgement and sense of equity (i, 41–2).

[34] John Dunbar, *Essays on the History of Mankind in Rude and Cultivated Ages* (London, 1780), 156.

[35] Samuel Estwick, *Considerations on the Negroe Cause Commonly So Called Addressed to the Right Honourable Lord Mansfield* (2nd edn, London, 1773), 79 n.; Edward Long, *The History of Jamaica*, 3 vols (London, 1774), ii, 477 n.

[36] As a Hanoverian subject, teaching at the electorate's principal university, Meiners had ready access to British publications while possessing a dual English and German identity of which he was clearly proud.

and the Aristotelian notion of the natural slave, suggesting that 'Mr. Hume argues nearly in the same manner [as Aristotle] in regard to the superiority of white men over black'. By 'proving' the natural inferiority of Negroes, Hume contradicted British values and traditions: 'Let it never be said, that slavery is countenanced by a people the bravest and most generous on earth, and who are animated with that heroic passion, the love of liberty, beyond all nations ancient and modern'.[37]

Hume's argument is in some respects surprising given the alternative account of diversity that he provides in 'A Dialogue' appended to the *Enquiry concerning the Principles of Morals* (1751). Here he focuses not on national character but on the diversity of moral and cultural practices apparent around the world. Economic and political circumstances have some effect in producing diversity in this context, as does national character itself, but he upholds the notion of a unified human nature; although human beings draw different conclusions, they reason from the same moral principles.[38] This may make the racism in the essay 'Of National Characters' more stark, but it suggests a disjunctive pattern which complicates received assumptions about universalism and diversity. By differentiating Africans, Hume at the same time fixes them so that they remain unchanging; his 'universalism' with respect to human nature and knowledge offers, by contrast, a more hopeful prospect.

II Kant's universalism

Discussion of the question of human nature and diversity in the German Enlightenment was equally widespread, engaging with many of the same questions of race, national character, and stadial history. The fact that the two dominant figures of this period, Immanuel Kant and Johann Gottfried Herder, came to such different conclusions tells us something about the scope of possible alignments and oppositions within what remains an identifiably Enlightenment problematic. Postcolonial historiography has focused particularly on Kant, not only on the racism of his remarks on Africans and

---

[37] James Beattie, *An Essay on the Nature and Immutability of Truth; in Opposition to Sophistry and Scepticism* (Edinburgh, 1770), 479, 484.

[38] David Hume, 'A Dialogue', in *An Enquiry concerning the Principles of Morals*, ed. Tom L. Beauchamp (Oxford: Oxford University Press, 1998), 110–23.

others but also, as Gayatri Spivak has emphasized, on Kant's prospective foreclosure from the realms of reason and culture of the 'raw man', the native or savage not yet elevated to the status of subject of philosophy. The inconsistency in Kant's position, if there is one, comes from his conspicuous tendency to universalize his moral and aesthetic philosophy.

A proper analysis of the polarities between univeralism and diversity in German Enlightenment thought requires a fuller account of Kant and some of his contemporaries. The following three sections of our essay explore different aspects of the German tradition as it confronts these problems. We begin with the imposing figure of Kant. His comments on native peoples in the *Critique of Judgement* have been the focus of Spivak's critical discussion, but they need to be set in a more thorough context which qualifies her argument. Although Spivak's conclusions about the *Critique of Judgement* cannot be sustained on closer reading, the questions raised in her account lead to a wider consideration of Kant's work. We reconnect his position with earlier discussion in this essay concerned with race, national character, and stadial history, in which a universal history of progress incorporates and synthesizes difference (as appears, for example, in Kant's 'Conjectures on the Beginning of Human History' and his *Anthropology from a Pragmatic Point of View*).

Herder famously rejected this approach, but to appreciate his intervention we first examine a less familiar context of theorizing about cultural difference and history—German *Ethnographie* and the creation of a new domain of enquiry, the history of peoples (*Völkergeschichte*), which formed part of universal history in the work of Johann Christoph Gatterer and August Ludwig von Schlözer. Herder also supplied a critique of this tradition, setting out a scheme for a diversified history of peoples as an alternative to the familiar European bias of such accounts.

This reconstruction leads to a reconsideration of the story of German Enlightenment thought. The universalizing bias of some of the key figures confirms aspects of postcolonial analysis while complicating other conclusions. In particular, the assumption that a universal narrative of reason and history (predicated on exclusion as much as assimilation) supports the interests of colonialism or derives, in Spivak's phrase, from the 'axiomatics of imperialism', must be revisited. Substantial consensus existed among German thinkers *against* colonialism and its consequences. This is true not only of Herder, from whom we might expect it, but also of Kant and a range of others. German Enlightenment thinkers of different stripes were linked in their condemnation of European practices in pursuing avid colonial expansion.

Among postcolonial scholars, Gayatri Spivak has devoted considerable effort to challenging Kant's Enlightenment universalism as exclusionary. A lengthy opening section of her *Critique of Postcolonial Reason* focuses on Kant's *Critique of Judgement* (1790), specifically the predicament of the 'raw man' (*der rohe Mensch*)—the 'savage' who is 'not yet or simply not' the subject of Kant's critiques and awaits the transforming effects of culture.[39] However, careful attention to the argument discloses some problematic features of her discussion. This is not to say that serious questions should not be asked of Kant on this issue, here and elsewhere in his work, as we will shortly see.

In her analysis of Kant, Spivak concentrates on Kant's treatment of teleological judgement in the *Critique of Judgement*. According to Spivak, Kant excludes the native from participation in the status of subject. The key passage she cites from Kant to prove this thesis invokes aboriginal peoples of Australia and Argentina in a parenthetical remark (note that the insertions in square brackets are provided by Spivak):

Grass is needful for the ox, which again is needful for man as a means of existence; but then we do not see why it is necessary that men should exist (a question which is not so easy to answer if we cast our thoughts by chance [*wenn man etwa . . . in Gedanken hat*] on the New Hollanders or the inhabitants of Tierra del Fuego). Such a thing is then [*alsdem (sic: alsdann) ist ein solches Ding*] not even a natural purpose; for it (or its entire species [*Gattung*—the connotation of 'race' as in 'human race' cannot be disregarded here]) is not to be regarded as a natural product.[40]

[39] Gayatri Chakravorty Spivak, *A Critique of Postcolonial Reason: Toward a History of the Vanishing Present* (Cambridge, Mass.: Harvard University Press, 1999), 14.

[40] Spivak, *Critique of Postcolonial Reason*, 26. She modifies J. H. Bernard's translation of the *Critique of Judgment* (1892; New York: Hafner, 1951), 225. For the original, see *Kants gesammelte Schriften*, ed. Königliche Preußische (now Deutsche) Akademie der Wissenschaften (Berlin: Georg Reimer [now De Gruyter], 1902–), known as the Akademie Ausgabe (cited hereafter as AA),v, 378 (§67). Our quotation begins at an earlier stage than Spivak's passage in order for the discussion to be intelligible. We have also placed in italics the missing sentence from Spivak's quoted portion: 'Die innere Form eines bloßen Grashalms kann seinen bloß nach der Regel der Zwecke möglichen Ursprung für unser menschliches Beurtheilungsvermögen hinreichend beweisen. Geht man aber davon ab und sieht nur auf den Gebrauch, den andere Naturwesen davon machen, verläßt also die Betrachtung der innern Organisation und sieht nur auf äußere zweckmäßige Beziehungen, wie das Gras dem Vieh, wie dieses dem Menschen als Mittel zu

For Spivak, the passage warrants several troubling conclusions: 'The subject as such in Kant is geopolitically differentiated'. The natives of New Holland or Argentina '*cannot* be the subject of speech or judgment in the world of the *Critique*'.[41] The native, in short, has been *foreclosed.*[42]

This interpretation depends on a number of mistaken assumptions and on the elision of an important sentence from the passage without indication. We can begin with Spivak's statement in a footnote that 'The question as to whether these peoples were human was part of a general European debate. Kant was simply answering in the negative'.[43] But there is no evidence to support the view that Kant denied humanity to New Hollanders or Fire-landers. On the contrary, he invokes them precisely because they *are* human to make a different point.

If we want to understand what Kant is trying to say in this passage we have to consider the argument of the section (§67) in which it occurs. He addresses the complex question of whether we can judge nature teleologically as constituting a system of ends (*Zwecke*), a view he of course wishes to defend. In order to establish this, we must first show that things in nature exist as ends of nature (*Endzwecke*). Two possible ways for doing so suggest themselves: on the basis of (1) what he calls the *external* purposiveness of things, or (2) their *internal* purposiveness. The route which focuses on external purposive-ness tries to explain why things exist in terms of their usefulness. For example, rivers make communication between different peoples possible, and mountains in turn create the flows of water that form rivers. But to explain the existence of rivers on this basis never overcomes an infinite regress of what is serving what, and why.

Internal purposiveness is very different. Under this conception of (organic) nature we recognize things as products of nature that possess an organized

seiner Existenz nöthig sei; und man sieht nicht, warum es denn nöthig sei, daß Menschen existiren (welches, wenn man etwa die Neuholländer oder Feuerländer in Gedanken hat, so leicht nicht zu beantworten sein möchte): *so gelangt man zu keinem kategorischen Zwecke, sondern alle diese zweckmäßige Beziehung beruht auf einer immer weiter hinauszusetzenden Bedingung, die als unbedingt (das Dasein eines Dinges als Endzweck) ganz außerhalb der physisch=teleologischen Weltbetrachtung liegt.* Alsdann aber ist ein solches Ding auch nicht Naturzweck; denn es ist (oder seine ganze Gattung) nicht als Natur-product anzusehen.'

[41] Spivak, *Critique of Postcolonial Reason*, 26–7.

[42] She borrows the figure of 'foreclosure' from Lacan and uses it to determine the gesture of expulsion. For further interpretation see Dina Al-Kassim, 'The Face of Foreclosure', *Interventions*, 4/2 (2002), 168–74.

[43] Spivak, *Critique of Postcolonial Reason*, 27 n.

internal form, with the parts serving the whole teleologically, in which entities generate themselves both as individuals and as members of a species.[44] The latter mode of explanation considers the entity as a natural end (*Naturzweck*)—an important advance—but this is still not the same as conceiving it as an end of nature (*Endzweck*). To get there, we need not just the concept of something as an end (*Zweck*), but also cognition of a final end (*Endzweck*), which exceeds all our teleological conceptions, because, as Kant puts it, the 'end of the existence of nature itself must be sought beyond nature'.[45]

Take a blade of grass. Its internal form can be judged by us as purposive, but if we move to the (inadequate) way of contemplating its external purposiveness, what do we get? Here we come to the passage quoted by Spivak. Grass, considered externally, is necessary for livestock, and livestock for human beings, but we still don't know why human beings exist (in which context the New Hollanders or Firelanders are mentioned parenthetically). Kant's point is about the problems intrinsic to explanations reliant on external purposiveness. They lead to an infinite regress and never get us to the real issue of *why* something exists. Spivak's interpretation is based on a misreading of Kant but also, crucially, on the failure to include a sentence from the middle of the passage (elided without indication). After the parenthetical remark about New Hollanders and Firelanders, Kant states:

thus one does not arrive at any categorical end, but all of this [external] purposive relation rests on a condition that is always to be found further on, and which, as unconditioned, (the existence of a thing as a final end [*Endzweck*]) lies entirely outside of the physical-teleological way of considering the world.[46]

---

[44] Kant is also arguing here against a purely mechanistic account of nature: 'the concept of the combinations and forms of nature in accordance with ends is still at least one more principle for bringing its appearances under rules where the laws of causality about the mere mechanism of nature do not suffice'. ('Der Begriff von Verbindungen und Formen der Natur nach Zwecken ist doch wenigstens ein Princip mehr, die Erscheinungen derselben unter Regeln zu bringen, wo die Gesetze der Causalität nach dem bloßen Mechanism derselben nicht zulangen'.) Immanuel Kant, *Critique of the Power of Judgment*, ed. Paul Guyer, trans. Paul Guyer and Eric Matthews (Cambridge: Cambridge University Press, 2000), 234 (§61), AA, v, 360.

[45] 'Denn der Zweck der Existenz der Natur selbst muß über die Natur hinaus gesucht werden' (§67), AA, v. 378.

[46] *Critique of the Power of Judgment*, 250. Spivak follows Bernard's translation, which restructures the sequence of Kant's argument. The consequence is that she quotes Bernard's text (but not Kant's) correctly. However, as she modifies Bernard's translation and often interpolates the German original, the unacknowledged elision from Kant is presumably intentional.

Kant indicates that the way of explaining things on the basis of external purposiveness never provides us with a 'categorical end' but rests on the condition of something else in a sequence (grass, oxen, men, etc.). As he goes on to say, we cannot conceive of a thing as a natural end (*Naturzweck*) under this mode of explanation because it, or the entire species it belongs to, is not even regarded as natural product.

What does Kant conclude from this? Internally organized matter brings with it the notion of a natural end (*Naturzweck*), since its specific form is a product of nature. This in turn suggests that nature as a whole must be understood as a system of ends. Yet it must be recognized that we engage in reflective or subjective judgement in this context, which is merely regulative, not determinant judgement.[47] Nonetheless, the example of (the internal purposiveness of) organic products justifies the view that nothing in nature is without purpose in the whole. Human beings, including New Hollanders and Firelanders, form part of this system.

For Spivak, Kant's purpose in the passage is to single out the 'raw man' (in her view, this is the figure named in Kant's reference to New Hollanders and Firelanders) for exclusion. Ostensibly, the raw man is here 'not only not the subject as such; he also does not quite make it as an example of the thing or its species as natural product'.[48] But this interpretation would only make sense if we ignored the context and paraphrased Kant, without warrant, as saying something like 'we do not see why it is necessary that some men should exist (such as New Hollanders and Firelanders), whereas the existence of other human beings (like Europeans) is much easier to explain'. Yet Kant is making a more general point about our inability to explain the existence of human beings in general (he uses the word *Menschen*) with this faulty kind of reasoning.[49] Spivak's remark that 'Kant's text cannot quite say this and

---

[47] Kant, *Critique of the Power of Judgment*, 234 (§61), AA, v, 360–1. For discussion see John H. Zammito, *The Genesis of Kant's Critique of Judgment* (Chicago: University of Chicago Press, 1992), ch. 10, esp. 222–4.

[48] Spivak, *Critique of Postcolonial Reason*, 26.

[49] Spivak's remark that this passage is the 'one and only' example in Kant's *Critique* of a 'legally adjusted and grounded determinant judgment' in which we find ourselves unable to prove that 'he [the raw man], or a species of him, need exist' (*Critique of Postcolonial Reason*, 26) is also mistaken. Kant is here discussing the problem of explaining nature on the basis of external purposiveness, not describing how determinant judgements work. Such judgements are adequate for making purely mechanistic explanations. Teleological judgement is required to explain natural entities

indeed cannot develop this argument' is telling.[50] The announcement at the outset of her discussion that her reading is a 'scrupulous travesty' turns out to contain surprising truth.[51]

The question remains why Kant would mention the New Hollanders or Firelanders even in an aside.[52] To answer this, it is important to keep the 'transcendental' and the 'empirical' (or anthropological) levels distinct, not as an alibi for Kant but to do justice to his position. According to Kant, neither the New Hollanders, Firelanders, Europeans, nor humankind as a whole can claim that they are a final end (*Endzweck*) based on external purposiveness. Kant's argument is 'transcendental', that is, it is based on what is accessible to our 'human' faculty of judgement. The parenthesis, instead, is an empirical (that is, non-transcendental) illustration and is not meant to express Kant's view here. Rather, he addresses those who argue in terms of external purposiveness and exposes an infinite regress that comes into play even in the case of 'man'. If it is impossible to make empirical sense of why the New Hollanders or Firelanders exist, this is because the manner of approaching the question is absurd.[53] A transcendental perspective is required.

Kant may also refer to these examples of humanity because they are considered closer to nature empirically. But transcendentally they are just the same. The rhetorical structure of the argument in section 67 is paralleled in section 63 of the *Critique* when Kant observes that Laplanders survive in harsh conditions by relying on reindeer, which in turn survive on moss. Other people who live in icy conditions nourish themselves with the produce of the sea. Kant says, 'Now here is an admirable confluence of so

properly, but it remains regulative rather than constitutive. Kant states explicitly that 'It is self-evident that this is not a principle for the determining but only for the reflecting power of judgement, that it is regulative and not constitutive' ('Es versteht sich, daß dieses nicht ein Princip für die bestimmende, sondern nur für die reflectirende Urtheilskraft sei'). *Critique of the Power of Judgment*, 250 (§67), AA, v, 379.

[50] Spivak, *Critique of Postcolonial Reason*, 27.

[51] Ibid. 9. This statement is based on her readiness to reintroduce the empirical into the philosophical, which Kant had kept separate.

[52] Kant probably obtained some knowledge of the New Hollanders from Georg Forster, 'Neuholland und die Brittische Colonie Botany-Bay', appended to Matthias Christian Sprengel (ed.), *Jahrbuch der merkwürdigsten Weltbegebenheiten für 1787, enthaltend die Geschichte der wichtigsten Staats- und Handelsveränderungen von Ostindien* (2nd edn, Leipzig, 1786), 300–22.

[53] We are grateful to Angelica Nuzzo for her advice and thoughts on this question.

many relations of nature for one end: and this is the Greenlander, the Lapp, the Samoyed, the Yakut, etc. But one does not see why human beings have to live there at all.'[54] On this occasion, the question that exposes the philosophical problem is: why is it necessary for human beings to live in such places? In section 67 the question is: why is it necessary for human beings to exist? In neither instance is Kant issuing a rebuke to these native peoples but rather clarifying—in the present case—that it would be 'a very bold and arbitrary judgment' ('ein sehr gewagtes und willkürliches Urtheil') to explain the existence of sea animals and other things on the basis of their external purposiveness or usefulness to man.

Although the *Critique of Judgement* does not yield the evidence that Spivak supposes, the irony is that a wider search of kant's work would have produced sufficient testimony to raise doubts about the inclusiveness of his philosophy. Yet here too the complexity of his position means that we need to investigate his work as a whole with care. How rigorous is his univeralism? What role does difference play in his philosophical system? To consider these issues we need to look elsewhere, to his discussion of race, species, and cultural development. This enquiry will take us, eventually, to Kant's anthropology and his account of historical progression. We may grant that he introduces some form of 'geopolitical differentiation', but is the condition permanent?

Throughout his writings, some intended for publication, others based on lectures or notes, Kant issued judgements on the accomplishments and shortcomings of various peoples and races. Many of these reflect a deep-seated prejudice and racial bias in favour of white Europeans. In his lectures on physical geography, for example, Kant maintained that

In a hot climate man matures faster [physically] in every respect, but he does not reach the same perfection as [peoples living] in temperate zones. The white race is the most perfect of mankind. The yellow Indians are already less talented. Negroes are situated far below [them], and at the bottom are some of the peoples of America.[55]

---

[54] *Critique of the Power of Judgment*, 241 (§63), AA, v, 369. ('Hier ist nun eine bewundernswürdige Zusammenkunft von so viel Beziehungen der Natur auf einen Zweck; und dieser ist der Grönländer, der Lappe, der Samojede, der Jakute u. s. w. Aber man sieht nicht, warum überhaupt Menschen dort leben müssen'.)

[55] Kant, *Physische Geographie*, AA, ix, 316 ('In den heißen Ländern reift der Mensch in allen Stücken früher, erreicht aber nicht die Vollkommenheit der temperirten Zonen. Die Mensch-

The placing of native Americans at the bottom may reflect the influence of
Buffon (whose impact on him is apparent elsewhere in his notion of species
and generation); in other writings, Kant's disparagement of Africans is
especially stark and may owe a debt to Hume.[56] It remains unclear, however,
whether the predicament would change with an alteration of climate, or is
endemic in certain races. The same ambiguity appears in his 'Lectures on
Pedagogy', where Kant observes that savage nations

never get used to a European way of life even if they have served them for a long
time. But it is not a noble inclination to freedom, as Rousseau and others suggest,
but their tendency to rawness [*Rohigkeit*], in the sense that the animal has not yet
fully developed humanity. For this reason man must get accustomed to obeying the
instructions of reason at an early age.[57]

heit ist in ihrer größten Vollkommenheit in der Race der Weißen. Die gelben Indianer haben
schon ein geringeres Talent. Die Neger sind weit tiefer, und am tiefsten steht ein Theil der
amerikanischen Völkerschaften').

[56] For Kant's disparaging comments on the Negro race, see e.g. AA, ix, 419: 'Die Abyssinier
sind von arabischer Abkunft, witzig, wohlgebildet, aber schwarzfalb mit wollichtem Haar,
ehrlich, nicht zanksüchtig. Es giebt unter ihnen auch einige weiße Mohren; die Kaffern aber,
die in ihrem Gebiete wohnen, sind nicht nur häßlich, sondern auch so ungestaltet und boshaft
wie die übrigen Neger' ('The Abyssinians are of Arabic descent, [they] are witty, [physically] well-
shaped, but dun-coloured, with woollen hair, upright, not quarrelsome. There are some white
moors among them; yet the Kaffirs who dwell in these places [of the Abyssinians] are not only
ugly, but also as misshapen and malicious as the other Negroes'). Kant then refers to Le Vaillant
as his source (François Le Vaillant, *Voyages de F. Le Vaillant dans l'intérieur de l'Afrique, 1781–1785*). See
also his *Observations on the Feeling of the Beautiful and the Sublime* (*Beobachtungen über das Gefühl des Schönen und
Erhabenen*, 1764), 'Die Negers von Afrika haben von der Natur kein Gefühl, welches über das
Läppische stiege' ('The Negroes from Africa do not by nature possess a feeling that reaches
beyond the trivial'). AA, ii, 253. Another crushing verdict occurs in one of his notebooks from
the 1780s: 'Der Neger kan disciplinirt und cultivirt, niemals aber ächt civilisirt werden. Er verfällt
von selbst in die Wildheit' ('The Negro can become disciplined and cultivated, but he can never
become truly civilized. He automatically reverts to savagery again'). AA, xv, 878: *Handschriftlicher
Nachlaß, Anthropologie, Entwürfe zu dem Colleg—über Anthropologie aus den 70er und 80er Jahren*. The
connection with Hume is suggested by Robert B. Louden, *Kant's Impure Ethics: From Rational Beings
to Human Beings* (New York: Oxford University Press, 2000), 99.

[57] AA, ix, 442 ('Man sieht es auch an den wilden Nationen, daß, wenn sie gleich den
Europäern längere Zeit hindurch Dienste thun, sie sich doch nie an ihre Lebensart gewöhnen.
Bei ihnen ist dieses aber nicht ein edler Hang zur Freiheit, wie Rousseau und Andere meinen,
sondern eine gewisse Rohigkeit, indem das Thier hier gewissermaßen die Menschheit noch nicht
in sich entwickelt hat. Daher muß der Mensch frühe gewöhnt werden, sich den Vorschriften
der Vernunft zu unterwerfen'.)

While discounting Rousseau's interpretation of the situation, Kant returns to the fate of the so-called 'raw' man. The permanence of his relegation to a subordinate condition appears to be confirmed by the fact that he never assimilates to European standards, but the final sentence qualifies this suggestion: instruction in reason from an early age may transform his prospects. On either interpretation of Kant, of course, the narrative he supplies is predicated on a European model of history, geography, and reason, with the white race occupying a privileged position.

Kant's comments on Poles, Russians, and Turks are not much more complimentary, it must be said, where deficiencies of government militate against their capacity for civilization.[58] This highlights that for Kant the correct form of government (combining freedom, law, and authority— ultimately, the republic) is among the crucial factors bearing on the realization of human potentialities. The limited number of races capable of producing culture is bound up with an absence of government or imperfect articulations of it.

Although Kant held racist beliefs, he argued against the polygenetic thesis that Hume, Meiners, and others adopted to support their position.[59] Kant maintained that all human beings were members of the same species. This point is not unimportant. It enabled him to speak of the destiny of the species as a whole, a future in which human beings would moralize themselves, according to Kant, beyond their current level of civilization, through the influences of education, government, and religion. From this perspective, rawness is a stage within human development. His narrative of progress is an inclusive one because his account of the species is emphatically inclusive. While Kant displays prejudice and contradictory impulses, the logic of the system is not exclusionary.[60]

[58] See remarks quoted in Louden, *Kant's Impure Ethics*, 89–91; 99–100.

[59] Mankind exists in a single species (*Gattung*) divided into four different races: the white, Negro, Hun (Mongol or Kamuck), and Hindu or Hindustani races. AA, ii, 432. For Kant, race is defined by skin colour, and it was differentiated in order to accommodate human beings to the different climates and terrains they were destined to inhabit: '... various germs [*Keime*] and natural predispositions must lie restrained in him to be on occasion either unfolded or restrained, so that he would become adapted to his place in the world'. AA, ii, 435, quoted in Louden, *Kant's Impure Ethics*, 104.

[60] Ibid. 104–5. The importance for Kant's anthropology of his biological and monogenetic perspective is missing from Todd Hedrick's otherwise insightful account in 'Race, Difference, and Anthropology in Kant's Cosmopolitanism', *Journal of the History of Philosophy*, 46/2 (2008), 245–68.

To appreciate that logic we must return to Kant's teleological perspective in the *Critique of Judgement*, discussed above, and his organic conception of human-kind in which human beings constitute a single species. Nature's purpose becomes clear not merely, as Angelica Nuzzo puts it, 'in man's biological and natural existence but rather in those human dispositions that reveal what man is able to purposively do with himself in society and history.'[61] Culture is the ultimate purpose of nature, a formal capacity consistent with human freedom. To explain this purpose, Kant turns to history and politics in the formation of a cosmopolitan order.[62] He works out the details theoretically and historically elsewhere in an account that bears some reminders of Scottish stadial history. But unlike the Scottish narrative, Kant does not acknowledge that a full realization of potentialities has yet occurred (as might be thought with the Scottish emphasis on the era of commerce as a social culmination). His version is more agonistic and is beset by a darker view of human nature in many ways. But above all the distinction resides in his overtly teleological and cosmopolitan analysis.[63] The question, then, is not whether Kant's philosophy is inclusive, but on what terms.

For mankind as a whole, the capacity for realizing its potential involves a *Bestimmung* (determination or purpose) of human progress.[64] Kant's 'Conjectures on the Beginning of Human History' ('Mutmaßlicher Anfang der Menschengeschichte', 1786) provides his variant of conjectural history. In this work, together with his discussion of 'The Character of the Species' (the concluding section of his *Anthropology from a Pragmatic Point of View [Anthropologie in*

For further discussion, see Alix Cohen, 'Kant on Epigenesis, Monogenesis and Human Nature: The Biological Premises of Anthropology', *Studies in History and Philosophy of Biological and Medical Sciences*, 37 (2006), 675–93.

[61] Angelica Nuzzo, *Kant and the Unity of Reason* (West Lafayette, Ind.: Purdue University Press, 2005), 358.

[62] Ibid. 359–60. See also Pheng Cheah, *Spectral Nationality: Passages of Freedom from Kant to Postcolonial Literatures of Liberation* (New York: Columbia University Press, 2003), ch. 2; Rudolf A. Makkreel, *Imagination and Interpretation in Kant: The Hermeneutical Import of the 'Critique of Judgment'* (Chicago: University of Chicago Press, 1990), ch. 7.

[63] For further discussion, see Bertrand Binoche, *Les trois sources des philosophies de l'histoire, 1764–1798* (Paris: Presses Universitaires de France, 1994).

[64] '. . . die Bestimmung des *menschlichen Geschlechts im Ganzen* ist unaufhörliches Fortschreiten, und die Vollendung derselben ist eine bloße, aber in aller Absicht sehr nützliche Idee von dem Ziele, worauf wir der Absicht der Vorsehung gemäß unsere Bestrebungen zu richten haben.' Kant, 'Recensionen von Johann Gottfried Herders Ideen zur Philosophie der Geschichte der Menschheit Theil 1.2', AA, viii, 65 (emphasis added).

pragmatischer Hinsicht] 1798), which has close connections with the 'Conjectures', Kant assessed the potentialities of mankind as a whole through different stages of development (while responding at the same time to Herder and Rousseau). Both works indicate Kant's distinctive balancing of antisocial and social tendencies in human nature with the progressive realization of reason and moral understanding, in an ultimately redemptive framework. The 'Conjectures' ironizes an orthodox monogeneticism by tying the narrative expressly to Genesis 2–6. The growth of reason (in the appreciation that man is distinguished from animals in being an 'end of nature' [*Zweck der Natur*] who must, at the same time, treat others as ends and not as means) coincides with the transition from a 'rude' existence conditioned by instinct to one of rationality and freedom.[65] As a reader of Rousseau, Kant was aware of loss and gain as part of the proposition but he nonetheless reconciled the demands of culture and nature, confirming the moral destiny of the species as a whole as one of '*progress* toward perfection'.[66] Yet Kant's model is agonistic rather than sanguine, as the struggle realizes potentialities while also creating inequalities. Culture and education proceed unevenly over time since they lack a plan, or rather the plan is left in human hands to execute. The consequence is an inequality in terms of 'universal *human rights*': 'Man was meant to rise, by his own efforts, above the barbarism [*Rohigkeit*] of his natural abilities, but to take care not to contravene them even as he rises above them. He can expect to attain this skill only at a late stage and after many unsuccessful attempts; and in the meantime, the human race groans under the evils which it inflicts on itself as a result of its own inexperience'.[67]

The movement from one stage to another is marked by ongoing strife. As the savage life of the hunter is superseded by pastoral and agricultural life, Kant conjectures, the farmer must use force to prevent the depredations of

---

[65] Immanuel Kant, 'Conjectures on the Beginning of Human History' ('Mutmaßlicher Anfang des Menschengeschichte'), in Immanuel Kant, *Political Writings*, ed. Hans Reiss, trans. H. B. Nisbet (2nd edn, Cambridge: Cambridge University Press, 1991), 225–6. See AA, viii, 111–15.

[66] Kant, 'Conjectures', 227, AA, viii, 115 ('Fortschreiten zur Vollkommenheit').

[67] Kant, 'Conjectures', 229 n., AA, viii, 116. ('Der Mensch sollte sich aus der Rohigkeit seiner Naturanlagen selbst herausarbeiten und, indem er sich über sie erhebt, dennoch Acht haben, daß er nicht wider sie verstoße; eine Geschicklichkeit, die er nur spät und nach vielen mißlingenden Versuchen erwarten kann, binnen welcher Zwischenzeit die Menschheit unter den Übeln seufzt, die sie sich aus Unerfahrenheit selbst anthut.')

the herdsmen's animals if they live near one another, which leads to the creation of village communities for protection. The settlement of communities close to one another generates in turn culture and art, but above all government, law, and justice. In this context, 'all human aptitudes could naturally develop, the most beneficial of these being *sociability and civil security*'. Yet because these conditions foster population growth, they provide the impetus for the dispersal of peoples and inhabiting of the earth. This epoch is one of inequality, the source of 'so much evil but also everything good'.[68] This account is far from self-congratulatory, however, since a pattern of ongoing conflict and war continues, until human freedom is attained, one of his ultimate objectives, in a cosmopolitan era of perpetual peace.[69]

Kant's affirmation, in his *Anthropology*, that concord is the *end* but discord is the *means* 'to bring about the perfection of the human being through progressive culture' opens up a worrying prospect from a postcolonial perspective.[70] For although Kant recognizes civil or foreign wars as an evil, he argues that they provide 'the incentive to pass from the crude state of nature to the *civil* state'.[71] But it would be easy to misinterpret him here. What he means is that, by creating the need for protection, the fact of war provides the impetus for certain forms of social and economic organization, in much the same way as civil war answers the despotism that would

---

[68] Kant, 'Conjectures', 230, AA, viii, 119 ('Von dieser ersten und rohen Anlage konnte sich nun nach und nach alle menschliche Kunst, unter welcher die der Geselligkeit und bürgerlichen Sicherheit die ersprießlichste ist, allmählich entwickeln, das menschliche Geschlecht sich vermehren und aus einem Mittelpunkte wie Bienenstöcke durch Aussendung schon gebildeter Colonisten überall verbreiten. Mit dieser Epoche fing auch die Ungleichheit unter Menschen, diese reiche Quelle so vieles Bösen, aber auch alles Guten, an und nahm fernerhin zu').

[69] See Kant, *Critique of the Power of Judgment*, §83; and Kant, 'Perpetual Peace: A Philosophical Sketch' ('Zum ewigen Frieden: Ein philosophischer Entwurf', 1795), in *Political Writings*, 93–130, AA, viii, 341–86.

[70] Immanuel Kant, 'Anthropology from a Pragmatic Point of View', trans. Robert B. Louden, in *Anthropology, History, and Education*, ed. Günther Zöller and Robert B. Louden (Cambridge: Cambridge University Press, 2007), 417, AA, vii, 322 ('die Perfectionirung des Menschen durch fortschreitende Cultur').

[71] Kant, 'Anthropology', 425, AA, vii, 330 ('die Triebfeder aus dem rohen Naturzustande in den bürgerlichen überzugehen'). There is a parallel of sorts in the fact that 'The human being must therefore be educated to the good; but he who is to educate him is on the other hand a human being who still lies in the crudity [*Rohigkeit*] of nature and who is now supposed to bring about what he himself needs' ('Der Mensch muß also zum Guten erzogen werden; der aber, welcher ihn erziehen soll, ist wieder ein Mensch, der noch in der Rohigkeit der Natur liegt und nun doch dasjenige bewirken soll, was er selbst bedarf') (*Anthropology*, 420, AA, vii, 325).

overcome freedom. To interpret this aspect of Kant's theory as authorizing or naturalizing colonial conquest is thus misleading. In a more explicit statement in the *Metaphysics of Morals* (*Metaphysik der Sitten*, 1797), Kant argues that in European encounters with pastoral or hunting peoples (such as the Hottentots, Tongas, or American Indians), no justification existed for using violent means to impose 'culture' on them or to occupy land other than by contracts which did not exploit their ignorance, a stance consistent with his opposition to utilitarian moral theory.[72]

III German *Ethnographie* and universal history

Aside from this important concluding chapter of his *Anthropology*, Kant presented his anthropological theses as deliberately ahistorical. Even in the historical sequence he maintained, as we have seen, a relatively abstract and universal mode of argument. As he remarked elsewhere, 'Anthropology is not a local but a general anthropology. One becomes acquainted in it not with the condition of man but with the nature of mankind, for the local characteristics of men are always changing, but the nature of man does not'.[73] Human nature remained a uniform concept. The tendency of anthropology to take this form in Germany meant that discussion of cultural diversity occurred in other contexts. The most important of these is that of *Ethnographie* and universal history.

The German term for the art of describing (other) cultures and societies on the basis of eyewitness observation, *Ethnographie*, derived from the Greek word *ēthnos* for 'people'. This academic sub-discipline developed from German historiography, not from anthropology. While the 'invariable laws' of human nature were the subject of anthropological study, the varying forms of man's institutions, or the diversity of cultures, became central to

---

[72] Kant, *Metaphysical Elements of Justice: Part I of the Metaphysics of Morals*, 2nd edn, trans. John Ladd (Indianapolis: Hackett, 1999), 161, AA, vi, 353. For discussion, see Catherine Wilson, 'Savagery and the Supersensible: Kant's Universalism in Historical Context', *History of European Ideas*, 24/4–5 (1998), 323.

[73] Kant, [*Anthropologie-*] *Vorlesungen des Wintersemesters 1775/76*, quoted in John H. Zammito, *Kant, Herder and the Birth of Anthropology* (Chicago: University of Chicago Press, 2002), 299.

Ethnographie.[74] *Ethnographie* was much more restricted in scope than anthropology because it reduced the quintessential and all-embracing study of humankind to the *historical* study of a single people. In this sense it also differed from geography, so a new term became necessary. *Ethnographie* was later fully translated into German as *Völkerkunde*. The principal objects of early German ethnography were the peoples settling at Europe's peripheries. Germany may have been a country without colonies but there were various enclaves scattered across east and central Europe that were subject to one of the German states. At that stage, the term *Volk* still lacked the nationalistic connotations of nineteenth-century German Romanticism. On the contrary, it was used to denote the equality of peoples, because even the smallest people or tribe deserved to be called *Volk*; every *Volk* was a centre.[75]

Two prominent rival professors at Göttingen University established ethnography as an ancillary science for the study of universal history: Johann Christoph Gatterer (1727–90) and August Ludwig von Schlözer (1735–1809), both of whom (wrongly) claimed to have invented the term. Gatterer founded Göttingen's Royal Historical Institute, where he concentrated on questions of historical methodology and published several works on the theory of history. His primary concern was to draw up a 'historical plan' for sound scholarship, which had to be based on the 'science of rules' (*Wissenschaft von den Regeln*).[76] For Gatterer, the only adequate way to write history was *Völkergeschichte* (history of the peoples), essentially a synonym for universal history. It was a radically pluralized version of history, which in theory comprised the histories of all peoples—'a work not yet written'.[77]

---

[74] The Latin term *ethnographia* first appeared in 1767 in a book on local history: Johann Friedrich Schöpperlin, *Sveviae veteris per temporum periodos descriptae primae Lineae* (Nördlingen, 1767), which referred in its title to the taxonomic system of Linnaeus. For the conceptual history of 'ethnography' and related terms ('Ethnos-Begriffe'), see Justin Stagl, *Eine Geschichte der Neugier: Die Kunst des Reisens 1550–1800* (Vienna: Böhlau, 2002), 253–69.

[75] Mohammed Rassem, *Die Volkstumswissenschaften und der Etatismus* (Mittenwald: Mäander, 1979).

[76] '[Die] Wissenschaft von den Regeln, lesenswerte Geschichtsbücher zu verfertigen'; Gatterer, quoted in Jörn Rüsen, *Konfigurationen des Historismus: Studien zur deutschen Wissenschaftskultur* (Frankfurt: Suhrkamp, 1993), 55.

[77] Rudolf Vierhaus, 'Die Universität Göttingen und die Anfänge der modernen Geschichtswissenschaft im 18. Jahrhundert', in Hartmut Boockmann and Hermann Wellenreuther (eds), *Geschichtswissenschaft in Göttingen: Eine Vorlesungsreihe* (Göttingen: Vandenhoeck & Ruprecht, 1987), 20–1.

In a similar manner, the philologist and historian Schlözer, who held a chair in Göttingen from 1770, advocated the idea of a descriptive and comparative historical study of *all* peoples, including those of the non-Western world, and presented a theoretical outline of this idea in his *Introduction to Universal History*,[78] written as a response to global developments of his time. Europe's knowledge of the world had grown considerably since the age of discoveries, in the light of efforts to establish a global economy and to consolidate or expand colonial empires in the Americas and Asia. With this, an awareness of cultural diversity and the history of the countries outside Europe also emerged in eighteenth-century Germany. It was evident that historiography had to widen its perspective to cope with the masses of new historical information about peoples inhabiting the globe. For Schlözer, European history was no longer the sole object of history but became a particularly significant case subsumed under a wider category that he called *Völkergeschichte* (history of peoples) or *Universalgeschichte* (universal history). Schlözer introduced statistical methods to historiography to create some order in the growing body of data he was collecting, his most significant historical contribution. There was little space for questions of *philosophical* anthropology in his historical work, since he did not consider the universal nature of man. In this respect, Schlözer's work was, in Kant's words, 'merely empirical historiography' ('bloß empirisch... abgefaßte Historie').[79] But the questions raised by philosophical anthropology became relevant to what Schlözer called his *Metapolitik*, his conception of the formation of the state, in which he described the physical and mental features of mankind ('körperliche[s] und geistige[s] Wesen') which compelled the realization of Right (*Recht*) and the development of state society (*Staatsgesellschaft*).[80]

Schlözer's historical approach was decidedly anti-nationalistic and cosmopolitan in perspective. 'Global history', he wrote in his *Introduction*, 'comprises all countries and nations of the world.... Without fatherland and national

---

[78] August Ludwig Schlözer, *Vorstellung seiner Universal-Historie (1772/73)*, ed. Horst Walter Blanke (Waltrop: Hartmut Spenner, 1997).

[79] Kant, 'Idee zu einer allgemeinen Geschichte in weltbürgerlicher Absicht', AA, viii, 30.

[80] August Ludwig von Schlözer, *Theorie der Statistik: Nebst Ideen über das Studium der Politik überhaupt* (Göttingen: Vandenhoek & Ruprecht, 1804), 29. In terms of methodology, Linnaeus's taxonomies (which Schlözer also employed in his own systematic ordering of peoples, or *Völkersystem*) remained a link between physical anthropology and universal history. Following Leibniz, the main distinguishing feature was language; see Stagl, *Eine Geschichte der Neugier*, 264–5.

pride it covers all the places where human societies dwell'.[81] He stressed that every people was worthy of description in universal historiography, though he made a distinction between major peoples (the Persians, Romans, Spanish, and Chinese, for example) and perhaps unexpectedly minor ones (Egyptians, Greeks, or Hebrews).[82] For Schlözer, world history was a continuous process of worldwide integration. He left no doubt that Europe was its driving force, a position he had in common with most other contemporary European historians.

This sort of teleological perspective collided with the historical views of Johann Gottfried Herder (1744–1803). Herder (whose interests ranged from philosophy to philology, poetry, history, and theology) doubted the value of empirical data in this context and questioned the way in which it was used. His short but venomous review of Schlözer's *Introduction* made an enemy of him for several years to come and dented Herder's own academic career.[83] Leaving aside the polemical tone of the review, Herder raised an important objection. He did not believe that sufficient information on human nature and history would ever exist to support the conclusion that history develops in a uniform direction, with Europe as the spearhead of progress. For Herder, God's will alone determined human history, so how could someone like Schlözer pretend to know the course of the history of mankind?[84] He also rejected Schlözer's term 'Ethnographisch' ('one of the hard words we sometimes have no grindstone for').[85] Schlözer responded to Herder's critique in a powerfully eloquent second volume of his universal history (1773) and stood his ground, at least in the eyes of contemporary observers.

[81] Schlözer, *Vorstellung seiner Universal-Historie*, 28 ('Weltgeschichte ... umfasst alle Völker und Staaten der Welt. ... Ohne Vaterland, ohne Nationalstolz verbreitet sie sich über alle Gegenden, wo gesellschaftliche Menschen wohnen').

[82] Ibid. 106 ff.

[83] Johann Gottfried Herder, 'A. L. Schlözers Vorstellung seiner *Universal-Historie*', in *Sämmtliche Werke*, ed. Bernhard Suphan, 33 vols (Berlin: Weidmann'sche Buchhandlung, 1877–1913) (hereafter SW), v, 436–40.

[84] Ibid. 438: 'Where is the end? What's the straight way to it? What does it mean: "progress of humankind"? Is it Enlightenment? Is it improvement? Perfection? Greater happiness? What is the measure? Where do we find proper data for measuring given that there are so many different peoples and times to consider ... ?' ('[W]o steht der Eine, große Endpfahl? wo geht der gerade Weg zu ihm? was heists, "Fortgang des menschlichen Geschlechts["]? Ists Aufklärung? Verbesserung? Vervollkommnung? mehrere Glückseligkeit? Wo ist Maaß? wo sind Data zum Maaße in so verschiednen Zeiten und Völkern ... ?').

[85] Ibid.

In retrospect, Schlözer's methodological work on statistics prepared the way for political science and sociology in Europe. But Herder's impact on European thought was certainly more profound. In particular, his philosophy of history added new depth to current notions of *Volk* (people): 'Whereas for Schlözer', Hans Vermeulen notes, '*Volk* was a taxonomical unit, a subgroup of the larger unity of humankind, Herder regarded *Volk* as something natural and organic in which humanity expressed itself'.[86] In one respect, Herder's account of *Volk* reconceived the object of study by delegating it capacities and significance it had not previously enjoyed. The collective entity *Volk* became a focal point, possessing an internal soul which communicated itself, above all, in the particularity of language. While Kant had set in place a universal progressive history associated with the development of mankind as a whole, led by a kind of *Bestimmung* or purpose, Herder's different *Völker* could not be coordinated in such a fashion other than as an expression of humanity. Cultural difference was built into his system, in this respect, as a basic principle and value. The shared nature of human beings was productive of this diversity.

The practical and methodological implication of this for Herder meant that the 'soul' of a people could not be grasped through political history or the history of wars between nations ('revolutions' in Schlözer's terminology),[87] but only through the study of a people's poetry.[88] And he put his ideas into practice. His collections of German folk songs (*Volkslieder*) set the stage for nineteenth-century *Volkskunde*.[89]

For Herder, a people's distinctiveness therefore resided in language:

Those who have been educated in the same language, who have learned to pour out their hearts and to express their souls through it, belong to the people of that language … a nation is educated through language; through language it acquires a liking for neatness and tidiness; [through language] it becomes honest, obedient,

---

[86] Hans F. Vermeulen, 'The German Invention of *Völkerkunde*: Ethnological Discourse in Europe and Asia, 1740–1798', in Sara Eigen and Mark J. Larrimore (eds), *The German Invention of Race* (New York: SUNY Press, 2006), 134.

[87] Schlözer, *Vorstellung seiner Universal-Historie*, 1–44, passim.

[88] Johann Gottfried Herder, *Briefe zur Beförderung der Humanität*, Sammlung 8, Brief 107 (1796), in SW, xviii, 137. This work is a series of public letters by Herder ('Letters for the advancement of humanity'), numbered consecutively and organized in ten collections (*Sammlungen*).

[89] See Heinz Rölleke, 'Nachwort', in Johann Gottfried Herder, *Stimmen der Völker in Liedern: Volkslieder. Zwei Teile 1778/79*, ed. Heinz Rölleke (Stuttgart: Reclam, 1974), 463–503.

polite, affable, famous, diligent, and powerful. Who despises the language of his nation . . . will become the most dangerous murderer of its spirit.[90]

There are many implications in this passage that deserve comment. To begin with, we can reinforce the point that Herder's focus on the diversity of cultures, with its attendant cultural relativism, necessarily conflicted with the idea of universal progress. (He even defended national prejudice against its enlightened enemies because 'It pushes peoples together to their [cultural] centre'.[91]) Herder pledged to judge each time and each culture by its own canon of values and customs, and turned against any *raison universelle* that propelled a uniform development of civilization.[92] The emergence of a new conception of culture may also be glimpsed here. For Kant this notion was associated with *Bildung*, a form of cultivation or raising up and education (required of the raw man but potentially beyond his reach). In Herder's account, language plays a constitutive role in the formation of culture, which anticipates a potential pluralization of the concept.

At the same time, shared language ensures that the unity of a people derives not from an ossified condition of race or from the alternative of climate, but from a source which is historical. Language is not a genetic trait; although it implies the contiguity of people, the determinant is not geography but communication. However, we cannot overlook the association already present in the passage between language and nation. Elsewhere Herder deplored the mixing of peoples as a threat to the integrity of languages. The destructive power of ethnocentrism, the ranking of peoples, and validation of the nation as agent of empire, which appear in the nineteenth century and beyond, becomes visible.

[90] Herder, *Briefe zur Beförderung der Humanität*, Sammlung 5, Brief 57, Beilage (1795), in SW, xvii, 294–5 ('Wer in derselben Sprache erzogen ward, wer sein Herz in sie schütten, seine Seele in ihr ausdrücken lernte, der gehört zum Volk dieser Sprache. . . . Mitterls der Sprache wird eine Nation erzogen und gebildet; mittels der Sprache wird sie ordnungs- und ehrliebend, folgsam, gesittet, umgänglich, berühmt, fleißig und mächtig. Wer die Sprache seiner Nation verachtet, . . . wird ihres Geistes gefährlichster Mörder').

[91] Herder, *Auch eine Philosophie der Geschichte zur Bildung der Menschheit* (1774), in SW, xiii, 510 ('Das Vorurteil ist gut, zu seiner Zeit: denn es macht glücklich. Es drängt Völker zu ihrem Mittelpunkte zusammen').

[92] Herder, *Briefe, das Studium der Theologie betreffend*, in SW, x, 373 ('eine menschliche Geschichte müsse man menschlich, nach ihrem natürlichen Zusammenhange, in ihrer eigenen Farbe, nach ihrem eignen Geist beurtheilen; nicht ihr den unsrigen, und mit ihm den Zusammenhang unsers Wahn, unsrer Willkühr, so wie die Säfte unsers Herzens leihen').

Herder did not anticipate this development but offered instead a pluralistic version of history, and it was this that inevitably incurred Kant's displeasure. Herder had been a student in Königsberg and attended Kant's lectures in the early 1760s, but his theory accommodated diversity in a very different way from Kant's. In 1785, Kant reviewed the first instalments of Herder's *Ideen zur Philosophie der Geschichte der Menschheit* (published between 1784 and 1791). He was respectful in tone but rejected Herder's central arguments. According to Kant, the human race was, as we have seen, destined for continuous progress, and his idea of human perfection left no room for cultural relativism.[93] He also did not share Herder's view on *Volk*, which in Kant's philosophy came to be subsumed under the more important category of the *state*. And in contrast to Herder, Kant defined the state not on the basis of its people but on the basis of law.[94]

IV The German critique of colonialism

In the light of his critical remarks on universal history and the stadial account of human history, as well as his objection to the category of race, Herder's opposition to colonialism is not unexpected.[95] What may come as more of a surprise is the fact that most of the German *philosophes* in the latter half of the eighteenth century, including Kant, were open critics of European imperialism.[96] Evidently no necessary conceptual connection existed between the adoption of Enlightenment views on historical progress, race, or polygenesis and an imperialist conclusion. Kant and Georg Forster disagreed over the concept of race and monogenesis, for example (Forster upheld

[93] Kant, 'Recensionen von Johann Gottfried Herders Ideen', AA, viii, 65: 'die Bestimmung des menschlichen Geschlechts im Ganzen ist unaufhörliches Fortschreiten, und die Vollendung derselben ist eine bloße, aber in aller Absicht sehr nützliche Idee von dem Ziele, worauf wir der Absicht der Vorsehung gemäß unsere Bestrebungen zu richten haben.' For an English translation, see 'Reviews of Herder's Ideas on the Philosophy of the History of Mankind', in Herder, *Political Writings*, 201–20.

[94] See Kant, 'Über den Gemeinspruch: Das mag in der Theorie richtig sein, taugt aber nicht für die Praxis' (1793), AA, viii, 297 ff.

[95] It adds to the irony that his plea for tolerance and deep respect for cultural diversity eventually gave rise to aggressive forms of European nationalism in the following centuries.

[96] See Sankar Muthu, *Enlightenment against Empire* (Princeton: Princeton University Press, 2003), chs 4–6 on Kant and Herder.

polygenesis, which Kant denied, but Forster rejected Kant's views on race on other grounds).[97] Herder, meanwhile, regarded 'race' an unnecessary category and an 'ignoble term'. In his *Ideen*, he considered various theories of race then current in Europe and explicitly turned against both Blumenbach and Kant: 'In short, there are neither four or five different races, nor exclusive varieties, on this earth'.[98] Yet they all coincided on the subject of imperalism.

Both Kant and Engelbert Kaempfer praised the Japanese for their policy of isolation,[99] and Georg Forster thought most highly of those peoples who had managed to escape European attention as long as possible.[100] In 1762, the German economist Johann Heinrich Gottlob von Justi based his rejection of European colonialism on moral and economic principles. Looking at international trade, he suggested that prosperity and stability were possible without it: 'The purity of morals, the love of the fatherland, a real sense of honour, and other virtues can emerge or be preserved in a nation that has no intercourse with other peoples'.[101] Such a nation was less likely, in any event,

[97] Following Samuel Thomas Soemmering's views on the topic, Forster defended polygenesis and argued that there were important physiological differences between Europeans and Africans that made them closely related but not identical. He criticized Kant's definition of race as lacking sufficient empirical foundation. See 'Noch etwas über die Menschenraßen', *Der teutsche Merkur* (4.Vierteljahr 1786), 57–86; 'Beschluß der im vorigen Monat angefangenen Abhandlung über die Menschenrassen', ibid. 150–66. Kant later dismissed Forster's arguments in his essay 'On the Use of Teleological Principles in Philosophy' ('Über den Gebrauch teleologischer Principien in der Philosophie', 1788), AA, viii, 157–84. See also Harry Liebersohn, *The Travelers' World: Europe to the Pacific* (Cambridge, Mass.: Harvard University Press, 2006), 197–208.

[98] Herder, *Ideen zur Philosophie der Geschichte der Menschheit*, in SW, xiii, 275 ('Kurz, weder vier oder fünf Rassen, noch ausschließende Varietäten gibt es auf der Erde').

[99] Engelbert Kaempfer, *Geschichte und Beschreibung von Japan* [1777–79], 2 vols, ed. C. W. Dohm (Stuttgart: F. A. Brockhaus, 1964), ii, 396; Kant, 'Zum ewigen Frieden', AA, viii, 359.

[100] See Wolfdietrich Schmied-Kowarzig, 'Der Streit um die Einheit des Menschengeschlechts: Gedanken zu Forster, Herder und Kant', in Claus-Volker Klenske (ed.), *Georg Forster in interdisziplinärer Perspektive* (Berlin: Akademie-Verlag, 1994), 117. Georg Forster accompanied his father Reinhold on Cook's second voyage in 1772–5. See his *A Voyage Round the World*, 2 vols (London, 1777) (for a new edition, see that by Nicholas Thomas and Oliver Berghof (Honolulu: University of Hawai'i Press, 2000)).

[101] Johann Heinrich Gottlob von Justi, *Vergleichungen der europäischen mit den asiatischen und andern vermeintlich barbarischen Regierungen. In drey Büchern verfasset* (Berlin, Stettin and Leipzig, 1762), 312–13 ('Die Reinigkeit der Sitten, die Liebe des Vaterlandes, die wahre Ehrgbegierde, und andre Heldentugenden, können bey einem Volke, das allen Umgang mit andern Völkern vermeidet, in einem ungleich größern Grad bewirkt und erhalten werden: jedenfalls ist ein solches Volk nicht so sehr dem Verderben unterworfen').

to be ruined by the effects of luxury and self-interest promoted by that trade. Countries like pre-conquest Mexico and Peru or present-day Japan showed that it was possible to feed their people, remaining populous and powerful on the basis of agriculture and domestic trade alone. Even Schlözer, who usually advocated intercontinental trade, feared that Europe's overseas expansion could make a serious dent in people's morality. Europe's technological advances and its cultural achievements, he declared, have raised the Western nations over all other peoples on earth, but he qualified that remark by saying that *'with the help of these inventions we discovered three new worlds, and subjugated, plundered, educated, or devastated them'.*[102] We have already noted Kant's critical remarks in the *Metaphysik der Sitten* (1797). In his well-known essay 'Perpetual Peace' (1795), he accused the European powers of inciting Indian states 'to wars, famine, insurrection, treachery and the whole litany of evils that can afflict the human race'.[103]

Of course we might attribute the relative anti-colonial consensus to the fact that German participation in eighteenth-century colonial expansion was so limited,[104] which in turn relates to the decentralized political structure of the country.[105] Spivak remarks on these distinctive features of Germany in

[102] August Ludwig von Schlözer, *Weltgeschichte nach ihren Haupt Theilen im Auszug und Zusammenhange*, 2 vols (Göttingen, 1785–9), i, 116 ff.

[103] Kant, 'Zum ewigen Frieden', AA, viii, 341–86. Kant's engagement with the question of racial and cultural difference produces a decidedly mixed record. What keeps him from extending the logic of prejudice to a colonial policy is, ultimately, a commitment to a more liberatory politics, worked out in a European context and later inspired by the French Revolution. Enlightenment, it seems, cuts both ways, inevitably complicating our relationship to this complex inheritance.

[104] Aside from the Welser enterprise in Venezuela (1528–46), Germany did not engage in colonial projects in the New World. Of course individuals from German states did participate in the great European trading companies, especially the Dutch East India Company (like Johan Nieuhof), and a variety of important German travel accounts were published. In 1751, Frederick II established his Royal Prussian Asiatic Trade Company (Königlich-Preußische Asiatische Handlungscompanie), a development which Voltaire welcomed. But only a few Prussian ships seem to have travelled between China and Prussia before the company was closed down after the end of the Seven Years War in 1765. On Germany's later history of colonialism see George Steinmetz, *The Devil's Handwriting: Precoloniality and the German Colonial State in Qingdao, Samoa, and Southwest Africa* (Chicago: University of Chicago Press, 2007). See also Susanne Zantop, *Colonial Fantasies: Conquest, Family, and Nation in Pre-Colonial Germany, 1770–1870* (Durham, NC: Duke University Press, 1997) for the German fantasy of colonial possessions.

[105] Until 1806, Germany was divided into Catholic and Protestant territories and embedded in the rather loose (though highly sensitive) structures that formed the Holy Roman Empire—

the period, before suggesting that German separation from the rest of Europe in this respect made it the source of scholarly reflection on difference as it developed the comparative study of philology, religion, and literature without 'direct involvement in the utilization of that other difference, between the colonizer and the colonized'. She cites Herder's capacity for 'thinking alterity by way of language/culture' in this context. But she sets up a contrast here with the domain of philosophy, which in Germany produced ' "universal" narratives where the subject remained unmistakably European'. She never explains the reason for this anomaly or disjunction between philosophy and comparative studies. But she later says of Kant's invocation of the *Neuholländer* and *Feuerländer* in the *Critique of Judgement* that 'We find here the axiomatics of imperialism as a natural argument to indicate the limits of the cognition of (cultural) man'.[106] While we may debate Kant's circumscription of the native and the limits of his own cognition in this regard, the notion of an 'axiomatics of imperialism' should nonetheless give us pause. Whatever else we may conclude, the connection between Kant's position and imperialism is far from axiomatic in the sense of being 'self-evident' or 'indisputably true'.[107] The mistake in her reading, then, may not be the deliberate one of recalling the empirical into the philosophical, which she defends on the grounds of needing to disrupt the deployment of philosophy in the 'narrativization of history'. Rather, the problem lies with what she calls her own 'historical fable', namely the claim that the end of the eighteenth century in Germany sees the fabrication of new versions of self and world 'that would provide alibis for the domination, exploitation, and epistemic violation entailed by the establishment of colony and empire'.[108]

according to Samuel von Pufendorf's dictum of 1667 a 'body that conforms to no rule and resembles a monster' (*irregulare aliquod corpus et monstro simile*). Samuel Freiherr von Pufendorf, *De statu imperii Germanici*, ed. Fritz Salomon (Weimar: Böhlau, 1910), 126. On the nature of the Holy Roman Empire see Volker Press, *Das alte Reich: Ausgewählte Aufsätze* (Berlin: Duncker & Humblot, 1997).

[106] Spivak, *Critique of Postcolonial Reason*, 8, 26.

[107] *OED*. See also the passage where Spivak notes the changing relationship between 'European discursive production and the axiomatics of imperialism' in the century spanning from Kant to Marx, but finds that this 'axiomatics' continues to make itself 'appear the only negotiable way' (*Critique of Postcolonial Reason*, 4). She describes her methodology as one in which 'the aporia between the discontinuous texts of the raw man and the subject as such' is made readable by 'passing through it by way of the axiomatics of imperialism' (ibid. 34).

[108] Ibid. 7. Spivak's conclusion coincides with Zantop. On Kant, see Zantop, *Colonial Fantasies*, 41 and passim.

V Universalism *and* diversity?

The inclination historiographically has been to separate Kant and Herder on a fault line between Enlightenment and Counter-Enlightenment, as the instance just noted from Spivak suggests: one stands for an oppressive universalism and the other for diversity, with Kant called into question in a postcolonial moment and Herder endorsed for his capacity to 'think alterity'. We might respond by questioning whether Herder is quite so at odds with the *Aufklärung* or emerges from it, by way of Leibniz, Locke, and Condillac, in his reflections on language.[109] But rather than pursue that argument, let us assume for the moment the validity of the opposition and consider its implications.

At the end of *Provincializing Europe*, Chakrabarty explains his purpose as one of employing 'universals' in order to 'produce critical readings of social injustices' while balancing this with what he calls the hermeneutic tradition, which articulates the relationship 'between thought and dwelling' and makes possible the writing of 'some very particular ways of being-in-the-world'.[110] As the latter phrase suggests, he draws on Heidegger to realize this possibility, but he might just as easily have called on Herder, whose important contribution to historiography Heidegger emphasized on various occasions.[111] For Herder, language provides the repository of cultural identity and specificity; the uniqueness of peoples resides in their speech and poetry, which resist translation, or for that matter universalization. It follows that respect and an assumption of equal status are also due to the diverse languages of the world.

If we accept the antithesis that Chakrabarty sets up between the universalism of the Enlightenment and the particularity of a hermeneutic tradition, the question remains whether a reconciliation can be effected in which we somehow retain the good of the Enlightenment and the good of diversity, the universal *and* the particular. Chakrabarty's attempt concentrates on creating a conjoint hermeneutics. But in this final section we would like to pose the problem in political terms. Can we retain the universalism of the

[109] This is the argument of Bob Chase, 'Herder and the Postcolonial Reconfiguring of the Enlightenment', *Bucknell Review*, 41/2 (1998), 172–96.

[110] Chakrabarty, *Provincializing Europe*, 254–5.

[111] See e.g. Martin Heidegger, *Zur Bestimmung der Philosophie*, ed. Bernd Heimbüchel, in *Martin Heidegger Gesamtausgabe*, lvi–lvii (Frankfurt: Vittorio Klostermann, 1987), 132–4.

Enlightenment as expressed, for example, in natural rights to be extended to all, while also protecting cultural difference?

This problem has been addressed explicitly in a political context largely overlooked in postcolonial debates, the contemporary political theory of multiculturalism. This body of work, which has emerged in the last twenty years, has set itself the task of reconciling the claims of cultural difference with the needs of a consensual constitution. And it has been written in many cases with the express intention of resolving the contradictions in Western democracies acquired by a legacy of colonialism. As such it realizes the potential for a sophisticated examination of Enlightenment by attempting to contain difference within a democratic form of association.

Among the leading theorists in this field, James Tully has brought to the discussion an especially sharp focus on the colonial past of modern nations which has left a legacy of injustice. In particular, he responds to the stadial theory of history (discussed in this essay above) and its influence on the liberal tradition, running from Locke to Mill. An imposed narrative of historical progression authorized the destruction of primitive cultures in favour of assimilation to a European standard of civility. By contrast, Tully conceives of the very purpose of contemporary constitutions as the 'accommodation of cultural diversity', in accordance with principles of mutual recognition, consent, and continuity, predicated on 'intercultural dialogue' as a means of reaching negotiated agreement.[112] To make the case he returns to Enlightenment and liberal democratic values of freedom, autonomy, and self-respect, arguing that if these are to be honoured and achieved, then a liberal constitution must 'protect the cultures of its members and engender the public attitude of mutual respect for cultural diversity that individual self respect requires',[113] partly by providing this recognition within 'public institutions, histories and symbols': 'Far from being a threat to liberal values, the recognition and protection of cultural diversity is a necessary condition of the primary good of self respect, and so of the individual freedom and autonomy that it underpins, in a manner appropriate to a post-imperial

---

[112] James Tully, *Strange Multiplicity: Constitutionalism in an Age of Diversity* (Cambridge: Cambridge University Press, 1995), 184. For discussion, see Duncan Ivison, *Postcolonial Liberalism* (Cambridge, Cambridge University Press, 2002), 82–3.

[113] Ibid. 190. Will Kymlicka, *Multicultural Citizenship: A Liberal Theory of Minority Rights* (Oxford: Clarendon Press, 1995), ch. 5, similarly embeds culture within a liberal polity by arguing that participation in a societal culture is an essential requirement for achieving a liberal goal of making meaningful choices.

age.'[114] Tully argues that these values require the protection of diversity, and that autonomy and self-respect need a cultural foundation in which the self takes shape and experiences meaning. Yet he resists the image of cultures as separate and distinct entities, coextensive with the 'nation' in certain forms of nineteenth-century thinking (and often said to derive from Herder); rather, he sees cultures as diverse entities in themselves, composed of patterns of interlinking experience, values, and commitments.[115] The model of cultural hybridity, while speaking to the identity of postcolonial subjects, undercuts the possibility of radical political disaggregation.

The most sustained deliberation over these questions has come from Will Kymlicka. For Kymlicka, the defining characteristics of a multicultural state include abandonment of the notion that the state exists to foster the identity and interests of a single dominant group; acknowledgement of the need to recognize and accommodate cultural difference; and the will to rectify injustices visited on indigenous peoples, members of annexed states, and immigrants. The specific remedies vary with the context of each country, but they require, in his analysis, a 'supplement' of rights for disenfranchised or marginal groups. In part the imperative serves to rebalance the state and constitution by recognizing that majority groups typically ignore the ways in which they impose the culture of their own group on others while assuming (conveniently) that the state remains neutral in such matters. By protecting the existence and future of aboriginal groups, multicultural policies in places such as Canada, New Zealand, Scandinavia, and Greenland represent part of a 'gradual but real process of decolonization', according to Kymlicka, 'as indigenous peoples regain rights regarding their lands, legal norms, and self-government'.[116]

Kymlicka traces these developments in political theory and practice to a realization of the implications of human rights. The equality of human beings calls for the preservation rather than assimilation of cultural difference in so far as culture is integral to our understanding of humanity. In this way, universal ideals of the Enlightenment are seen as logically connected to diversity. But the relationship between universalism and diversity is also

---

[114] Tully, *Strange Multiplicity*, 190–1.

[115] Ibid. 11–13, passim.

[116] Will Kymlicka, *Multicultural Odysseys: Navigating the New International Politics of Diversity* (Oxford: Oxford University Press, 2007), 67.

dialectical. Group-differentiated minority rights may derive, on the one hand, from a basic elaboration of human rights, but on the other hand, human rights also impose constraints. As Kymlicka puts it:

In fact, the human rights revolution is a double-edged sword. It has created political space for ethnocultural groups to contest inherited hierarchies. But it also requires groups to advance their claims in a very specific language—namely, the language of human rights, civil rights liberalism, and democratic constitutionalism, with their guarantees of gender equality, religious freedom, racial non-discrimination, gay rights, due process, and so on.[117]

To understand this development in political theory we can return to the dimension of Enlightenment thought about diversity with which we began. Toleration of religious difference was central to the conception of Enlightened politics, although toleration was typically conceived at the time as a grant rather than a right. Contemporary theories of multiculturalism share with this tradition a sense that diversity is irreducible but they create a more active constitutional effort to recognize difference. This recognition is constituted as a right not a grant, and is no longer confined to religion but extends to cultural practices more generally. There is a further analogy worth remarking upon: theorists of toleration like Locke set a limit by refusing to tolerate the intolerant. Kymlicka imposes a parallel restriction in extending a civil right protecting diversity on condition that those who benefit from it likewise respect the rights of others.

Universalism and diversity find themselves coexisting in this political context, not as hostile forces but as necessary to one another. With this development in constitutional theory, the Enlightenment, often characterized in postcolonial scholarship with suspicion, may prove a less intractable inheritance.

[117] Ibid. 92–3.

8

'These Nations Newton Made his Own'

Poetry, Knowledge, and British Imperial Globalization

Karen O'Brien

Among the many ways of looking at the coincidence and involvement of the Enlightenment with the rise of modern European empires, two current, apparently incompatible approaches command particular attention: on the one hand, the ongoing postcolonial critique of the Enlightenment as the progenitor of an unexamined and highly exclusive myth of the universal human subject, and of unilinear trajectories of modernization that serve to legitimate imperial and other forms of global domination; and, on the other, some of the recent, persuasive intellectual-historical work that has restated the centrality of the Enlightenment critique of empire and established a significant degree of discontinuity between the Enlightenment and nineteenth-century imperialism.[1] In the historical domain, studies by Sankar Muthu, Jennifer Pitts, and others have foregrounded the Enlightenment

---

[1] Jennifer Pitts, *A Turn to Empire: The Rise of Imperial Liberalism in Britain and France* (Princeton: Princeton University Press, 2005) and Sankar Muthu, *Enlightenment against Empire* (Princeton: Princeton University Press, 2003).

hostility to empire for various reasons: humanitarian concerns (Voltaire, Diderot); the injustice and inefficiency of monopoly capitalism (Smith, Hume, Montesquieu, Gibbon); the derogation of the right to communal self-determination (Burke, Bentham, Paine); personal autonomy (Kant); and the domestic impact of corporate imperial interests (Burke). Nineteenth-century apologists for empire may have deployed the theoretical tools created by the Enlightenment, but something happened inbetween to transform eighteenth-century projects for liberty and progress *in* Britain, France, and other European countries into exportable projects for *British* or *French* liberty and progress. Something happened, also, to make possible a theoretical adjustment whereby the possibility of geographical transfer implicit in the abstract Enlightenment handling of concepts such as liberty and progress was foreclosed, to the point where even the liberal inheritors of the Enlightenment (J. S. Mill among them) doubted the feasibility of extending those benefits to peoples at a less 'advanced' state of civilization. For Muthu, the Enlightenment engendered a 'multiplicity of universalisms with distinct foundational claims' favourable to pluralistic notions of human agency, which partly fell casualty to the growing national self-confidence and diminishing tolerance of those writing within nineteenth-century imperial states.[2] The fact that continuities between the Enlightenment view of empire and nineteenth-century imperialisms have so often been asserted is attributable, in part, to the reinvention of the Enlightenment by English Victorians (Henry Thomas Buckle among them) and French Third Republicans (such as Ernest Lavisse) as the prehistory of their own brands of liberalism and positivism.

Recognizing this, Muthu, Duncan Ivison, and others have sought to demonstrate that the cosmopolitan world-view of Enlightenment intellectuals, with their sense of ethical obligation beyond the boundaries of the state and their (highly selective) respect for difference and autonomy, can still be salvaged in the context of globalization in our own time.[3] On this point, they have something in common with those postcolonial theorists, including Homi Bhabha, Kwame Anthony Appiah, and Arjun Appadurai, who have seen possibilities and resources in cosmopolitanism as a means of imagining

---

[2] Muthu, *Enlightenment against Empire*, 18.
[3] Duncan Ivison, *Postcolonial Liberalism* (Cambridge: Cambridge University Press, 2002).

and bringing into being a global civil society beyond national boundaries.[4]
Theirs is a postcolonial Enlightenment cosmopolitanism of a kind, in the
sense that it centres upon the shared values of a publicly accountable politics,
tolerance, and personal freedom, and asserts an ethic of mutual obligation,
beyond the setting of the state, that does not necessarily require metaphysical grounding. Others, however, have been sceptical about the lingering
legacy of Enlightenment cosmopolitanism in postcolonial theory, notably
Timothy Brennan, who warns of 'the drift of a good cosmopolitanism into
imperial apologetics'.[5] Brennan is careful to distinguish between the 'historically novel cosmopolitanism' engendered by contemporary economic globalization and that of the past, but rightly points out that 'to understand the
history of cosmopolitanism is to learn something about the elusiveness of
imperial attitudes themselves'.[6]

Such elusiveness was certainly a feature of the British and French Enlightenment languages of cosmopolitanism or world citizenship, and of the
related language of Scottish conjectural history which tentatively identified
universal patterns in human social development. These languages, in Britain
as elsewhere in Europe, bore witness to the geographically extended and
economically connected world of the eighteenth century. They evolved in a
complex and conflicted relationship to the major engine of that intercon-
nectedness, imperial expansion: on the one hand seeming to offer the
historical trajectories needed to underwrite a project of European global
dominance, but on the other hand deeply critical, on both economic and
humanitarian grounds, of enforced individual or communal membership in
that world order. Above all, Enlightenment cosmopolitanism was insistently
Eurocentric, and sought to mobilize, in the interests of regional peace, a
sense of shared European identity, galvanized by an awareness of cultural
competitiveness, and of common racial origins.[7] The sceptical handling, by

[4] Kwame Anthony Appiah, *Cosmopolitanism: Ethics in a World of Strangers* (New York: Norton,
2006); Arjun Appadurai, *Modernity at Large: Cultural Dimensions of Globalization* (Minneapolis: University of Minnesota Press, 1996).

[5] Timothy Brennan, *At Home in the World: Cosmopolitanism Now* (Cambridge, Mass.: Harvard
University Press, 1997), 147.

[6] Ibid. 1, 11.

[7] Karen O'Brien, *Narratives of Enlightenment: Cosmopolitan History from Voltaire to Gibbon* (Cambridge:
Cambridge University Press, 1997); Colin Kidd, *British Identities before Nationalism: Ethnicity and
Nationhood in the Atlantic World, 1600–1800* (Cambridge: Cambridge University Press, 1999).

Enlightenment writers, of cherished national myths and prejudices paradox-ically exemplified the kind of philosophical mastery that could be deployed in contexts where intellectual superiority was paraded as evidence of imperial entitlement. Allied to cosmopolitanism was the Enlightenment faith in commerce as the potential solvent of (aggressively defended) nation states, as an agent of peaceful cooperation and as the progenitor of new, trans-national forms of civil identity. Contemporary postcolonial theorists and philosophers consistently probe and problematize the relationship between economic and cultural globalization, whether or not they celebrate the 'vernacular modernities' (in Appadurai's phrase) and vibrant cultural forms created by the partial dissolving of national identities.[8] That probing offers an indirect critique of Enlightenment cosmopolitanism, and of the faith of Enlightenment writers in the capacity of a reformed economic globalization to create new civil identities, allegiances, and responsibilities without the need for radically new forms of distributive justice.

What is clear is that the conceptual framework of globalization has made possible a new kind of dialogue between the Enlightenment and the post-colonial in relation to questions of cosmopolitan culture and identity, and to the question of the singular or multiple nature of modernity itself. It enables us to see that, in addressing transoceanic contact, trade, and imperial intervention, the Enlightenment created a spectrum of supranational con-cepts and languages that ranged from the universal to the cosmopolitan, and that evaluated non-European cultures with differing degrees of respect for local specificity and difference. The word 'spectrum' is, I think, helpful here, rather than positing cosmopolitanism (of the kind advocated by Appiah) as an *alternative* to universal notions of reason and humanity, even though a number of recent critics have made productive use of this contrast.[9] The concept works well for political theorists of postcolonial liberalism seeking a selective appropriation of the humanist and universal aspects of Enlighten-ment thought, even as they disengage them from the Eurocentric historical

---

[8] See e.g. Fredric Jameson, 'Notes on Globalization as a Philosophical Issue', in Fredric Jameson and Masao Miyoshi (eds), *The Cultures of Globalization* (Durham, NC: Duke University Press, 1998), 54–77.

[9] E.g. Sharon Marcus, 'Anne Frank and Hannah Arendt: Universalism and Pathos', in Vinay Dharwadker (ed.), *Cosmopolitan Geographies: New Locations in Literature and Culture* (London: Routledge, 2001), 89–132, esp. 90.

trajectories in which they were originally embedded.[10] The notion of a spectrum also captures the profound ambiguity of the Enlightenment attempt to separate out a project for a global civil society and economic order from the 'bad' globalization brought about by warfare, colonial conquest and slave trading—an ambiguity abundantly evident, as Lynn Festa has shown, in the most substantial (albeit equivocal) anti-imperial statement of the Enlightenment, Raynal's *Histoire philosophique des deux Indes*.[11] At issue in the project for a cosmopolitan world, also, is the place of the local (customs, traditions, knowledges) either as superfluous residue or as a constituent part of an aggregate whole. It is here that the Enlightened *philosophe*—writing as a self-authorizing intellectual rather than as a delegated member of a national community—provides the global imagination needed to integrate parts into an intelligible whole. As Festa writes of Raynal:

For Raynal, commerce not only creates a global system; it also furnishes the imaginative tools that enable readers to conceive of that system. Not unlike Raynal's omnivoyant philosophe, the merchant possesses the extraordinary capacity to consider the world as a whole: in tracing the progress of commercial peoples across the planet, he shows 'the same understanding that Newton had to calculate the motion of the stars'. . . . Yet even the merchant's ability to cast beyond the local does not itself constitute a global perspective. . . . The philosophe alone is impartial enough and feeling enough to paint a true picture of the world.[12]

Enlightenment cosmopolitanism in Raynal, as elsewhere, is a matter of information, or rather, the synthesis of that information into an order of knowledge. It is the creation of an order of knowledge (of the kind possessed by Newton in the quotation from Raynal above) that precedes and has the potential to bring into being the world civil society that the *philosophe* hopes will come about. To the extent that Enlightenment thinkers considered themselves as belonging to a movement or as living (as they phrased it in the eighteenth century) in an 'Enlightened age', the creation, synthesis, and dissemination of knowledge was paramount. The fact that this order of knowledge was, throughout the Enlightenment period, so insistently associated with European science limited the degree to which Enlightenment

---

[10] See Ivison, *Postcolonial Liberalism*.

[11] Lynn Festa, *Sentimental Figures of Empire in Eighteenth-Century Britain and France* (Baltimore: Johns Hopkins University Press, 2006).

[12] Ibid., 216.

thinkers (with the honourable exception of Adam Ferguson) were able to imagine modernization as either multiple or internal to a particular country.

This essay explores, through a very particular set of literary examples, the kinds of imperial and anti-imperial perspectives that issue from a cosmopolitanism centred upon a sense of knowing more than upon a sense of transnational identity and belonging. Its purpose is to add something to the current complication, in postcolonial theory, of notions of Enlightenment universalism and cosmopolitanism, particularly as they bear upon imperial practices in the modern world and on the knowledge orders that underwrite them. It sheds some light on the prehistory of modern globalization as it surfaces in the works of literary writers of the eighteenth century, and on the distinctive intertwining of science, emotional rapture, and global imagining in their writings. And it seeks to point up the ambivalent, underdetermined relationship of that global imagining to incipient imperialism. The intellectual-historical context for this critical reading is that of the Newtonian English Enlightenment. By this, I mean not only the transformation of scientific knowledge by Newton's works, but, in his wake, the philosophical relegation of older concepts of rationality in favour of empirical methods, and the extension of those methods (Lockean as well as Newtonian) into many areas of theological and social enquiry, as well as into those of cultural production.[13] Newtonianism had a delayed but significant impact on the Continent from the 1730s, and, as Margaret C. Jacob has argued in a recent study, *Strangers Nowhere in the World*, informed a particular kind of cosmopolitics in which scientific knowledge functioned as a marker of European cultural citizenship.[14] The essay traces a movement, from the second to the final decade of the eighteenth century, from an imperially minded cosmopolitanism based upon empirically derived, universal principles to one that conceived of itself in more openly collaborative terms. It suggests ways in which British writers, living at a time when the British Empire, especially in India, was not yet fully part of the state, were able to

[13] See Margaret C. Jacob, *The Newtonians and the English Revolution, 1689–1720* (London: Harvester Press, 1976) and Betty Jo Teeter Dobbs and Margaret C. Jacob, *Newton and the Culture of Newtonianism* (Atlantic Highlands, NJ: Humanities Press, 1995).

[14] See Jonathan I. Israel, *Radical Enlightenment: Philosophy and the Making of Modernity, 1650–1750* (Oxford: Oxford University Press, 2001), ch. 27; Margaret C. Jacob, *Strangers Nowhere in the World: The Rise of Cosmopolitanism in Early Modern Europe* (Philadelphia: University of Pennsylvania Press, 2006).

misrecognize or subsume the nature of their country's changing involvement with the world within a global consciousness inflected by the Enlightenment. Drawing on specific examples from prominent eighteenth-century poets such as James Thomson and William Cowper, the essay explores the imaginative interpenetration of the scientific culture of the British Enlightenment with ideas of global trade, discovery, and empire. It begins, in the early eighteenth century, with the articulation of a distinctively 'Newtonian' kind of global consciousness that pictured Britain instigating and upholding a worldwide knowledge order based on scientific laws, and thereby imposing political modernization on the rest of the world. It charts a shift, in the later eighteenth century—as Britain engaged in more aggressive imperial activity and as its public became more critically concerned with colonial abuses—to more cosmopolitan (yet, on occasions, imperially enabling) ideals of global citizenship; also to an intensified interest in the relationship between the global awareness fostered by imperial expansion, discoveries, and import consumption and the need to develop new, cosmopolitan models of moral agency.

I Newtonian laws of empire

Recent historians have characterized early modern European empires as powerful agents of early globalization, and have focused upon their role in effecting new distributions of capital, peoples, technologies, and natural resources around the world.[15] This phase of what is often now called 'proto-globalization', occurring between the 'archaic globalization' of ancient trading networks and the 'modern globalization' of the mid nineteenth century onwards, was strongly Eurocentric in its origins and orientation and, it is argued, laid the foundations for the global interdependence of our

<hr/>

[15] See A. G. Hopkins (ed.), *Globalization in World History* (London: Pimlico, 2002). Particularly relevant in this volume is Tony Ballantyne, 'Empire, Knowledge and Culture: From Proto-Globalization to Modern Globalization', 115–40. See also Felicity Nussbaum (ed.), *The Global Eighteenth Century* (Baltimore: Johns Hopkins University Press, 2003), and Janet Sorensen's illuminating study *The Grammar of Empire in Eighteenth-Century British Writing* (Cambridge: Cambridge University Press, 2000).

own era on economic terms enormously favourable to the West.[16] Many eighteenth-century writers portrayed the British Empire as an effect, rather than a motor, of globalization, which was then understood as the bringing together of dispersed resources and peoples for the common good of all. In *The Spectator*, for instance, Addison painted an idealized portrait of the Royal Exchange as a community of merchants from all over the world at work in the creation of an 'additional empire' of trade. In doing so, the merchant community compensates for each region's ecological differences and disadvantages:

Nature seems to have taken a particular Care to disseminate her Blessings among the different Regions of the World, with an Eye to this mutual Intercourse and Traffick among Mankind, that the Natives of the several Parts of the Globe might have a kind of Dependence upon one another, and be united together by their common Interest.[17]

Merchants, in this (by Addison's time, well-worn) account of globalization, are the agents of a natural or divinely intended process of human and market integration, a privileged position made possible by technical knowledges and economic institutions centred upon London ('this metropolis [is] a kind of *emporium* for the whole earth'), as well as, paradoxically, by the paucity of English natural resources: 'If we consider our own Country in its natural Prospect, without any of the Benefits and Advantages of Commerce, what a barren uncomfortable Spot of Earth falls to our Share!'[18] Addison positions merchants and factors here, not as adjuncts of the state, but as an alternative, multinational commonwealth of men ('Factors in the Trading World are what Ambassadors are in the Politick World'), as well as, implicitly, models for a future civil society based upon successful private enterprise, rather than traditionally ascribed social status.[19] He provides us here with one well-known, early example of the kind of global consciousness at work in the eighteenth century, one that subsumes, under a rubric of natural harmony,

[16] See C. A. Bayly, *The Birth of the Modern World, 1780–1914* (Oxford: Blackwell, 2004), 41–7. See also Ballantyne, 'Empire, Knowledge and Culture', 133, and H. V. Bowen, 'British Conceptions of Global Empire, 1756–83', *Journal of Imperial and Commonwealth History*, 26/3 (1988), 1–27.

[17] Joseph Addison and Richard Steele, *The Spectator*, 69 (1711), in *The Spectator*, ed. Donald F. Bond, 5 vols (Oxford: Clarendon Press, 1965), i, 294–5.

[18] Addison, in *Spectator*, ed. Bond, i, 295.

[19] Ibid. i, 293.

the colonial and monopoly trading company framework within which significant parts of global human and economic exchange were then taking place. The Royal Exchange is the place where individually dispersed local knowledges are concentrated under a single point of oversight.

Addison's conception of this kind of knowledge is not explicitly scientific here, but there were many other writers of the early eighteenth century who certainly did envisage merchants as natural philosophers able to understand and therefore master the global distribution of natural resources. One famous example is Edward Young, who, in his *Imperium Pelagi. A Naval Lyrick* of 1730, robustly defended the merchant class ('Is *Merchant* an inglorious Name?') as the possessors of exceptional knowledge of natural and human geography, of navigation and astronomy.[20] The merchant, he writes:

> *Trade* Art's *Mechanick, Nature's* Stores
> Well-weighs; to *Starry Science* soars:
> Reads warm in *Life*, (dead-colour'd by the *Pen*)
> The *Sites, Tongues, Interests* of the Ball:
> Who studies *Trade*, He studies All;
> Accomplish'd *Merchants* are accomplish'd Men.[21]

Young specifically designates the scientific 'accomplishment' of merchants as Newtonian in its grasp of wave motion and astronomy and, by extension, of order and regularity in the workings of trade. Such knowledge, he insists, should form the basis of a new collaboration between entrepreneurs and the state ('King's Merchants are in League, and Love'), again on a Newtonian analogy of regularity and attraction:

> *Planets* are Merchants, take, return
> Lustre, and Heat; by *Traffick* burn;
> The whole *Creation* is one vast *Exchange*.[22]

Young's poem, clumsy though it is, gives a clear insight into the broader intertwining of the idea of Newtonian physics and the Georgian commercial

---

[20] [Edward Young], *Imperium Pelagi. A Naval Lyrick: Written in Imitation of Pindar's Spirit* (London, 1730), strain III, xxiv. 1. This poem is discussed by Suvir Kaul in his *Poems of Nation, Anthems of Empire: English Verse in the Long Eighteenth Century* (Charlottesville: University Press of Virginia, 2000), 200–11.

[21] *Imperium Pelagi*, strain III, xxviii.

[22] Ibid., strain III, xxiv. 1 and 4–6.

order, recently described by Margaret Jacob and Larry Stewart.[23] It shows how, at least to the early eighteenth-century Whig mind, a particular kind of knowledge seemed to underpin the expanding regime of global order. This knowledge regime is predicated, for Addison's merchants and factors, on information gathering and sharing. But for Young, it yields up an intuition of global economic attraction and dependence that, in the last instance, discloses a providential distribution of unequal resources and human talents (God has destined Africa, in Young's poem, as a labour resource for other slave-owning nations). Nor is Young's parallel, in *Imperium Pelagi*, between Britain's mastery of overseas trade and Newton's masterful grasp of the solar system and the stars ('These Nations *Newton* made his own; / All *Intimate* with Him alone') merely a passing conceit.[24] The process by which Newton and merchants gathered information was similar. Newton drew extensively upon data retrieved from overseas sites, many of them in strategic and colonial locations. As Jacob and Stewart write, 'Newton's achievement can be tied to the vast increase in general knowledge that overseas trade and exploration had brought the Europeans in areas such as tidal changes, astronomical observations and so on'.[25] From empirical and experimental data came his inductive knowledge of the fixed and simple laws at work in the ordering of the world. Roger Cotes in his famous preface to the second edition of the *Philosophiae naturalis principia mathematica* (1713) drew attention to global information-gathering and the peculiar sense of global synchronicity conveyed by Newton's discoveries:

For if gravity be the cause of the descent of a stone in *Europe*, who doubts that it is also the cause of the same descent in America? If there is a mutual gravitation between the stone and the earth in *Europe*, who will deny the same to be mutual in *America*?[26]

---

[23] Margaret C. Jacob and Larry Stewart, *Practical Matter: Newton's Science in the Service of Industry and Empire, 1687–1851* (Cambridge, Mass.: Harvard University Press, 2005).

[24] *Imperium Pelagi*, strain III, xii. 1–2.

[25] Stewart and Jacob, *Practical Matter*, 16.

[26] Roger Cotes, preface to Sir Isaac Newton, *Principia* (2nd edn, Cambridge, 1713), p. xvi (translated from the Latin: 'Quis enim dubitat, si Gravitas sit causa descensus Lapidis in *Europa*, quin eademsit causa descensus in *America*? . . . Si vis attractiva Lapidis et Terrae componatur, in *Europa*, ex viribus attractivis partium; quis negabit similem esse compositionem in *America*?').

Young's merchants, too, perceive the '*Sites, Tongues, Interests* of the Ball' (iii. 4) as simultaneously obedient to predictable laws, and are able to harness these laws to the project of a British trading empire.

Numerous other writers anticipated or echoed Young's equation between Newton's laws of motion and the British imperial global order. Among these was the Scottish poet Allan Ramsay, who, having drawn the same equation between science and empire, advocated a colonial civilizing mission for Britain. In his 'Ode to the Memory of Sir Isaac Newton' (1731) he offered this encouragement to the members of the Royal Society (of which Newton himself had been president):

> May from your *Learned Band* arise,
> *Newtons* to shine thro' future times,
> And bring down knowledge from the skies,
> To plant on wild *Barbarian* climes.
> 'Til nations, few degrees from brutes,
> Be brought into each proper road,
> Which leads to wisdom's happiest fruits,
> To know their Saviour and their God.[27]

Like Young, Ramsay wrote in the white heat of the Newtonian Enlighten-ment when Newtonian natural philosophy served as a governing paradigm, not only for commercial empire and the state (witness J. T. Desaguliers's poem *The Newtonian System of the World, the Best Model of Government*, 1728), but also for theological enquiry, including (as in Ramsay's poem above) the applica-tion of inductive reasoning to the question of a final, metaphysical cause.[28] Newton offered not only a model of knowledge acquisition, but also a means of transforming that knowledge into a non-discursive, self-evidently truthful

[27] 'To the Memory of Sir Isaac Newton', in *Poems by Allan Ramsay*, 2 vols (London, 1731), ii, 177. See also the poem by an anonymous contributor to a competition run by the *Gentleman's Magazine* to commemorate the setting-up of a monument to Newton in Richmond Gardens: 'High on the List of Fame . . . Newton stands / Whose spreading Beams enlighten Foreign Lands. . .'. 'On the Five Bustoes erected by her Majesty in the Hermitage at Richmond', *Gentleman's Magazine*, 3 (Apr. 1733), 207.

[28] On the rise of Newton's reputation, see Patricia Fara, *Newton: The Making of a Genius* (New York: Columbia University Press, 2002), esp. ch. 7, 'Myths'. On Newtonian theology, see B. W. Young, *Religion and Enlightenment in Eighteenth-Century England: Theological Debate from Locke to Burke* (Oxford: Clarendon Press, 1998). The original study of Newton's *Opticks* and poetry is Marjorie Hope Nicolson, *Newton Demands the Muse: Newton's Opticks and the Eighteenth-Century Poets* (Princeton: Princeton University Press, 1946).

medium of utterance. For Newton's *Principia* contained a general theory of dynamics which was derived from empirical observations, but which set out that theory deductively in mathematical language in ways that occluded those observations. This mode of utterance greatly appealed to creative writers who saw knowledge imparted in this way as a radically new form of the sublime. Addison stated that:

there are none who more gratifie and enlarge the Imagination, than the Authors of the new Philosophy. . . . The Understanding, indeed, opens an infinite space on every side of us, but the Imagination after a few faint Efforts, is immediately at a stand, and finds her self swallowed up in the Immensity of the Void that surrounds it . . . [29]

As Patricia Fara and others have shown, Newton was quickly and lastingly assimilated by eighteenth-century writers as a solitary genius possessed of extraordinarily sublime qualities of vision.[30] This trope was in place from the outset. Edmund Halley's ode, prefixed to the first edition of the *Principia*, opened with a reference to Newton's marvellous gaze:

> En tibi norma Poli, et divae libramina Molis,
> Computus atque Jovis.
>
> Lo, for your gaze, the pattern of the skies!
> What balance of the mass, what reckonings Divine![31]

Paintings of Newton by Thornhill, Kneller, and others tended to show him staring with dreamy intensity out of one side of the canvas. Poets associated Newton's blinding vision with Milton's visionary blindness, and, particularly in the many poems commemorating Newton's death in 1727, created a kind of composite Miltonic–Newtonian figure whose encompassing vision they sought to link to their own. One of the best-known of these is Richard Glover's 'Poem on Sir Isaac Newton', prefixed to Henry Pemberton's landmark general introduction to Newton's work. Here Glover, writing in Miltonic blank verse, calls upon Newton to raise him up to a sublime prospect of the globe:

[29] Addison, *The Spectator*, 420 (1712), in *The Spectator*, ed. Bond, iii, 574–6.

[30] Fara, *Newton*, 159–66. See also Maureen McNeil, 'Newton as National Hero', in John Fauvel et al. (eds), *Let Newton Be!* (Oxford: Oxford University Press, 1988), 223–39.

[31] Edmund Halley, 'In Viri Praestantissimi D. Isaaci Newtoni', in Isaac Newton, *Philosophiae naturalis principia mathematica* (London, 1687), p. iv.

Chiefly Newton let me soar with thee,
And while surveying all yon starry vault
With admiration I attentive gaze,
Thou shalt descend from thy celestial seat,
And waft aloft [sic!] my high-aspiring mind.[32]

The Newtonian sublime offered the *ne plus ultra* of the kind of commanding prospect that, in so many eighteenth-century descriptive poems, asserted aesthetic and social mastery over a landscape surveyed from too great a height to reveal its human detail.[33] When it came to the idea of a global trading empire, the Newtonian sublime also effected a reversing of the flows of knowledge that made trade possible in the first place. This is to say that, instead of an idea of global trade based upon locally sourced commodities and networks of information, they upheld a Newtonian vision of globalization in which knowledge flows from centre to periphery, and brings in its wake a decidedly British version of Enlightenment and world order.

To illustrate this trajectory, and to understand how a version of Newtonian natural philosophy became entangled with aesthetic practice, I will turn to Mark Akenside's 'Hymn to Science', first printed in the *Gentleman's Magazine* in 1739. Akenside is of particular interest because, as a Whig physician, he warmly embraced the Newtonian Enlightenment culture of the mid century.[34] His 'Hymn to Science' came out before his highly successful collection of self-consciously sublime Pindaric odes (1745), and shortly after his poetic call for imperial war against Spain, *A British Philippic* (1738). Like many of the later odes, the 'Hymn' takes the form of an invocation to an abstract power (in this case, all of human knowledge), in which the speaker both seeks and dramatizes his own rapturous identification with his subject. One important item of knowledge he seeks is that of the Newtonian laws of gravity and motion:

Give me to learn each secret cause;
Let number's, figure's, motion's laws
Reveal'd before me stand;

---

[32] Richard Glover, 'Poem on Sir Isaac Newton', in Henry Pemberton, *A View of Sir Isaac Newton's Philosophy* (London, 1728), pp. xiii–xiv.

[33] On landscape prospect and its ideological implications, see John Barrell, 'An Unerring Gaze: The Prospect of Society in the Poetry of James Thomson and John Dyer', in *English Literature in History, 1730–80: An Equal, Wide Survey* (London: Hutchinson, 1983), ch. 1.

[34] On these aspects of Akenside, see Dustin Griffin, *Patriotism and Poetry in Eighteenth-Century Britain* (Cambridge: Cambridge University Press, 2002), ch. 4.

> These to great Nature's scenes apply,
> And round the globe, and thro' the sky,
> Disclose her working hand.[35]

He then asks for knowledge of the living world and of society (the 'policies of men'), implicitly on the model of Newtonian mechanics, as well as for an understanding of the human mind that seeks constantly to

> Dive thro' th'infinity of space,
> And strain to grasp THE WHOLE.[36]

This understanding of man's aspiring mind in turn leads to an inductive knowledge of God's existence, itself the highest form of rational self-awareness, and it is this higher 'science' that acts as the motivational force behind all material and artistic progress:

> Of wealth, pow'r, freedom, thou! the cause;
> Foundress of order, cities, laws,
> Of arts inventress, thou![37]

Here, as so often in his poem *The Pleasures of Imagination* (1744), Akenside moves from invocation to apostrophe as he seeks to excite an affective and aesthetic attachment to the idea of knowledge in both himself and his reader which they will experience as 'rapture'. For him, Newtonian and poetical cognitive paths are the same, from experimental and detailed observation of natural phenomena to a unitary and emotionally compelling apprehension of the truth. That truth, reached without prior hypotheses through the free play of mind, then becomes the inspiration for national self-improvement.

The connection, in eighteenth-century British culture, between this cognitive path to knowledge, national self-improvement, and scientific models of global empire becomes clearer when we turn to James Thomson, like Akenside a patriot Whig and enthusiastic advocate of the new scientific culture. Thomson's *A Poem Sacred to the Memory of Sir Isaac Newton* was among the many poems commemorating Newton's burial at Westminster Abbey in 1727, but stands out as work of extraordinary accomplishment and artistic

---

[35] 'Hymn to Science' [1739, repr. 1775], ll. 19–24, in *The Poetical Works of Mark Akenside*, ed. Robin C. Dix (Madison, NJ: Fairleigh Dickinson University Press, 1996).

[36] Ibid., ll. 56, 35–6.

[37] Ibid., ll. 85–7.

promise. Thomson conjures up a Newton possessed of Miltonic creative power, an intuitive genius whose 'piercing mental eye' found unity and order where others had found only

> Romantic schemes, defending by the din
> Of specious worlds, and tyranny of names.[38]

Bypassing old, Aristotlelian forms of discursive and collaborative knowledge, Newton's intellectual journey takes him from isolated, attentive observation ('bidding his amazing mind attend, / And with heroic patience years on years / Deep searching') to blinding insight and then rapture:

> [he] saw at last the SYSTEM dawn
> And shine, of all his race, on him alone.
> WHAT were his raptures then! How pure! How strong![39]

Like Akenside's, Newton's path to knowledge is hastened by his aesthetic alertness to the grandeur, sounds and colours of the natural world ('Did ever poet image aught so fair, / Dreaming in whispering groves, by the hoarse brook!').[40] For Thomson, as for Akenside, Newtonian and poetical ways of knowing are the same, and they impose a sense of coherence upon the disparate natural phenomena of the world.

Thomson likens Newton's mental mastery to a modern kind of peaceful world-domination: instead of the 'triumphs of old GREECE and ROME' with their

> Shatter'd parcels of this earth usurp'd
> By violence unmanly, and sore deeds
> Of cruelty and blood

Newton has only to command assent ('Nature herself / Stood all subdu'd by him').[41] Now that Newton is dead and definitively 'in rapture lost', Thomson can invoke him as a tutelary genius for Britain, and ask him to provide national inspiration at a time when the country is 'deprav'd and sunk'.[42] The national striving that Thomson has in mind here is mainly in relation to

---

[38] James Thomson, *A Poem Sacred to the Memory of Sir Isaac Newton* [1727], ll. 139 and 24–5, in *Liberty, The Castle of Indolence and Other Poems*, ed. James Sambrook (Oxford: Clarendon Press, 1986).

[39] Ibid., ll. 25–6, 28–30.

[40] Ibid., ll. 119–20.

[41] Ibid., ll. 31, 34–7.

[42] Ibid., ll. 195, 204.

moral and spiritual improvement. The connection between Thomson's often discussed 'physico-theology' and what we might call his 'physico-imperialism', made in the comparison between Britain and Greece and Rome above, becomes much clearer in 'Summer'. This poem was first published in the same year as the poem on Newton, and was greatly expanded in subsequent editions of *The Seasons* (1730, 1744, 1746). From its earliest version, 'Summer' contained a patriotic panegyric, modelled on Virgil's praise of Italy in the *Georgics*, that included Newton among the list of men who had made Britain great. Thomson's panegyric centres upon the English countryside, but opens out vistas on to the seas beyond ('Thy crowded ports, / Where rising masts and endless prospect yield'), and alludes to Britain's naval supremacy ('thy generous youth /.../ Scattering the nations where they go; and first / Or in the listed plain or stormy seas').[43] Then follows the list of national heroes first of liberty and art, then when

> The light of dawning Science spread
> Her orient ray

of natural philosophy, such as Bacon, Newton, and Boyle.[44] All this leads up to Thomson's famous celebration of the British 'Island of bliss!' as a military fortress with global strategic range:

> At once the wonder, terror, and delight
> Of distant nations, whose remotest shore
> Can soon be shaken by thy naval arm.[45]

From this climactic moment, there follows a description of sunset and the arrival of night in which Thomson again reflects upon the aesthetic possibilities of a global and scientific way of seeing the world. He describes, with his usual feeling for the spacious and vertiginous, the stars and comets visible at night ('The life-infusing suns of other worlds', and the 'rushing comet, from the dread immensity of space / Returning with accelerated course').[46] To the superstitious, such sights are ominous, but to

[43] Thomson, 'Summer', ll. 1461–2 and 1469–70, in *The Seasons and The Castle of Indolence*, ed. James Sambrook (Oxford: Oxford University Press, 1972).
[44] James Thomson, 'Summer', *The Seasons*, ll. 1533–4.
[45] Ibid., ll. 1595, 1596–9.
[46] Ibid., ll. 1705–8.

>   the enlightened few,
>   Whose godlike minds philosophy exalts

they are intelligible, in a Newtonian way, as signs of a benign, divine order.[47] This in turn leads to Thomson's apostrophe to 'serene Philosophy' (by which he means rational knowledge) as the 'effusive source of evidence and truth', as the spring of men's mental development in general, and as the principal source of knowledge and inspiration to poets:

>   Tutored by thee, hence Poetry exalts,
>   Her voice to ages; and informs the page
>   With music, image, sentiment, and thought...[48]

Like Akenside in the 'Hymn to Science', Thomson sees both poetry and natural philosophy as partners in the processes of mental awakening and civilizing that take man forward from savagery to Enlightenment. Enlightened modernity, as Thomson's poem *Liberty* (1735–6) makes clear in still greater detail, consists of composite elements of economic development (beyond the hunter-gatherer and agricultural stages to the commercial stage), technological and scientific progress, and the refinement of political institutions, affective ties, and religious beliefs that regulate civil society. Thomson attributes these apparently disparate components of modernity to the single inspiration of 'philosophy'. Like Newton, who uncovered the set of gravitational laws behind diverse natural phenomena, Thomson grasps intuitively, as a poet, the underlying and evolving knowledge order behind modern Enlightenment:

>   Without thee [philosophy] what were unenlightened man?
>   A savage, roaming through the woods and wilds
>   In quest of prey; and with the unfashioned fur
>   Rough-clad; devoid of every finer art
>   And elegance of life. Nor happiness
>   Domestic, mixed of tenderness and care,
>   Nor moral excellence, nor social bliss,
>   Nor guardian law were his; nor various skill
>   To turn the furrow, or to guide the tool
>   Mechanic; nor the heaven-conducted prow

[47] Ibid., ll. 1714–15.   [48] Ibid., ll. 1753–5.

> Of Navigation bold, that fearless braves
> The burning line or dares the wintry pole...[49]

Thomson's poetry is, in the closing part of 'Summer', presented as both an expression and an aesthetic mediation of a stage of Enlightenment that brings with it an altered disposition towards the rest of the world. Nations which, like Britain, live under the regime of philosophy are the paradoxical enforcers of cosmopolitan global harmony:

> taught by thee,
> Ours are the plans of policy and peace;
> To live like brothers, and, conjunctive all,
> Embellish life.[50]

By clear implication, others are excluded from this enlightenment, like the Africans whom Thomson describes earlier in the same poem, who know nothing of

> the softening arts of peace,
> Whate'er the humanizing Muses teach,
> The godlike wisdom of the tempered breast,
> Progressive truth....[51]

Thomson's poetry bears witness, and may well have helped to give imaginative colouring, to a new kind of global consciousness in mid-eighteenth-century Britain. To the extent that this was based upon scientific universalism, rather than universal ideas of kingship or religion, it belongs to a 'modern' rather than an 'archaic' phase of global cultural awareness. It articulates an idea of the British Empire as a benign agent of globalization by picturing Britain as the initiator, rather than the recipient, of world-wide flows of scientific knowledge. Thomson's poetry had an enduring influence upon later eighteenth-century writers, even as Britain entered, from the 1760s, a new, more aggressive phase of imperial activity, and this influence withstood the new image of the empire that emerged as the East India Company became a territorial power, the American colonies won independence, and the Cook voyages to the South Seas utterly transformed

---

[49] James Thomson, 'Summer', *The Seasons*, ll. 1758–69.
[50] Ibid., ll. 1774–7.   [51] Ibid., ll. 875–8.

the geographical and ethnic map of the globe.[52] The Cook voyages, in particular, were instigated and publicly received in a spirit of scientific improvement to which commercial and territorial objectives were held to be subordinate.[53] Even so, the humanitarian optimism that greeted the Cook voyages coincided with growing public unease about slavery in North America and the Caribbean and about the depredations in India and exorbitant domestic political influence of East India Company magnates, as well as a sense of national crisis over the impending loss of the American colonies.

II Cowper and the moral order of knowledge

Among the literary works attempting to make sense of these geo-political developments, the most substantial was undoubtedly William Cowper's *The Task* (1785). This poem was, despite its inauspicious opening reflections on sofas, the late eighteenth century's most searching attempt to explore the impact of the global on the domestic, from British politics and patriotism right down to Cowper's own intimate, subjective experience of life in a small Buckinghamshire town. Cowper was, as Kevis Goodman has argued, one of the first writers to record the ways in which the individual sense of the global was filtered through the print news media, and *The Task* includes an account of Cowper's excited reaction to the delivery of *The Morning Chronicle*:

> What are its tidings? have our troops awaked?
> Or do they still, as if with opium drugg'd,
> Snore to the murmurs of th'Atlantic wave?
> Is India free?[54]

---

[52] On Thomson's influence, see Richard Terry (ed.), *James Thomson: Essays for the Tercentenary* (Liverpool: Liverpool University Press, 2000), pt 2, 'Posterity', and Griffin, *Patriotism and Poetry*, 181–6.

[53] See David Mackay, *In the Wake of Cook: Exploration, Science and Empire* (New York: St Martin's Press, 1985) and John Gascoigne, *Joseph Banks and the English Enlightenment: Useful Knowledge and Polite Culture* (Cambridge: Cambridge University Press, 1994).

[54] Kevis Goodman, *Georgic Modernity and British Romanticism: Poetry and the Mediation of History* (Cambridge: Cambridge University Press, 2004), 78–81; William Cowper, *The Task*, iv. 25–8, in *The Poems of William Cowper*, ed. John D. Baird and Charles Ryskamp, 3 vols (Oxford: Clarendon Press, 1995), ii, 187.

Cowper registers this inflow of information from the 'noisy world' as a cacophony in need of sifting and management, yet ultimately not susceptible to philosophical synthesis.[55] Unlike Thomson and Akenside, Cowper is wary of rapturous imaginative access to an integrated, verbally unmediated sense of the world. Rather he claims, elsewhere in *The Task* in a passage (iii. 221–60) that alludes directly to Newton's *Opticks* and indirectly to Thomson on Newton, to have formulated his own, evangelical version of Newtonian philosophy:

> never yet did philosophic tube
> That brings the planets home into the eye
> Of observation, and discovers, else
> Not visible, his family of worlds,
> Discover him that rules them....[56]

There can be, Cowper insists, no inductive path to metaphysical knowledge, no rational discernment of patterns of underlying order in the natural or human worlds that sufficiently evince a deity. This, he adds, is something that Newton himself understood:

> Such was thy wisdom, Newton, childlike sage!
> Sagacious reader of the works of God
> And in his word sagacious....[57]

However much he drew attention to the incoherent, information-saturated and newspaper-mediated way in which we experience the world, Cowper was not entirely sceptical about the possibility of global economic integration and order. He regarded slavery and despotic imperial governance, as practised by the British East India Company (e.g. i. 736–8), as enormous impediments to this and contrary to God's purpose for the world. Yet in his earlier poem 'Charity' (1782), he celebrated trade as the 'golden girdle of the globe', and claimed, in terms that Addison would have recognized, that the uneven worldwide distribution of raw materials and production was God's way of ensuring interdependence between the nations. He added that international contact and trade are the stimuli of the civilizing process:

> God opens fruitful nature's various scenes,
> Each climate needs what other climes produce,

[55] *The Task*, iv. 5, in *The Poems of William Cowper*, ii, 187.
[56] *The Task*, iii. 229–33, in *The Poems of William Cowper*, ii, 168.
[57] *The Task*, iii. 252–4, in *The Poems of William Cowper*, ii, 169.

And offers something to the gen'ral use;
No land but listens to the common call,
And in return receives supply from all;
This genial intercourse and mutual aid,
Cheers what were else an universal shade,
Calls nature from her ivy-mantled den,
And softens human rockwork into men.
Ingenious Art with her expressive face
Steps forth to fashion and refine the race...[58]

Behind the knowledge order requisite to international economic exchange (more dispersed in terms of its centres of production than Thomson's British-centred version), there must be, Cowper argues, a moral order of charity, or love. The sources of charity must always lie in the moral disposition of individual men towards their fellow creatures. Cook was one such individual ('He spurn'd the wretch that slighted or withstood / The tender argument of kindred blood') who implemented God's 'social plan' that 'attaches man to man' without violating the 'rights of man'.[59] Yet, ironically, Cook's disinterested, scientific approach to exploration in the South Seas may not, in the end, have served the ends of charity. In *The Task*, in a famous passage that conjecturally recreates the feelings of the repatriated Polynesian Mai (or Omai as the poem styles him), Cowper laments Britain's lack of economic interest in the Society Islands as the reason for its apparent abandonment of them:

We found no bait
To tempt us in thy country. Doing good,
Disinterested good, is not our trade.
We travel far 'tis true, but not for nought;
And must be brib'd to compass earth again
By other hopes and richer fruits than yours.[60]

The failure of trade and charity to converge, in ways that Cowper had envisaged in 'Charity', leaves Omai a stranded and deracinated casualty of

[58] 'Charity', ll. 88–98, in *The Poems of William Cowper*, i, 339.
[59] 'Charity', ll. 31–2, 15–16, in *The Poems of William Cowper* i, 338, 337.
[60] *The Task*, i. 673–77, in *The Poems of William Cowper* ii, 134. Mai was brought to England in 1774 at the end of Cook's second voyage, and in 1777 he returned to the Society Islands, where he died four years or so later. Cowper was not aware of his death at the time of writing *The Task*.

incomplete globalization. Cowper pictures Omai back at home, unable to reintegrate himself into his homeland, unsettled by all the trappings of civilization he has seen in London, and yet incapable of perceiving these trappings, as Cowper does, as superficial and vain:

> And having seen our state,
> Our palaces, our ladies, and our pomp
> Of equipage, our gardens, and our sports,
> And heard our music; are thy simple friends,
> Thy simple fare, and all thy plain delights
> As dear to thee as once? And have thy joys
> Lost nothing by comparison with ours?[61]

Cowper does not treat this dissatisfaction with his former simple life and yearning for English sophistication as false consciousness on the part of Omai. Omai has seen enough in England to understand that his own people are isolated from contact with the rest of the world ('From all that science traces, art invents, / Or inspiration teaches; and inclosed / In boundless oceans never to be pass'd / By navigators uninform'd as they'), and that he, as a lone intermediary, can do nothing to remedy his country's lack of civilization:

> I see thee weep, and thine are honest tears,
> A patriot's for his country. Thou art sad
> At thought of her forlorn and abject state,
> From which no power of thine can raise her up.[62]

Cowper's Omai (who bears little relation to the historical figure) looks hopelessly out to sea for English ships that never come. Neither a noble savage nor a deluded, mimic Englishman, he stands as a figure for thwarted global citizenship. Cowper is at one with contemporary Enlightenment thinkers in regarding civilization, for good and ill, not as a process internal to each nation, but as the result of sustained contact and economic exchange. That contact and exchange must eventually encompass the whole world if God's civilizing purpose is to be fulfilled. The British Empire

---

[61] *The Task*, i. 642–8, in *The Poems of William Cowper*, ii, 133. On Mai's visit and return, see Harriet Guest, 'Ornament and Use: Mai and Cook in London', in Kathleen Wilson (ed.), *A New Imperial History: Culture, Identity, and Modernity in Britain and the Empire, 1660–1840* (Cambridge: Cambridge University Press, 2004), 317–44.

[62] *The Task*, i. 627–30, 657–60, in *The Poems of William Cowper*, ii, 133.

may be an agent of global connectedness, and, however much it stands in need of moral reformation, it may be better than no agent at all.

Cowper sought to moralize the idea of empire as a regime of knowledge, and to imagine that regime as one with multiple, often unfamiliar, geographical centres. The idea of empire as one potential realization of benevolent global consciousness, articulated by a number of eighteenth-century writers, overlapped with and steadily mutated into the nineteenth-century idea of British imperial trusteeship.[63] That idea of trusteeship entailed putting into imperial effect of an originally Enlightenment model of the world as distributed into different, incompatible temporalities, in which nations at the modern, commercial stage would supervise those at earlier, more primitive stages of development. Yet at this earlier point, eighteenth-century British writers such as Thomson and Cowper were not so much inclined to imagine global expansion in terms of a conflict of historical stages—of European modernity versus non-European premodernity. For them, global consciousness was a conceptualizing system that sought to transform the contemporary fact of transoceanic commercial networks into an order of knowledge or an order of universal citizenship. This was to treat the outward reaching of the imagination as an ethical gesture, bound up, in an unspecified way, with the desire to salvage Enlightenment from the imperial context within which globalization occurred.

[63] Karen O'Brien, 'Poetry and Political Thought: Liberty and Benevolence in the Case of the British Empire, c.1680–1800', in David Armitage (ed.), *British Political Thought in History, Literature and Theory, 1500–1800* (Cambridge: Cambridge University Press, 2006), 168–90.

Coda

How to Write Postcolonial
Histories of Empire?

Suvir Kaul

Postcolonial scholarship begins with the assumption that postcolonial histories of empire originate in modes of consciousness and critique developed during the anticolonial struggles of the early twentieth century and the bloody processes of mid- and late twentieth-century decolonization in European colonies across the globe. This origin reminds us that the specifically *post*colonial dimensions of such revisionary historiography—including the aspiration to cast off European political control, to re-examine and rebuild economies and societies, to rethink and remake cultural structures as well as modes of collective and individual subject-formation—are not simply acts of the intellect. Postcolonial historiography is informed by active processes of political engagement that derive their intellectual priorities from dynamic contemporary challenges; from the knowledge that the colonial history of the independent nation, sedimented into state and institutional practices, militates against some changes and encourages others; and from the understanding that the political economy of the globe forged by over two centuries of European imperialism will continue to structure international relations in the foreseeable future.[1]

---

[1] To claim this genealogy for postcolonial studies is not to deny that many of its character-istic concerns and assumptions derive from the instance of earlier anticolonial actors and texts, some going back to early moments of violent European contact with non-European societies. It

Postcolonial scholarship recognizes varied intellectual and cultural debts, in effect extending and complicating the lessons learned by anticolonial nationalists in the early twentieth century. As these nationalists forged the political, organizational, and intellectual tools necessary for successful movements for national independence, they did so by reacting against the dehumanizing language of the many Europeans who advocated and built empire, while drawing encouragement from the more muted idiom of those Europeans who questioned its methods or effects. Postcolonial scholarship inherits this legacy, and also continues to speak in the name of native and non-European traditions of enquiry, including those that were extirpated by, or at the very least delegitimated by, the coercion of colonial administrators and pedagogues.[2] However, it is also the case that postcolonial thought, articulated several decades after formal independence, recognizes that movements of national independence often extended colonial systems of governance, and continued to perpetuate hierarchies cemented during colonial rule. Postcolonial scholarship, then, seeks to make possible more equitable rearrangements of power and culture even after the celebrations of independence. In turn, postcolonial histories of empire thus diagnose the past with a robust sense of the present, that is, with a clear understanding of the particular forms in which the colonial past impinges on, and continues to shape, the politically decolonized present.

Little I have written so far will be unfamiliar to those who keep abreast of postcolonial studies, which has ranged, in the last three decades, from studies of colonial political economy, administrative and military operations, and cultural and educational practices to the psychic burdens of modern empire on both colonized and metropolitan peoples. These studies have extended

is a reminder, however, that postcolonial modes of thought are not solely derived from, or endlessly trapped within, Eurocentric frames and histories, and are energized by the priorities of both political and intellectual decolonization, both in once-colonized societies and in once-imperial nations. Further, it allows us to see how local histories and pre-colonial formations play a crucial role in shaping the forms of anticolonial and postcolonial thought.

[2] In *The Dynamics of Global Dominance: European Overseas Empires 1415–1980* (New Haven: Yale University Press, 2000), David B. Abernethy describes modern empire as the European 'triple assault on other societies: on indigenous institutions of governance, on long-standing patterns of generating and distributing economic assets, and on ideas and values that gave meaning to life' (p. 12). Postcolonial activism and scholarship attempt to develop life-renewing alternatives to the historical effects of each of these forms of assault.

from the microanalysis of literary enunciation in a seventeenth-century male poet's lyrics that imagine the female body as a new-found land to be discovered and possessed to macro-estimations of the connections between modern empires and late twentieth-century neocolonial international relations and globalization.[3] The history of white Europeans ruling over and occasionally decimating non-white populations across the globe has been remarked upon at length, as has been the power of racism to warp both those discriminated against and those whose self-image was celebrated as the hallmark of a natural or civilizational superiority. Postcolonial scholars have explored the epistemological and ideological difficulties faced by those who can no longer unquestioningly accept the asymmetry between the 'tradition' of once-colonized societies (to be left behind) and the 'modernity' of the 'West' (to be aspired to as the proper condition of historical subjectivity). Nor has there been any easy consensus about the scope and proper form of postcolonial studies: like any other vital intellectual or academic terrain, this too has been defined by its debates and disagreements.

Against this breadth and quality of writing, it seems both presumptuous and unnecessary to ask the question 'How to write postcolonial histories of empire?' But the question has taken on a redoubled force in the last few years, particularly as Anglo-US adventurism in Iraq has been accompanied (and perhaps prepared for) by provocative justifications not only of the war but of the model of imperial rule itself (which involves, most consequentially, the rehabilitation of the British Empire). A convenient instance is the following passage from Niall Ferguson:

The British Empire has had a pretty lousy press from a generation of 'postcolonial' historians anachronistically affronted by its racism. But the reality is that the British were significantly more successful at establishing market economies, the rule of law and the transition to representative government than the majority of postcolonial governments have been. The policy 'mix' favored by Victorian imperialists reads like something just published by the International Monetary Fund, if not the World Bank: free trade, balanced budgets, sound money, the common law, incorrupt

---

[3] See R. V. Young, '"O My America, My New-Found-Land": Pornography and Imperial Politics in Donne's "Elegies"', *South Central Review*, 4/2 (1987), 35–48, and Shankar Raman, '"Can't Buy Me Love": Money, Gender, and Colonialism in Donne's Erotic Verse', *Criticism*, 43/2 (2001), 135–68.

administration and investment in infrastructure financed by international loans. These are precisely the things the world needs right now.[4]

These sentiments, and the policy prescriptions that accompany them, are heard often now, as the ideal of Western domination that was rejected categorically by the wave of successful decolonization and freedom struggles in the second half of the twentieth century is rehabilitated as appropriate ideological cover for US and Anglo-American military and political-economic dominance. The destructive, even genocidal histories of modern empires are whitewashed, and we are back once more with Rudyard Kipling's 1899 exhortation to Anglo-Saxon imperialism:

> Take up the White Man's burden—
>   Send forth the best ye breed—
> Go, bind your sons to exile
>   To serve your captives' need;
> To wait, in heavy harness,
>   On fluttered folk and wild—
> Your new-caught sullen peoples,
>   Half devil and half child.[5]

Except that we are not quite there, for Ferguson writes his essay to bemoan the fact that 'the same fiction that underpinned American strategy in

[4] Niall Ferguson, 'The Empire Slinks Back', *New York Times Magazine* (27 Apr. 2003), 54. Niall Ferguson was born in Scotland and educated at Oxford, and is now Professor of History at Harvard University, where he has a joint appointment in the Business School. He is also a Senior Fellow of the Hoover Institution at Stanford University.

[5] Rudyard Kipling, 'The White Man's Burden', first pub. in *McClure's Magazine* (Feb. 1899), repr. in *Collected Poems of Rudyard Kipling* (London: Wordsworth Editions, 1994), 334–5. I note in passing Kipling's frank and populist avowal of the racism that Ferguson thinks is found *anachronistically* by postcolonial commentators on the British Empire. Kipling is re-emerging as a touchstone for public commentators (particularly Britons) on the US imperium, who find in his writing valuable historical lessons along the lines of 'with imperial enrichment and power come imperial duties and obligations'. This is the new language of post-Cold War realpolitik: like it or not (and many do like it), the US is an imperial power, which means that scholars must get beyond the problem that 'Imperialism now has a very bad name' and make the 'distinction between responsible and irresponsible imperialism; between investment and asset-stripping' (Philip Hensher, 'Exceedingly Good Advice from Mr Kipling', *The Independent* (London, 14 May 2003), 16). There are many political ironies at play in this invitation to the US (and the UK) to assume the 'full duties of a responsible imperialism', to not be too 'self-conscious', and 'to just run the damned place', but I will point only to a literary-critical paradox: postcolonial critics

Vietnam—that the United States was not trying to resurrect French colonial rule in Indochina—is peddled in Washington to rationalize what is going on in Iraq'. He wants the American Empire to do what Kipling did, which is to act upon its imperial convictions and to 'dare' to 'speak its own name'.[6]

If Victorian imperialism drives Ferguson's imagination, eighteenth-century conceptions of the British empire of the seas and of divinely sanctioned imperial destiny inform the pronouncements of that other holy warrior of Anglo-American expansionism, Paul Johnson:

Britain, which is not so much an ally of America as it is a member of the same family, will continue to serve as the geographical center of the Anglosphere and as America's offshore island to the Eurasian landmass. Other than that, the U.S. should put its trust in the seas and oceans, which offer a home and a friendly environment to its forces and do not change with the treacherous winds of opinion. The military lessons to be learned from the lead-up to the Iraq operation are profound, and all point in the same direction: America should always have the means to act alone, in any area of the globe where danger threatens and with whatever force is necessary . . .

The U.S. must not merely possess the means to act alone if necessary; it must also cultivate the will. Fate, or Divine Providence, has placed America at this time in the position of sole superpower, with the consequent duty to uphold global order and to punish, or prevent, the great crimes of the world . . .

It must continue to engage the task imposed upon it, not in any spirit of hubris but in the full and certain knowledge that it is serving the best and widest interests of humanity.[7]

---

have recently reread Kipling's writing to trace the arrogance, the paranoia, and the delusional desires that structure the racist and self-aggrandizing texts of high imperialism in order to argue 'never again'; advocates of neo-imperialism revisit these texts to derive from them lessons in the 'proper' management of a necessary and inevitable Anglocentric empire. (For instances of such postcolonial criticism, see the essays collected in Zohreh Sullivan (ed.), *Rudyard Kipling's 'Kim': Authoritative Text, Backgrounds, Criticism* (New York: Norton, 2002)).

[6] Ferguson, 'The Empire Slinks Back', 57. Ferguson's nostalgia for Victorian Britain has him virtually quoting Lord Alfred Douglas's 1892 poem 'Two Loves' (which spoke of 'the love that dare not speak its name,' a line understood then, as now, as referring to homosexuality). In a travesty of the politics and vocabulary of gay liberation struggles, Ferguson imagines Empire in the closet, now seeking redemption in an unsympathetic world!

[7] Paul Johnson, 'Five Vital Lessons from Iraq', *Forbes Magazine* (17 Mar. 2003), <http://www.forbes.com/forbes/2003/0317/037.html> accessed 6 July 2008. Johnson is a prolific English writer and journalist whose political and cultural views have won him a following in conservative trans-Atlantic circles. President George Bush awarded him the Presidential Medal of Freedom in 2006.

Johnson's crusading zeal and Ferguson's more pragmatic realpolitik replicate views of the world developed over three centuries of European expansionism, and, what is more germane to us here, derive from an imperialist histori-ography whose teleological certainties result in, and from, narratives of a storytelling simplicity best exemplified by the many novels of G. H. Henty. Decolonization has, however, not been kind to such narcissistic bedtime stories, and as intellectuals and academics in both the once-colonized world and in colonizing nations have examined the historical record of modern empires to exhume both their international crimes and, perhaps even more important, their connections to continuing postcolonial socio-economic inequities across the globe, conceptual complexity and challenge have re-placed storytelling ease.[8]

The likes of Ferguson and Johnson arrive at their neo-imperialism by ignoring the murderous record of colonial history in favour of an emphasis on the failure to thrive, in the last three to five decades, of many decolonized nation states.[9] What standards of historical accuracy and scholarship might, after all, allow for a formulation like Ferguson's nostalgic celebration of

[8] Perhaps it needs to be said that this complexity is not to be admired for itself, but recognized as the difficult product of attempts to disinter the histories of people and sub-national communities from imperialist triumphalism and, in many cases, to disaggregate these local histories from the univocal narratives of anticolonial nationalist historiography. Critics of postcolonial historiography occasionally return to traditional forms of historical explanation by producing narratives that feature European men and women as flawed and vulnerable agents of imperial history. Such storytelling eschews all analysis of the systems or power-relations of empire (I return to this point later in this essay).

[9] Ferguson's mendacious claims about the historical benefits of empire, elaborated at some length in his *Colossus: The Price of America's Empire* (New York: Penguin, 2004), have been systematically dismantled in Vivek Chibber's review 'The Good Empire', *Boston Review*, 30/1 (Feb.–Mar. 2005), 30–4. The failure of many postcolonial states to thrive is understood by Ferguson and Johnson, among others, in total isolation from the colonial histories of these states, the dead weight of Cold War allegiances, and, perhaps most importantly, the neocolonial power of banking, corporate, and military-industrial systems to intensify and perpetuate in-equalities within once-colonized societies and across international borders. In so many cases, far from being the 'modernizing' or egalitarian force that the Fergusons of the world claim it was, the British Empire, like other European empires, functioned by legitimating and giving institutional form to the most atavistic and exploitative sectors of colonized societies. The movement towards democracy thus becomes the task of postcolonial societies, a task hampered until recently by Cold War priorities and today by the economic and foreign policy priorities of the US-led imperium. To recount the continuing power of imperial divisions is not to discount the culpability of native elites in benefiting from, and perpetuating, inequality and human misery in once-colonized countries. Both imperialists and their collaborators have to be understood

Victorian imperial rule, which, as we have seen, he believes implemented 'free trade, balanced budgets, sound money, the common law, incorrupt administration?' Only a wilful disregard of well-documented facts. For instance, as Mike Davis has written in *Late Victorian Holocausts*, 'If the history of British rule in India were to be condensed into a single fact, it is this: there was no increase in India's per capita income from 1757 to 1947. Indeed, in the last half of the nineteenth century, income probably declined by more than 50 percent.'[10] Further, during the 'age of Kipling, that "glorious imperial half century" from 1872 to 1921, the life expectancy of ordinary Indians fell by a staggering 20 percent'.[11] Davis goes on to explore several paradoxes that have an enormous relevance for the 'globalizing' world today: 'Where were the fruits of modernization, of the thousands of miles of railroad track and canal?' he asks, and

where were the profits of the great export booms that transformed the subcontinent's agriculture in the second half of the nineteenth century? Here, if anywhere in rural Asia, integration into the world market should have resulted in significant local increases in local agricultural productivity and profitability. Apart from the plantation crops of tea and indigo, most export production—opium, wheat, rice and cotton—remained in native hands under a regime of modern property rights ...

Yet, as macroeconomic statistics demonstrate, such prosperity was usually ephemeral and quickly reabsorbed into the huge inertia of rural poverty. Peasant agriculture, even in the most dynamic cash-crop sectors, remained radically undercapitalized. Only moneylenders, absentee landlords, urban merchants, and a handful of indigenous industrialists seemed to have benefited consistently from India's renewed importance in world trade. 'Modernization' and commercialization were accompanied by pauperization.[12]

The point is not that already poor Indians stayed poor under imperial British rule; it is that their living conditions actively worsened as economic and administrative systems conducive to British authority were put into place. As evidence Davis offers a case study of the province of Berar, where traditional agricultural practices were transformed by the government of India, on the

for what they are, just as—in a postcolonial moment—we need an accounting of both transnational and national power in order best to analyse local as well as global political-economic and sociocultural relations today.

[10] Mike Davis, *Late Victorian Holocausts: El Niño Famines and the Making of the Third World* (London: Verso, 2001), 311.

[11] Ibid. 312.

[12] Ibid. 312.

urging of the Manchester Chamber of Commerce, into cotton monoculture. Laxman Satya and others have shown how this shift also required the reshaping of agriculture and land relations, such that in Berar between 1861 and 1877 the British government became 'the supreme landlord with peasant tenure . . . strictly conditional upon payment of revenue'.[13] I will cut a complicated story of 'high taxes, chronic debt and subsistence instability'[14] short here, and repeat only a few conclusions about transformations in peasant lives in Berar (and in other parts of the Deccan more generally):

A society formerly celebrated for its rich cotton fabrics was virtually unclothed by poverty as per capita textile consumption plummeted in inverse ratio to soaring exports of raw cotton. . . . Similarly local food security was eroded by the advance not only of cotton production . . . but of grain exports as well. During the famine of 1899–1900, when 143,000 Beraris died directly from starvation, the province exported not only tens of thousands of bales of cotton but an incredible 747,000 bushels of grain.[15]

All this, and more, was the direct result of the imposition after 1857 in India of what the Victorians thought of as 'Free Trade'. None of this is particularly new information: indeed both colonial and anticolonial historians and political commentators from the late nineteenth century on argued about these agricultural and landownership policies, and postcolonial work has been assiduous in documenting the collaboration between local elites and the British government in the creation of systemic poverty and human misery. Davis too derives his conclusions from the archival and empirical work of a host of economic historians, whose work he footnotes, a scholarly protocol that seems to be dropping out of favour with those historians of empire who wish to suggest that Victorians abroad were either on ceremonial picnics where festoons and ribbons abounded or were selfless and tireless workers on behalf of impoverished non-white millions. David Cannadine's *Ornamentalism*, for instance, which describes itself as 'characteristically entertaining and provocatively original',[16] achieves both by scrupulously refusing to engage with the conclusions of economic historians or indeed of those

---

[13] Ibid. 313.   [14] Ibid. 314.   [15] Ibid. 315.

[16] David Cannadine, *Ornamentalism: How the British Saw their Empire* (London: Penguin Press, 2001), inside jacket flap. The polemical thrust of Cannadine's argument is that historians need to 'recognize that there were other ways of seeing the empire than in the oversimplified categories

scholars whose writing on politics and culture have been central to recent revisions of the imperial record. In his book *Empire*, Ferguson goes one better by simply omitting precise references to other scholarship (he does, however, provide a list of books which he says he has consulted during his writing).

Neocolonial and neoconservative theorists who turn to nineteenth-century British imperialism to define their sense of what the world needs today do so in part because they assume imperialists then brought to fruition geopolitical and sociocultural ideas first proposed by eighteenth-century Enlightenment intellectuals, whose commitment to progress, rationality, and reform is thought unquestionable. What is missing is any awareness that Enlightenment reformists were as much the products of, and the instruments of, the flows of goods, bodies, and knowledge that resulted from the first English (and European) colonies of the seventeenth and eighteenth centuries, as Victorian imperialists were of the larger nineteenth-century empire. The views of the globe and of its peoples that are the characteristic products of eighteenth-century sociology, anthropology, and cultural studies (which is one way to disaggregate into today's terms the more seamless enquiries of that time) are inextricably

of black and white with which we are so preoccupied. It is time we reoriented orientalism' (p. 125). Cannadine's preferred mode is to see '*imperialism as ornamentalism*' (p. 122). It is odd to see Edward Said's *Orientalism* invoked as authorizing a theory of empire which argues that the British Empire was founded on and legitimized simply by white racism, a claim that is to be found nowhere in the book. Cannadine spends no time reading or responding to the details of Said's many essays on the cultures of empire; nor does he detail instances of the kind of historical analysis he finds unacceptable. In his effort to shift attention away from the role played by racist superiority in the making of British governance overseas, Cannadine points to instances of strategic upper-class cross-race 'individual cooperation based on a shared recognition of equal social status' (p. 126). India's first Prime Minister, Jawaharlal Nehru, of Harrow, Trinity College, and the Inner Temple might be considered a prime instance of the kind of individual understood by British imperialists to be more like them than dissimilar. This is what Nehru writes in his *The Discovery of India* (1946): 'Biologists tell us that racialism is a myth and there is no such thing as a master race. But we in India have known racialism in all its forms ever since the commencement of British rule. The whole ideology of this rule was that of the herrenvolk and the master race, and the structure of government was based upon it; indeed the idea of a master race is inherent in imperialism. There was no subterfuge about it; it was proclaimed in unambiguous language by those in authority. More powerful than words was the practice that accompanied them . . . .' Jawaharlal Nehru, *The Discovery of India* (Delhi: Oxford University Press, 1989), 326. Nehru wrote these lines in 1944, and his vocabulary suggests no compunctions in equating the racism of British imperialists with that of Nazi supremacists.

involved with European commercial and territorial expansion.[17] To ignore this impoverishes historical analysis, but, more importantly, it allows neoconservative historians to be selective in their understanding of the political economy of modern empires, and to deny avoid the unavoidable conclusion that the neoclassical splendours of eighteenth- and nineteenth-century Europe might derive from the surplus extracted from colonies and commerce across the globe.[18] Nor are they concerned that the very international systems put into place to create and ensure colonial inequality continue to function equally efficiently (or not) in a postcolonial world. Those are of course authorial decisions that reflect a particular world-view, one which is now underwritten by US military authority in many of the same theatres of influence where the Union Jack once flew.[19]

These ideological blinkers are further narrowed in narratives that feature an anecdotal, storytelling style and which, in acts of academic bad faith, gesture towards complex intellectual difficulties while refusing to engage with them.[20] The history that results erects a cordon sanitaire around philosophical and intellectual complexity, or indeed around speculative thought that questions those assumptions of conventional historiography that are experienced as the unexamined certainties of the discipline itself. The many epistemological questions that should give us pause—the questions about the shifting and often interrelated forms of dominance and resistance; about the constitution of the colonial archive, and the search

[17] These issues have been defined in a variety of books, as for instance in P. J. Marshall and Glyndwr Williams, *The Great Map of Mankind: British Perceptions of the World in the Age of Enlightenment* (London: Dent, 1982).

[18] Even tiny Belgium had its Congo (or rather, King Leopold had his private colony). For a superb account of one instance of the competitive will to imperial power among otherwise undistinguished nineteenth-century European nations, see Adam Hochschild's *King Leopold's Ghost* (New York: Houghton Mifflin, 1998).

[19] Since this essay was first written, military reverses, corruption, and the destruction of Iraqi civil society have caused some propagandists of the US-led invasion to rethink their neocolonial enthusiasms. There is no discernible change in US strategic ambitions in Iraq yet.

[20] In that they are legatees of the 'jodhpurs and white flannels' school of storytellers which contributed to the 'Raj revival' and 'heritage culture' industry in the UK in the 1980s. Salman Rushdie comments on the former in 'Outside the Whale', in *Imaginary Homelands: Essays and Criticism, 1981–1991* (New York: Penguin, 1991), 87–101. For an interesting 'reception studies' analysis of the latter, see Concetta Sidoti, 'An Evening with Jane Austen. National Pride and Audience Prejudice: Re-Writing the Heritage Text', *Cultural Studies from Birmingham*, 2/1 (1998), archived at <http://web.archive.org/web/20040224120412/artsweb.bham.ac.uk/bccsr/issue1/sidoti.htm> accessed 28 June 2006.

for alternative traces of social being; about the mutating, interdependent play of race and class; about the significance of gender and sexuality; about the complex forms in which subjectivities are experienced and collectivities mobilized; about representation itself; or about the ethnographic translation of cultures—seem to make little dent in these histories, except as irritating elements of the 'lousy press' that the British Empire has been getting of late, to be noticed and then set aside, or to be used as a rhetorical staging post for nostalgic evocations of Empire Lite, Empire Brite.

There are of course many intellectuals who have wondered about, in conversations and in writing, the course that some forms of postcolonial theory—or the colonial discourse studies influenced by its philosophical and historical speculations—have been taking, but their disagreements are as nought when compared with the lack of purchase they have on these histories of empire.[21] Conversely, scholars might actually now be able to see with renewed clarity what the point is in thinking about the economic and human dynamics of empire in ways that are at once sceptical about easy forms of storytelling, vigilant about their own investments in the critical discourse of empire and its aftermath, and committed to engaging with the past as if the past really matters, as if there is a vital connection between the embattled state of international relations today and the even more repressive organization of the globe fifty or a hundred years ago.

Neoimperialist historiography also reminds us that universities are vital to the making of public opinion, but that they also supply the men and women who are and who will be at the front lines of Anglo-American governmental and non-governmental engagement with the world. Ironically, the power and achievement of the educational establishment in the US and the UK also mean that these universities produce a significant element of the future elites of countries all over the world. These are the institutions within which many postcolonial scholars also do academic work, and this is where they participate in larger, and more visibly important, public policy conversations. Most academics have in recent years been hesitant—perhaps rightly so—to claim that their writing and teaching (particularly their theoretical and conceptual

---

[21] The debates and contested positions that mark the recent history and progress of postcolonial studies are traced in the Introduction to, and in the essays collected in, Ania Loomba, Suvir Kaul, Matti Bunzl, Antoinette Burton, Jed Esty (eds), *Postcolonial Studies and Beyond* (Durham, NC: Duke University Press, 2005).

flourishes!) have consequences beyond the academy, but it is university students whom Ferguson has in mind when he calls for 'the products of America's elite educational institutions' to go overseas to rule the new American empire as once the new 'Oxbridge-educated, frock-coated mandarins' ran the British Empire.[22] Unabashed neo-imperialists have no anxieties about the privileged isolation of universities from their communities; since they are no democrats, they have no qualms in seeing 'ivory towers' as appropriate training grounds for future imperialists.[23] Progressive academics are used to thinking of the university as a site of intellectual and institutional conflicts, but they need to remember that it is also, importantly, home to the development and negotiation of consequential ideas about national and international culture and political economy.

So how to write postcolonial histories of modern (and indeed contemporary) empire? First, scholars must continue to work with the idea that Great Britain (or any other European national agglomeration, including the United States, in the eighteenth century) was forged both via internal commerce, conflict, and treaty, and via overseas trade, warfare, and colonization. This means that—in the instance of Britain—the frames of reference, whether in an analysis of an English lyric or a parliamentary document, or changes in land relations or the making of financial institutions, will not simply be the poet or the parliamentarian, or the landowner and financier, the Whig or the Tory, the Londoner or the provincial, but will expand to incorporate questions about the making of national subjects and civic and military institutions adequate to the demands of international trade and a burgeoning (if on occasion uncertain) empire. Our analyses will continue to illuminate the foundational material and cultural importance of overseas trade and colonies in the making of modern bourgeois culture, in land and class relations, and in

[22] Ferguson, 'The Empire Slinks Back', 56.

[23] James Atlas has pointed to the fact that a great many 'neocon' ideologues in Washington think tanks and in the Bush administration see themselves as an elite trained into the defence of 'Western civilization' as it was defined by Leo Strauss in his work on Greek philosophers ('Leo-Cons; A Classicist's Legacy: New Empire Builders', *New York Times* 'Week in Review' (4 May 2003), 1. Ancient Greek philosophy has many lessons to offer, as do 'Enlightenment' values and philosophy, but it is important to teach world-views different from those embodied by Strauss and his epigones. Ann Norton's *Leo Strauss and the Politics of American Empire* (New Haven: Yale University Press, 2004) is a pointed account of Straussians in their roles as theoreticians, institutional performers, and politicians.

the development of industry—both in Europe and in colonized territories. Equally, critics will continue to explore archives and records inside and outside the metropolitan centres of empire, particularly those from once-colonized spaces, and will trace in them histories not only of resistance to or collaboration with rulers from across the seas, but also of the historical mutations of indigenous collectivities, of socioeconomic and cultural formations, in response to this powerful transformative presence.

Several years ago Dane Kennedy surveyed the historiography of British imperialism, and suggested that its 'adamant empiricism' had led to its 'reputation for insularity and inattention to the methodological advances made both by historians in related fields and by scholars in related disciplines'.[24] He remarked on the fact that literary and cultural critics, 'armed with the latest post-structuralist theories', had 'opened up and exploited some surprisingly rich and provocative intellectual terrain', but warned that without 'serious engagement' between historians and literary scholars, neither the methodological narrowness of historians nor the 'theoretical excesses' of literary scholars would be checked.[25] Kennedy did not propose a facile reconciliation of intellectual and methodological differences, and in fact even as his essay addresses the insularity of mainstream historiography, it also offers critiques of the hyperbolic claims made by some postcolonial theorists for the 'relationship between language and liberation',[26] their 'recondite literary analysis', and their dissolution of historical specificity into the ready-mix soup of semiotics or psychoanalysis. His essay is, in short, a sympathetic and clear-sighted call for the systematic dialogue that will contribute 'to the task of restoring the relationship between centre and periphery, of recovering the connection between the history of Britain and the history of its imperial dependencies'.[27]

---

[24] Dane Kennedy, 'Imperial History and Post-Colonial Theory', *Journal of Imperial and Commonwealth History*, 24/3 (1996), 345. Just in case readers are tempted to believe that Kennedy's account of such historiography is out of date, there is the example of Linda Colley's recent essay 'What is Imperial History Now?' which quotes Dane Kennedy approvingly, but goes on to ignore systematically, even at the level of footnotes, the substantive conceptual and ideological challenges of different varieties of postcolonial enquiry. Perhaps the most glaring absence is her refusal to register the work of the subaltern studies historians and their great influence on the recent study of precolonial, colonial, and postcolonial societies in South Asia, South Africa, and Latin America. David Cannadine (ed.), *What is History Now?* (Basingstoke: Palgrave Macmillan, 2002), 132–47.

[25] Kennedy, 'Imperial History', 346.

[26] Ibid. 349.   [27] Ibid. 359.

As I mentioned earlier, postcolonial analyses of the eighteenth-century cultures of empire have a particular legacy to deal with: that of the 'Enlightenment' (which, in literary studies at least, is a signifier of British humanism second only to the talismanic 'Shakespeare'.) Equally, in a European frame, Enlightenment functions as the 'Renaissance' once did, as a term that offers itself as historical description while in fact being an expression of self-approbation. Indeed one can argue that the very idea of 'European', with its geographical and cultural exclusions—of all that is east of Germany and Italy, for instance—is crucially dependent on the cultural and philosophical self-description made possible by eighteenth-century Enlightenment thinkers.[28] When the term is deployed in an unexamined, unqualified, or self-congratulatory and Eurocentric way, it functions as the celebratory common sense of several modern disciplines ranging from anthropology to zoology, all of which are meant to have originated under its benign aegis. Equally often, the Enlightenment is touted as the exclusive intellectual and ethical legacy in whose name citizens and scholars are enjoined to liberal thought and action in the present. It is of course entirely anachronistic to expect to find in the contentious philosophical, scientific, and sociocultural debates of eighteenth-century thinkers in France, Germany, Britain, and elsewhere (including British America) templates for progressive politics or cultural performance in different parts of the globe today. It is also a historiographical failing for us to shield scholarly engagement with the Enlightenment—whether that term is understood as shorthand for a series of debates between consequential philosophers, or more broadly as zeitgeist—from its location in the world brought into being by late seventeenth- and eighteenth-century European imperialism.[29]

---

[28] While the term 'European' is found in English literary texts from the early seventeenth century, the term took its particular modern valence when it was invoked as the geographical and historical location of the highest form of 'civilization', which itself was a crucial comparative idea developed fully in the eighteenth century. In *Civilization and its Contents* (Stanford: Stanford University Press, 2004), Bruce Mazlish provides a genealogy for the term 'civilization' that points to its conceptual centrality to Enlightenment, colonial, and racist discourses.

[29] In their introduction to Peter Hulme's essay 'The Spontaneous Hand of Nature: Savagery, Colonialism, and the Enlightenment', the editors suggest the need to reinstate, for instance, 'the Enlightenment discussion of "savagery" into a colonial history, looking, at least briefly, at the *practice* associated with these ideas and trying to see just how they formed part of an extended ideological justification for colonial appropriation of non-European writers. No major Enlightenment figure had direct experience of the colonies but several, foremost among them John Locke, worked closely with the private and state bodies which were responsible for formulating

An eloquent recent instance of the liberal desire to return to Enlightenment principles is to be found in Stephen Eric Bronner's *Reclaiming the Enlightenment*, which rehabilitates the political history and critical functions of the Enlightenment (which he believes ought to be spoken of in the singular, as a recognizable and even coherent historical phenomenon) in order to confront both the ascendancy of right-wing philosophies today and as the philosophical power of critical theorists (in particular members of the Frankfurt School) who have interrogated or disavowed Enlightenment paradigms. His book does not engage with particular Enlightenment thinkers and their writing but speaks on behalf of 'the political spirit of the Enlightenment', which he argues 'crystallized around the principles connected with fostering the accountability of institutions, reciprocity under the law, and a commitment to experiment with social reform. Not in imperialism, or racism, or the manipulation of liberty, but in these ideals lies the basis of Enlightenment universalism.'[30] Bonner insists rightly that the political and scientific 'ethos' of the Enlightenment was responsible for major progressive developments in European social organization, political systems, scientific thought, and pedagogy (all in the face of dogged and violent opposition from various interests that he labels the Counter-Enlightenment). However, there is little mention in his book of the even more violent histories of European imperialism that ought to complicate his restoration of a liberal Enlightenment world-picture (though he does on occasion complain that postcolonial theorists distrust the legacy of the European Enlightenment). Postcolonial scholars of course do not have the luxury of keeping the historical record of empire separate from the history of philosophical and political debate in modern Europe, especially since those debates were exported to the colonies via, and *embodied in*, the mechanisms of imperial surplus extraction, administration, and pedagogy.[31]

the colonial policies of European countries during the period.' Peter Hulme and Ludmilla Jordanova (eds), *The Enlightenment and its Shadows* (London: Routledge, 1990), 17.

[30] Stephen Eric Bronner, *Reclaiming the Enlightenment: Toward a Politics of Radical Engagement* (New York: Columbia University Press, 2004), 9.

[31] Dorinda Outram reminds us that 'in spite of all the ways in which Enlightenment interpretation has changed over the past decades, Enlightenment scholars have yet to come to terms with the issues of the relationship between the Enlightenment and the creation of a global world'. *The Enlightenment* (2nd edn, Cambridge: Cambridge University Press, 2005), 8. Outram's discussion of slavery and Enlightenment thinking turns on her insight that the latter is 'centrally concerned with the meaning and manipulation of difference' (p. 74).

The limits of the theorists of the Enlightenment were the limits of thought in their historical moment, just as the tensions between different strands of argument, including in their views of human and species difference, were interrelated with the world brought into view by merchants and colonists, as well as by the writers and painters who accompanied them. Their knowledge systems, indeed the understanding of what constituted knowledge, were simultaneously expansive (in that they brought more and more of nature and society into the purview of rational investigation), instrumental (that is, devoted to harnessing natural products across the globe to serve European desires), and ideological (since they were designed to facilitate such desires). A similar coupling of instrumentality and ideology shaped even progressive Enlightenment discussions about gender and class relations at home, which were always understood within an international frame, as when women in eighteenth-century Britain compared their station to that of slaves abroad.[32] It did not follow that such a metaphoric linkage led immediately to an abolitionist politics (that politics came later), but it does remind us that the imagination, and the contradictions, of self-understanding and self-interest in this historical moment are derived from the practices of modern European empires.[33]

I chose this 'domestic' example also to nudge the discussion of Enlightenment thought away from its obsessive focus on male *philosophes* and towards a recognition that shifts in everyday discourse and institutional practices are as compelling for the understanding of Enlightenment legacies as, for

[32] A representative instance is Sarah Fyge Egerton's 'The Emulation', in *Poems on Several Occasions, Together with a Pastoral* (London, [1703]), 108–9, which derives its poetic energy and proto-feminist passion from the idea of women being enslaved by men. Egerton complains in particular about 'Tyrant Custom' denying women the sciences, arts, philosophy, and poetry, which makes this poem an early instance of the intellectual aspirations associated with the Enlightenment.

[33] Abolitionism too drew upon crucial Enlightenment and imperial tropes to fashion its optative rhetoric: the light of British Liberty would one day shine on all equally, benignly extending both the empire and Christianity. Hannah More begins her important *Slavery, A Poem* (1788) by figuring slavery as the absence of the 'Bright intellectual Sun': 'If heaven has into being deign'd to call / Thy light, O LIBERTY! to shine on all; / Bright intellectual Sun! why does thy ray / To earth distribute only partial day?' (ll. 1–4). She ends with a vision of freed African slaves, who are now voluntarily drawn into the circle of British and Christian 'Liberty': 'Oppression's fall'n, and Slavery is no more! / The dusky myriads crowd the sultry plain, / And hail that mercy long invok'd in vain. / Victorious Pow'r! she bursts their two-fold bands, / And FAITH and FREEDOM spring from Mercy's hands' (ll. 290–4).

instance, are treatises by the Marquis de Condorcet or Adam Smith. The same universalist ambitions that allow these philosophers to speak of the progress of civilization and of the inauguration of the modern and to pontificate on the proper subjectivity of human beings are available in a less self-assured, less narcissistic idiom when women in Europe claim rights based on their humanity, or when Phyllis Wheatley or Olaudah Equiano does the same. The 'Enlightenment', not surprisingly, reads differently when attention is paid to the language of those who had to demand admission to full philosophical and legal subjectivity from the way it does when scholars only read the writing of those who legislated the terms of such admission. Further, the particular modernity made possible by the overlap between imperialism and Enlightenment discourses was not a choice for its subjects in many parts of the globe (or even for substantial sections of the European population); rather, such a modernity became, as David Scott puts it, 'itself one of the fundamental *conditions* of choice'. For Scott, this peculiar conjuncture meant that even powerful Enlightenment thinkers and actors like Toussaint Louverture and his colleagues in Haiti were 'conscripts—not volunteers—of modernity'.[34]

So if many postcolonial critics have chosen not to develop a detailed engagement with those European writers who are gestured at by the term 'Enlightenment', this is hardly surprising (there is much other, more com- pelling, work to be done). There are those who chose simply to list the term within the bankrupt lexicon of European imperialist self-representation (along with cognate terms like 'civilization' and 'liberalism'). There are also those who feel the need to reinflect and perhaps rehabilitate the term, if only by pointing to a number of key writers who, working within the philosoph- ical terms that defined Enlightenment debates, strenuously critiqued the business of empire.[35] And there are of course many ways of taking seriously the Enlightenment precisely by disaggregating and historicizing the

---

[34] David Scott, *Conscripts of Modernity: The Tragedy of Colonial Enlightenment* (Durham, NC: Duke University Press, 2004), 19.

[35] One convincing recent instance is Sankar Muthu's *Enlightenment against Empire* (Princeton, Princeton University Press, 2003), in which Muthu reminds us that 'while imperialist arguments surface frequently in eighteenth-century European political debates, this period is anomalous in the history of modern political philosophy in that it includes a significant anti-imperialist strand, one moreover that includes not simply marginal figures, but some of the most prominent and innovative thinkers of the age' (pp. 5–6). Muthu's primary instances of anti-imperialist thinkers are Diderot, Kant, and Herder, whose anti-imperialism was based, in part, on their conviction

phenomenon, and by questioning the self-image of the term provided by its celebrants. Historians have pointed to the hollowness of its ethical claims, or at the very least to their exclusionary scope (a pointed national instance being the contrast between British 'Liberty' and the British slave trade), and literary critics have made visible the self-interest that motivates the characteristic rhetoric of key Enlightenment texts. Political theorists have shown that 'improved' systems of governance (including taxation and revenue extraction) crafted at home had pernicious consequences when implemented in the colonies, and, even more consequentially, they have shown how colonies functioned as captive laboratories for the administrative fantasies of European liberalism, particularly when those fantasies could find no institutional home in Europe. Another crucial move in rethinking the Enlightenment derives from the recognition that some crucial sociological and scientific advances came from conversations between non-Europeans and Europeans, and were based on the learning and practices of non-European communities everywhere.[36] This is a model of interaction and exchange—forced and unidirectional as the largest part of it might have been—that counters the relentless self-representation of imperial and neo-imperial vainglory, in which an enlightened and militarized 'West' brings its principles of economic organization, its politics, its science, and its culture to the rescue of peoples mired in unchanging local stupor.

The postcolonial study of empire thus by definition engages with more than just imperial attitudes or power; it in fact understands cultures and peoples everywhere as continually active, for better and for worse, in their accrual of knowledge, and thus as participants in processes of social and self-definition, albeit within the constraints imposed by local elites and imperial governors. Postcolonial critics have also learned to be suspicious of the philosophical consensus that is indicated by the term 'Enlightenment' (used in the singular), for that consensus is often the product of a historiography cleansed of dissent and prescriptively certain of its civilizational values, which is to say that many received notions of the Enlightenment

that 'European states...throughout the globe...routinely and oppressively denied individuals and whole peoples the freedoms necessary for the cultivation of their humanity, that is, for the workings of their cultural agency, and thus for a flourishing pluralism' (p. 282).

[36] See, for a compelling instance of such scholarship, Richard H. Grove, *Green Imperialism: Colonial Expansion, Tropical Island Edens, and the Origins of Environmentalism, 1600–1860* (Cambridge: Cambridge University Press, 1995), esp. 73–94.

were crafted retrospectively to suit the purposes of high imperialism during the nineteenth and early twentieth centuries. As Muthu points out,

In this respect, the nineteenth-century European political and philosophical discourse on empire marked a return to the frequently held imperialist sentiments of pre-Enlightenment political thought. While the dominance of languages of race and nation in the nineteenth century was new, the virtual consensus about the necessity and justice of imperialism among European political thinkers recalls the pre-Enlightenment discourse on empire. It is perhaps by reading popular nineteenth-century political views of progress, nationality, and empire back into the eighteenth century that 'the Enlightenment' as a whole has been characterized as a project that ultimately attempted to efface or marginalize difference, a characterization that has hidden from view the anti-imperialist strand of Enlightenment-era political thought.[37]

Imperialist historiography and philosophy, not surprisingly, achieved their putative coherence and pieties via acts of reading, by setting aside traditions of dissent and resistance at home and in the colonies.

Today, there is even more that progressive scholars have to keep in mind, for our postcolonial priorities demand not only historical clarity and a fuller accounting of the material and ideological processes at work in the making of modern empire, but precise and urgent responses to the continuing and bloody ambition of the world-creating power of Western capital and weapons.[38] As postcolonial intellectuals responding to the world-knowing, world-creating legacies of eighteenth-century Enlightenment thinkers (most of whom—with exceptions along the lines that Muthu details—saw no contradiction between the progressive values and rationality they advocated and the hierarchical, indeed imperial, taxonomies of human collectivity they articulated), we have to be responsible also for the cultural and political struggles that define the social being of once-colonized nations today. Writing the histories of unsuccessful or successful colonization, of anti-colonial nationalisms, and of the state of nations after independence—the history of empire and its aftermath, that is—requires an awareness of the

[37] Muthu, *Enlightenment against Empire*, 6.
[38] For the past half-century, multinational capital has originated in many sectors of the globe (Japan, now China, and also India and Brazil), including the once-colonized world. However, the financial institutions that regulate the flows of such capital are themselves Western or follow policies mandated (or 'negotiated') by regulators in Washington, London, and the European Union.

struggles that define the present as much as those that characterized the past. It is very important, then, that we make explicit once again why we write, and to what institutional and ideological purposes, in the same way as Niall Ferguson unabashedly writes on behalf of what he calls 'Anglobalization'.[39]

Such a restatement of the ethical and political impulses that guide the postcolonial reimagining of the past in the name of History might seem a simple exercise, but it is indispensable in reminding our audiences of the stakes of scholarship that engages with empires past and present. Imperialist ideologies have been enormously successful in translating self-centred and parochial views of the world into explanatory paradigms whose universal force is hard to shake, but this is precisely the task of postcolonial historio-graphical and cultural analyses. The material apparatus of empire is examined not only for its own sake but to register the fact that much of it, often in scarcely mutated forms, is the apparatus of the global economy and of nation states (including postcolonial nations) today. Postcolonial scholars examine the forms of racist domination embedded into the ideology and protocols of empire because continuing racisms everywhere draw sustenance from such domination; similarly, we ask what lessons the simultaneous development of modern European capitalism and empires might offer for our analyses of the political economy of nations and transnational formations today. And we ask what it might mean that European Enlightenment thinkers and policy makers were products of, and helped bring into being, modern empires, for that allows us to rethink intellectual formations in both colonial and postcolonial cultures. An awareness of the past and the present, the past-in-the-present, allows us to give the lie to the argument that large parts of the globe still need the tutelage of their former masters, even when we argue that the wealthy nations of the world (most of which are located in Europe or North America) have an economic and political responsibility to those colonial subjects whose lives and communities they impoverished. And finally, such awareness guards against the revitalization of the claims of today's proselytizers and practitioners of imperialism.

In a revealing moment in Ferguson's book, he admits he cannot imagine what the world would have looked like today without the British Empire.[40]

[39] Niall Ferguson, *Empire: The Rise and Demise of the British World Order and the Lessons for Global Power* (London: Basic Books, 2002), 368.
[40] Ibid., p. xxix. He does attempt an exercise in 'counterfactual' vision though, and can only see 'glimpses of world empires that might have been'—the Dutch, the French, the Mughal (!),

That admission is an instance of lazy thinking which cannot imagine intriguing or challenging counterfactual scenarios, and in that a testimonial to an impoverished historical imagination confined within the heavy-walled citadels of modernity erected by empire.[41] Ferguson is not alone among British historians in believing that, in the eighteenth century at least, empire was the only international (and indeed national) political formation that deserves historical attention today. Linda Colley has recently argued in *The Nation* that postcolonial critiques of the British Empire are both unfair and analytically suspect because postcolonialists do not realize that empire, which she describes as 'one of the oldest, most recurrent forms of political organization in global history', 'was markedly in fashion at the turn of the eighteenth century'. Colley grants that the 'eighteenth and early nineteenth centuries were an era both of strident and complacent British nationalism and unparalleled imperial aggression' (a phenomenon that she documented partially in her book *Britons: Forging the Nation 1707–1837*) but argues that everyone from the Americans to the Russians to the Chinese were playing the same game, and that if the 'British imperial elite' needed ideological justification for their actions, they turned to the history of the Ottomans and the Mughals, and indeed to the more ancient Grecian and Roman empire-builders.[42]

Colley seems to offer an odd explanatory metaphor: empire as fashion (which might be thought of here as a cursory extension of Cannadine's conceit of Ornamentalism). However, fashion turns out not to be Colley's metaphor-of-choice for the rise and fall of empire, for she goes on to argue that empire is properly understood not as analogous to historicizable phenomena like fascism or slavery, but in comparison to 'war or religious zealotry', with the implication that these are states of mind and being endemic to the historical condition of humanity. This being the case, she argues (and here she enlists herself in the ranks of postcolonial analysts of neo-imperialism) that empire is still with us. As an instance, she offers not

the Japanese (pp. xxv–xxvi). Not a world given shape by non-imperialist practices and visions, then, only one in which readers are asked to choose between the dominances of different empires.

[41] For a review-essay on counterfactual scenarios and their utility, one that points out just how limited Ferguson's efforts in this vein are, see Richard Ned Lebow, 'What is so Different about a Counterfactual', *World Politics*, 52 (July 2000), 550–85.

[42] Linda Colley, 'Empire as a Way of Life', *The Nation* (31 July 2006), 7.

only the US, but also Russia, China, and India, each of which holds territories and peoples against their will.

All of which is true, but hardly unnoticed or unexamined. If Colley had spent time engaging with the postcolonialists whose analyses she thinks misguided, she would have known that the density of their examination of modern empire and its aftermath in the last fifty years follows from their analyses of postcolonial nation states, particularly of those practices of the state which have subjected entire populations within and adjoining these nations to forms of internal colonialism and resource extraction. Thus her aperçu about imperial state formations in the present moment is both belated and, given the concerns of her own extensive scholarship, opportunistic. Her attempt is, after all, to get postcolonial scholars to pay more sympathetic attention to modern European colonialism: 'It follows that the tendency to approach empire as a peculiarly European psychosis, occurring only in particular centuries in the past, is misleading' (p. 7). No postcolonialists I know of, even those whose analytical methods draw heavily upon psychoanalytical vocabularies, believe that empire is the product of psychosis, European or otherwise. Several have, however, advanced the argument that many of the spectacular, psychotic cruelties of colonial derangement, and the everyday fears of both colonizers and colonized subjects, derive from the racist hierarchies and socioeconomic differences institutionalized by European imperialists across the globe. Colley rightly suggests that postcolonial academics based in the US should pay more attention to US imperial history; in just such a critical spirit, she might well wish for sustained attention to the history of Anglo-American imperial collaboration in the shaping of the contemporary world.

Empires, in the past or in the present, have their defenders—too much is at stake, materially and ideologically, for it to be otherwise. On the other hand, progressive and postcolonial critics must work with the occasionally despairing sense that the egalitarian global and national futures envisioned by the independence movements that defeated European empires have, at best, come to thin fruition. Their work then is twofold: to explain the arrangements of international power and revenue extraction that characterized modern empires, and to do so (in part) with a view to explain the continuing overlaps between imperialism and neo-imperialism, and the power sharing arrangements of globalizing elites today. It is true that modern imperialism hijacked millions of people across the world away from more local transformational processes and into a world in which capitalist Europe authored the coercive script of historical change, but this historical record is also replete with coruscating instances of alternative visions of human and social betterment. These are the visions that need to energize postcolonial analyses of imperial power. Doing so will allow us to become better historians, literary critics, political economists, anthropologists, and philosophers, but also, with any luck, people with imaginations no longer in thrall to the legacies of the British Empire, or indeed to the pernicious ideal of Empire per se.

BIBLIOGRAPHY

Primary Sources

Addison, Joseph, and Richard Steele, *The Spectator*, ed. Donald F. Bond, 5 vols (Oxford: Clarendon Press, 1965).

Akenside, Mark, *The Poetical Works of Mark Akenside*, ed. Robin C. Dix (Madison, NJ: Fairleigh Dickinson University Press, 1996).

Bayle, Pierre, *De la tolérance: commentaire philosophique sur ces paroles de Jésus-Christ 'Contrains-les-d'entrer'*, ed. Jean-Michel Gros (n.p.: Presses Pocket, 1992); trans. as *A Philosophical Commentary on These Words of the Gospel, Luke 14.23, 'Compel Them to Come In, That My House May be Full'*, ed. John Kilcullen and Chandran Kukathas (Indianapolis: Liberty Fund, 2005).

Beattie, James, *An Essay on the Nature and Immutability of Truth; in Opposition to Sophistry and Scepticism* (Edinburgh, 1770).

Behn, Aphra, *Oroonoko; or, The Royal Slave*, ed. Catherine Gallagher with Simon Stern (Boston: Bedford/St Martin's, 2000).

Blumenbach, Johann Friedrich, *De generis humani varietate nativa* (Göttingen, 1775; 3rd edn, 1795); trans. as 'On the Natural Variety of Mankind', in *The Anthropological Treatises of Johann Friedrich Blumenbach*, trans. Thomas Bendyshe (London: Published for the Anthropological Society by Longman, Green, Longman, Roberts, & Green, 1865).

Bougainville, Louis Antoine, comte de, *Voyage autour du monde par la frégate du Roi, la Boudeuse et la flûte l'Etoile*, ed. Jacques Proust (Paris: Gallimard, 1982).

Burke, Edmund, *A Philosophical Enquiry into the Origin of our Ideas of the Sublime and Beautiful* (2nd edn, 1759; facs. edn, Menston: The Scolar Press, 1970).

Champlain, Samuel de, *Des Sauvages, ou, Voyage de Samuel Champlain, de Brouage, fait en la France nouvelle, l'an mil six cens trois: contenant les moeurs, façon de vivre, mariages, guerres, & habitations des Sauvages de Canadas [sic]* (Paris, 1604).

Clarendon, Edward Hyde, Earl of, *A Brief View and Survey of the Dangerous and Pernicious Errors to Church and State of Mr. Hobbes's Book, entitled Leviathan* (Oxford, 1676).

Colden, Cadwallader, *The History of the Five Indian Nations* (New York, 1727).

Condorcet, Jean-Antoine-Nicolas de Caritat, marquis de, *Esquisse d'un tableau historique des progrès de l'esprit humain* (Paris: Garnier-Flammarion, 1988); trans. as *Outlines of a History of the Progress of the Human Mind* (London, 1795).

Condorcet, Jean-Antoine-Nicolas de Caritat, marquis de, *Réfléxions sur l'esclavage des Nègres* (Neufchatel, 1781).

Cowper, William, *The Poems of William Cowper*, ed. John D. Baird and Charles Ryskamp, 3 vols (Oxford: Clarendon Press, 1995).

Crébillon, Claude-Prosper Jolyot de, *Le Sopha, conte morale*, 2 vols (Paris, 1742); trans. as *The Sopha: A Moral Tale. Translated from the French Original of Monsieur Crebillon*, 2 vols (London, 1742).

Crisp, Elizabeth Marsh, 'Journal of a Voyage by Sea from Calcutta to Madras, and of a Journey from thence back to Dacca, was written by my deceased Sister Elizabeth Crisp, and given to me by her Daughter Elizabeth Maria Shee, on her arrival in England from Bengal in the Year 1788', University of California at Los Angeles Library, Special Collections, MS 170/604.

Cushman, Robert, *A Sermon Preached at Plimmouth* (London, 1622).

Dalrymple, Sir John, *An Essay towards a General History of Feudal Property in Great Britain* (London, 1757).

Defoe, Daniel, *Defoe's Review*, ed. Arthur Wellesley Secord, 22 vols, (New York: Columbia University Press, 1938).

—— *The Farther Adventures of Robinson Crusoe; Being the Second and Last Part of His Life, and of the Strange Surprising Account of his Travels Round Three Parts of the Globe. Written by Himself* (7th edn, London, 1747).

—— *Jure Divino: A Satyr* (London, 1706).

—— *Robinson Crusoe* (London: J. M. Dent & Sons, 1945).

—— *Serious Reflections during the Life and Surprising Adventures of Robinson Crusoe* (London, 1720).

Diderot, Denis, *Political Writings*, trans. and ed. John Hope Mason and Robert Wokler (Cambridge: Cambridge University Press, 1992).

—— *Supplément au Voyage de Bougainville*, ed. Gilbert Chinard (Paris: Librairie E. Droz, 1935); in *Oeuvres philosophiques*, ed. Paul Vernière (Paris: Bordas, 1990), 455–516.

Doig, David, *Two Letters on the Savage State* (London, 1792).

Donne, John, *A Sermon upon the VIII Verse of the I Chapter of the Acts of the Apostles Preached to the Honourable Company of the Virginian Plantation 13 November 1622* (London, 1622).

Dow, Alexander (trans.), *The History of Hindostan, second revised, corrected and enlarged edition with a prefix on Ancient India based on Sanskrit Writings, translated from Persian*, 3 vols (London, 1770; repr. New Delhi: Today & Tomorrow's Printers & Publishers, 1973).

—— *The History of Hindostan translated from the Persian*, in Michael J. Franklin (ed.), *Representing India: Indian Culture and Imperial Control in Eighteenth-Century British Orientalist Discourse*, 9 vols, Sources and Perspectives of the Eighteenth Century (London: Routledge, 2000), ii.

Dunbar, John, *Essays on the History of Mankind in Rude and Cultivated Ages* (London, 1780).

Egerton, Sarah Fyge, *Poems on Several Occasions, Together with a Pastoral* (London, [1703]).

Estwick, Samuel, *Considerations on the Negroe Cause Commonly So Called Addressed to the Right Honourable Lord Mansfield* (2nd edn, London, 1773).

Fay, Eliza, *Original Letters from India (1779–1815)*, ed. E. M. Forster (New York: Harcourt Brace and Company, 1925).

Ferguson, Adam, *An Essay on the History of Civil Society*, ed. Duncan Forbes (Edinburgh: Edinburgh University Press, 1966).

Forrest, George W. (ed.), *Selections from the State Papers of the Governors-General of India*, 4 vols (Oxford: B. H. Blackwell; London: Constable & Co., Ltd, 1910–26), ii: *Warren Hastings Documents*.

Forster, Georg, 'Beschluß der im vorigen Monat angefangenen Abhandlung über die Menschenrassen', *Der teutsche Merkur* (4.Vierteljahr, 1786), 150–66.

—— 'Neuholland und die Brittische Colonie Botany-Bay', appended to Matthias Christian Sprengel (ed.), *Jahrbuch der merkwürdigsten Weltbegebenheiten für 1787, enthaltend die Geschichte der wichtigsten Staats- und Handelsveränderungen von Ostindien*, (2nd edn, Leipzig, 1786), 300–22.

—— 'Noch etwas über die Menschenraßen', *Der teutsche Merkur* (4.Vierteljahr, 1786), 57–86.

—— *A Voyage Round the World*, 2 vols (London, 1777), ed. Nicholas Thomas and Oliver Berghof (Honolulu: University of Hawai'i Press, 2000).

Glover, Richard, 'Poem on Sir Isaac Newton', in Henry Pemberton, *A View of Sir Isaac Newton's Philosophy* (London, 1728), pp. xi–xxv.

Godwin, William, *Enquiry Concerning Political Justice*, ed. Isaac Kramnick (Harmondsworth: Penguin Books, 1976).

Grotius, Hugo, *The Free Sea*, trans. Richard Hakluyt, ed. and introd. by David Armitage (Indianapolis: Liberty Fund, 2004).

Halhed, Nathaniel Brassey, *A Code of Gentoo Laws, or, Ordinations of the Pundits*, in Michael J. Franklin (ed.), *Representing India: Indian Culture and Imperial Control in Eighteenth-Century British Orientalist Discourse*, 9 vols, Sources and Perspectives of the Eighteenth Century (London: Routledge, 2000), iv.

Halley, Edmund, 'In Viri Praestantissimi D. Isaaci Newtoni', in Isaac Newton, *Philosophiae naturalis principia mathematica* (London, 1687).

Hamor, Ralph, *A True Discovrse of the Present Estate of Virginia* (London, 1615).

Harrington, James, *The Commonwealth of Oceana*, ed. J. G. A. Pocock (Cambridge: Cambridge University Press, 1993).

Harriot, Thomas, *A briefe and true report of the new found land of Virginia* (Frankfurt, 1590).

Hastings, Warren, 'Letter to Nathaniel Smith, from *The Bhagvat-Geeta*', in P. J. Marshall, *The British Discovery of Hinduism in the Eighteenth Century* (Cambridge: Cambridge University Press, 1970), 184–91.

Hastings, Warren, *Memoirs of the Life of the Right Hon. Warren Hastings, First Governor-General of Bengal*, ed. G. R. Gleig, 3 vols (London: R. Bentley, 1841).

Herder, Johann Gottfried, *Sämmtliche Werke*, ed. Bernhard Suphan, 33 vols (Berlin: Weidmann'sche Buchhandlung, 1877–1913).

—— *Stimmen der Völker in Liedern: Volkslieder. Zwei Teile 1778/79*, ed. Heinz Rölleke (Stuttgart: Reclam, 1974).

Hobbes, Thomas, *Elementorvm philosophiae sectio tertia de cive* (Paris, 1642), trans. and ed. Richard Tuck and Michael Silverthorne as *On the Citizen* (Cambridge: Cambridge University Press, 1998).

—— *Leviathan* (London, 1651), ed. Richard Tuck (Cambridge: Cambridge University Press, 1991).

Holwell, John Zephaniah, evidence given on 30 Mar. 1767, British Library, Add. MS 18,469.

—— *Interesting Historical Events, Relative to the Provinces of Bengal, and the Empire of Indostan. With A Seasonable Hint and Perswasive To the Honourable The Court of Directors of the East India Company. As Also The Mythology and Cosmogony, Fasts and Festivals of the Gentoo's, followers of the Shastah. And A Dissertation on the Metempsychosis, commonly, though erroneously, called the Pythagorean Doctrine*, 3 vols (London, 1765–71), in Michael J. Franklin (ed.), *Representing India: Indian Culture and Imperial Control in Eighteenth-Century British Orientalist Discourse*, 9 vols, Sources and Perspectives of the Eighteenth Century (London: Routledge, 2000), i.

Honorius Philoponus [Caspar Plautius], *Nova typis transacta navigatio: novi orbis Indiae Occidentalis* ([Linz], 1621).

Hughes, Lewes, *A Letter Sent into England from the Summer Ilands* (London, 1615).

—— *A Plaine and True Relation of the Goodness of God towards the Sommer Ilands* (London, 1621).

Hume, David, *An Enquiry concerning the Principles of Morals*, ed. Tom L. Beauchamp (Oxford: Oxford University Press, 1998).

—— *Essays Moral, Political, and Literary*, rev. edn, ed. Eugene F. Miller (Indianapolis: Liberty Fund, 1987).

Inchbald, Elizabeth, *The Mogul Tale; or, the Descent of the Balloon* (1784; Dublin, 1788).

Ives, Edward, *A Voyage from England to India, in the Year MDCCLIV and an Historical Narrative of the Operations of the Squadron and Army in India, under . . . Watson . . . and Colonel Clive* (London, 1773).

Johnson, Samuel, *Rasselas and Other Tales*, ed. Gwin J. Kolb, in *The Yale Edition of the Works of Samuel Johnson*, 16 (New Haven: Yale University Press, 1990).

Jones, William, *A Grammar of the Persian Language* (1771; Menston: Scolar Press, 1969).

—— 'A Hymn to Náráyana', in Jerome McGann (ed.), *New Oxford Book of Romantic Period Verse* (Oxford: Oxford University Press, 1993).

Jones, William, *Institutes of Hindu Law: or, the Ordinances of Menu, according to the Gloss of Cullúca. Comprising the Indian System of Duties, Religious and Civil* (Calcutta and London, 1796), in Michael J. Franklin (ed.), *Representing India: Indian Culture and Imperial Control in Eighteenth-Century British Orientalist Discourse*, 9 vols, Sources and Perspectives of the Eighteenth Century (New York: Routledge, 2000), ix.

—— *The Letters of Sir William Jones*, ed. Garland Cannon, 2 vols (Oxford: Clarendon Press, 1970).

—— 'On the Gods of Greece, Italy, and India', in *Asiatick Researches*, i (Calcutta, 1788), ch. 9.

—— *Poeseos Asiaticae Commentariorum* (London, 1774).

—— *Sacontala, or the Fatal Ring* (Calcutta, 1789).

—— *Sir William Jones: A Reader*, ed. Sayta S. Pachori (New York: Oxford University Press, 1993).

—— *Sir William Jones: Selected Poetical and Prose Works*, ed. Michael Franklin (Cardiff: University of Wales Press, 1995).

—— *The Works of Sir William Jones*, ed. Lord Teignmouth, 13 vols (London, 1807).

Jourdain, Silvester, *A Plaine Description of the Barmudas, Now Called Sommer Ilands* (London, 1613).

Justi, Johann Heinrich Gottlob von, *Vergleichungen der europäischen mit den asiatischen und andern vermeintlich barbarischen Regierungen. In drey Büchern verfasset* (Berlin, Stettin, and Leipzig, 1762).

Kaempfer, Engelbert, *Geschichte und Beschreibung von Japan*, ed. C. W. Dohm, 2 vols, (1777–9; Stuttgart: F. A. Brockhaus, 1964).

Kames, Henry Home, Lord, *Essays on the Principles of Morality and Natural Religion* (2nd edn, London, 1758).

—— *Historical Law-Tracts*, 2 vols (Edinburgh, 1758).

—— *Sketches of the History of Man*, ed. James A. Harris, 3 vols (Indianapolis: Liberty Fund, 2007).

Kant, Immanuel, 'An Answer to the Question: What is Enlightenment?', in James Schmidt (ed.), *What is Enlightenment?: Eighteenth-Century Answers and Twentieth-Century Questions* (Berkeley: University of California Press, 1996), 58–64.

—— *Anthropology, History, and Education*, ed. Günther Zöller and Robert B. Louden (Cambridge: Cambridge University Press, 2007).

—— *Correspondence*, trans. and ed. Arnulf Zweig (Cambridge: Cambridge University Press, 1999).

—— *Critique of Judgment*, trans. J. H. Bernard (1892; New York: Hafner, 1951); trans. James Creed Meredith (Oxford: Clarendon Press, 1952).

—— *Critique of the Power of Judgment*, ed. Paul Guyer, trans. Paul Guyer and Eric Matthews (Cambridge: Cambridge University Press, 2000).

—— *Kants gesammelte Schriften*, ed. Königliche Preußische [now Deutsche] Akademie der Wissenschaften (Berlin: Georg Reimer [now De Gruyter], 1902–).

Kant, Immanuel, *Metaphysical Elements of Justice: Part I of the Metaphysics of Morals*, 2nd edn, trans. John Ladd (Indianapolis: Hackett, 1999).

—— *Political Writings*, ed. Hans Reiss, trans. H. B. Nisbet (2nd edn, Cambridge: Cambridge University Press, 1991).

[Kayll, Robert], *The Trades Increase* (London, 1615).

Kindersley, Jemima, *Letters from the Island of Teneriffe, Brazil, the Cape of Good Hope, and the East Indies* (London, 1777).

Kingsbury, Susan Myra (ed.), *Records of the Virginia Company*, 4 vols (Washington, DC: Library of Congress, 1906–35).

Kipling, Rudyard, 'The White Man's Burden', first pub. in *McClure's Magazine* (Feb. 1899), repr. in *Collected Poems of Rudyard Kipling* (London: Wordsworth Editions, 1994), 334–5.

Lahontan, Louis Armand de Lom d'Arce, baron de, *Dialogues avec un sauvage* (Paris: Éditions Sociales, 1973).

—— *Nouveaux voyages de M. Le Baron de Lahontan, dans l'Amérique Septentrionale*, 2 vols (The Hague, 1703).

—— *Oeuvres complètes*, ed. Réal Ouellet, 2 vols (Montreal: Presses Universitaires de Montréal, 1990).

—— *Suite du Voyage, de l'Amérique, ou Dialogues de Monsieur le baron de Lahontan et d'un sauvage, dans l'Amerique. Contenant une description exacte des moeurs et des coutumes de ces peuples sauvages. Avec les voyages du même en Portugal et en Danemarc, dans lesquels on trouve des particularitez trés curieuses, et qu'on n'avoit point encore remarquées* (Amsterdam, 1704).

Le Jeune, Paul, *Relation de ce qui s'est passé en la Nouvelle France* (Paris, 1634).

Léry, Jean de, *Histoire d'un voyage faict en la terre du Bresil (1578)*, ed. Frank Lestringant (Paris: Librairie Générale Française, 1994).

Le Vaillant, François, *Voyages de F. Le Vaillant dans l'intérieur de l'Afrique, 1781–1785*, ed. Jacques Boulenger (Paris: Plon, 1932).

Linnaeus, Carl von, *Systema naturae, sive regna tria naturae systematice proposita per classes, ordines, genera, et species* (Leiden, 1735).

Locke, John, *A Letter concerning Toleration*, trans. William Popple, ed. James Tully (Indianapolis: Hackett, 1983).

—— *Two Treatises of Government*, ed. Peter Laslett (Cambridge: Cambridge University Press, 1988).

—— *Two Tracts on Government*, ed. and introd. by Philip Abrams (Cambridge: Cambridge University Press, 1967).

Long, Edward, *The History of Jamaica*, 3 vols (London, 1774).

Ludolphus, Job [Hiob Ludolf], *A New History of Ethiopia. Being a Full and Accurate Description of the Kingdom of Abessinia, Vulgarly, though Erroneously called the Empire of Prester John. In Four Books . . . Made English by J. P. Gent* (London: Samuel Smith, 1682).

Marx, Karl, *A Contribution to the Critique of Political Economy*, trans. S. W. Ryazanskaya, ed. Maurice Dobb (Moscow: Progress Publishers, 1970).

Miller, James, *Mahomet, the Imposter* (London, 1744).

Montaigne, Michel de, *Les Essais*, ed. André Tournon, 3 vols (Paris: Imprimerie Nationale Éditions, 1998).

More, Hannah, *Slavery, A Poem* (London, 1788).

Morton, Thomas, *New English Canaan, or New Canaan* (London, 1637).

Newton, Isaac, Sir, *Philosophiae naturalis principia mathematica* (London, 1687; 2nd edn, London, 1713).

'On the Five Bustoes erected by her Majesty in the Hermitage at Richmond', *Gentleman's Magazine*, 3 (Apr. 1733), 207.

Orders and constitutions, partly collected out of his Maiesties letters patents; and partly by authority, and in vertue of the said letters patents: ordained vpon mature deliberation, by the gouernour and company of the city of London, for the plantation of the Summer-Islands: for the better gouerning of the actions and affaires of the said company and plantation. 6. Febr. 1621. (London, 1622).

Prichard, James Cowles, 'Of the Causes which Have Produced the Diversities of the Human Species', 1813, in Peter J. Kitson (ed.), *Slavery, Abolition and Emancipation: Writings in the British Romantic Period*, viii: *Theories of Race* (London: Pickering & Chatto, 1999), 269–308.

Pufendorf, Samuel, Freiherr von, *De statu imperii Germanici*, ed. Fritz Salomon (Weimar: Böhlau, 1910).

Purchas, Samuel, *Hakluytus Posthumus or Purchas His Pilgrimes*, 4 vols (London, 1625).

—— 'Virginias Verger: Or a Discourse shewing the benefits which may grow to this Kingdome from American English Plantations, and specially those of Virginia and Summer Ilands', in *Hakluytus Posthumus, or, Purchas His Pilgrimes*, 20 vols (Glasgow: James MacLehose and Sons, 1905–7), xix, 218–67.

Ramsay, Allan, 'To the Memory of Sir Isaac Newton', in *Poems by Allan Ramsay*, 2 vols (London, 1731), ii, 175–7.

Raynal, Guillaume-Thomas-François, abbé, *Histoire philosophique et politique des Etablissements et du Commerce des Européens dans les deux Indes*, 3rd edn (Neuchâtel and Geneva, 1780); ed. Yves. Bénot (Paris: François Maspero, 1981), trans. J. Justamond as *A Philosophical and Political History of the Settlements and Trade of the Europeans in the East and West Indies. 2nd ed. Revised and Corrected. With Maps Adapted to the Work, and a Copious Index*, 5 vols (London, 1776).

Schiller, Friedrich von, *Werke in drei Bänden*, ed. Herbert G. Göpfert (Munich: Hanser, 1966).

Schlözer, August Ludwig von, *Theorie der Statistik: Nebst Ideen über das Studium der Politik überhaupt* (Göttingen: Vandenhoek & Ruprecht, 1804).

—— *Vorstellung seiner Universal-Historie (1772/73)*, ed. Horst Walter Blanke (Waltrop: Hartmut Spenner, 1997).

—— *Weltgeschichte nach ihren Haupt Theilen im Auszug und Zusammenhange*, 2 vols (Göttingen, 1785–9).

Schöpperlin, Johann Friedrich, *Sveviae veteris per temporum periodos descriptae primae Lineae* (Nördlingen, 1767).

Selden, John, *Mare clausum* (London, 1635).

Shaftesbury, Anthony Ashley Cooper, third Earl of, *Characteristics of Men, Manners, Opinions, Times*, ed. Lawrence E. Klein (Cambridge: Cambridge University Press, 1999).

S[harpe], E[dward], *Britaines Busse* (London, 1615).

Smith, John, *The Generall Historie of Virginia, New-England and the Summer Isles* (London, 1631).

Speed, John, *The Theatre of the Empire of Great-Britaine* (London, 1676).

Starke, Mariana, *The Sword of Peace* (Dublin, 1790); repr. in Jeffrey N. Cox (ed.), *Slavery, Abolition and Emancipation: Writings in the British Romantic Period*, v: *Drama* (London: Pickering & Chatto, 1999).

Stewart, Dugald, 'Account of the Life and Writings of Adam Smith, LL.D', in *The Collected Works of Dugald Stewart*, ed. Sir William Hamilton, 10 vols (Edinburgh: T. Constable, 1858), x, 5–98.

Symonds, William, *Virginia. A Sermon Preached at White-Chappel* (London, 1609).

Thomson, James, *A Poem Sacred to the Memory of Sir Isaac Newton*, 1727, in *Liberty, The Castle of Indolence and Other Poems*, ed. James Sambrook (Oxford: Clarendon Press, 1986).

—— *The Seasons and The Castle of Indolence*, ed. James Sambrook (Oxford: Clarendon Press, 1972).

Voltaire, *Traité sur la tolerance* ([Geneva], 1763).

Waterhouse, Edward, *A Declaration of the State of the Colony and Affaires in Virginia. With a Relation of the Barbarous Massacre in the Time of Peace* (London, 1622).

Welwood, William, *An Abridgement of all Sea-Lawes* (London, 1613).

Wood, William, *New Englands Prospect* (London, 1634).

[Young, Edward], *Imperium Pelagi. A Naval Lyrick: Written in Imitation of Pindar's Spirit* (London, 1730).

Secondary Sources

Aarsleff, Hans, *The Study of Language in England, 1780–1860* (Princeton: Princeton University Press, 1967).

Abernethy, David B., *The Dynamics of Global Dominance: European Overseas Empires 1415–1980* (New Haven: Yale University Press, 2000).

Abrams, M. H., *The Mirror and the Lamp: Romantic Theory and the Critical Tradition* (New York: Oxford University Press, 1953).

Ahmad, Aijaz, 'The Politics of Literary Postcoloniality', *Race and Class*, 36/3 (1995), 1–20.

Aldridge, A. Owen, *The Ibero-American Enlightenment* (Urbana: University of Illinois Press, 1971).

Al-Kassim, Dina, 'The Face of Foreclosure', *Interventions*, 4/2 (2002), 168–74.

Althusser, Louis, *For Marx*, trans. Ben Brewster (London: Allen Lane, 1969).

Anderson, Benedict, *Imagined Communities: Reflections on the Origin and Spread of Nationalism* (London: Verso, 1991).

Appadurai, Arjun, *Modernity at Large: Cultural Dimensions of Globalization* (Minneapolis: University of Minnesota Press, 1996).

Appiah, Kwame Anthony, *Cosmopolitanism: Ethics in a World of Strangers* (New York: Norton, 2006).

Aravamudan, Srinivas, 'Sovereignty: Between Embodiment and Detranscendental-ization', *Texas International Law Journal*, 41/3 (2006), 427–46.

—— *Tropicopolitans: Colonialism and Agency, 1688–1804* (Durham, NC: Duke University Press, 1999).

—— ' "The Unity of the Representer": Reading *Leviathan* against the Grain', in Alberto Moreiras (ed.), *Thinking Politically*, special issue of *South Atlantic Quarterly*, 104/4 (Fall 2005), 631–53.

Arendt, Hannah, 'The Crisis in Culture: Its Social and Political Significance', in *Between Past and Future: Six Exercises in Political Thought* (New York: Viking, 1961), 197–226.

Armitage, David, 'Hobbes and the Foundations of Modern International Thought', in Annabel Brett and James Tully with Holly Hamilton-Bleakley (eds), *Rethinking the Foundations of Modern Political Thought* (Cambridge: Cambridge University Press, 2006), 219–35.

—— *The Ideological Origins of the British Empire* (Cambridge: Cambridge University Press, 2000).

—— 'The New World and British Historical Thought: From Richard Hakluyt to William Robertson', in Karen Ordahl Kupperman (ed.), *America in European Consciousness, 1493–1750* (Chapel Hill: University of North Carolina Press, 1995), 52–75.

Ashcraft, Richard, '*Leviathan* Triumphant: Thomas Hobbes and the Politics of Wild Men', in Edward J. Dudley and Maximillian E. Novak (eds), *The Wild Man Within: An Image in Western Thought from the Renaissance to Romanticism* (Pittsburgh: University of Pittsburgh Press, 1972), 141–82.

Atlas, James, 'Leo-Cons; A Classicist's Legacy: New Empire Builders', *New York Times*, 'Week in Review' (4 May 2003), 1.

Ayers, Robert W., '*Robinson Crusoe*: "Allusive Allegorick History"', *Publications of the Modern Language Association*, 82/5 (1967), 399–407.

Baker, Keith, *Inventing the French Revolution: Essays on French Political Culture in the Eighteenth Century* (Cambridge: Cambridge University Press, 1990).

Ballantyne, Tony, 'Empire, Knowledge and Culture: From Proto-Globalization to Modern Globalization', in A. G. Hopkins (ed.), *Globalization in World History* (London: Pimlico, 2002), 115–40.

Barker, Francis, Peter Hulme, and Margaret Iversen, introduction in *Colonial Discourse / Postcolonial Theory* (Manchester: Manchester University Press, 1994), 1–23.

Barrell, John, *English Literature in History, 1730–80: An Equal, Wide Survey* (London: Hutchinson, 1983).

Bartels, Emily, 'Making More of the Moor: Aaron, Othello and Renaissance Re-fashionings of Race', *Shakespeare Quarterly*, 41/4 (Winter 1990), 433–54.

Barthelemy, Anthony, *Black Face, Maligned Race: The Representation of Blacks in English Drama from Shakespeare to Southerne* (Baton Rouge: Louisiana State University Press, 1987).

Barthes, Roland, 'Le dernier des écrivains heureux', in *Essais critiques* (Paris: Éditions du Seuil, 1964), 94–100; trans. Richard Howard as 'The Last Happy Writer', in *Critical Essays* (Evanston, Ill.: Northwestern University Press, 1972), 83–9.

Bartolovich, Crystal and Neil Lazarus (eds), *Marxism, Modernity and Postcolonial Studies* (Cambridge: Cambridge University Press, 2002).

Bayly, C. A., *The Birth of the Modern World, 1780–1914* (Oxford: Blackwell, 2004).

—— 'The British and Indigenous Peoples, 1760–1860: Power, Perception and Identity', in Martin Daunton and Rick Halpern (eds), *Empire and Others: British Encounters with Indigenous Peoples, 1600–1850* (London: UCL Press, 1999), 19–41.

—— *Imperial Meridian: The British Empire and the World, 1780–1830* (New York: Longman, 1989).

—— *Indian Society and the Making of the British Empire* (Cambridge: Cambridge University Press, 1988).

—— *Origins of Nationality in South Asia: Patriotism and Ethical Government in the Making of Modern India* (Oxford: Oxford University Press, 1998).

Beal, Timothy K., *Religion and its Monsters* (New York: Routledge, 2002).

Becker, G. C., *The Heavenly City of the Eighteenth-Century Philosophers* (1932; New Haven: Yale University Press, 1977).

Bell, David A., Ludmila Pimenova, and Stéphane Pujol (eds), *La Recherche dix-huitièmiste: raison universelle et culture nationale au siècle des Lumières / Eighteenth-Century Research: Universal Reason and National Culture during the Enlightenment* (Paris: Honoré Champion, 1999).

Benhabib, Seyla, ' "Nous" et "les autres": The Politics of Complex Cultural Dialogue in a Global Civilization', in Christian Joppke and Steven Lukes (eds), *Multicultural Questions* (Oxford: Oxford University Press, 1999), 44–62.

Bénot, Yves, *Diderot, de l'athéisme à l'anticolonialisme* (Paris: François Maspero, 1981).

Benrekassa, Georges, 'Le Dit et le non-dit idéologique: à propos du *Supplément au voyage de Bougainville*', in *Le Concentrique et l'excentrique: marges des Lumières* (Paris: Payot, 1980), 213–24.

Benton, Lauren A., *Law and Colonial Cultures: Legal Regimes in World History, 1400–1900* (Cambridge: Cambridge University Press, 2002).

Berlin, Ira, *Generations of Captivity: A History of African-American Slaves* (Cambridge, Mass.: Harvard University Press, 2003).

Bhabha, Homi K., *The Location of Culture* (London: Routledge, 1994).

Binoche, Bertrand, *Les trois sources des philosophies de l'histoire, 1764–1798* (Paris: Presses Universitaires de France, 1994).

Blackburn, Robin, *The Overthrow of Colonial Slavery, 1776–1848* (New York: Verso, 1988).

Blackburn, Timothy C., 'Friday's Religion: Its Nature and Importance in *Robinson Crusoe*', *Eighteenth-Century Studies*, 18/3 (1985), 360–82.

Blewett, David, *The Illustration of Robinson Crusoe, 1719–1920* (Gerrard's Cross: Colin Smythe, 1995).

Bobbio, Norberto, *Thomas Hobbes and the Natural Law Tradition*, trans. Daniela Gobetti (Chicago: University of Chicago Press, 1993).

Bose, Sugata, 'Space and Time on the Indian Ocean Rim: Theory and History', in Leila Tarazi Fawaz and C. A. Bayly (eds), *Modernity & Culture: From the Mediterranean to the Indian Ocean* (New York: Columbia University Press, 2002), 365–88.

Boulle, Pierre, 'In Defense of Slavery: Eighteenth-Century Opposition to Abolition and the Origins of a Racist Ideology in France', in Frederick Krantz (ed.), *History from Below: Studies in Popular Protest and Popular Ideology in Honour of George Rudé* (Montreal: Concordia University, 1985), 221–41.

Boulukos, George E., *The Grateful Slave: The Emergence of Race in Eighteenth-Century British and American Culture* (Cambridge: Cambridge University Press, 2008).

Bowen, H. V., 'British Conceptions of Global Empire, 1756–83', *Journal of Imperial and Commonwealth History*, 26/3 (1988), 1–27.

Brantlinger, Patrick, *Crusoe's Footprints: Cultural Studies in Britain and America* (London: Routledge, 1990).

Braverman, Richard, 'Crusoe's Legacy', *Studies in the Novel*, 18/1 (1986), 1–26.

Breckenridge, Carol A., and Peter van der Veer (eds), *Orientalism and the Postcolonial Predicament: Perspectives on South Asia* (Philadelphia: University of Pennsylvania Press, 1993).

Brennan, Timothy, *At Home in the World: Cosmopolitanism Now* (Cambridge, Mass.: Harvard University Press, 1997).

Brewer, Daniel, *The Discourse of Enlightenment in Eighteenth-Century France: Diderot and the Art of Philosophizing* (Cambridge: Cambridge University Press, 1993).

Brockington, J. L., 'Warren Hastings and Orientalism', in Geoffrey Carnall and Colin Nicholson (eds), *The Impeachment of Warren Hastings* (Edinburgh: Edinburgh University Press, 1989), 91–108.

Bronner, Stephen Eric, *Reclaiming the Enlightenment: Toward a Politics of Radical Engagement* (New York: Columbia University Press, 2004).

Brooks, Joanna, *American Lazarus: Religion and the Rise of African-American and Native American Literatures* (New York: Oxford University Press, 2003).

Brown, Laura, *Ends of Empire: Women and Ideology in Early Eighteenth-Century English Literature* (Ithaca: Cornell University Press, 1993).

—— *Fables of Modernity: Literature and Culture in the English Eighteenth Century* (Ithaca: Cornell University Press, 2001).

—— 'The Romance of Empire: *Oroonoko* and the Trade in Slaves', in Felicity Nussbaum and Laura Brown (eds), *The New Eighteenth Century: Theory, Politics, English Literature* (New York: Methuen, 1987), 41–61.

Butler, Marilyn, 'Orientalism', in David Pirie (ed.), *The Romantic Period* (New York: Penguin, 1994), 395–447.

Byrne, Peter, *Natural Religion and the Nature of Religion: The Legacy of Deism* (New York: Routledge, 1989).

Cain, P. J., and A. G. Hopkins, *British Imperialism, 1688–2000* (London: Longman, 2002).

Cañizares-Esguerra, Jorge, *How to Write the History of the New World: Histories, Epistemologies, and Identities in the Eighteenth-Century Atlantic World* (Stanford: Stanford University Press, 2001).

Cannadine, David, *Ornamentalism: How the British Saw their Empire* (London: Penguin Press, 2001).

Cannon, Garland, *The Life and Mind of Oriental Jones: Sir William Jones, the Father of Modern Linguistics* (Cambridge: Cambridge University Press, 1990).

—— 'Oriental Jones: Scholarship, Literature, Multiculturalism, and Humankind', in Garland Cannon and Kevin R. Brine (eds), *Objects of Enquiry: The Life, Contributions, and Influences of Sir William Jones, 1746–1794* (New York: New York University Press, 1995), 25–50.

—— and Kevin R. Brine (eds), *Objects of Enquiry: The Life, Contributions, and Influences of Sir William Jones, 1746–1794* (New York: New York University Press, 1995).

Carey, Daniel, *Locke, Shaftesbury, and Hutcheson: Contesting Diversity in the Enlightenment and Beyond* (Cambridge: Cambridge University Press, 2006).

Chakrabarty, Dipesh, *Habitations of Modernity: Essays in the Wake of Subaltern Studies* (Chicago: University of Chicago Press, 2002).

—— *Provincializing Europe: Postcolonial Thought and Historical Difference* (Princeton: Princeton University Press, 2000).

Chakravarti, Uma, 'Whatever Happened to the Vedic *Dasi*? Orientalism, Nationalism and a Script for the Past', in Kumkum Sangari and Sudesh Vaid (eds), *Recasting Women: Essays in Indian Colonial History* (New Brunswick: Rutgers University Press, 1990), 27–87.

Chartier, Roger, *Cultural History: Between Practices and Representations*, trans. Lydia Cochrane (Ithaca: Cornell University Press, 1988).

Chase, Bob, 'Herder and the Postcolonial Reconfiguring of the Enlightenment', *Bucknell Review*, 41/2 (1998), 172–96.

Chatterjee, Partha, *Nationalist Thought and the Colonial World: A Derivative Discourse?* (1986; Minneapolis: University of Minnesota Press, 1993).

Cheah, Pheng, *Spectral Nationality: Passages of Freedom from Kant to Postcolonial Literatures of Liberation* (New York: Columbia University Press, 2003).

Cheek, Pamela, *Sexual Antipodes: Enlightenment Globalization and the Placing of Sex* (Stanford: Stanford University Press, 2003).

Chibber, Vivek, 'The Good Empire', review of Niall Ferguson, *Colossus: The Price of America's Empire* (New York: Penguin, 2004), in *Boston Review*, 30/1 (Feb.–Mar. 2005), 30–4.

Chinard, Gilbert, introduction in Denis Diderot, *Supplément au voyage de Bougainville*, ed. Gilbert Chinard (Paris: Librairie E. Droz, 1935), 13–96.

Chow, Rey, 'The Politics of Admittance: Female Sexual Agency, Miscegenation, and the Formation of Community in Frantz Fanon', in *Ethics after Idealism: Theory—Culture—Ethnicity—Reading* (Bloomington and Indianapolis: Indiana University Press, 1998), 53–73.

Chrisman, Laura, 'The Imperial Unconscious? Representations of Imperial Discourse', *Critical Quarterly*, 32/3 (Autumn 1990), 38–58.

Clarke, J. J., *Oriental Enlightenment: The Encounter between Asian and Western Thought* (London: Routledge, 1997).

Coclanis, Peter A., review of Ira Berlin, *Generations of Captivity: A History of African-American Slaves* (Cambridge, Mass.: Belknap Press of Harvard University Press, 2003), in *William and Mary Quarterly*, 3rd ser., 61/3 (July 2004), 544–55.

Cohen, Alix, 'Kant on Epigenesis, Monogenesis and Human Nature: The Biological Premises of Anthropology', *Studies in History and Philosophy of Biological and Medical Sciences*, 37 (2006), 675–93.

Cohn, Bernard S., 'The Command of Language and the Language of Command', in Ranajit Guha (ed.), *Subaltern Studies IV* (Delhi: Oxford University Press, 1985), 276–329.

—— 'Law and the Colonial State in History', in June Starr and Jane F. Collier (eds), *History and Power in the Study of Law: New Directions in Legal Anthropology* (Ithaca: Cornell University Press, 1989), 131–52.

—— 'Notes on the History of the Study of Indian Society and Culture', in Milton Singer and Bernard S. Cohn (eds), *Structure and Change in Indian Society* (Chicago: Aldine, 1968), 3–28.

Colley, Linda, *Captives: Britain, Empire and the World 1600–1850* (London: Jonathan Cape, 2002).

—— 'Empire as a Way of Life', *The Nation* (31 July 2006), 7.

—— 'What is Imperial History Now?', in David Cannadine (ed.), *What is History Now?* (London: Palgrave, 2002), 132–47.

Coulet, Henri, 'Deux confrontations du sauvage et du civilisé: les *Dialogues de Lahontan* et le *Supplément au voyage de Bougainville* de Diderot', *Man and Nature: Proceedings of the Canadian Society for Eighteenth-Century Studies*, 9 (1990), 122–7.

Cowley, Robert L. S., *Hogarth's 'Marriage A-la-Mode'* (Ithaca: Cornell University Press, 1983).

Cragg, Gerald R., *Reason and Authority in the Eighteenth Century* (Cambridge: Cambridge University Press, 1964).

Craven, Wesley Frank, *Dissolution of the Virginia Company: The Failure of a Colonial Experiment* (New York: Oxford University Press, 1932).

—— *An Introduction to the History of Bermuda* (Bermuda: Bermuda Maritime Museum Press, 1990).

Dabydeen, David, *Hogarth's Blacks: Images of Blacks in Eighteenth-Century English Art* (Kingston-on-Thames, Surrey: Dangeroo Press, 1985).

Dalleo, Raphael, 'Emplotting Postcoloniality: Usable Pasts, Possible Futures, and the Relentless Present', *Diaspora*, 13/1 (2004), 129–40.

Darnton, Robert, *The Business of Enlightenment: A Publishing History of the 'Encyclopédie,' 1775–1800* (Cambridge, Mass.: Harvard University Press, 1979).

Davis, David Brion, 'Catching the Conquerors', review of Linda Colley, *Captives: Britain, Empire and the World 1600–1850* (London: Jonathan Cape, 2002), in *New York Review of Books*, 50/9 (29 May 2003), 38.

—— *The Problem of Slavery in the Age of Revolution 1770–1823* (Ithaca: Cornell University Press, 1975).

Davis, Mike, *Late Victorian Holocausts: El Niño Famines and the Making of the Third World* (London: Verso, 2001).

Davis, Robert C., *Christian Slaves, Muslim Masters: White Slavery in the Mediterranean, the Barbary Coast, and Italy, 1500–1800* (New York: Palgrave, 2003).

Dayan, Joan, *Haiti, History, and the Gods* (Berkeley: University of California Press, 1995).

Deane, Seamus, *Foreign Affections: Essays on Edmund Burke* (Cork: Cork University Press, 2005).

Delon, Michel, 'L'appel au lecteur dans l'*Histoire des deux Indes*', in Hans-Jürgen Lüsebrink and Manfred Tietz (eds), *Lectures de Raynal: 'L'Histoire des deux Indes' en Europe et en Amérique au XVIIIe siècle* (Oxford: Voltaire Foundation, 1991), 53–66.

Dharwadker, Aparna, 'Nation, Race, and the Ideology of Commerce in Defoe', *The Eighteenth Century: Theory and Interpretation*, 39/1 (1998), 63–84.

Dieckmann, Herbert, introduction in Denis Diderot, *Supplément au voyage de Bougainville* (Geneva: Droz, 1955), pp. xi–clv.

Dirks, Nicholas, 'From Little King to Landlord: Colonial Discourse and Colonial Rule', in Nicholas Dirks (ed.), *Colonialism and Culture* (Ann Arbor: University of Michigan Press, 1992), 175–208.

Dirlik, Arif, 'The Postcolonial Aura: Third World Criticism in the Age of Global Capitalism', *Critical Inquiry*, 20/2 (1994), 328–56.

Dobbs, Betty Jo Teeter, and Margaret C. Jacob, *Newton and the Culture of Newtonianism* (Atlantic Highlands, NJ: Humanities Press, 1995).

Dodson, Michael, *Orientalism, Empire, and National Culture: India, 1770–1880* (New York: Palgrave Macmillan, 2007).

Douthwaite, Julia, *Exotic Women: Literary Heroines and Cultural Strategies in Ancien Régime France* (Philadelphia: University of Pennsylvania Press, 1992).

Dubey, Madhu, 'Racial Difference in Postmodern Theory', paper presented at University of California at Los Angeles, Nov. 2002.

—— *Signs and Cities: Black Literary Postmodernism* (Chicago: University of Chicago Press, 2003).

Duchet, Michèle, *Anthropologie et histoire au siècle des Lumières* (Paris: François Maspero, 1971).

—— *Diderot et 'L'Histoire des deux Indes', ou l'écriture fragmentaire* (Paris: Éditions A.-G. Niget, 1987).

—— '*L'Histoire des deux Indes*: sources et structure d'un texte polyphonique', in Hans-Jürgen Lüsebrink and Manfred Tietz (eds), *Lectures de Raynal: 'L'Histoire des deux Indes' en Europe et en Amérique au XVIIIe siècle* (Oxford: Voltaire Foundation, 1991), 9–16.

Dunn, John, *The Political Thought of John Locke: An Historical Account of the Argument of the 'Two Treatises of Government'* (Cambridge: Cambridge University Press, 1969).

Dupré, Louis, *The Enlightenment and the Intellectual Foundations of Modern Culture* (New Haven: Yale University Press, 2004).

Eagleton, Terry, *The Ideology of the Aesthetic* (Oxford: Blackwell, 1990).

Egan, Jim, *Authorizing Experience: Refigurations of the Body Politic in Seventeenth-Century New England Writing* (Princeton: Princeton University Press, 1999).

Eisenberg, José, 'Cultural Encounters, Theoretical Adventures: The Jesuit Missions to the New World and the Justification of Voluntary Slavery', *History of Political Thought*, 24/3 (2003), 375–96.

Ellingson, Ter, *The Myth of the Noble Savage* (Berkeley: University of California Press, 2001).

Engell, James, *The Creative Imagination: Enlightenment to Romanticism* (Cambridge, Mass.: Harvard University Press, 1981).

Eze, Emmanuel Chukwudi, 'The Color of Reason: The Idea of "Race" in Kant's Anthropology', in Emmanuel Chukwudi Eze (ed.), *Postcolonial African Philosophy: A Critical Reader* (Oxford: Blackwell, 1997), 103–40.

—— 'Hume, Race, and Human Nature', *Journal of the History of Ideas*, 61/4 (2000), 691–8.

Fanon, Frantz, *Black Skin, White Masks*, foreword by Homi Bhabha, trans. Charles Lam Markham (London: Pluto Press, 1986).

—— 'Racism and Culture', in *Toward the African Revolution: Political Essays*, trans. Haakon Chevalier (New York: Grove Press, 1988), 29–33.

—— *The Wretched of the Earth*, pref. by Jean-Paul Sartre, trans. Constance Farrington (New York: Grove Press, 1968).

Fara, Patricia, *Newton: The Making of a Genius* (New York: Columbia University Press, 2002).

Farr, James, 'Locke, Natural Law, and New World Slavery', *Political Theory*, 36/4 (2008), 495–522.

—— ' "So Vile and Miserable an Estate": The Problem of Slavery in Locke's Political Thought', *Political Theory*, 14/2 (1986), 263–89.

Ferguson, Niall, *Colossus: The Price of America's Empire* (New York: Penguin, 2004).

—— *Empire: How Britain Made the Modern World* (London: Allen Lane, 2003).

—— *Empire: The Rise and Demise of the British World Order and the Lessons for Global Power* (London: Basic Books, 2002).

—— 'The Empire Slinks Back', *New York Times Magazine* (27 Apr. 2003), 52–7.

Ferrar, Nicholas, *Sir Thomas Smith's Misgovernment of the Virginia Company* (Cambridge: Roxburghe Club, 1990).

Ferreira da Silva, Denise, *Toward a Global Idea of Race* (Minneapolis: University of Minnesota Press, 2007).

Festa, Lynn, *Sentimental Figures of Empire in Eighteenth-Century Britain and France* (Baltimore: Johns Hopkins University Press, 2006).

Fischer, Sibylle, *Modernity Disavowed: Haiti and the Cultures of Slavery in the Age of Revolution* (Durham, NC: Duke University Press, 2004).

Fisher, Humphrey J., *Slavery in the History of Muslim Black Africa* (London: Hurst and Company, 2001).

Fleck, Andrew, 'Crusoe's Shadow: Christianity, Colonization and the Other', in John C. Hawley (ed.), *Historicizing Christian Encounters with the Other* (Basingstoke: Macmillan, 1998), 74–89.

Foucault, Michel, 'Of Other Spaces', trans. Jay Miskowiec, *Diacritics*, 16/1 (Spring 1986), 22–7.

—— 'What is Enlightenment?', in *The Foucault Reader*, ed. Paul Rabinow (New York: Pantheon, 1984), 32–50.

Fox, Robert (ed.), *Thomas Harriot: An Elizabethan Man of Science* (Burlington, Vt.: Ashgate, 2000).

France, Peter, *Rhetoric and Truth in France: Descartes to Diderot* (Oxford: Clarendon Press, 1972).

Franklin, Michael John, introduction in Alexander Dow, *The History of Hindostan Translated from the Persian Volumes I and II*, in Michael John Franklin (ed.), *Representing India: Indian Culture and Imperial Control in Eighteenth-Century British Orientalist Discourse*, 9 vols (New York: Routledge, 2000), ii, pp. v–xiii.

—— introduction in John Zephaniah Holwell, *Interesting Historical Events, Relative to the Provinces of Bengal, and the Empire of Indostan Parts I and II*, in Michael John Franklin (ed.), *Representing India: Indian Culture and Imperial Control in Eighteenth-Century British Orientalist Discourse*, 9 vols (New York: Routledge, 2000), i, pp. xii–xix.

—— introduction in Nathaniel Brassey Halhed, *A Code of Gentoo Laws, or, Ordinations of the Pundits*, in Michael John Franklin (ed.), *Representing India: Indian Culture and Imperial Control in Eighteenth-Century British Orientalist Discourse*, 9 vols (New York: Routledge, 2000), iv, pp. v–xii.

—— introduction in Sir William Jones, *Institutes of Hindu Law or, The Ordinances of Menu, According to the Gloss of Cullúca. Comprising the Indian System of Duties, Religious and Civil*, in Michael John Franklin (ed.), *Representing India: Indian Culture and Imperial Control in Eighteenth-Century British Orientalist Discourse*, 9 vols (New York: Routledge, 2000), ix, pp. v–xiii.

—— introduction in *Sir William Jones: Selected Poetical and Prose Works*, ed. Michael John Franklin (Cardiff: University of Wales Press, 1993), pp. xv–xxx.

Furet, François, *Interpreting the French Revolution*, trans. Elborg Forster (Cambridge: Cambridge University Press, 1981).

Fuss, Diana, 'Interior Colonies: Frantz Fanon and the Politics of Identification', in *Identification Papers* (New York: Routledge, 1995), 141–72.

Gargett, Graham, *Voltaire and Protestantism* (Oxford: Voltaire Foundation, 1980).

Garrard, Graeme, *Counter-Enlightenments: From the Eighteenth Century to the Present* (London: Routledge, 2006).

Garrett, Aaron, 'Hume's "Original Difference": Race, National Character and the Human Sciences', *Eighteenth-Century Thought*, 2 (2004), 127–52.

Gascoigne, John, *Joseph Banks and the English Enlightenment: Useful Knowledge and Polite Culture* (Cambridge: Cambridge University Press, 1994).

Gautier, Gary, 'Slavery and the Fashioning of Race in *Oroonoko, Robinson Crusoe*, and Equiano's *Life*', *The Eighteenth Century: Theory and Interpretation*, 42/2 (2001), 161–79.

Gay, Peter, *The Enlightenment: An Interpretation*, i: *The Rise of Modern Paganism* (New York: Vintage, 1966).

Gellner, Ernest, *Nations and Nationalism* (Oxford: Blackwell, 1983).

Ghosh, Amitav, and Dipesh Chakrabarty, 'A Correspondence on *Provincializing Europe*', *Radical History Review*, 82 (2002), 146–72.

Gibbons, Luke, *Edmund Burke and Ireland: Aesthetics, Politics and the Colonial Sublime* (Cambridge: Cambridge University Press, 2003).

—— 'Towards a Postcolonial Enlightenment: The United Irishmen, Cultural Diversity and the Public Sphere', in Clare Carroll and Patricia King (eds), *Ireland and Postcolonial Theory* (Cork: Cork University Press, 2003), 81–91.

Gierke, Otto Friedrich von, *Community in Historical Perspective*, trans. Mary Fischer, ed. Antony Black (Cambridge: Cambridge University Press, 1990).

Gilroy, Paul, *The Black Atlantic: Modernity and Double Consciousness* (Cambridge, Mass: Harvard University Press, 1993), 255–87.

Glausser, Wayne, 'Three Approaches to Locke and the Slave Trade', *Journal of the History of Ideas*, 51 (1990), 199–216.

Gliozzi, Giuliano, 'Poligenismo e razzismo agli albori del secolo dei lumi', *Rivista di filosofia*, 70 (1979), 1–31; repr. in Gliozzi, *Differenze e uguaglianza nella cultura europea moderna* (Naples: Vivarium, 1993), 255–87.

Gooding-Williams, Robert, *Look, A Negro! Philosophical Essays on Race, Culture, and Politics* (New York: Routledge, 2006).

Goodman, Dena, *Criticism in Action: Enlightenment Experiments in Political Writing* (Ithaca: Cornell University Press, 1989).

Goodman, Kevis, *Georgic Modernity and British Romanticism: Poetry and the Mediation of History* (Cambridge: Cambridge University Press, 2004).

Gossman, Lionel, 'What Was Enlightenment?', in Denis Hollier (ed.), *A New History of French Literature* (Cambridge, Mass.: Harvard University Press, 1989), 487–95.

Gramsci, Antonio, *Selections from the Prison Notebooks*, ed. and trans. Quintin Hoare and Geoffrey Nowell Smith (New York: International Publishers, 1971).

Gray, John, *Enlightenment's Wake: Politics and Culture at the Close of the Modern Age* (London: Routledge, 1995).

Gray, Peter, 'The Peculiarities of Irish Land Tenure, 1800–1914: From Agent of Impoverishment to Agent of Pacification', in Donald Winch and Patrick K. O'Brien (eds), *The Political Economy of British Historical Experience, 1688–1914* (Oxford: Oxford University Press, 2002), 139–64.

Green, Martin, *The Robinson Crusoe Story* (University Park: Pennsylvania State University Press, 1990).

Greene, Jack, *Pursuits of Happiness: The Social Development of Early Modern British Colonies and the Formation of American Culture* (Chapel Hill: University of North Carolina Press, 1988).

Griffin, Dustin, *Patriotism and Poetry in Eighteenth-Century Britain* (Cambridge: Cambridge University Press, 2002).

Grove, Richard, *Green Imperialism: Colonial Expansion, Tropical Island Edens, and the Origins of Environmentalism, 1600–1860* (Cambridge: Cambridge University Press, 1995).

Grundy, Isobel, *Lady Mary Wortley Montagu: Comet of the Enlightenment* (Oxford: Oxford University Press, 1999).

Guest, Harriet, 'Ornament and Use: Mai and Cook in London', in Kathleen Wilson (ed.), *A New Imperial History: Culture, Identity, and Modernity in Britain and the Empire, 1660–1840* (Cambridge: Cambridge University Press, 2004), 317–44.

Guha, Ranajit, *History at the Limit of World-History* (New York: Columbia University Press, 2002).

—— *An Indian Historiography of India: A Nineteenth-Century Agenda and Its Implications* (Calcutta: Published for Centre for Studies in Social Sciences, Calcutta, by K. P. Bagchi & Co., 1988).

—— 'On Some Aspects of the Historiography of Colonial India', in Ranajit Guha (ed.), *Subaltern Studies I* (Delhi: Oxford University Press, 1982), 1–8.

—— preface in Ranajit Guha (ed.), *Subaltern Studies I* (Delhi: Oxford University Press, 1982), pp. vii–viii.

—— 'The Prose of Counter-Insurgency', in Ranajit Guha and Gayatri Chakravorty Spivak (eds), *Selected Subaltern Studies* (New York: Oxford University Press, 1988), 45–86.

—— *A Rule of Property for Bengal: An Essay on the Idea of Permanent Settlement* (1963; Durham, NC: Duke University Press, 1996).

Gura, Philip, 'The Study of Colonial American Literature, 1966–87: A Vade Mecum', *William and Mary Quarterly*, 3rd ser., 45 (1988), 305–41.

Hall, Kim, ' "Troubling Doubles": Apes, Africans, and Blackface in *Mr. Moore's Revels*', in Joyce Green MacDonald (ed.), *Race, Ethnicity, and Power in the Renaissance* (Madison, NJ: Fairleigh Dickinson University Press, 1997), 120–44.

Hall, Max, *Benjamin Franklin and Polly Baker: The History of a Literary Deception* (Chapel Hill: University of North Carolina Press, 1960).

Hall, Richard, *Empires of the Monsoon: A History of the Indian Ocean and its Invaders* (London: HarperCollins, 1998).

Hall, Stuart, 'New Ethnicities', in David Morley and Kuan-Hsing Chen (eds), *Critical Dialogues in Cultural Studies* (London: Routledge, 1996), 441–9.

Hammond, J. R., *A Defoe Companion* (Lanham, Md.: Barnes & Noble, 1993).

Harvey, David, *The New Imperialism* (New York: Oxford University Press, 2003).

Hawari, R., 'Antoine Galland's Translation of the *Arabian Nights*', *Revue de littérature comparée*, 54 (1980), 150–64.

Hayes, Julie Candler, *Reading the French Enlightenment: System and Subversion* (Cambridge: Cambridge University Press, 1999).

Hazard, Paul, *La Pensée européenne au dix-huitième siècle: de Montesquieu à Lessing*, 3 vols (Paris: Boivin & Cie, 1946).

Hechter, Michael, *Internal Colonialism: The Celtic Fringe in British National Development, 1536– 1966* (Berkeley: University of California Press, 1975).

Hedrick, Todd, 'Race, Difference, and Anthropology in Kant's Cosmopolitanism', *Journal of the History of Philosophy*, 46/2 (2008), 245–68.

Heidegger, Martin, *Zur Bestimmung der Philosophie*, ed. Bernd Heimbüchel, in *Martin Heidegger Gesamtausgabe*, lvi–lvii (Frankfurt: Vittorio Klostermann, 1987).

Hensher, Philip, 'Exceedingly Good Advice from Mr Kipling', *The Independent* (London, 14 May 2003), 16.

Hochschild, Adam, *King Leopold's Ghost* (New York: Houghton Mifflin, 1998).

Hont, Istvan, *Jealousy of Trade: International Competition and the Nation-State in Historical Perspective* (Cambridge, Mass.: Harvard University Press, 2005).

Hopkins, A. G. (ed.), *Globalization in World History* (London: Pimlico, 2002).

Horkheimer, Max, and Theodor Adorno, *Dialectic of Enlightenment*, trans. John Cumming (New York: Continuum, 1999).

Hudson, Nicholas, 'From "Nation" to "Race": The Origin of Racial Classification in Eighteenth-Century Thought', *Eighteenth-Century Studies*, 29 (1996), 247–64.

Hulme, Peter, *Colonial Encounters: Europe and the Native Caribbean, 1492–1797* (London: Methuen, 1986).

—— 'Imperial Counterpoint', review essay on Edward Said, *Culture and Imperialism* (New York: Alfred A. Knopf, 1993), *Wasafiri*, 18 (Autumn 1993), 57–61.

—— 'Postcolonial Theory and Early America: An Approach from the Caribbean', in Robert Blair St George (ed.), *Possible Pasts: Becoming Colonial in Early America* (Ithaca: Cornell University Press, 2000), 33–48.

—— 'The Spontaneous Hand of Nature: Savagery, Colonialism, and the Enlightenment', in Peter Hulme and Ludmilla Jordanova (eds), *The Enlightenment and its Shadows* (London: Routledge, 1990), 15–34.

Hulton, Paul, and David Beers Quinn, *The American Drawings of John White, 1577–1590*, 2 vols (London: The Trustees of the British Museum and Chapel Hill: University of North Carolina Press, 1964).

Hunter, J. Paul, *The Reluctant Pilgrim* (Baltimore: Johns Hopkins University Press, 1966).

Hutchinson, John, and Anthony O. Smith (eds), *Nationalism* (New York: Oxford University Press, 1994).

Ibbetson, David, 'Sir William Jones as a Comparative Lawyer', in Alexander Murray (ed.), *Sir William Jones, 1746–1794: A Commemoration* (Oxford: Oxford University Press, 1998), 17–42.

Immerwahr, John, 'Hume's Revised Racism', *Journal of the History of Ideas*, 53/3 (1992), 481–6.

Irwin, Robert, *For Lust of Knowing: The Orientalists and their Enemies* (London: Allen Lane, 2006).

Islam, Sirajul, *The Permanent Settlement in Bengal: A Study of its Operation, 1790–1819* (Dacca: Bangla Academy, 1979).

Islam, Syed Manzurul, *The Ethics of Travel: From Marco Polo to Kafka* (Manchester: Manchester University Press, 1996).

Israel, Jonathan I., *Radical Enlightenment: Philosophy and the Making of Modernity, 1650–1750* (Oxford: Oxford University Press, 2001).

Ivison, Duncan, *Postcolonial Liberalism* (Cambridge: Cambridge University Press, 2002).

Jacob, Margaret C., *The Newtonians and the English Revolution, 1689–1720* (London: Harvester Press, 1976).

—— and Larry Stewart, *Practical Matter: Newton's Science in the Service of Industry and Empire, 1687–1851* (Cambridge, Mass.: Harvard University Press, 2005).

—— *Strangers Nowhere in the World: The Rise of Cosmopolitanism in Early Modern Europe* (Philadelphia: University of Pennsylvania Press, 2006).

Jameson, Fredric, 'Notes on Globalization as a Philosophical Issue', in Fredric Jameson and Masai Miyoshi (eds), *The Cultures of Globalization* (Durham, NC: Duke University Press, 1998), 54–77.

JanMohamed, Abdul, 'The Economy of Manichean Allegory: The Function of Racial Difference in Colonialist Literature', *Critical Inquiry*, 12 (1985), 59–87.

Jennings, Francis, *The Invasion of America: Indians, Colonialism, and the Cant of Conquest* (Chapel Hill: Published for the Institute of Early American History and Culture by the University of North Carolina Press, 1975).

Johnson, Paul, 'Five Vital Lessons from Iraq', *Forbes Magazine* (17 Mar. 2003) <http://www.forbes.com/forbes/2003/0317/037.html>.

Jooma, Minaz, 'Robinson Crusoe Inc(corporates): Domestic Economy, Incest and the Trope of Cannibalism', *Literature, Interpretation, Theory*, 8/1 (1997), 61–81.

Joseph, Betty, 'Re(playing) Crusoe/Pocahontas: Circum-Atlantic Stagings in *The Female American*', *Criticism*, 42/3 (Summer 2000), 317–35.

Kahn, Victoria, *Wayward Contracts: The Crisis of Political Obligation in England, 1640–1674* (Princeton: Princeton University Press, 2004).

Kamdar, Mira, 'Subjectification and Mimesis: Colonizing History', *American Journal of Semiotics*, 7/3 (1990), 91–100.

—— 'Poétique et politique: le paradoxe de la représentation de l'autre dans le *Supplément au voyage de Bougainville*', *Qui parle*, 1 (1985), 71–86.

Kaplan, Richard Paul, 'Daniel Defoe's Views on Slavery and Racial Prejudice', Ph.D. diss., New York University, 1970.

Kaul, Suvir, *Poems of Nation, Anthems of Empire: English Verse in the Long Eighteenth Century* (Charlottesville: University Press of Virginia, 2000).

—— 'Provincials and Tropicopolitans: Eighteenth-Century Literary Studies and the Un-Making of "Great Britain" ', *Diaspora*, 9/3 (2000), 421–37.

Keane, Patrick J., 'Slavery and the Slave Trade: Crusoe as Defoe's Representative', in Roger D. Lund (ed.), *Critical Essays on Daniel Defoe* (New York: G. K. Hall, 1997), 97–120.

Kennedy, Dane, 'Imperial History and Post-Colonial Theory', *Journal of Imperial and Commonwealth History*, 24/3 (1996), 345–63.

Kidd, Colin, *British Identities before Nationalism: Ethnicity and Nationhood in the Atlantic World, 1600–1800* (Cambridge: Cambridge University Press, 1999).

—— *The Forging of Races: Race and Scripture in the Protestant Atlantic World, 1600–2000* (Cambridge: Cambridge University Press, 2006).

Kitson, Peter J., introduction in Peter J. Kitson (ed.), *Slavery, Abolition and Emancipation: Writings in the British Romantic Period*, ii: *The Abolition Debate* (London: Pickering & Chatto, 1999), pp. ix–xxv.

—— introduction in Peter J. Kitson (ed.), *Slavery, Abolition and Emancipation: Writings in the British Romantic Period*, viii: *Theories of Race* (London: Pickering & Chatto, 1999), pp. vii–xxvi.

—— and Debbie Lee, 'General Introduction', in Peter J. Kitson and Debbie Lee (general eds), *Slavery, Abolition and Emancipation: Writings in the British Romantic Period* (London: Pickering & Chatto, 1999), i, pp. ix–xxix.

Kohn, Margaret, and Daniel I. O'Neill, 'A Tale of Two Indias: Burke and Mill on Empire and Slavery in the West Indies and America', *Political Theory*, 34/2 (2006), 192–228.

Kolb, Gwin J. (ed.), *Samuel Johnson: Rasselas and Other Tales*, The Yale Edition of the Works of Samuel Johnson, 16 (New Haven: Yale University Press, 1990).

Kopf, David, *British Orientalism and the Bengal Renaissance: The Dynamics of Indian Modernization, 1773–1835* (Berkeley: University of California Press, 1969).

—— 'The Historiography of British Orientalism, 1772–1992', in Garland Cannon and Kevin R. Brine (eds), *Objects of Enquiry: The Life, Contributions, and Influences of Sir William Jones (1746–1794)* (New York: New York University Press, 1995), 141–60.

Kupperman, Karen Ordahl, *Indians and English: Facing Off in Early America* (Ithaca: Cornell University Press, 2000).

Kymlicka, Will, *Multicultural Citizenship: A Liberal Theory of Minority Rights* (Oxford: Clarendon Press, 1995).

—— *Multicultural Odysseys: Navigating the New International Politics of Diversity* (Oxford: Oxford University Press, 2007).

Laclau, Ernesto, 'Identity and Hegemony: The Role of Universality in the Constitution of Political Logics', in Judith Butler, Ernesto Laclau, and Slavoj Žižek, *Contingency, Hegemony, Universality: Contemporary Dialogues on the Left* (London: Verso, 2000), 44–89.

Lazarus, Neil, 'The Fetish of "the West" in Postcolonial Theory', in Crystal Bartolovich and Neil Lazarus (eds), *Marxism, Modernity and Postcolonial Studies* (Cambridge: Cambridge University Press, 2002), 43–64.

Lebow, Richard Ned, 'What is so Different about a Counterfactual', *World Politics*, 52 (July 2000), 550–85.

Lee, Debbie (ed.), *Slavery, Abolition and Emancipation: Writings in the British Romantic Period*, iii: *The Emancipation Debate* (London: Pickering and Chatto, 1999).

Liebersohn, Harry, *Aristocratic Encounters: European Travelers and North American Indians* (Cambridge: Cambridge University Press, 2001).

—— *The Travelers' World: Europe to the Pacific* (Cambridge, Mass: Harvard University Press, 2006).

Liedman, Sven-Eric, *The Postmodern Critique of the Project of Enlightenment* (Amsterdam: Rodopi, 1997).

Liu, Lydia H., 'Robinson Crusoe's Earthenware Pot', *Critical Inquiry*, 25/4 (1999), 728–57.

Lloyd, David, 'Analogies of the Aesthetic: The Politics of Culture and the Limits of Materialist Aesthetics', *New Formations*, 10 (Spring 1990), 109–26.

—— 'Foundations of Diversity: Thinking the University in a Time of Multiculturalism', in John Carlos Rowe (ed.), *'Culture' and the Problem of the Disciplines* (New York: Columbia University Press, 1998), 15–43.

—— 'Kant's Examples', *Representations*, 28 (Fall 1989), 34–54.

—— 'Race under Representation', *Oxford Literary Review*, 13/1–2 (1991), 62–94.

—— 'Representation's Coup', in Swati Chattopadhyay and Bhaskar Sarkar (eds), *The Subaltern and the Popular* (London: Routledge, forthcoming).

—— and Paul Thomas, *Culture and the State* (London: Routledge, 1997).

Loar, Christopher F., 'How to Say Things with Guns: Military Technology and the Politics of *Robinson Crusoe*', *Eighteenth-Century Fiction*, 19/1–2 (2006), 1–20.

Loomba, Ania, 'Overworlding the Third World', *Oxford Literary Review*, 13/1–2 (1991), 164–91.

—— Suvir Kaul, Matti Bunzl, Antoinette Burton, and Jed Esty (eds), *Postcolonial Studies and Beyond* (Durham, NC: Duke University Press, 2005).

Louden, Robert B., *Kant's Impure Ethics: From Rational Beings to Human Beings* (New York: Oxford University Press, 2000).

Lovejoy, Paul, *Transformations in Slavery: A History of Slavery in Africa* (Cambridge: Cambridge University Press, 1983).

Lowe, Lisa, *Critical Terrains: French and British Orientalisms* (Ithaca: Cornell University Press, 1991).

—— *Immigrant Acts: On Asian American Cultural Politics* (Durham, NC: Duke University Press, 1996).

Ludden, David, 'Orientalist Empiricism: Transformations of Colonial Knowledge', in Carol A. Breckenridge and Peter van der Veer (eds), *Orientalism and the Postcolonial Predicament* (Philadelphia: University of Pennsylvania Press, 1993), 250–78.

McClintock, Anne, *Imperial Leather: Race, Gender, and Sexuality in the Colonial Context* (New York: Routledge, 1995).

Macfie, A. L., *Orientalism* (New York: Longman, 2002).

McGrane, Bernard, *Beyond Anthropology: Society and the Other* (New York: Columbia University Press, 1989).

McInelly, Brett C., 'Expanding Empires, Expanding Selves: Colonialism, the Novel, and *Robinson Crusoe*', *Studies in the Novel*, 35/1 (2003), 1–21.

Mackay, David, *In the Wake of Cook: Exploration, Science and Empire* (New York: St Martin's Press, 1985).

MacKenzie, John M., *Orientalism: History, Theory and the Arts* (Manchester: Manchester University Press, 1995).

McLane, John R., *Land and Local Kingship in Eighteenth-Century Bengal* (Cambridge: Cambridge University Press, 1993).

McMahon, Darrin, *Enemies of the Enlightenment: The French Counter-Enlightenment and the Making of Modernity* (Oxford: Oxford University Press, 2001).

MacMillan, Ken, *Sovereignty and Possession in the English New World: The Legal Foundations of Empire, 1576–1640* (Cambridge: Cambridge University Press, 2006).

McNeil, Maureen, 'Newton as National Hero', in John Fauvel et al. (eds), *Let Newton Be!* (Oxford: Oxford University Press, 1988), 223–39.

McVeagh, John, ' "The Blasted Race of Old *Cham*": Daniel Defoe and the African', *Ibadan Studies in English*, 1 (1969), 85–109.

Majeed, Javed, *Ungoverned Imaginings: James Mill's 'The History of British India' and Orientalism* (Oxford: Clarendon Press, 1992).

Makdisi, Saree, *Romantic Imperialism: Universal Empire and the Culture of Modernity* (Cambridge: Cambridge University Press, 1998).

Makkreel, Rudolf A., *Imagination and Interpretation in Kant: The Hermeneutical Import of the 'Critique of Judgment'* (Chicago: University of Chicago Press, 1990).

Malcolm, Noel, *Aspects of Hobbes* (Oxford: Clarendon Press, 2002).

Manning, Patrick, *Slavery and African Life: Occidental, Oriental, and African Slave Trades* (Cambridge: Cambridge University Press, 1990).

Mannoni, O., *Prospero and Caliban: The Psychology of Colonization*, trans. Pamela Powesland (New York and Washington: Frederick A. Praeger, 1964).

Manuel, Frank, *The Eighteenth Century Confronts the Gods* (Cambridge, Mass.: Harvard University Press, 1959).

Marcus, Sharon, 'Anne Frank and Hannah Arendt: Universalism and Pathos', in Vinay Dharwadker (ed.), *Cosmopolitan Geographies: New Locations in Literature and Culture* (London: Routledge, 2001), 89–132.

Marshall, John, *John Locke, Toleration and Early Enlightenment Culture: Religious Intolerance and Arguments for Religious Toleration in Early Modern and 'Early Enlightenment' Europe* (Cambridge: Cambridge University Press, 2006).

Marshall, P. J., *Bengal. The British Bridgehead: Eastern India, 1740–1828* (Cambridge: Cambridge University Press, 1987).

—— (ed.), *The British Discovery of Hinduism in the Eighteenth Century* (Cambridge: Cambridge University Press, 1970).

—— and Glyndwr Williams, *The Great Map of Mankind: British Perceptions of the World in the Age of Enlightenment* (London: Dent, 1982).

Massey, Doreen, *Space, Place, and Gender* (Minneapolis: University of Minnesota Press, 2001).

Mat, Michèle, 'Le *Supplément au voyage de Bougainville*: une aporie polyphonique', *Revue internationale de philosophie*, 38/148–9 (1984), 158–70.

Matar, Nabil, *Turks, Moors, and Englishmen in the Age of Discovery* (New York: Columbia University Press, 1999).

May, H. F., *The Enlightenment in America* (New York: Oxford University Press, 1976).

Mazlish, Bruce, *Civilization and its Contents* (Stanford: Stanford University Press, 2004).

Meek, Ronald L., *Social Science and the Ignoble Savage* (Cambridge: Cambridge University Press, 1976).

Mehta, Uday Singh, *Liberalism and Empire: A Study in Nineteenth-Century British Liberal Thought* (Chicago: University of Chicago Press, 1999).

Metcalf, Thomas, *Ideologies of the Raj* (Cambridge: Cambridge University Press, 1994).

Mignolo, Walter, *Local Histories/Global Designs: Coloniality, Subaltern Knowledges, and Border Thinking* (Princeton: Princeton University Press, 2000).

—— '(Post)Occidentalism, (Post)Coloniality, and (Post)Subaltern Rationality', in Fawzia Afzal-Khan and Kalpana Seshadri-Crooks (eds), *The Pre-Occupation of Postcolonial Studies* (Durham, NC: Duke University Press, 2000), 86–118.

Moore, Catherine E., 'Robinson and Xury and Inkle and Yarico', *English Language Notes*, 19 (Sept. 1981), 24–9.

Moore, James, 'Montesquieu and the Scottish Enlightenment', in Rebecca Kingston (ed.), *The Legacy of Montesquieu* (Albany: SUNY Press, forthcoming).

Moskal, Jeanne, 'English National Identity in Mariana Starke's "The Sword of Peace": India, Abolition, and the Rights of Women', in Catherine Burroughs (ed.), *Women in British Romantic Theatre: Drama, Performance, and Society, 1790–1840* (Cambridge: Cambridge University Press, 2000), 102–31.

Mukherjee, S. N., *Sir William Jones: A Study in Eighteenth-Century British Attitudes to India* (Cambridge: Cambridge University Press, 1968).

Mukherji, Abhijit, 'European Jones and Asiatic Pandits', *Journal of the Asiatic Society*, 27/1 (1985), 43–58.

Mukhopadhyay, Subhas Chandra, *The Agrarian Policy of the British in Bengal: The Formative Period, 1698–1772* (Allahabad: Chugh Publications, 1987).

Murray, David, *Forked Tongues: Speech, Writing, and Representation in American Indian Texts* (Bloomington: Indiana University Press, 1991).

Muthu, Sankar, *Enlightenment against Empire* (Princeton: Princeton University Press, 2003).

Nehru, Jawaharlal, *The Discovery of India* (Delhi: Oxford University Press, 1989).

Nicolson, Marjorie Hope, *Newton Demands the Muse: Newton's Opticks and the Eighteenth-Century Poets* (Princeton: Princeton University Press, 1946).

Niranjana, Tejaswini, *Siting Translation: History, Post-Structuralism, and the Colonial Context* (Berkeley: University of California Press, 1992).

Norton, Ann, *Leo Strauss and the Politics of American Empire* (New Haven: Yale University Press, 2004).

Novak, Maximillian E., *Daniel Defoe: Master of Fictions: His Life and Ideas* (Oxford: Oxford University Press, 2001).

—— *Defoe and the Nature of Man* (Oxford: Oxford University Press, 1963).

Nussbaum, Felicity A., introduction in Saree Makdisi and Felicity Nussbaum (eds), *The Arabian Nights in Historical Context: Between East and West* (Oxford: Oxford University Press, 2008), 1–24.

—— *The Limits of the Human: Fictions of Anomaly, Race, and Gender in the Long Eighteenth Century* (Cambridge: Cambridge University Press, 2003).

—— 'Slavery, Blackness, and Islam: *The Arabian Nights* in the Eighteenth Century', in Brycchan Carey and Peter J. Kitson (eds), *Slavery and the Cultures of Abolition: Essays Marking the Bicentennial of the British Abolition Act of 1807* (Woodbridge, Suffolk: Boydell & Brewer, 2007), 150–72.

—— *Torrid Zones: Maternity, Sexuality and Empire in Eighteenth-Century English Narratives* (Baltimore: Johns Hopkins University Press, 1995).

—— (ed.), *The Global Eighteenth Century* (Baltimore: Johns Hopkins University Press, 2003).

Nuzzo, Angelica, *Kant and the Unity of Reason* (West Lafayette, Ind.: Purdue University Press, 2005).

O'Brien, Karen, *Narratives of Enlightenment: Cosmopolitan History from Voltaire to Gibbon* (Cambridge: Cambridge University Press, 1997).

O'Brien, Karen, 'Poetry and Political Thought: Liberty and Benevolence in the Case of the British Empire, c.1680–1800', in David Armitage (ed.), *British Political Thought in History, Literature and Theory, 1500–1800* (Cambridge: Cambridge University Press, 2006), 168–90.

Ouellet, Réal, and Alain Beaulieu, introduction in Louis Armand de Lom d'Arce, baron de Lahontan, *Oeuvres complètes*, ed. Réal Ouellet, 2 vols (Montreal: Presses Universitaires de Montréal, 1990), i, 11–199.

Outram, Dorinda, *The Enlightenment* (Cambridge: Cambridge University Press, 1995; 2nd edn, 2005).

Overton, Bill, 'Countering *Crusoe*: Two Colonial Narratives', *Critical Survey*, 4/3 (1992), 302–10.

Oz-Salzberger, Fania, *Translating the Enlightenment: Scottish Civic Discourse in Eighteenth-Century Germany* (Oxford: Clarendon Press, 1995).

Pagden, Anthony, *European Encounters with the New World: From Renaissance to Romanticism* (New Haven: Yale University Press, 1993).

—— *The Fall of Natural Man: The American Indian and the Origins of Comparative Ethnology* (Cambridge: Cambridge University Press, 1982).

—— 'The Savage Critic: Some European Images of the Primitive', *Yearbook of English Studies*, 13 (1983), 32–45.

Palmer, Robert R., *Catholics and Unbelievers in Eighteenth-Century France* (1939; New York: Cooper Square Publishers, 1961).

Palter, Robert, 'Hume and Prejudice', *Hume Studies*, 21 (1995), 3–23.

Parker, Geoffrey, *The Military Revolution: Military Innovation and the Rise of the West, 1500–1800* (Cambridge: Cambridge University Press, 1996).

Parry, Benita, 'Problems in Current Theories of Colonial Discourse', *Oxford Literary Review*, 9/1–2 (1987), 27–58.

—— 'Signs of our Times: Discussion of Homi Bhabha's *The Location of Culture*', *Third Text*, 28–9 (1994), 5–24.

Peabody, Sue, *'There are no slaves in France': The Political Culture of Race and Slavery in the Ancien Régime* (New York: Oxford University Press, 1996).

Phillips, Richard, *Mapping Men and Empire: A Geography of Adventure* (London: Routledge, 1997).

Pitts, Jennifer, *A Turn to Empire: The Rise of Imperial Liberalism in Britain and France* (Princeton: Princeton University Press, 2005).

Pocock, J. G. A., *Barbarism and Religion*, ii: *Narratives of Civil Government* (Cambridge: Cambridge University Press, 1999).

Pocock, J. G. A., *Barbarism and Religion*, iv: *Barbarians, Savages, and Empires* (Cambridge: Cambridge University Press, 2005).

——— 'Enthusiasm: The Antiself of Enlightenment', in Lawrence Klein and Anthony La Vopa (eds), *Enthusiasm and Enlightenment in Europe, 1650–1850* (San Marino: Henry E. Huntington Library and Art Gallery, 1998), 7–28.

Pointon, Marcia, *Hanging the Head: Portraiture and Social Formation in Eighteenth-Century England* (New Haven: Yale University Press, 1993).

Popkin, Richard H., 'Hume's Racism', *Philosophical Forum*, 9 (1977–8), 211–26.

Porter, Roy, and Mikulas Teich (eds), *Enlightenment in National Context* (Cambridge: Cambridge University Press, 1981).

Prakash, Gyan, 'Postcolonial Criticism and Indian Historiography', *Social Text*, 31–2 (1992), 8–19.

——— 'Who's Afraid of Postcoloniality?', *Social Text*, 49 (Winter 1996), 187–203.

——— 'Writing Post-Orientalist Histories of the Third World: Perspectives from Indian Historiography', *Comparative Studies in Society and History*, 32/2 (1990), 383–408.

Pratt, Mary Louise, *Imperial Eyes: Travel Writing and Transculturation* (London: Routledge, 1992).

Press, Volker, *Das alte Reich: Ausgewählte Aufsätze* (Berlin: Duncker & Humblot, 1997).

Raman, Shankar, ' "Can't Buy Me Love": Money, Gender, and Colonialism in Donne's Erotic Verse', *Criticism*, 43/2 (2001), 135–68.

Rassem, Mohammed, *Die Volkstumswissenschaften und der Etatismus* (Mittenwald: Mäander, 1979).

Rex, Walter E., *Essays on Pierre Bayle and Religious Controversy* (The Hague: M. Nijhoff, 1965).

Ridley, Hugh, *Images of Imperial Rule* (London: Croom Helm, 1983).

Roach, Joseph, *Cities of the Dead: Circum-Atlantic Performance* (New York: Columbia University Press, 1996).

Robinson, la robinsonnade et le monde des choses, special issue of *Études françaises*, 35/1 (1999).

Rocher, Rosane, 'British Orientalism in the Eighteenth Century: The Dialectic of Knowledge and Government', in Carol A. Breckenridge and Peter van der Veer (eds), *Orientalism and the Postcolonial Predicament: Perspectives on South Asia* (Philadelphia: University of Pennsylvania Press, 1993), 215–49.

——— foreword in *Sir William Jones: A Reader*, ed. Satya S. Pachori (New York: Oxford University Press, 1993), 3–7.

——— 'Weaving Knowledge: Sir William Jones and Indian Pandits', in Garland Cannon and Kevin R. Brine (eds), *Objects of Enquiry: The Life, Contributions, and Influences of Sir William Jones (1746–1794)* (New York: New York University Press, 1995), 51–79.

Roelens, Maurice, introduction in Louis Armand de Lom d'Arce, baron de Lahon-tan, *Dialogues avec un sauvage* (Paris: Éditions Sociales, 1973), 7–81.

Rölleke, Heinz, 'Nachwort', in Johann Gottfried Herder, *Stimmen der Völker in Liedern: Volkslieder. Zwei Teile 1778/79*, ed. Heinz Rölleke (Stuttgart: Reclam, 1974), 463–503.

Rousseau, G. S., and Roy Porter (eds) *Exoticism in the Enlightenment* (Manchester: Manchester University Press, 1990).

Rubiés, Joan-Pau, 'Oriental Despotism and European Orientalism: Botero to Montesquieu', *Journal of Early Modern History*, 9/1–2 (2005), 109–80.

Rüsen, Jörn, *Konfigurationen des Historismus: Studien zur deutschen Wissenschaftskultur* (Frankfurt: Suhrkamp, 1993).

Rushdie, Salman, 'Outside the Whale', in *Imaginary Homelands: Essays and Criticism, 1981–1991* (New York: Penguin, 1991), 87–101.

Ryan, Vanessa L., 'The Physiological Sublime: Burke's Critique of Reason', *Journal of the History of Ideas*, 62/2 (2001), 265–79.

Said, Edward, *Culture and Imperialism* (New York: Alfred A. Knopf, 1993).

—— *On Late Style: Music and Literature against the Grain* (New York: Vintage, 2007).

—— *Orientalism* (New York: Vintage, 1978; 25th anniversary edn, New York: Vintage, 2003).

St George, Robert Blair (ed.), *Possible Pasts: Becoming Colonial in Early America* (Ithaca: Cornell University Press, 2000).

Sardar, Ziauddin, *Orientalism* (Buckingham and Philadelphia: Open University Press, 1999).

Sarkar, Sumit, 'The Decline of the Subaltern in *Subaltern Studies*', in Sumit Sarkar (ed.), *Writing Social History* (Delhi: Oxford University Press, 1997), 82–108.

Sassen, Saskia, *Globalization and its Discontents* (New York: The New Press, 1998).

Sayre, Gordon, *Les Sauvages Américains: Representations of Native Americans in French and English Colonial Literature* (Chapel Hill: University of North Carolina Press, 1997).

Schlatter, Richard (ed.), *Hobbes's Thucydides* (New Brunswick, NJ: Rutgers University Press, 1975).

Schmidt, James. 'What Enlightenment Project?', *Political Theory*, 28/6 (2000), 734–57.

Schmied-Kowarzig, Wolfdietrich, 'Der Streit um die Einheit des Menschengeschlechts: Gedanken zu Forster, Herder und Kant', in Claus-Volker Klenske (ed.), *Georg Forster in interdisziplinärer Perspektive* (Berlin: Akademie-Verlag, 1994), 115–32.

Schwab, Raymond, *Oriental Renaissance: Europe's Rediscovery of India and the East, 1680–1880* (New York: Columbia University Press, 1984).

Schwartz, Stuart B., *Sugar Plantations in the Formation of Brazilian Society: Bahia, 1550–1835* (Cambridge: Cambridge University Press, 1985).

Scott, David, *Conscripts of Modernity: The Tragedy of Colonial Enlightenment* (Durham, NC: Duke University Press, 2004).

Sebastiani, Silvia, 'Race and National Characters in Eighteenth-Century Scotland: The Polygenetic Discourses of Kames and Pinkerton', *Cromohs*, 8 (2003), 1–14.

Serequeberhan, Tsenay, 'The Critique of Eurocentrism and the Practice of African Philosophy', in Emmanuel Chukwudi Eze (ed.), *Postcolonial African Philosophy: A Critical Reader* (New York: Blackwell, 1997), 141–61.

Shirley, John W., *Thomas Harriot: A Biography* (Oxford: Clarendon Press, 1983).

Shklar, Judith N., 'Politics and the Intellect', in Stanley Hoffman (ed.), *Political Thought and Political Thinkers* (Chicago: University of Chicago Press, 1998), 94–104.

Shohat, Ella, 'Notes on the "Post-Colonial" ', in Fawzia Afzal-Khan and Kalpana Seshadri-Crooks (eds), *The Pre-Occupation of Postcolonial Studies* (Durham, NC: Duke University Press, 2000), 126–39.

Sidoti, Concetta, 'An Evening with Jane Austen. National Pride and Audience Prejudice: Re-Writing the Heritage Text', *Cultural Studies from Birmingham*, 2/1 (1998), archived at <http://web.archive.org/web/20040224120412/artsweb.bham.ac.uk/bccsr/issue1/sidoti.htm>.

Skinner, Quentin, *The Foundations of Modern Political Thought*, 2 vols (Cambridge: Cambridge University Press, 1978).

—— *Reason and Rhetoric in the Philosophy of Hobbes* (Cambridge: Cambridge University Press, 1996).

Sloan, Kim, *A New World: England's First View of America* (London: The British Museum Press, 2007).

Slotkin, James S. (ed.), *Readings in Early Anthropology* (Chicago: Aldine Publishing, 1965).

Smith, David, 'Orientalism and Hinduism', in Gavin Flood (ed.), *The Blackwell Companion to Hinduism* (Oxford: Blackwell, 2003), 45–64.

Sollors, Werner, *Neither Black nor White yet Both: Thematic Explorations of Interracial Literature* (New York: Oxford University Press, 1997).

Soncini, Sara, 'The Island as Social Experiment: A Reappraisal of Daniel Defoe's Political Discourse(s) in *Robinson Crusoe* and *The Farther Adventures*', in Marialuisa Bignami (ed.), *Wrestling with Defoe: Approaches from a Workshop on Defoe's Prose* (Bologna: Cisalpino, 1997), 11–43.

Sorensen, Janet, *The Grammar of Empire in Eighteenth-Century British Writing* (Cambridge: Cambridge University Press, 2000).

Spaas, Lieve, and Brian Stimpson (eds), *Robinson Crusoe: Myths and Metamorphoses* (Basingstoke: Macmillan, 1996).

Späth, Eberhard, 'Defoe and Slavery', in Wolfgang Binder (ed.), *Slavery in the Americas* (Würzburg: Königshausen & Neumann, 1993), 453–69.

Spivak, Gayatri Chakravorty. 'Can the Subaltern Speak?', in Patrick Williams and Laura Chrisman (eds), *Colonial Discourse and Postcolonial Theory: A Reader* (New York: Columbia University Press, 1994), 66–112.

—— *A Critique of Postcolonial Reason: Toward a History of the Vanishing Present* (Cambridge, Mass.: Harvard University Press, 1999).

Spivak, Gayatri Chakravorty. 'Subaltern Studies: Deconstructing Historiography', in Ranajit Guha and Gayatri Chakravorty Spivak (eds), *Selected Subaltern Studies* (New York: Oxford University Press, 1988), 3–32.

Stagl, Justin, *Eine Geschichte der Neugier: Die Kunst des Reisens 1550–1800* (Vienna: Böhlau, 2002).

Starr, G. A., *Defoe and Spiritual Autobiography* (Princeton: Princeton University Press, 1965).

Steinmetz, George, *The Devil's Handwriting: Precoloniality and the German Colonial State in Qingdao, Samoa, and Southwest Africa* (Chicago: University of Chicago Press, 2007).

Streeby, Shelley, *American Sensations: Class, Empire, and the Production of Popular Culture* (Berkeley: University of California Press, 2002).

Sudan, Rajani, *Fair Exotics: Xenophobic Subjects in English Literature, 1720–1850* (Philadelphia: University of Pennsylvania Press, 2002).

Suleri, Sara, *The Rhetoric of English India* (Chicago: University of Chicago Press, 1992).

Sullivan, Zohreh (ed.), *Rudyard Kipling's 'Kim': Authoritative Text, Backgrounds, Criticism* (New York: Norton, 2002).

Sypher, Wylie, *Guinea's Captive Kings: British Anti-Slavery Literature of the XVIIIth Century* (Chapel Hill: University of North Carolina Press, 1942).

Teltscher, Kate, *India Inscribed: European and British Writing on India, 1600–1800* (Delhi: Oxford University Press, 1995).

Tennenhouse, Leonard, 'The Case of the Resistant Captive', *South Atlantic Quarterly*, 95/4 (1996), 919–46.

——— 'Diaspora and Empire', in *The Importance of Feeling English: American Literature and the British Diaspora, 1750–1850* (Princeton: Princeton University Press, 2007), 1–18.

Terry, Richard (ed.), *James Thomson: Essays for the Tercentenary* (Liverpool: Liverpool University Press, 2000).

Thapar, Romila, 'Communalism and the Writing of Ancient Indian History', in Romila Thapar, Harbans Mukhia, and Bipan Chandra, *Communalism and the Writing of Indian History* (Delhi: People's Publishing House, 1969), 1–21.

——— 'Imagined Religious Communities? Ancient History and the Modern Search for a Hindu Identity', *Modern Asian Studies*, 23/2 (1989), 209–31.

Thomas, Hugh, *The Slave Trade: The Story of the Atlantic Slave Trade 1440–1870* (New York: Simon and Schuster, 1997).

Thomas, Nicholas, *Colonialism's Culture: Anthropology, Travel, and Government* (Cambridge: Polity Press, 1994).

Thompson, F. M. L., 'Changing Perceptions of Land Tenures in Britain, 1750–1914', in Donald Winch and Patrick K. O'Brien (eds), *The Political Economy of British Historical Experience, 1688–1914* (Oxford: Oxford University Press, 2002), 119–38.

Thomson, Ann, *Barbary and Enlightenment: European Attitudes towards the Maghreb in the Eighteenth Century* (Leiden: E. J. Brill, 1987).

Tiffin, Helen, 'Post-Colonial Literature and Counter-Discourse', in Bill Ashcroft, Gareth Griffiths, and Helen Tiffin (eds), *The Post-Colonial Studies Reader* (London: Routledge, 1995), 95–8.

Todorov, Tzvetan, *On Human Diversity: Nationalism, Racism, and Exoticism in French Thought*, trans. Catherine Porter (Cambridge, Mass.: Harvard University Press, 1993).

Trautmann, Thomas, *Aryans and British India* (Berkeley: University of California Press, 1997).

Travers, Robert, 'Ideology and British Expansion in Bengal, 1757–72', *Journal of Imperial and Commonwealth History*, 33/1 (2005), 7–27.

Travers, Robert, ' "The Real Value of the Lands": The *Nawabs*, the British and the Land Tax in Eighteenth-Century Bengal', *Modern Asian Studies*, 38/3 (2004), 517–58.

Tricaud, François, 'Hobbes's Conception of the State of Nature from 1640 to 1651: Evolution and Ambiguities', in G. A. J. Rogers and Alan Ryan (eds), *Perspectives on Thomas Hobbes* (Oxford: Clarendon Press, 1988), 107–23.

Trouillot, Michel-Rolph, *Silencing the Past: Power and the Production of History* (Boston: Beacon Press, 1995).

Tuck, Richard, 'Hobbes and Democracy', in Annabel Brett and James Tully with Holly Hamilton-Bleakley (eds), *Rethinking the Foundations of Modern Political Thought* (Cambridge: Cambridge University Press, 2006), 171–90.

—— 'Hobbes and Tacitus', in G. A. J. Rogers and Tom Sorell (eds), *Hobbes and History* (London: Routledge, 2000), 99–111.

—— *Natural Rights Theories: Their Origin and Development* (Cambridge: Cambridge University Press, 1979).

—— *Philosophy and Government 1572–1651* (Cambridge: Cambridge University Press, 1993).

Tully, James, *An Approach to Political Philosophy: Locke in Contexts* (Cambridge: Cambridge University Press, 1993).

—— *Strange Multiplicity: Constitutionalism in an Age of Diversity* (Cambridge: Cambridge University Press, 1995).

Turley, Hans, 'Protestant Evangelicalism, British Imperialism, and Crusonian Identity', in *A New Imperial History: Culture, Identity, and Modernity in Britain and the Empire, 1660–1840* (Cambridge: Cambridge University Press, 2004), 176–93.

—— 'The Sublimation of Desire to Apocalyptic Passion in Defoe's Crusoe Trilogy', in Philip Holden and Richard R. Ruppel (eds), *Imperial Desire: Dissident Sexualities and Colonial Literature* (Minneapolis: University of Minnesota Press, 2003), 3–20.

Van Den Abbeele, Georges, 'Utopian Sexuality and its Discontents: Exoticism and Colonialism in *Le Supplément au Voyage de Bougainville*', *L'Esprit créateur*, 24/1 (1984), 43–52.

Van der Veer, Peter, 'Sati and Sanskrit: The Move from Orientalism to Hinduism', in Mieke Bal and Inge Boer (eds), *The Point of Theory: Practices of Cultural Analysis* (Amsterdam: Amsterdam University Press, 1994), 251–9.

Van Ittersum, Martine Julia, *Profit and Principle: Hugo Grotius, Natural Rights Theories and the Rise of Dutch Power in the East Indies, 1595–1615* (Boston and Leiden: Brill, 2006).

Vasconcelos, Pedro de Almeida, *Salvador de Bahia (Brésil): transformations et permanences (1549–2004)* (Paris: L'Harmattan, 2005).

Vaughan, Alden T., ' "Expulsion of the Salvages": English Policy and the Virginia Policy of 1622', in *The Roots of American Racism: Essays on the Colonial Experience* (New York: Oxford University Press, 1995), 105–27.

—— *Transatlantic Encounters: American Indians in Britain, 1500–1776* (Cambridge: Cambridge University Press, 2006).

Verges, Françoise, *Monsters and Revolutionaries: Colonial Family Romance and Métissage* (Durham, NC: Duke University Press, 1999).

Vermeulen, Hans F., 'The German Invention of *Völkerkunde*: Ethnological Discourse in Europe and Asia, 1740–1798', in Sara Eigen and Mark J. Larrimore (eds), *The German Invention of Race* (New York: SUNY Press, 2006), 123–45.

Vierhaus, Rudolf, 'Die Universität Göttingen und die Anfänge der modernen Geschichtswissenschaft im 18. Jahrhundert', in Hartmut Boockmann and Hermann Wellenreuther (eds), *Geschichtswissenschaft in Göttingen: Eine Vorlesungsreihe* (Göttingen: Vandenhoeck & Ruprecht, 1987), 9–29.

Vinicius de Freitas, Marcus, 'The Image of Brazil in *Robinson Crusoe*', *Portuguese Literary and Cultural Studies*, 4–5 (2001), 453–9.

Viswanathan, Gauri, 'Colonialism and the Construction of Hinduism', in Gavin Flood (ed.), *The Blackwell Companion to Hinduism* (Oxford: Blackwell, 2003), 23–44.

Voegelin, Eric, *From Enlightenment to Revolution*, ed. John H. Hallowell (Durham, NC: Duke University Press, 1975).

Vyverberg, Henry, *Human Nature, Cultural Diversity, and the French Enlightenment* (New York: Oxford University Press, 1989).

Wallerstein, Immanuel, 'Bourgeois(ie) as Concept and Reality', in Étienne Balibar and Immanuel Wallerstein, *Race, Nation, Class: Ambiguous Identities* (London: Verso, 1991), 135–52.

Ward, J. R., 'The Industrial Revolution and British Imperialism, 1750–1850', *Economic History Review*, new ser., 47/1 (1994), 44–65.

Warner, Marina, *Fantastic Metamorphoses, Other Worlds: Ways of Telling the Self* (New York: Oxford University Press, 2002).

Warner, Michael, 'What's Colonial about Colonial America?', in Robert Blair St George (ed.), *Possible Pasts: Becoming Colonial in Early America* (Ithaca: Cornell University Press, 2000), 49–72.

Weber, David J., *Bárbaros: Spaniards and their Savages in the Age of Enlightenment* (New Haven: Yale University Press, 2005).

Wheeler, Roxann, *The Complexion of Race: Categories of Difference in Eighteenth-Century British Culture* (Philadelphia: University of Pennsylvania Press, 2000).

Williams, Patrick, and Laura Chrisman, introduction in Patrick Williams and Laura Chrisman (eds), *Colonial Discourse and Post-Colonial Theory: A Reader* (New York: Columbia University Press, 1994), 1–20.

Willis, John R., *Slaves and Slavery in Muslim Africa* (London: Frank Cass, 1985).

Wilson, Catherine, 'Savagery and the Supersensible: Kant's Universalism in Historical Context', *History of European Ideas*, 24/4–5 (1998), 315–30.

Wilson, Diana de Armas, *Cervantes, the Novel, and the New World* (Oxford: Oxford University Press, 2000).

Wilson, George M., 'Edward Said on Contrapuntal Reading', *Philosophy and Literature*, 18/2 (1994), 265–73.

Wilson, Kathleen, *The Island Race: Englishness, Empire, and Gender in the Eighteenth Century* (London: Routledge, 2002).

—— (ed.), *A New Imperial History: Culture, Identity and Modernity in Britain and the Empire, 1660–1840* (Cambridge: Cambridge University Press, 2004).

Withers, Charles W. J., *Placing the Enlightenment: Thinking Geographically about the Age of Reason* (Chicago: University of Chicago Press, 2007).

Wokler, Robert, 'The Enlightenment Project as Betrayed by Modernity', *History of European Ideas*, 24/4–5 (1998), 301–13.

Wolin, Sheldon, *Hobbes and the Epic Tradition of Political Theory*, introd. by Richard Ashcraft (Los Angeles: Clark Memorial Library, University of California at Los Angeles, 1970).

Wolpe, Hans, *Raynal et sa machine de guerre* (Paris: Librairie de Médicis, 1956).

Young, B. W., *Religion and Enlightenment in Eighteenth-Century England: Theological Debate from Locke to Burke* (Oxford: Clarendon Press, 1998).

Young, Robert, *Postcolonialism: An Historical Introduction* (Oxford: Blackwell, 2001).

—— *White Mythologies: Writing History and the West* (London: Routledge, 1990).

Young, R. V., ' "O My America, My New-Found-Land": Pornography and Imperial Politics in Donne's "Elegies" ', *South Central Review*, 4/2 (1987), 35–48.

Zammito, John H., *The Genesis of Kant's Critique of Judgment* (Chicago: University of Chicago Press, 1992).

—— *Kant, Herder and the Birth of Anthropology* (Chicago: University of Chicago Press, 2002).

Zantop, Susanne, *Colonial Fantasies: Conquest, Family, and Nation in Pre-Colonial Germany, 1770–1870* (Durham, NC: Duke University Press, 1997).

Zhiri, Oumelbanine, 'Fractured Africa: Space, Time and Intelligibility in the European Conception of Africa', paper presented at conference 'Race in the Early Modern Period', University of California, Santa Cruz, spring 1997.

INDEX

Boldface numerals indicate illustrations.

7084678R00217

Printed in Great Britain
by Amazon.co.uk, Ltd.,
Marston Gate.